Quatremère de Quincy

Quatremère de Quincy

*Art and Politics during
the French Revolution*

DAVID GILKS

Great Clarendon Street, Oxford, OX2 6DP,
United Kingdom

Oxford University Press is a department of the University of Oxford.
It furthers the University's objective of excellence in research, scholarship,
and education by publishing worldwide. Oxford is a registered trade mark of
Oxford University Press in the UK and in certain other countries

© David Gilks 2024

The moral rights of the author have been asserted

All rights reserved. No part of this publication may be reproduced, stored in
a retrieval system, or transmitted, in any form or by any means, without the
prior permission in writing of Oxford University Press, or as expressly permitted
by law, by licence or under terms agreed with the appropriate reprographics
rights organization. Enquiries concerning reproduction outside the scope of the
above should be sent to the Rights Department, Oxford University Press, at the
address above

You must not circulate this work in any other form
and you must impose this same condition on any acquirer

Published in the United States of America by Oxford University Press
198 Madison Avenue, New York, NY 10016, United States of America

British Library Cataloguing in Publication Data

Data available

Library of Congress Control Number: 2023946682

ISBN 978–0–19–874556–3

DOI: 10.1093/oso/9780198745563.001.0001

Printed and bound by
CPI Group (UK) Ltd, Croydon, CR0 4YY

Links to third party websites are provided by Oxford in good faith and
for information only. Oxford disclaims any responsibility for the materials
contained in any third party website referenced in this work.

Preface

I first heard Quatremère's name mentioned twenty years ago in a seminar on cross-cultural aesthetics. Given the burgeoning interest in the history of museums and collecting, this founding father of 'museophobia' seemed a curious subject for further study. But as a doctoral student I discovered that Quatremère's attitude towards museums was ambivalent, and that he wrote relatively little about them. If Quatremère was no museum theorist, I wondered, who was he, why did he matter, and why was he misrepresented? I sought answers in René Schneider's biographies, Sylvia Lavin's reflections on the language of architecture, and Édouard Pommier's work on art theories and institutions during the French Revolution. And I read Quatremère's writings despite their inaccessibility and bewildering range. In search of a unifying thread for my dissertation, I wrote about eighteenth-century proposals to 'regenerate' the arts; in the shadow of Pommier's *L'art de la liberté*, I approached Quatremère as Winckelmann's follower and treated his interventions as sincere attempts to perfect the arts during an era of collective euphoria.

Sceptical about the merit of my dissertation, I jettisoned both my manuscript and Quatremère when I began a post-doctoral fellowship. However, over the next years I encountered him repeatedly when I taught the French Revolution and researched eighteenth-century debates about intellectual and cultural property. I found these encounters baffling. Did Quatremère, friend of the regicide Jacques-Louis David and architect of the Republic's most emblematic monument, the Panthéon, really join the royalist Feuillant and Clichy clubs? How, I asked, could the advocate of the 'liberty of theatres' and purported 'enemy' of the Royal Academies in the early Revolution later support censorship and become the permanent secretary of the Academy of the Fine Arts? It made no sense to square the circle by repeating that Quatremère was a 'moderate' or 'liberal' who later became a Catholic royalist.

My research on artists' petitions in the quarrel over plundering Rome helped to sketch the outlines of a more satisfactory portrait. Although Quatremère depicted himself as a man of principles whose reflections transcended their immediate circumstances, my research revealed that, in summer 1796 at least, he was a polemicist who exploited the language of his republican opponents to attract support from artists and republicans whose politics differed from his own. His strategy, I realized, helped explain why the Directory ostracized him for writing his *Letters on the Plan to Abduct Monuments of Art from Italy* even though ostensibly he defended the same 'republic of the arts and sciences' and 'civilization' that the regime claimed to protect and advance.

vi PREFACE

Since Quatremère was clearly a more engaged thinker than I had previously imagined, I endeavoured to restore the context of political action to his other writings and interventions. I wanted to explain his contradictions, document his affairs, reconstruct his milieux and political alliances, establish what he read, reinterpret his most famous writings, and recover his forgotten writings.

I have incurred many debts over the course of the book's gestation and composition. Courses and conversations with Irene Winter, Christina Tarnopolsky, Richard Tuck, and Peter Galison at Harvard played a greater role in the book's genesis than will be apparent from the resulting text. The AHRC funded my doctorate at Cambridge, supervised sagely and humanely by Tim Blanning and examined by Peter Mandler and Stephen Bann. I was fortunate to spend a year of my doctorate in Paris as a *pensionnaire étranger* at ÉNS Ulm where Gilles Pécout and Élisabeth Décultot encouraged me to investigate Quatremère's milieux in Italy and Germany. Trinity College, Cambridge, not only provided me with a home and community during my formative years as a student but also subsidized my efforts to learn foreign languages and kept the wolf from the door while I finished my dissertation. Special thanks to Marian Hobson, Richard Serjeantson, Boyd Hilton, and Sachiko Kusukawa for their support during this critical stage of my career.

Most of the research that I ended up using for this book was, however, undertaken thanks to a Junior Research Fellowship at Christ Church, Oxford. I am grateful to the former Dean, Reverend Christopher Lewes, and Students of the House for awarding me this exceptional privilege and thank, in particular, Brian Young, Henry Mayr-Harting, Jacqueline Thalmann, Chris Pelling, Chris Haigh, Tommy Karshan, Oliver Thomas, Wendy Warren, and John Paton for memorable lunchtime chats. Kate Tunstall and Lawrence Brockliss kindly invited me to present several rather nebulous research papers at Oxford's Besterman Centre for the Enlightenment that subsequently evolved into parts of the present book. Many thanks also to Caroline Warman, Pietro Corsi, John Robertson, Ritchie Robertson, and Alastair Wright for words of support and constructive criticism during my time at Oxford.

I formulated the proposal for the current work during a Leverhulme Early Career Fellowship at QMUL, where I profited enormously from the inspiring and dynamic School of History. Many thanks to Julian Jackson, Gareth Stedman Jones, Miri Rubin, Richard Bourke, Amanda Vickery, James Baldwin, Mark Curran, Jérémie Barthas, and Alex Fairfax-Cholmeley for their advice and informative conversations about France and eighteenth-century history. I am especially grateful to Colin Jones for his mentorship during this time: without his encouragement, I would have abandoned Quatremère altogether. The greater part of the book has been written since I joined UEA as a Lecturer. I thank my past and present colleagues-in-arms in the School of History. I am especially grateful to Cathie Carmichael and Nick Vincent for taking a chance on me; to the late

Richard Deswarte for showing me the ropes with characteristic enthusiasm and kindness when I started; to Katy Cubitt, Tony Howe, and Tom Licence for their intellectual curiosity and their encouragement through some vexatious moments whilst writing; to Rob Liddiard for his candidly droll mentorship; and to Mark Thompson and Jan Vermeiren for sharing an office with me despite my foibles and follies.

Other collaborators, colleagues, and fellow students contributed to this book in different ways. Jon Conlin encouraged me to read Quatremère when I was looking for a dissertation subject. Thibault Dornon, Rabah Ghezali, and Mariana Saad provided the gift of friendship, hospitality, and patient assistance with the French language. Jeff Schwegman, fellow *pensionnaire étranger*, was an exceptionally encouraging and thoughtful research companion in the BnF and Ulm during a year in Paris. Over Chinese dumplings in the vingtième, Alan Potofosky shared his expertise on the Panthéon and construction trade and helped convince me that a book on Quatremère and the Revolution would be a worthwhile endeavour. Damian Valdez, Jeevan Deol, Belinda Beaton, Tom Stammers, Ambrogio Caini, and Joseph Clarke commented on work in progress or invited me to speak about Quatremère at seminars and conferences. Chris Miller, peerless as a translator of early modern art historical sources and scholarship, sharpened my thinking through his exceptional grasp of the specificities and eccentricities of texts that we translated for the Getty Research Institute. Dominique Poulot helpfully and succinctly described different approaches to Quatremère, convincing me that I might develop a reading of Quatremère embedded in historical context, even if such a reading hardly negates the legitimacy of other approaches. Stephen Bann, Oren Margolis, and the anonymous readers at Oxford University Press read my manuscript at different stages; I am indebted to their invaluable suggestions, which have improved this book substantially. At the Press, Robert Faber contracted the book and Cathryn Steele awaited its completion with patience before Imogene Haslam saw it through production. I am grateful to UEA for funding the maps. I thank Duke University Press for permission to draw upon my article 'Civilization and Its Discontents: Quatremère de Quincy and Directorial Political Culture', *French Historical Studies*, vol. 45, no. 3, pp. 481–510, in Chapter 8 of the present work.

The book has been enriched by digitized sources and other online resources provided by the Bibliothèque nationale de France, Institut national d'histoire de l'art, the Stanford-BnF French Revolution Digital Archive, and the University of Chicago's ARTFL Project. However, much of my research was undertaken in physical libraries and archives. I am grateful to librarians at the Bibliothèque nationale de France, Bibliothèque de l'Arsenal, Bibliothèque de l'Institut de France, British Library, Cambridge University Library, Bodleian Libraries in Oxford, and Robarts Library in Toronto; and to archivists at the Bibliothèque historique de la ville de Paris, Archives nationales, Archives de Paris, National Archives, and Balliol College Historic Collections.

It is standard practice to thank students in prefaces, but my gratitude goes beyond convention because the humour, resilience, and inquisitiveness of successive cohorts over the last decade has sustained me against bureaucratic nihilism. My *grand remède* of choice, however, has been my wife's company. Just as her own research on early modern perfume and bathing provided refreshing views across an alternative intellectual landscape, she has been the most incisive supporter and critic of an endeavour that has usurped upon summer holidays. Our sons, Aidan and Clement, are too young to offer their opinions on my profession or on Quatremère, but they have been a joyful distraction from both. Our extended families in Britain and Canada provided the continuous moral and logistical support that made it possible for me to write this book.

Contents

Abbreviations	xi
Note on Names and Language	xiii
Biographical and Political Chronology	xv
Introduction: An Unconventional History of the Revolution	1
1. The Making of a Missionary of Antiquity, 1755–85	15
2. The Friend of the Arts, 1785–9	32
3. Art in a Regenerated Nation, 1789–91	48
4. The Nation's Temple, 1791	72
5. Devoted to the King, 1791–2	89
6. Republicanizing the Panthéon, 1792–4	116
7. Standing for the Counter-Revolution, 1794–6	135
8. Justice to the Papacy, 1796	154
9. The Mask of Constitutionalism, 1796–9	179
Conclusion: Art, Crown, and Altar	200
Maps	208
Bibliography	211
Index	247

Abbreviations

AN	Archives nationales
AP	*Archives parlementaires*
BHVP	Bibliothèque historique de la ville de Paris
BnF	Bibliothèque nationale de France
CAFR	*Correspondance de l'Académie de France à Rome avec les surintendants des bâtiments*
PVCIP	*Procès-verbaux du comité d'instruction publique de l'assemblée législative*
EMA	*Encyclopédie méthodique. Architecture*

Note on Names and Language

For the sake of brevity, I usually refer to Antoine-Chrysosthôme Quatremère de Quincy simply as 'Quatremère' except when distinguishing him from family members. However, this convenient practice should not lead us to ignore how he presented himself in his writings. Before summer 1791, he called himself 'Quatremère de Quincy'. In September 1791, he started using the less aristocratic-sounding 'Quatremère-Quincy' and by 1793 he opted for 'Antoine Quatremère'. During the Consulate, he reverted to 'Quatremère de Quincy'. I also simplify other names. For example, I refer to 'Quatremère-Disjonval' rather than 'Quatremère d'Isjonval. For the sake of accessibility and readability, I use English-language terms when there is a suitable equivalent to the French original. I therefore refer to the 'Academy of Fine Arts' rather than the 'Académie des beaux-arts'. The 'Church' generally refers to the Catholic Church in France, whereas 'church' refers to a specific place of worship. Translations are my own unless otherwise indicated.

Biographical and Political Chronology

1755	Antoine-Chrysostôme Quatremère is born on 21 October into a Parisian family of cloth merchants and sent to a wetnurse in the village of Quincy.
1758	Death of his mother, Marie-Anne Bourjot.
*c.*1767–72	Studies at Collège Louis-le-Grand.
*c.*1772–6	Apprentice under Pierre Julien in the studio of sculptor Guillaume Coustou le Jeune.
1774	Accession of Louis XVI.
1775	Giovanni Angelo Braschi becomes Pope Pius VI.
1776–80	First Italian voyage.
1780–2	Returns to Paris.
1782–5	Second Italian voyage; writes about the Doric order.
1785	Returns to Paris and lives at 57 rue Sainte-Croix-de-la-Bretonnerie; wins the Prix Caylus for his essay on what the ancient Greeks borrowed from Egyptian architecture.
1786	Charles Panckoucke contracts him to produce an architecture dictionary for the *Encyclopédie méthodique*.
1787	*Journal de Paris* (11 Feb.) publishes his letter urging the authorities to save the Fountain of the Innocents.
1788	Publishes first volume of *Encyclopédie méthodique: architecture* (covering 'Abajour' to 'Coloris des Fleurs'). Moves to 25 rue des Fossés-du-Temple by rue de Ménilmontant.
1789	
March	*Mercure de France* publishes his 'Dissertation on Italian opera bouffa' defending the Théâtre de Monsieur.
April–June	First voyage to England coincides with the opening of the General Estates.
July	Returns around when the Bastille falls (14 July) and is elected to the Assembly of Representatives of the Commune of Paris.
Aug.	National Constituent Assembly abolishes feudalism, privileges, and venality and proclaims the Declaration of the Rights of Man and the Citizen.
1790	
April	Delivers to the Assembly of Representatives his reflections on the 'liberty of theatres' attacking privileged theatres to advance the interests of the Théâtre de Monsieur.
July	Civil Constitution of the Clergy and Festival of the Federation.
Oct.	Resigns from the Assembly of Representatives.
Nov.	Commune of the Arts founded.

xvi BIOGRAPHICAL AND POLITICAL CHRONOLOGY

1791

Jan.–May — Contributes to the debate about reforming the Royal Academies, starting with *Considerations on the Arts of Drawing in France; Followed by a Plan for the Academy or the Public School, and a Plan for a System of Encouragements.*

April — Defends the Constituent Assembly's decision to convert the church of Sainte-Geneviève into a temple dedicated to the nation's 'great men'. He is also appointed to the Department of Paris's Committee of Public Instruction, chaired by Talleyrand.

May–July — Investigates and reports how to transform the church of Sainte-Geneviève.

20–1 June — Flight to Varennes.

July — Directory of the Department of Paris appoints him 'commissioner of the administration and general direction of works' to transform the former church of Sainte-Geneviève. During the next year he hands important commissions to the sculptors Moitte, Dejoux, and Boichot and oversees much of his vision for what is soon known as the Panthéon.

Aug. — Joins the committee organizing the first open Salon of painting and sculpture.

Sept. — Elected a national representative for the Legislative Assembly and sits among the right-wing caucus when it opens in October. Over the next ten months he votes consistently on the right, defends the royal veto and past and present ministers, and opposes the Jacobins and measures against refractory priests and émigrés.

Oct. — Joins the Legislative Assembly's Committee of Public Instruction, chaired by Condorcet.

Nov. — On behalf of the Committee of Public Instruction he reports on the complaints of artists who exhibited in the Salon.

Nov.–Dec. — Name appears on membership lists for the Sainte-Chapelle and Feuillant clubs, which he may have joined several months earlier.

1792

Feb. — On behalf of the Committee of Public Instruction, he reports on the intellectual property of playwrights and theatre directors' complaints.

20 Feb.–20 March — Secretary to the president of the Legislative Assembly.

March — Louis XVI appoints a Girondin ministry.

20 April — Votes with the majority in the Assembly for war against Austria.

May — Organizes the Festival of the Law.

June — Investigates the Petits-Augustins repository and recommends selling artefacts unsuitable for the national museum.

July — National representative François-Valentin Mulot attacks his direction of the Panthéon. He is expelled from the Commune of the Arts, and joins Feuillant efforts to hamper the war effort.

Early Aug. — Defends Lafayette's return to Paris and threat to crush the Jacobins and helps defeat the proposed indictment of Lafayette, but popular violence prevents him and other conservative representatives returning to the Manège.

BIOGRAPHICAL AND POLITICAL CHRONOLOGY xvii

10 Aug.	Insurrectionists storm the Tuileries Palace, leading to the suspension and then abolition of the monarchy.
Aug.–Sept.	Hides in Paris and Cernay during the fall of the monarchy, the September Massacres, and elections by universal adult male suffrage for the National Convention.
Oct.	Resumes work directing the Panthéon to demonstrate his patriotic credentials, but he also joins a secret counter-revolutionary committee.
Dec.	Tries to exclude his elder brother, Denis-Bernard Quatremère-Disjonval, from their father's will through a notary's deed labelling him an émigré.
1793	
21 Jan.	Louis XVI is executed after a trial held by the Convention.
June–July	Overthrow of the Girondin faction enables the Montagnards to dominate the Convention, but the 'Federalist revolt' spreads as a result.
Sept.	Committee of General Security warrants his arrest, but he avoids detention by paying for his own house arrest.
Oct.	Dechristianization campaign and revolutionary calendar introduced.
Nov.	Defends his direction of the Panthéon in his last published report.
1794	
Jan.	Cousin Marc-Étienne Quatremère is guillotined.
Jan.–Feb.	Designs sculpture group representing 'The French Republic', which is executed in ephemeral materials and displayed in the Panthéon.
March	Committee of General Security orders his detention; he is taken to the Madelonettes prison where he befriends Francisco Miranda in July.
27 July	Fall of Robespierre and start of the 'Thermidorian reaction'.
Aug.	Released from Madelonettes; lives on rue Saint-Dominique-Saint-Germain.
Sept.	Becomes president of the primary assembly of section Fontaine-de-Grenelle.
Dec.	Writes *Précis pour Miranda*, which criticizes foreign policy and asks the Convention to release Miranda. Joins jury awarding prizes for painting, sculpture, and architecture and serves as its president between February and September 1795.
1795	
2 April	His father, François-Bernard Quatremère de l'Épine, dies.
April	First publication of Condorcet's posthumous *Sketch for a Historical Picture of the Human Spirit*; Quatremère acquires two copies.
June	Death of Louis XVII; Louis XVIII issues the Verona Declaration.
22 Aug.	Constitution of Year III and Law of Two Thirds approved.
Sept.	Attacks the Law of Two Thirds, declares that Paris's primary assemblies can discuss as one body this law, and urges citizens to arm themselves against the Convention.
4 Oct.	Orders section Fontaine-de-Grenelle to mobilize national guard units against the Convention, but the following day the army crushes the Vendémiaire insurrection.

xviii   BIOGRAPHICAL AND POLITICAL CHRONOLOGY

Oct.	Hides after a military tribunal finds him guilty in absentia of an act of revolt and condemns him to death; he spends ten months hiding (until August 1796).
2 Nov.	Start of the rule of the Directory; Louis-Marie de La Révellière-Lépeaux is the Director chosen by most national representatives.

1796

4 April	Inaugural meeting of the National Institute (decreed in October 1795).
23 June	Bologna armistice signed between the French Republic and the papacy after Bonaparte, General of the Army of Italy, scores rapid victories, advances across northern Italy, and demands artworks, antiquities, and other precious objects.
June–July	Publishes several anonymous writings—including *Letters on the Plan to Abduct Monuments of Art from Italy* (printed in late July)—to discredit and divide the Directory, criticize the National Institute, and argue that seizing cultural property from Italy will undermine the 'civilization' that the French Republic claims to represent.
Aug.	Criminal Tribunal's Jury of Accusation tries him for conspiring against the regime. Once freed he lives at 209 rue Saint-Domingue.
19 Aug.	*Journal de Paris* publishes a petition signed by him and many famous artists requesting a commission to report on the seizure of artworks from Italy.
3 Oct.	Counter-petition by artists who favour seizing artworks.
Oct.	Publishes anonymously a letter in *Journal littéraire* that responds to the counter-petition and attacks museums created during the Revolution.

1797

Feb.	Writes *The Veritable List of Candidates* as an electoral manifesto serving the Clichy club's strategy of winning legislative majorities to restore monarchy.
March	Dufourny asks his advice about an ancient statue for the Central Museum of the Arts.
April–Sept.	Serves on the committee that helps the Central Museum of the Arts determine what to display in the Special Museum of the French School in Versailles.
20 May	Benefits from royalist electoral gains and is chosen by the Seine Department as a national representative.
May–Sept.	Sits on the right of the Council of Five Hundred as one of the most experienced and active clichyeans. He opposes selling rectories, supports tax exemptions for painters and sculptors, tries to remove impediments to royalist electoral gains, argues that the Constitutional circles should be banned, and conspires against the Republic with other 'absolutist' members of the Clichy club.
3–4 Sept. 1797	The Fructidor coup removes him from office and obliges him to leave France, but he hides in Paris and joins plots to undermine the Directory and form a provisional government until Louis XVIII returns.

BIOGRAPHICAL AND POLITICAL CHRONOLOGY xix

1798

27 Nov.
Travels to Frankfurt in disguise with a passport obtained by Talleyrand; the state seizes his collection of artworks and books in Paris.

Dec.
Arrives in Frankfurt with few contacts and no German and leaves for Hamburg a week later.

1799

Jan.
Accepts Mathieu Dumas's invitation to visit Holstein and remains in Eutin as Friedrich Stolberg's guest alongside Charles Vanderbourg and Friedrich Jacobi.

9–10 Nov.
Brumaire coup leads to the Consulate and allows some exiles to return.

1800

Feb.
Leaves Holstein for Paris with Portalis and Dumas. Lives in Chaillot and struggles to retrieve property.

8 May
He and seventy other artists, writers, and scientists petition against demolishing the church of Saint-Nicolas-du-Chardonnet.

20 July
Appointed general secretary of the General Council of the Seine Department.

1800–4
Active on the Council throughout the Consulate, making arguments for cemeteries, repairing public monuments, regulating the 'mania for collections', and creating a triumphal arch honouring the First Consul on the site of the Grand Châtelet.

1801
Concordat agreed between Pope Pius VII and Napoleon Bonaparte. Publishes *Encyclopédie méthodique: architecture*, volume 2, part 1 ('Colossal' to 'Escalier'). (Publishes part 2 of volume 2 in 1820 and the third volume in 1825.)

1802
Leaves Chaillot for 31 rue Basse in Passy.

1803
Publishes a longer version of his 1785 prize-winning essay on Egyptian architecture.

1804
Elected to the National Institute's Class of History and Ancient Literature in February, and over the next decade presents memoranda on ancient art. In December, he attends the Coronation of Napoleon marking the end of the Republic and start of the Empire.

1804–7
Publishes in *Archives littéraires de l'Europe* nine new articles on Canova, landscape painting, nudity in sculpture, Cornelis de Pauw's theory about female beauty, Parrhasius's picture of the Demos, the Temple of Olympian Jupiter in Agrigento, and the ideal in the arts.

1806
His lectures on the 'moral considerations on the destination of artworks' (published in 1815) criticize how the Empire commissions and displays artworks, and how the Museum of French Monuments accumulates disembodied religious sculptures.

1812–14
Joins plots preparing Napoleon's downfall.

1814
Publishes *The Olympian Jupiter* before the Restoration, but copies printed after May are dedicated to Louis XVIII. Awarded the Legion of Honour and appointed royal censor. Appointed general intendant of the arts and public monuments, but the post is short-lived.

xx BIOGRAPHICAL AND POLITICAL CHRONOLOGY

1815	Refuses roles during the Hundred Days (March–June). After the second Restoration he lives briefly at 13 rue de la Ville l'Evêque, joins the Royal Council of Public Instruction, Honorary Museum Council, and Office for Improvements in the General Council of the Seine.
1816	Elected permanent secretary of the Academy of Fine Arts after Dufourny declines the role. He uses his influence to close the Museum of French Monuments. He moves to 14 rue de Condé, which will remain his home for the rest of his life.
1818	Second English voyage to study the Parthenon sculptures in the British Museum, subject of his pseudo-epistolary *Letters Written from London to Canova in Rome on the Elgin Marbles*.
1819	Publishes *Collection of Dissertations on Different Subjects of Antiquity*.
1820–2	Elected by the Seine Department to serve in the Chamber of Deputies.
1823	Publishes *Essay on the Nature, the End and the Means of Imitation in the Fine Arts*.
1824	Publishes a biography of Raphael and an edition of Poussin's letters.
1827–9	Designs and partly finances a pulpit for Saint-Germain-des-Prés, Paris.
1830	Bedridden for months after the July Revolution.
1834	Publishes a biography of Canova.
1835	Publishes a biography of Michelangelo.
1837	Publishes *Essay on the Ideal*.
1839	Retires as permanent secretary of the Academy of Fine Arts.
1848	Revolution and Second Republic.
1849	Dies in Paris on 28 December aged ninety-four and is buried in Montparnasse cemetery.

Introduction: An Unconventional History of the Revolution

Antoine-Chrysosthôme Quatremère de Quincy was celebrated during his lifetime as 'the person in France and even in Europe who writes best on the arts'. His biographies of artists, reconstructions of ancient masterpieces, and writings on the theory, practice, and history of art and architecture led his compatriots to call him 'our Winckelmann' and earned him the respect of distinguished foreigners.[1] Just as Soane admired his essay on Egyptian architecture, Hegel praised his 'masterpiece' on ancient Greek polychromy.[2]

However, as I argue, Quatremère was never simply an esoteric antiquarian and theoretician; he was also a zealous functionary and skilled publicist whose ostensibly impartial writings on the arts often served a political agenda. This was clearly the case during the Revolution, the subject of this book, when he was twice elected to the national legislature and spent several years hiding, imprisoned, or exiled because of his royalist politics. Influential political figures during the 1790s recognized his 'intelligence, probity and knowledge', 'excellent mind', and contribution to the counter-revolution.[3] But after the Restoration younger generations saw him simply as the permanent secretary of the Academy of Fine Arts and the defender of outdated institutional and stylistic norms. The art critic Auguste Jal thus described him as a 'tiring nightmare' whilst Stendhal dismissed him as 'the most boring of all members of the Institute'.[4]

---

[1] A.-F. Artaud de Montor, *Histoire du pape Pie VII*, vol. 1 (Paris, 1837), p. 381; R. Schneider, *L'esthétique classique chez Quatremère de Quincy (1805–1823)* (Paris, 1910), p. 88.

[2] D. Watkin, 'Quatremère de Quincy', in idem, *Sir John Soane: Enlightenment Thought and the Royal Academy Lectures* (Cambridge, 1996), pp. 171–8; G. W. F. Hegel, *Hegel's Aesthetics. Lectures on Fine Art* [1823–30], vol. 2, trans. T. Knox (Oxford, 1998), p. 773.

[3] C.-M. de Talleyrand, *Extraits des mémoires du prince de Talleyrand-Périgord*, vol. 2 (Paris, 1838), p. 323; P.-L. Roederer, *Journal d'économie publique, de morale et de politique*, vol. 2, no. 20, 10 March 1797, p. 66; P. Barras, *Mémoires de Barras, membre du Directoire*, vol. 2 (Paris, 1895), pp. 396–7. Quatremère's first biographers devoted around half of their accounts to his life during the revolutionary decade: A. Arnault et al, 'Quatremère de Quincy (Antoine-Chrysosthôme)', *Dictionnaire historique et raisonné de tous les hommes depuis la Révolution française*, vol. 17 (Paris, 1827), pp. 167–9; F. Barrière, 'M. Quatremère de Quincy', *Revue de Paris*, vol. 5, May 1850, p. 286; A. Maury, 'Quatremère de Quincy', in L. Michaud, ed., *Biographie universelle ancienne et moderne, nouvelle édition*, vol. 34 (Paris, n.d. [post-1853]), pp. 608–12.

[4] A. Jal, *Esquisses, croquis, pochades, ou tout ce qu'on voudra sur le Salon de 1827* (Paris, 1828), pp. 244, 538; Stendhal, 'Esquisses de la société parisienne, de la politique et de littérature: Esquisse XV', in Stendhal, *Paris-Londres: Chroniques*, ed. R. Dénier (Paris, 1997), pp. 767, 807.

Quatremère de Quincy: Art and Politics during the French Revolution. David Gilks, Oxford University Press.
© David Gilks 2024. DOI: 10.1093/oso/9780198745563.003.0001

2 QUATREMÈRE DE QUINCY

The way that Quatremère was remembered after his death in 1849, aged ninety-four, tended to reinforce the reputation that he acquired during his last decades. Members of the Institute staked out his legacy as their exclusive property when they commissioned his portrait bust and addressed his deeds as an academician in their obituaries and eulogies.[5] This was partly because they knew little about the first half of his life, despite the efforts of Étienne-Marc Quatremère, who abandoned writing a biography of his father's cousin after publishing a first segment covering up until 1789.[6] During the second half of the nineteenth century, Quatremère fell into relative obscurity even if his writings on architecture and ancient colossal sculptures were reference works for experts and his biography of Raphael was read outside the academe.[7]

Despite Quatremère's diminished standing, during the decades before the Great War the emergence of Art History as an academic discipline, combined with the wider initiative to gather, verify, and publish historical documents, created favourable conditions that led to several important studies of him. First came short biographies by Henri Jouin (secretary of the School of Fine Arts) and Henri Wallon (permanent secretary of the Academy of Inscriptions), which focused on his deeds after 1815 and depicted him as an effective administrator whose name honoured both the Academy of Fine Arts and the Academy of Inscriptions.[8] However, whilst previous academic eulogizers downplayed his life in the Revolution, Jouin and Wallon devoted a third of their accounts to his actions during this period. Until the present study, they provided the most detailed overview of these years, but they avoided spelling out his Catholic faith or support for the counter-revolution—appalling attributes in the context of the Third Republic.

---

[5] AN, F21 0048, dossier 7. The Institute commissioned Charles-François Nanteuil-Leboeuf to produce a white marble bust. Several academicians gave accounts of Quatremère's life that glossed over the Revolution: C. Magnin, *Funérailles de M. Quatremère de Quincy* (Paris, 1849); D. Raoul-Rochette, *Discours prononcés aux funérailles de Quatremère de Quincy le 30 décembre 1849* (Paris, 1850); J.-D. Guigniaut, *Notice historique sur la vie et les travaux de M. Quatremère de Quincy* (Paris, 1864). Guigniaut published a slightly longer biography in 1866.

[6] É. Quatremère, 'Notice historique sur la vie de M. Quatremère de Quincy. Premier article', *Journal des Savants* (1853), pp. 657–69.

[7] See, for example, G. Semper, *Die vier Elemente der Baukunst* (Brunswick, 1851), pp. 1, 12; E. Viollet-le-Duc, *Dictionnaire raisonné de l'architecture française du XIème au XVIème siècle*, vol. 6 (Paris, 1863), pp. 31–9; C. Blanc, *Grammaire des arts du dessin: architecture, sculpture, peinture, jardins* (Paris, [1880] 2000), pp. 119, 145, 206, 283, 353–4, 420; 'Raphael of Urbino', in *National Quarterly Review* (1873), vol. 27, pp. 252–72. Quatremère was occasionally cited in other contexts, such as in J. Renouvier, *Histoire de l'art pendant la Révolution* (Paris, 1863), pp. 2, 23, 34, 48, 75, 91, 97; and L. Avin, 'Quelques mots touchant l'application du droit le conquête aux monuments de l'art', *Bulletins de l'Académie royale des sciences, des lettres et des beaux-arts de Belgique*, vol. 41 (1872), pp. 263–91.

[8] H. Jouin, *Antoine-Chrysosthôme Quatremère de Quincy. Deuxième secrétaire perpétuel de l'Académie des beaux-arts* (Paris, 1892); H. Wallon, *Centenaire de l'élection de Quatremère de Quincy à l'Institut, classe d'histoire et de littérature ancienne* (Paris, 1903).

The art historian René Schneider followed Jouin and Wallon with more substantial works.[9] Schneider had no intention of rehabilitating Quatremère, whose apparent contempt for museums and medieval art belonged to a bygone era, but this critical distance did not help him to adopt a rounded approach to his subject. Since Schneider justified writing about Quatremère on the grounds that it would help explain the institutional and theoretical contexts in which artists worked, he naturally dwelled upon Quatremère the neo-classical aesthetician, the friend of artists, the 'superintendent of the arts' during the Restoration, the precursor of Haussmann in urban improvements, and the enemy of the Museum of French Monuments. By contrast, Schneider largely ignored Quatremère the politician and subtle polemicist. By organizing his studies of Quatremère thematically, Schneider depicted a character whose views remained oddly impervious to change, even though they were expressed over many decades in radically different circumstances. His portrait thus played into how Quatremère fashioned himself as a man of principle.

Interest in Quatremère declined further when fascism tainted neo-classicism. Between the 1920s and 1960s, his name rarely appeared in print except in several histories of aesthetics and studies of Jacques-Louis David and Antonio Canova.[10] Since the 1960s, however, Quatremère has been rediscovered thanks to a truly interdisciplinary and international effort in which Italian scholars were often pioneers. Architectural theorists found Quatremère's encyclopaedias and archaeological reconstructions fruitful sources for their own reflections.[11] Once historians of art and architecture revisited the eighteenth century, they encountered Quatremère as the biographer of artists, travel companion of David, friend of Canova, architect of the Panthéon, and influential theorist.[12] Historians of heritage

---

[9] R. Schneider, 'Quatremère de Quincy et l'art de la médaille (1806–1830)', *Gazette numismatique française*, vol. 12 (1908), pp. 363–86; idem, 'Un ennemi du Musée des Monuments françaises', *Gazette de beaux-arts* (1909), pp. 353–70; idem, *Quatremère de Quincy et son intervention dans les arts, 1788–1830* (Paris, 1910); idem, *L'esthétique classique chez Quatremère*.

[10] T. Mustoxydes, *Histoire de l'esthétique française, 1700–1900* (Paris, 1920), pp. 95–111; F. Will, 'Two Critics of the Elgin Marbles: William Hazlitt and Quatremère de Quincy', *Journal of Aesthetics and Art Criticism*, vol. 14, no. 4 (June 1956), pp. 462–74; R. Baschet, *E.-J Delécluze: Témoin de son temps 1781–1863* (Paris, 1942), p. 259; D. Dowd, *Pageant-Master of the Republic: Jacques-Louis David and the French Revolution* (Lincoln, Nebraska, 1948), pp. 11, 34, 77; H. Honour, 'Antonio Canova and the Anglo-Romans', *Connoisseur*, vol. 144 (1959), p. 225; A. Watt, 'Notes from Paris', *Apollo*, vol. 27, no. 157 (1938), p. 35; F. Luiso, 'L'ultima dimora a Parigi di A.Canova e l'ultima sua grande opera di sculptura', *Nuova antologia* (16 Aug. 1926), pp. 1–17.

[11] See, for example, G. Argan, 'On the Typology of Architecture', *Architectural Design*, vol. 33 (1963); A. Rossi, *L'architettura della città* (Padua, 1966); A. Vidler, 'The Idea of Type: The Transformation of the Academic Ideal, 1750–1830', *Oppositions*, vol. 8 (1977), pp. 95–115; O. Mazzei, *L'ideologia del restauro architettonico da Quatremère a Brandi* (Milan, 1984); V. Farinati, 'Storia e fortuna di un dizionario, Quatremère de Quincy in Italia', in Quatremère de Quincy, *Dizionario storico di architettura*, ed. V. Farinati and G. Teyssot (Venice, 1985), pp. 43–81; S. Lavin, *Quatremère de Quincy and the Invention of a Modern Language of Architecture* (Cambridge, MA, 1992).

[12] See, for instance, M. Messina, 'L'arte di Canova nella critica di Quatremère de Quincy', *Quaderni sul neoclassico*, vols 1–2 (1973), pp. 119–51; I. Wardropper, and F. Rowlands, 'Antonio Canova and Quatremère de Quincy: The Gift of Friendship', *Museum Studies*, vol. 15, no. 1 (1989), pp. 38–46;

4 QUATREMÈRE DE QUINCY

and museums rediscovered Quatremère's writings on the patrimonial upheavals of the Revolution, which stimulated philosophical reflection on the displacement and decontextualization of artworks.[13]

If Quatremère ceased to be an obscure figure by the 1980s, since the bicentenary of the Revolution his reputation has grown to the extent that he is now once again celebrated as the most important writer on the arts and antiquity at the end of the Enlightenment. Historians such as François Furet and Mona Ozouf paved the way, both by jettisoning socio-economic explanations of the Revolution in favour of discourses and symbols, and by challenging the idea that modern France could be traced back to the first supporters of the Republic. Such novel interpretations and approaches created the conditions for Édouard Pommier's paradoxical depiction of Quatremère as both the greatest writer on the arts during the revolutionary decade and the alternative to revolutionary orthodoxy.[14] By substantially advancing our understanding of Quatremère during the 1780s and 1790s, Pommier laid the foundations for recent scholarship that situates some of Quatremère's interventions within wider histories of museums, heritage, art plunder, and within the history of sculpture and architecture.[15] However, Pommier's attempt to understand Quatremère

---

P. Griener, 'Le génie et le théoricien. Canova selon Quatremère de Quincy', in P. Schneemann and P. Griener, eds, *De l'image de l'artiste* (Berne, 1998); C. Johns, *Antonio Canova and the Politics of Patronage in Revolutionary and Napoleonic Europe* (Los Angeles, 1998); H. Körner and F. Piel, '"A mon ami Antoine Quatremère de Quincy": Ein unbekanntes Werk Jacques-Louis Davids aus dem Jahre 1779', *Pantheon*, vol. 43 (1985), pp. 89–96; J. Laurent, *A propos de l'École des beaux-arts* (Paris, 1987), pp. 44–62; A. Becq, *Genèse de l'esthétique française moderne, 1680–1814* (Pisa, 1984), bk. 3; D. Watkin, *A History of Western Architecture* (London, [1986] 1996), p. 336; Y. Luke, 'The Politics of Participation: Quatremère de Quincy and the Theory and Practice of "Concours publiques" in Revolutionary France, 1791–1795', *Oxford Art Journal*, vol. 10, no. 1 (1987), pp. 15–43; T. Rowlands, 'Quatremère de Quincy, the Formative Years, 1785–1795', unpublished Ph.D. thesis, Northwestern University, 1987; J.-C. Lebensztejn, 'De l'imitation dans les beaux-arts', *Critique*, vol. 38, no. 416 (1982), pp. 3–21.

[13] A. Pinelli, 'Storia dell'arte e cultura della tutela. Les Lettres à Miranda di Quatremère de Quincy', *Ricerche di storia dell'arte*, vol. 8 (1975–6), pp. 43–62; A. Pinelli and A. Emiliani, eds, *Lo studio delle arti e il genio dell'Europa. Scritti di A.C. Quatremère de Quincy – Pio VII Chiaramonti (1796-1802)* (Bologna, 1989); D. Sherman, 'Quatremère/Benjamin/Marx: Art Museums, Aura, and Commodity Fetishism', in D. Sherman and I. Rogoff, eds, *Museum Discourses: Histories, Discourses, Spectacles* (Minneapolis, 1994), pp. 123–43.

[14] É. Pommier, 'La Révolution et le destin des ouvrages de l'art de l'Italie', in Quatremère, *Lettres à Miranda*, ed. É. Pommier (Paris, 1989), pp. 7–83; idem, *L'art de la liberté* (Paris, 1989), esp. pp. 63–91, 168–74, 415–49; idem, 'Quatremère de Quincy et le patrimoine', in G. Pavanello, ed., *Canova* (Venice, 2006), pp. 459–80; idem, 'Quatremère de Quincy et la destination des ouvrages de l'art', in R. Démoris, ed., *Les fins de la peinture* (Paris, 1990), pp. 31–51.

[15] See, for example, P. Griener, 'Carlo Fea and the Defence of the Museum of Rome, 1783–1815', *Georges-Bloch-Jahrbuch des Kunstgeschichtlichen Seminars der Universität Zürich*, vol. 7 (2000), pp. 96–109; L. Baridon, 'Le Dictionnaire d'architecture de Quatremère de Quincy: codifier le néoclassicisme', in C. Blanckaert, M. Porret, and F. Brandli, eds, *L'Encyclopédie méthodique (1782-1832). Des lumières au positivisme* (Geneva, 2006), pp. 691–718; R. Middleton and M.-N. Baudouin-Matuszek, *Jean Rondelet: The Architect as Technician* (New Haven, 2007), p. 331; A. Potofsky, *Constructing Paris in the Age of Revolution* (Basingstoke, 2009), p. 112; E. Naginski, *Sculpture and Enlightenment* (Los Angeles, 2009), esp. pp. 223–25, 232–39; B. Savoy, *Patrimoine annexé: les biens culturels saisis par la France en Allemagne autour de 1800* (Paris, 2003), vol. 1, esp pp. 203–14; D. Poulot, 'The Cosmopolitanism of Masterpieces', in A. Quatremère de Quincy, *Letters to Miranda and Canova on the Abduction of Antiquities from Rome and Athens* (Los Angeles, 2012),

INTRODUCTION 5

within and against discourses and debates during the Revolution overlooked how Quatremère's writings functioned within strategic political alliances. If many art historians share Pommier's confusion over Quatremère's politics, most historians of the Revolution have ignored him altogether.[16]

The revival of interest in Quatremère has rescued him from oblivion and underlined the range of his writings and their ability to inspire theorists, architects, and art historians. But the nature of this revival has also resulted in a fragmentary understanding of his life, a partial and often an anachronistic engagement with his writings, and confusion about his roles during the Revolution.

My book is the first comprehensive account of Quatremère's interventions, political alliances, and milieux during the Revolution. Rather than treating him as an esoteric and a categorical thinker, my book restores the context of political action to demonstrate that he was a strategic thinker, polemicist, and publicist who was involved in the cut-and-thrust of high politics and art-world politicking. The book reinterprets his most famous writings, but my attempts to explain what he was doing by writing them have led me to reconstruct his social circles, to sketch the events and arguments that compelled him to act, to scrutinize his less-known writings (including several that were published anonymously or never published) besides letters, pamphlets, articles, essays, treatises, reports, speeches, testimonies, and inventories of seized possessions. There were, as Werner Szambien notes, 'several Quatremères', and throughout this book I aim to depict a complex and contradictory figure with multiple agendas whose cultural and artistic interventions were sometimes politically motivated.[17]

What follows is a detailed contextual study of an eventful yet widely misunderstood period in Quatremère's life when he turned to public affairs after setting aside his antiquarian research and encyclopaedia of architecture. However, the book does not simply reboot how we think about Quatremère. Through immersing ourselves in his world during the Revolution, the book provides a window

---

pp. 1–91; idem, *Musée, nation, patrimoine (1789–1815)* (Paris, 1997), esp. pp. 277-81; idem, '*Surveiller et s'instruire': La Révolution française et l'intelligence de l'héritage historique* (Oxford, 1996), esp. pp. 485–92; K. Pomian, *Le Musée, une histoire mondiale*, vol. 2 (Paris, 2021), esp. pp. 153–65; A. Stara, *The Museum of French Monuments 1795–1816: 'Killing Art to Make History'* (Farnham, 2013), esp. ch. 4; C. Michel, *The Académie Royale de Peinture et de Sculpture: The Birth of the French School, 1648–1793*, trans. C. Miller (Los Angeles, [2012] 2018), pp. 198–207, 235–9.

[16] Pommier mischaracterized Quatremère as a moderate revolutionary who shared Francisco Miranda's politics; 'La Révolution et le destin des ouvrages de l'art de l'Italie'. Most art historians follow Pommier's verdict, but some also describe Quatremère as a dechristianizing vandal and an 'inflexible character', 'firm in his republican convictions', whose concept of the 'Republic of the Arts' was 'more republican than the Republic'; F. Souchal, *Le vandalisme de la Révolution* (Paris, 1993), pp. 54–6, 244, 288; and Lavin, *Quatremère*, pp. xiii, 158. However, Lavin recognises that his 'political career is difficult to characterise' because 'no comprehensive study of his political writings has been undertaken' (ibid., p. 149).

[17] W. Szambien, 'Quatremère de Quincy: lettres à Miranda sur le déplacement des monuments de l'art de l'Italie (1796)', *Revue de l'art*, no. 87 (1990), p. 88.

into revolutionary art and politics, art-world rivalries, institutional and legal reforms, and debates about state patronage for the arts. Most ambitiously, the book offers an unconventional history of the Revolution that foregrounds the royalist Feuillant and Clichy clubs, the right-wing press, successive Committees of Public Instruction, and debates about the purpose of the fine arts and future of the republic of letters. Looking at his life during the Revolution also reminds us that the Revolution was a lived experience whose participants made choices and compromises, formed friendships and alliances, and learned to reuse the language of their opponents to different ends. My contention is that a detailed biographical study can provide insights into the mental inventory of a participant, shed light on the contradictory and even hypocritical character of revolutionary politics, and overturn the assumption that individual revolutionary actors embodied a fixed ideology.

Even though I never tried to apply any one particular methodology, several historians have informed my approach to researching and writing this book. My efforts to read and contextualize Quatremère's writings and establish what they meant to his informed contemporaries pay homage to John Pocock's study of Edward Gibbon. Yet my choice of subject follows in the footsteps of art historians, and is partly inspired by Francis Haskell's exploration of the connections between artistic creation, rediscovery, patronage, collecting, and displaying. If these historians of ideas and art shaped the book's approach and scope, writings by historians of the Revolution—both historians of factions and contingencies and those of discourses and symbolism—provided invaluable interpretative prompts.

Two trends in scholarship on the Revolution mark this book. The first is the revival of biography. I have found especially instructive biographies of eccentric and even marginal revolutionary actors that shed light on the pathway from the Old Regime to the Revolution and that challenge convenient generalizations about this controversial period.[18] The second trend is the invigorated interest in

---

[18] Such biographies include M. Vovelle, *L'irrésistible ascension de Joseph Sec, bourgeois d'Aix* (Paris, 1975); P. Serna, *Antonelle, aristocrate révolutionnaire (1747–1817)* (Paris, 1997); A. Sepinwall, *The Abbé Grégoire and the French Revolution: The Making of Modern Universalism* (Los Angeles, 2005); J. Horn, *Alexandre Rousselin and the French Revolution* (Oxford, 2020); C. Le Bozec, *Boissy d'Anglas: un grand notable libéral* (Paris, 1993); L. Mason on Fréron, in 'The Culture of Reaction: Demobilizing the People after Thermidor', *French Historical Studies*, vol. 39, no. 3 (2016), pp. 1–26; J.-L. Chappey, 'Pierre-Louis Roederer et la presse sous le Directoire et le Consulat: l'opinion publique et les enjeux d'une politique éditoriale', *Annales historiques de la Révolution française*, no. 334 (2003), pp. 1–21; and I. Rademacher, 'La science sociale républicaine de Pierre-Louis Roederer', *Revue française d'histoire des idées politiques*, vol. 13 (2001), pp. 25–55, and idem, 'Élites et républicanisme: Pierre-Louis Roederer, critique de la campagne d'Italie et brumairien', in J.-P. Barbe and R. Bernecker, eds, *Les intellectuels européens et la campagne d'Italie, 1796–1798* (Munster, 1999), pp. 129–60; T. Tackett (on Adrien-Joseph Colson), in *The Glory and the Sorrow. A Parisian and His World in the Age of the French Revolution* (Oxford, 2022); and G. Matthew Adkins, 'The Renaissance of Peiresc: Aubin-Louis Millin and the Postrevolutionary Republic of Letters', *Isis*, vol. 99, no. 4 (2008), pp. 675–700; C. Trinchero, 'Regards sur l'Italie entre XVIIIe et XIXe siècles: le Magasin encyclopédique de Millin', *Annales historiques de la Révolution française*, no. 351 (2008), pp. 59–75.

the years between Thermidor 1794 and Brumaire 1799, the fruits of which helped me to reinterpret Quatremère's most famous writing from the Revolution. In particular, the last chapters of the book profit from recent scholarship that integrates the history of ideas with the study of political power and identifies a distinctive political culture based on republican attempts to distance the new Republic from the year II.[19]

The structure of the book is chronological, although several chapters partly transcend their place in the sequence. The first two chapters consider Quatremère's life before the Revolution and demonstrate that his ideas about the arts predated 1789. Chapter 1 documents his family, his schooling at Louis-le-Grand, and his apprenticeship in a sculptor's studio before turning to his Italian voyages, research into ancient sculpture and architecture, and conviction that papal Rome was the epicentre of the learned world. Chapter 2 reconsiders his first writings between 1785 and 1789: these consisted of his reflections on ancient Egyptian and Greek architecture and a first volume on architecture for the *Encyclopédie méthodique*, besides short contributions in periodicals to shape public opinion about certain issues in Paris.

The next four chapters explain how Quatremère navigated the Revolution between 1789 and 1794. This section of the book shows how in public he supported the Constitution of 1791 and paid lip service to the idea that liberty would regenerate the arts, but in private favoured handing greater powers to the king in 1791 and feared that the Revolution would harm venerable cultural institutions and artistic patronage. Chapter 3 focuses on his introduction to revolutionary politics as a municipal representative in the Paris Commune, showing how he used his position in 1789–90 to advance the interests of the Théâtre de Monsieur, one of the queen's cultural projects, by supporting the 'liberty of theatres'. The chapter then reinterprets his contributions in 1791 to the quarrel over the royal academies and their compatibility with the Revolution. I show that he: defended the Academy of Painting and Sculpture and its besieged leadership; reiterated the case for generous state patronage and the traditional academic hierarchy of genres; and proposed that the Academy control the national museum and state-funded art education. However, as the chapter concludes, intrigues against him and his association with the open Salon of 1791 earned him an ill-deserved reputation as a *vainqueur* of the academic Bastille.

---

[19] See, for example, P. Serna, *La République des girouettes. 1789-1815 et au-delà. Une anomalie politique: la France de l'extrême-centre* (Paris, 2005); J.-L. Chappey, 'Du peuple *enfant* au peuple *malheureux*. Questions sur les mutations des dominations sociales et politiques entre la république thermidorienne et l'Empire', *La Révolution française: cahiers de l'Institut d'histoire de la Révolution française*, no. 9 (2015), pp. 67–91; L. Chavanette, ed., *Le Directoire: forger la République (1795–1799)* (Paris, 2020); and V. Martin, 'Les enjeux diplomatiques dans le Magasin encyclopédique (1795–1799): du rejet des systèmes politiques à la redéfinition des rapports entre les nations', *La Révolution française: cahiers de l'Institut d'histoire de la Révolution française*, no. 2 (2012).

Chapter 4 reconsiders Quatremère's vision for transforming the church of Sainte-Geneviève. It explains how his reputation as a reform-minded savant in spring 1791 led him to join Talleyrand's Committee of Public Instruction just when the Constituent Assembly sought a temple for honouring great men such as the late Mirabeau. The chapter shows how Quatremère led the Committee's investigation into transforming Sainte-Geneviève and proposed changes that would, in his view, respect Soufflot's intentions whilst giving the edifice a sombre and unified character that befitted its new function. The far-reaching yet economical changes that Quatremère envisaged appealed to the Directory of the Department of Paris, which in July appointed him to direct what was soon called the Panthéon. Quatremère's reputation in 1791 also led Paris artists to help elect him to the Legislative Assembly. However, as Chapter 5 shows, many artists were disappointed when he used his position as a national representative for partisan purposes, such as organizing the Festival of the Law in June 1792 to check the radicalization of public opinion. In the Legislative Assembly, he voted consistently on the right and in 1792 helped the royalist press articulate a coherent anti-Jacobin discourse.

Chapter 6 explains how Quatremère realized his vision for the Panthéon between July 1791 and his incarceration in March 1794. The chapter argues that his principal decisions reflected the spirit of enlightened patriotism predating 1791 rather than the republicanism of 1792–4, but it also explains how he continued directing the project after the abolition of the monarchy. Although he left unchanged most of his iconographic programme, events compelled him to adapt and rename several sculptures and to design others to feign support for the Republic—gestures that did not prevent his house arrest in 1793 and imprisonment the following year.

The last chapters show how Quatremère served the counter-revolution against the Thermidorian Convention and Directory. Chapter 7 describes his imprisonment in 1794 and analyses his political interventions and writings between summer 1794 and summer 1796. The chapter shows how, after his release, he helped reform David's competition for artists and how he became militant when the Law of Two Thirds prevented royalists dominating the legislative chambers. Condemned to death in absentia for his role in the Vendémiaire uprising, the chapter documents how, whilst hiding, he wrote several attacks on the Directory. These writings show that we must place him amongst those conservative agitators who, consistent with the Clichy club's strategy, exploited press freedom to pen works intended to spread mistrust and scepticism, widen division, and fragment public opinion.

Chapter 8 reinterprets the most famous of these writings: Quatremère's pseudo-epistolary *Letters on the Abduction of Monuments of the Arts of Italy*, which attacked the Republic's attempt to perfect its museums through plundering cultural property. The chapter shows how his reflections about 'civilization' that at first glance appear moderate, even apolitical, actually attacked the Republic in both subtle and explicit ways. I show that he wrote this work to defend the papacy whilst also appealing to republican sceptics of the Directory's expansionist foreign policy by insisting that foreign plunder would undermine the Republic's civilizing mission.

Chapter 9 covers the period between summer 1796 and 1800. The chapter explains how sympathetic judges cleared him of participating in the Vendémiaire uprising, and how he then resumed efforts to undermine the Republic through his writings whilst feigning constitutionalism during the 1797 election campaigning. He was one of the most vocal clichyean deputies after his election to the Council of Five Hundred, but his outspoken politics and reputation for plotting meant that he was proscribed after the Fructidor coup. The chapter shows how he then hid in Paris for over a year, finally leaving for Germany in November 1798. The concluding section reconstructs his travels and his milieu in Holstein in 1799, examining the different ways that his exile partly changed and partly reinforced his thinking before the Brumaire coup allowed him to return to France.

Three arguments run through these chapters. The first is that Quatremère was a devout Catholic royalist who favoured a reformed and centralized monarchy. Just as he described himself as 'the least revolutionary man there is', his perceptive allies and critics alike recognized that he served the counter-revolution with distinction.[20] His description in 1797 of the ideal candidate for the legislative councils should thus be read as autobiographical: he proposed that electors choose an impartial student of the ancients whose honest and independent wealth, experience of government, and political record ensured that their representative would pursue 'order and justice', end 'war and revolution', and revive public finance, commerce, religion, and morality.[21] Given Quatremère's politics, understanding his biography means that we need to reconsider his membership of royalist clubs, identify his allies in national legislatives (such as Vincent-Marie Viénot de Vaublanc), examine his contact with royalist publicists (such as Jacques Mallet du Pan and Jean-Gabriel Peltier), explain his admiration for counter-revolutionary writers (such as Jean Richer de Sérizy), and interpret his steadfast belief that the papacy was the custodian of art and knowledge and that Catholicism was the greatest source of artistic inspiration. By contrast, his fraught relationship with David and fleeting friendship with Miranda were less significant than previous scholars have imagined.

---

[20] AN, F7 6285, no. 5819, paper 14; Letter from Quatremère de Quincy in Frankfurt to 'Monsieur Martin, 42 Broad St. London' [Miranda], 6 Dec. 1798; J. Mallet du Pan, 'Lettre...au comte de Sainte-Aldegonde' (19 April 1797), in *Mémoires et correspondance de Mallet du Pan*, ed. P.-A. Sayous (Paris, 1851), vol. 2, p. 299; Barras, *Mémoires*, vol. 2, p. 396.

[21] Quatremère, *La véritable liste des candidats, précédée d'observations sur la nature de l'institution des candidats, et son application au gouvernement représentatif* (Paris, 1797), pp. 57–67.

10   QUATREMÈRE DE QUINCY

The second argument is that modern scholars have misunderstood Quatremère's political convictions because his strategic compromises—both to survive and to advance his political aims and personal ambitions—sewed confusion. The book contends that he was an opportunistic and a dissembling figure who exploited the language of his opponents, often, as one rival complained, by hiding beneath a 'cloak of democracy and liberty'.[22] If Quatremère was never the turncoat depicted by his Restoration critics such as the Comte de Paroy, he nevertheless displayed several hallmarks of the 'weathervanes' identified by Pierre Serna because he was prone to devise right-wing political stands in private and then attempt to make these stands appear moderate in public.[23]

The third argument is that Quatremère's politics and reflections on the fine arts, culture, and education were often intertwined. As Sainte-Beuve recognized, he was 'an enemy of democracy in art' as much as in politics.[24] The book demonstrates, moreover, that his political convictions progressed logically from the architectural theory that he formed before the Revolution. During the 1780s, he contrasted the modern mania for innovation unfavourably with the Greek Doric order that resulted from centuries of gradual experimentation with wooden huts. After 1789, he duly contrasted the benefits of collective, organic, intergenerational social and political evolution to the dangers of radical leaps of faith, 'vapours of opinion', and 'experimental politics', which favoured unlimited liberty and destroyed institutions and monuments that earlier generations had created patiently.[25] Yet, as the book also shows, after 1789 he often used ostensibly artistic subjects in the service of his political ends.

The book's chronological structure and its treatment of Quatremère as an intellectual and political figure risk overlooking crucial facets of his biography such as his appearance, character, and mindset. We should now therefore piece together from scattered sources a sketch of Quatremère the individual—a surprisingly difficult task because he was reticent and disliked writing private letters or talking about himself (Fig. 0.1).[26]

His tall stature, hawk nose, elongated philtrum, and large oval head meant that he was easily recognized. His oratory was equally striking: his loud, nasally voice delivered slow and firm monologues that initially commanded respect

---

[22] A. Renou, *Réfutation de la seconde suite aux Considérations sur les arts de dessin par M. Quatremère de Quincy* (Paris, [20 June] 1791), p. 3.

[23] Serna, *La république des girouettes*, p. 19.

[24] C.-A. Sainte-Beuve, *Nouveaux lundis*, vol. 2 (Paris, 1883), p. 233.

[25] Quatremère, *Considérations sur les arts du dessin en France, suivies d'un plan d'Académie, ou d'école publique et d'un système d'encouragements* (Paris, 1791), p. 168; idem, *La véritable liste*, pp. 4–7; idem, *Quelques considérations pratiques et de circonstance, sur la constitution et la liberté de la presse* (Paris, 1814), pp. 6, 11.

[26] H. Lemonnier, 'Une lettre de Quatremère de Quincy [1828]', *Archives de l'art français*, vol. 1 (1907), pp. 189–92.

Fig. 0.1 François Bonneville, *Quatremère. Deputy of the Department of the Seine to the Council of Five-Hundred*. 1797. Stipple engraving. 15.4 × 10 cm. BnF.

but later invited ridicule.[27] He was blessed with robust health, despite suffering in his fifties from what he described as 'melancholy, hypochondria or apathy that drains every sort of enthusiasm for life'.[28] Although he fashioned himself as an impartial savant and 'friend of the arts', he was often prudent or opportunistic rather than principled. He was loyal but unlikeable: friends noted that he craved influence rather than popularity whilst unsympathetic acquaintances

---

[27] Several artists depicted Quatremère in portraits and caricatures, including David (1779), Françoise Bonneville (1797), François-André Vincent (c.1810), Julien-Léopold Boilly (c.1815–16 and 1820), François-Joseph Heim (1824), and Pierre-Jean David d'Angers (1834 and 1835). Contemporary descriptions of his voice and appearance include: V.-M. Vaublanc, *Mémoires sur la Révolution de France*, vol. 1 (Paris, 1833), pp. 349, 426; Guigniaut, *Notice historique*, pp. 40, 45, 61; Amaury-Duval, *L'atelier d'Ingres. Souvenirs* (Paris, 1878), p. 9; J.-P.-G. de Paroy, *Mémoires du comte de Paroy: souvenirs d'un défenseur de la famille royale pendant la Révolution* (Paris, 1895), p. 264; Stendhal, *Correspondance générale*, ed. V. del Litto, vol. 3 (Paris, 1999), p. 587; 'Sketches of Parisian Society, Politics and Literature, Paris, October 18, 1826', in *New Monthly Magazine and Literary Journal*, vol. 17 (London, 1826), pp. 422–3.

[28] *Carteggio*, pp. 169–71; *Procès-verbaux de l'Académie des beaux-arts*, ed. J.-M. Leniaud, vol. 5 (Paris, 2004), pp. 57, 127.

12 QUATREMÈRE DE QUINCY

found him short-tempered, ambitious, and supercilious. Letters that he wrote during his exile in Germany reveal his neurotic and intolerant character.[29]

Quatremère imbibed an orderly Jansenist mercantile mentality from his father that permitted little time for pleasure. However, he enjoyed reading La Fontaine's *Fables* and Greek and Roman epic poetry and listening to church verse and Pergolesi's comic operas. Sculpture was the artform that enthused him and that he practised—his oeuvre included allegorical figurines, bas-reliefs, neo-antique vases, architectural features, and designs for a colossal sculpture group in the Panthéon and for the pulpit in Saint-Germain-des-Prés.[30] Male friendship rather than family structured his social existence. If sexuality of any kind was never the motivating force in his life, his closest emotional attachments were to men such as Canova, Denis-Stanislas Gérard (with whom he cohabited for many years during the Restoration), and the actor Adolphe Leclère (a principal benefactor in his will). Other friends included artists, architects, actors, publicists, philosophers, and politicians, but women barely featured in his life after his mother and sister died during his childhood.[31] He was not close to his family as an adult: political differences and inheritance disputes poisoned his relationship with his brother; and one cousin recalled that extended family members 'did not approach him without difficulty, even though he was very good to them'.[32]

However weak these familial bonds, the fact that Quatremère was born into one of the wealthiest textile dynasties in Paris enabled his devotion to art, scholarship, and public affairs. He lived comfortably from his inheritance, investments, and rents; he rarely cared for money even after the Revolution harmed his finances; and at his death he was sufficiently rich to leave several individuals six-figure franc sums.[33] Despite his wealth, however, he disliked ostentatious luxury and preferred simple if well-furnished and spacious living quarters in central Paris rather than fashionable western faubourgs. He spent his last decades, for example, on the rue de Condé, near the Luxembourg gardens, in an *hôtel* filled with his books and modest collection of antiquities and sculptures that included Canova's gift of two 'ideal heads'.[34] His family had close ties to the parish of Saint-Germain l'Auxerrois

---

[29] P.-F.-L. Fontaine, *Journal, 1799–1853* (Paris, 1987), vol. 1, pp. 605–6, 659; Jouin, *Quatremère*, p. 36; C.-A. Sainte-Beuve, *Nouveaux lundis*, vol. 2 (Paris, 1866), p. 233; AN, F7 6285, no. 5819, papers 14–16; *Archivo del Miranda*, vol. 6 (Caracas, 1929–50), pp. 341–2, 355–7; J. Mallet du Pan, *Mémoires et correspondance de Mallet du Pan* (Paris, 1851), pp. 426–8.

[30] Jouin, *Quatremère*, pp. 5–6, n. 2, explains that most of his work was destroyed in 1870.

[31] AN, MC ET II 1061, wills of 25 June 1833 and 26 Feb. 1840; *Carteggio*, esp. p. 171. Guigniaut, *Notice historique*, p. 48, commented suggestively on his celibacy.

[32] B. Saint-Hilaire, 'Notice sur Étienne Quatremère', *Journal des savants* (1857), p. 721.

[33] At different moments Quatremère owned and rented properties in Paris and its surroundings, including one at no. 140 rue Honoré; Archives de Paris: DQ10 51, file 28, no. 5937; and DQ10 1396, dossier 1037; Bibliothèque de l'Institute, Ms 2555, dossier 4, pieces 52, 60, 107. See AN: MC ET II 1061, for wills dated 25 June 1833 and 26 Feb. 1840.

[34] G. Pavanello, ed., *Il carteggio Canova-Quatremère de Quincy (1785-1822)* (Venice, 2005), p. 186 (hereafter cited as *Carteggio*); Fournel, ed., *Catalogue d'objets d'arts: antiquités égyptiennes, grecques et*

on the right bank, but he lived on both sides of the Seine without an affiliation to any one neighbourhood. His identity was instead inseparable from Paris as a whole, the city of his birth and death where he spent almost all his life bar two voyages to Italy, two shorter visits to England, and a year in Holstein. He continued the family tradition of municipal service, but whereas his relatives were famous for philanthropy and local administration he exercised his civic duty by arguing for improvements and embellishments whilst preserving the city's historic and artistic monuments.[35]

Quatremère's books and prints shed light on how his intellectual interests evolved. Records of his first library (seized by the state in 1798) and second library (assembled between 1798 and 1849) suggest that he learned Latin and ancient Greek during his school years, Italian during his adolescence, and German and English later in life. His collections also reflect his piety: in the 1790s he decorated his apartments with engravings of the Vatican *stanze* and owned several editions of the Holy Bible and the spiritual exercises of the seventeenth-century Jesuit preacher Louis Bourdaloue. During the second half of his life, he amassed theological writings, histories of the papacy and Catholic Church, sermons by Bishop Denis de Frayssinous, and writings by Chateaubriand.[36]

His first library reveals his preoccupation with architecture, art theory, and history and antiquity, but it also betrays his youthful ignorance of the philosophes and his uninterest in politics and political economy. Indeed, this library is consistent with his belief that the real and positive Enlightenment resulted not from the triumph of secular reason but from the papacy's moral and intellectual leadership, the rediscovery of the past, the circulation of knowledge, and the advance of taste.[37] When he finally turned to public affairs in 1789, his library shows that he sought wisdom from foreign sources, such as commentaries on the English and American constitutions and writings by Emmerich de Vattel, Adam Smith, and Arthur Young. Several years later, he acquired works dear to the Idéologues by Étienne Bonnot de Condillac, Nicolas de Condorcet, and Charles-François Dupuis, but reading these writers was simply a means to

---

romaines, vases grecs, terres cuites, figurines en bronze, sculptures en marbre, dont deux bustes de Canova, médailles, miniatures, dessins et belles estampes anciennes et modernes, composant le cabinet de feu M. Quatremère de Quincy (Paris, 1850).

[35] BHVP, MS NA-121, fol. 77.

[36] Two documents (AN: F17 2780/2 and F17 1195) list what the Republican state seized from his first library and incorporated into its own collections. Religious texts included: *Novum Testamentum, ex Regiis aliisque optimis editionibus cum cura expressum* (Leiden, 1673); *Biblia Sacra vulgatæ editionis: Sixti V. pontif* (Lyon, 1732); L. Bourdaloue, *Retraite spirituelle à l'usage des communautés religieuses* (Paris, 1733). His second library was catalogued and sold after his death; Fournel, ed., *Bibliothèque de M. Quatremère de Quincy, la vente 27 mai–6 juin 1850* (Paris, 1850) (hereafter cited as *Bibliothèque*). It contained a large number of books on religion; ibid., esp. pp. 11, 13–15, 137–9.

[37] Quatremère expressed this last view most clearly in his *Letters on the Plan to Abduct Monuments of Art from Italy* [1796] (see Chapter 8) and review of Bernardi's *De l'origine et des progrès de la législation française* (*Journal des savants*, Dec. 1816, pp. 748–51).

understand his enemies. Convinced that the Revolution was 'bloody anarchy', his second library included counter-revolutionary classics by Edmund Burke, Louis de Bonald, and Joseph de Maistre.[38] His libraries together reflect the idiosyncrasies of his intellect, the combination of erudition, logic, and rhetoric that lay behind his polemical writings, and a systemic pattern of thought well suited to the patient yet imaginative work that he considered essential for his descriptions of lost ancient monuments.[39]

[38] Quatremère, *Recueil de notices historiques lues dans les séances publiques de l'Académie royale des beaux-arts à l'Institut* (Paris, 1834), p. 200; *Bibliothèque*, pp. 8, 12, 134–5, 135, 182, 184, 202.

[39] Quatremère, *Letters written from London to Canova in Rome on the Elgin Marbles or the Sculptures of the Temple of Minerva in Athens* [1818], trans C. Miller, in Quatremère, *Letters to Miranda and Canova on the Abduction of Antiquities from Rome and Athens* (Los Angeles, 2012), p. 130.

1

The Making of a Missionary
of Antiquity, 1755–85

Quatremère was born on 28 October 1755 into a merchant dynasty at the apex of right-bank bourgeois society.[1] Yet his family's roots in Paris were shallow, dating back only to the reign of Louis XIV. His ancestors were Burgundian wine merchants who moved to the city where his grandfather, Nicolas-Marc Quatremère, later created the textile business that would make the family's fortune. Nicolas-Marc made shrewd investments like buying the Baudin family's renowned shop on the rue Saint-Denis. He understood Jansenist mercantile social norms, wisely marrying his sons, Nicolas-Étienne Quatremère l'aîné (c.1723–93) and François-Bernard Quatremère de l'Épine (1727–95), to the daughters of a distinguished *marchand mercier* called Jacques Bourjot.[2] The brothers—Antoine Quatremère's uncle and father—expanded the business, paying 1.4 million livres for a Sedan cloth factory that supplied high-value cloth to the family's boutiques, and raised the family's status by serving as judge consuls, *marguillers* in Saint-Germain-l'Auxerrois parish, and *échevins* in the municipal government. Such was the family's local prominence that a street was renamed the rue Quatremère.[3]

The brothers' wealth and association with a prestigious corporation allowed them to overcome their family's undistinguished history. Towards the end of Louis XV's reign they acquired titles of nobility, but they did not move seamlessly from the Third to the Second Estate. The conditions of their ennoblement allowed their eldest sons to continue commerce: Marc-Étienne Quatremère (Antoine's cousin) therefore managed the business and lived in the family residence at 45 rue

---

[1] Bibliothèque de l'Institut de France, MS 2555, dossier 1, no. 1. On the family's status, see D. Garrioch, *The Formation of the Parisian Bourgeoisie, 1690–1830* (Cambridge, MA, 1996), p. 278; C. Sargentson, *Merchants and Luxury Markets: The Marchands Merciers of Eighteenth-Century Paris* (London, 1996), p. 102.

[2] N. Lyon-Caen, 'Territoire paroissial et investissement nobiliaire. Marc-Étienne Quatremère et les limites de Saint-Germain-l'Auxerrois', *Hypothèses 2005. Travaux de l'école doctorale d'histoire*, vol. 1 (Paris, 2006), p. 83; A.-P. Durnerin, *Table généalogique de la famille Quatremère* (Paris, 1896).

[3] I. Balsamo et al., ed., *La manufacture du Dijonval et la draperie sedanaise, 1650–1850* (Châlons-sur-Marne, 1984), p. 88; N. Lyon-Caen, 'Les jansénistes, le commerce, et l'argent au dix-huitième siècle', in F. Armannachi, ed., *Religion and Religious Institutions in the European Economy, 1000–1800* (Florence, 2012), pp. 592–3. The rue Quatremère later became part of the rue d'Anjou-Saint-Honoré—see J.-B. de Saint-Victor, *Tableau historique et pittoresque de Paris*, vol. 1 (Paris, 1808), p. 524.

Quatremère de Quincy: Art and Politics during the French Revolution. David Gilks, Oxford University Press.
© David Gilks 2024. DOI: 10.1093/oso/9780198745563.003.0002

16   QUATREMÈRE DE QUINCY

St Denis and Denis-Bernard Quatremère-Disjonval (Antoine's brother) oversaw the Sedan factory.[4] Other family members devoted themselves to piety, charity, law, or learning.[5]

Nicolas-Étienne and François-Bernard Quatremère bequeathed a culture of learning to the next generation despite their own lack of intellectual ambitions. Family friends included classical scholars, such as the permanent secretary of the Royal Academy of Inscriptions, Bon-Joseph Dacier, and the celebrated Hellenist and philologist Jean-Baptiste-Gaspard d'Ansse de Villoison.[6] The family also knew artists who belonged to their parish church of Saint-Germain-l'Auxerrois. The painter Nicolas-Bernard Lépicié even lived in Marc-Étienne Quatremère's household towards the end of his life. Lépicié's intimate group portrait of his hosts captured the warmth and decency of this branch of the family: he depicted Marc-Étienne with his young wife, Suzanne Sophie, cradling their baby whilst their daughter held a doll. Although set in an austere room, the high-quality if simple furnishings and clothing conveyed the family's wealth.[7]

The infant Antoine Quatremère spent his first years with a wet nurse in the village of Quincy, hence the 'de Quincy' added to his name—an affectation later mocked by humourists.[8] Bereavement and injury punctuated his childhood in Paris: his mother died before his third birthday; after turning five, a carriage accident left his leg fractured; and, several months before his tenth birthday, his only sister died, aged six. Women henceforth featured infrequently in his life.

His first efforts at sculpture impressed Jean-Baptiste Pigalle, according to a family legend, but his formal education followed a more conventional course. He received private tuition near the Place Saint-Michel and then, from the mid-1760s to the early 1770s, boarded at the College of Louis-le-Grand on the rue Saint-Jacques.[9] Although his contemporaries included Fréron, Robespierre, and Desmoulins, his only known friendship was with Marguerite-Louis-François Duport du Tertre, who later served as minister of justice.[10] The first years in the

---

[4] B. Saint-Hilaire, 'Notice sur Étienne Quatremère', *Journal des savants* (1857), p. 709.

[5] On the family's piety and charity, see A.-F. Ballet, *Éloge de M. Augustin-François Ballet, prêtre du diocèse de Paris* (Paris, 1808), pp. 6–9; P.-D. Labat, *Vie de demoiselle Anne-Charlotte Bourjot: épouse de M. Quatremère l'aîné* (Paris, 1791), pp. 31–5, 75, 112–17. Antoine Quatremère and his brother (commercial work aside) won academic prizes before the Revolution; their cousin Jean-Nicolas Quatremère de Roissy published novels, historical works, and a London travel guide; and Étienne-Marc Quatremère, their cousin once removed, became a distinguished orientalist.

[6] N. Lyon-Caen, *La boite à Perrette: le jansénisme parisien au XVIIIe siècle* (Paris, 2010), p. 227; Saint-Hilaire, 'Notice sur Étienne Quatremère'; Quatremère, *Institut de France. Funérailles de M. d'Ansse de Villoison, 8 floréal an XIII* (Paris, n.d.), p. 4.

[7] N.-B. Lépicié, *Portrait de Marc-Étienne Quatremère et sa famille* (1780). Oil on canvas. 51 × 61 cm. Musée du Louvre. RF2002-5.

[8] A.-L.-D. Martainville, *Merdiana, ou Manuel des chieurs, suite de l'Almanach des gourmands* (Paris, 1803), p. 27.

[9] É. Quatremère, 'Notice historique', pp. 658–9.

[10] Arnault et al, 'Quatremère de Quincy (Antoine-Chrysosthôme)', p. 167.

curriculum consisted mostly of Greek and Roman literature and devotional duties; the middle years included Latin and French grammar; and the final year included moral philosophy, mathematics, and natural science.[11] His father insisted that he remained to study law, which he went about with little enthusiasm.

His father and uncle purchased venal posts and encouraged their younger sons to became magistrates.[12] However, Antoine Quatremère defied his father and immersed himself in the history and theory of the fine arts. He read biographies of artists by Giorgio Vasari, Giovanni Bellori, André Felibien, Giovanni Bottari, and Louis-Abel Bonafous de Fontenay. He studied philosophical writings on beauty, taste, and the relationship between the arts, including those by Vincenzo Vittoria, Bottari, Charles Batteux, Louis Doissin, Daniel Webb, Alexandre Gérard, Jean-Baptiste Du Bos, Ludovico Dolce, and the conferences of the Royal Academy of Painting and Sculpture.[13] He also studied artworks in Paris: religious paintings in churches and monasteries; Rubens's Medici cycle in the Luxembourg Palace; bas-reliefs on fountains and triumphal arches; and freestanding sculptures in squares and gardens such as the Tuileries, which he later called a 'fertile seedbed of the arts'.[14] The young Quatremère perhaps also admired the collections of the Crown, Duc d'Orléans, and Academy of Painting and Sculpture besides temporary exhibitions and displays in dealers' boutiques, the biennial Salon, and Academy of Saint Luke's exhibition (the last of which was in 1774).[15] He later regretted losing this public and pluralistic display of artworks in Paris.

Quatremère's fascination with the arts led him spend three years between 1772 and 1775 as an apprentice in the Louvre studio of Guillaume Coustou le Jeune, a distinguished master of several genres.[16] Most apprentices started young and were the sons of sculptors or masons, but many apprentices paid for instruction and his decision reflected the prestige sculpture enjoyed as the most durable public medium that could stimulate patriotism, embellish cities, and make architecture speak.[17] He later recalled the spirit of emulation in the studio and the 'knowledge, wise taste and esteem for the correct doctrines' that Coustou inherited from his

---

[11] On the College and curriculum, see G. Émond, *Histoire du collège de Louis-le-Grand, ancien collège des jésuites à Paris* (Paris, 1845), pp. 226–7; R. Palmer, ed., *The School of the French Revolution: A Documentary History of the College of Louis-le-Grand and its Director, Jean-Francois Champagne 1762–1824* (Princeton, 1975).

[12] AN, MC ET II 624. In the early 1780s, Antoine Quatremère's cousins became a notary and a judge in the châtelet. Demand meant that the family paid 90 000 livres for the first position alone.

[13] É. Quatremère, 'Quatremère', pp. 659–60; AN: F17 2780/2 and F17 1195.

[14] Quatremère, *Considérations morales sur la destination des ouvrages de l'art* (Paris, 1815), pp. 69, 112; idem, *Recueil de notices historiques*, pp. 62, 393.

[15] On these sites, see inter alia T. Crow, *Painters and Public Life in Eighteenth-Century Paris* (New Haven, 1985); R. Berger, ed., *Public Access to Art in Paris: A Documentary History from the Middle Ages to 1800* (Philadelphia, 1999), pp. 138, 228, 241; J. Connelly, 'Forerunner of the Louvre', *Apollo*, vol. 45 (1972), pp. 382–9; D. Spieth, *Revolutionary Paris and the Market for Netherlandish Art* (Leiden, 2017), ch. 3; C. Guichard, *Les amateurs d'art à Paris au XVIIIe siècle* (Paris, 2008), pp. 122–35.

[16] Jouin, *Quatremère*, p. 4.

[17] R. Benhamou, *Public and Private Art Education in France: 1648–1793* (Oxford, 1993), p. 45.

father and transmitted to his students.[18] Like all apprentices, he learned certain skills and techniques: life drawing, adapting poses from antique models, finishing surfaces, scaling up models, creating casts, and hewing stone. More unusually, he formed a lasting friendship with his mentor, Pierre Julien.[19] He imbibed Julien's simple yet fashionable classical style and through him met the sculptors Claude Dejoux and Guillaume Moitte. Given Quatremère's later interventions, he was perhaps influenced by Julien's gratitude for Crown commissions and Marie-Antoinette's patronage, and, to a lesser extent, this mentor's frustrations with the Academy of Painting and Sculpture.[20]

One can speculate that Quatremère learned several lessons from the *Monument to the Dauphin* (1766–77) for Sens Cathedral, dedicated to the memory of Louis XV's devout son and his wife—the commission that preoccupied the studio during his apprenticeship.[21] For instance, seeing how the studio adapted Charles-Nicolas Cochin's design perhaps encouraged him to think of conception and execution as distinct stages in the creative process. Equally, the commission perhaps reinforced in his mind the belief that costly artworks in the highest genres required Crown patronage and should fulfil spiritual purposes and occupy pre-determined places.

Antoine Quatremère's paternal grandfather died in 1776, leaving his heirs assets that included properties on the right bank and nearby Auteuil.[22] Aged twenty, Quatremère left shortly afterwards for Italy on a voyage that would last four years.[23] Most French visitors who had received an education steeped in Latin and ancient authors considered travelling to Italy a sort of intellectual homecoming. However, he was an unusual traveller: just as his financial independence set him apart from French artists working in Italy as guides, illustrators, or prize-winners, his earnestness distinguished him from affluent young men seeking fashionable amusements.[24]

---

[18] Quatremère, *Recueil de notices historiques*, p. 76.

[19] J. Le Breton, *Notice historique sur la vie et les ouvrages de Pierre Julien* (Paris, 1805), p. 14; M. Worley, 'The Image of Ganymede in France, 1730–1820: The Survival of a Homoerotic Myth', *Art Bulletin*, vol. 76, no. 4 (1994), p. 642; Quatremère, *Discours, Institut de France. Funérailles de M. Moitte* (Paris, 1810).

[20] A. Pascal, *Pierre Julien, sculpteur (1731–1804): sa vie et son œuvre* (Paris, 1904), pp. 48–62; G. Scherf, 'Pierre Julien, "Le vrai statuaire"', in G. Grandjean and G. Scherf, eds, *Pierre Julien 1731–1804: sculpteur du roi* (Paris, 2004), pp. 23–5; M. Worley, *Pierre Julien: Sculptor to Queen Marie-Antoinette* (New York, 2003), pp. 1–15; C. Michel, *The Académie Royale de peinture et de sculpture: The Birth of the French School, 1648–1793*, trans. C. Miller (Los Angeles, 1999), pp. 232–40.

[21] C. Michel, *Charles-Nicolas Cochin et l'art des lumières* (Rome, 1993), p. 455; F. Souchal, 'Le monument funéraire du Dauphin, fils de Louis XV, à la cathédrale de Sens', in B. Barbiche and Y.-M. Bercé, eds, *Études sur l'ancienne France offertes en hommage à Michel Antoine* (Paris, 2003), pp. 369–87; E. Naginski, *Sculpture and Enlightenment* (Los Angeles, 2009), ch. 2.

[22] AN, ET/II 765.

[23] Quatremère, *Canova et ses ouvrages, ou Mémoires historiques sur la vie et les travaux de ce célèbre artiste* (Paris, 1834), p. 19.

[24] On the wider context of the Grand Tour, see esp. I. Bignamini and A. Wilton, *Grand Tour: The Lure of Italy in the Eighteenth Century* (London, 1996) and G. Bertrand, *Le grand tour revisité: pour une archéologie du tourisme: le voyage des Français en Italie (milieu XVIIIe siècle–début XIXe siècle)* (Rome, 2008).

Quatremère spent most of this voyage in Rome, but his library and references in his writings indicate that he saw several northern cities.[25] His excursions were mostly in the Grand Duchy of Tuscany, where, primed by reading Vasari, he saw that even 'the reign of the gothic' produced worthy art and architecture.[26] He later remarked that the thirteenth-century Campo Santo in Pisa was the 'model for all cemeteries', and reflected that Arnolfo di Cambio's Santa Maria dei Fiori, cathedral of Florence, was miraculous given its construction in 'the shadows of barbarism'.[27] He visited the Uffizi gallery and later praised its 'invaluable collection', 'diverse riches of art and curiosities', and 'tastefully decorated halls or rooms'.[28] This gallery opened to the public in 1765, but in recent years had been transformed to tell a Tuscan-centred art history—one that he would replicate in his history of early Renaissance architecture.[29]

Quatremère later advised that a good voyage required living in one place for an extended period.[30] Consistent with this dictum, he remained in Rome for the greater part of these years in Italy to study sculpture and immerse himself in the city's cultural and spiritual life. Since Rome was at the heart of his itinerary, over half the books useful for his voyage that he acquired before or during his stay in Italy concerned the city and its surroundings.[31] This was hardly surprising given Rome's reputation as 'the city worthiest of curiosity in the world' and given that most visitors to Italy wanted to see above all else its ancient monuments, ruins and antiquities and its modern piazzas, palaces, fountains, churches, and museums.[32]

Quatremère lived alongside his compatriots in the tight-knit milieu of nobles, savants, and artists that congregated around the embassy and the French Academy

---

[25] There is tentative evidence that he visited Bologna and Verona. His first library included Carlo Malvasia's *Le pitture di Bologna* (Bologna, 1754). He later described Verona's antiquities in what appear first-hand terms; 'Verona', *EMA*, vol. 3, pp. 574–6.

[26] Quatremère, *Letters on the Plan to Abduct Monuments of Art from Italy* [1796] (hereafter cited as *Letters*), trans D. Gilks, in Quatremère, *Letters to Miranda and Canova on the Abduction of Antiquities from Rome and Athens* (Los Angeles, 2012), p. 97.

[27] Quatremère, 'Cimetière', *EMA*, vol. 1, pp. 681–2; Quatremère, 'Arnolfo de Lapo', *EMA*, vol. 1, p. 136.

[28] Quatremère, 'Muséum', *EMA*, vol. 2:1, p. 742.

[29] G. Luciani, 'Les voyageurs français et les musées italiens', *Dix-huitième siècle*, no. 27 (1995), p. 99; P. Findlen, 'The Eighteenth-Century Invention of the Renaissance: Lessons from the Uffizi', *Renaissance Quarterly*, vol. 66, no. 1 (2013), pp. 9–23. More generally, Quatremère was influenced by scholarship valorising 'primitive' paintings. He owned a copy of G. Cambiagi, *L'Antiquario Fiorentino o sia guida per osservar con metodo le cose notabili della città di Firenze* (Florence, 1778). Revealingly, Quatremère chose only Tuscan examples to illustrate pre-1450 architecture in his *Histoire de la vie et des ouvrages des plus célèbres architectes*, vol. 1 (Paris, 1830).

[30] Quatremère, *Recueil de notices historiques*, p. 241.

[31] AN: F17 2780/2 and 1195. Inventories of his first library list thirteen titles useful for his voyage that were printed before 1780. Quatremère most likely acquired them before or during his stay in Italy. Most of these books were about Rome and its surroundings; only four titles were about other cities or regions. Other books included dictionaries and the *Dictionnaire historique et géographique portatif de l'Italie* (Paris, 1775).

[32] L. de Jaucourt, 'Rome', in D. Diderot and J.-B. d'Alembert, eds, *Encyclopédie, ou dictionnaire raisonné des sciences, des arts et des métiers*, vol. 14 (Neuchâtel, 1765), p. 347; R. Sweet, *Cities and the Grand Tour: The British in Italy, c. 1690–1820* (Cambridge, 2012), ch. 3.

20 QUATREMÈRE DE QUINCY

in the Palazzo Mancini.[33] He absorbed the spirit of discipline and classical learning imposed by the Academy's Director, Joseph-Marie Vien, but, unlike most of the French in Rome, he admired the papacy and contemporary Roman culture.

The increasingly secular culture of French elites jarred with the omnipresence of Catholicism in Rome. The Church owned a third of the city, one in three days were religious festivals, and one in fifteen inhabitants belonged to a monastic order. French visitors therefore gained a reputation for cultural chauvinism and impatience.[34] Many of them compared modern Rome unfavourably to ancient and Baroque Rome; they blamed the papal government for ruining the arts and censoring men of letters whilst failing to improve amenities, revive once fertile land surrounding Rome, and drain pestilent marshes. The result of this misrule, French critics complained, was an idle population wholly dependent on tourists, pilgrims, and court expenditure.[35] Worst of all in French eyes, the papacy neglected Europe's ancient heritage: over many centuries, the papacy had mutilated and repurposed monuments and then, in modern times, failed to prevent the sale and dispersal of antiquities.[36] Struck by the disconnect between ancient and modern Rome, critical French writers scorned the venerable teleology that the papacy was the legatee of pagan monuments because the Roman Empire was the precursor of God's reign.[37] They instead reasoned that contemporary Romans were 'barbarians', 'unworthy of possessing... beautiful monuments', who lacked ancient blood and virtue and lived like ignorant foreigners in their own city.[38]

---

[33] Quatremère, *Canova*, p. 30. On this milieu, see O. Michel, *Vivre et peindre à Rome au XVIIIe siècle* (Rome, 1996), pp. 42–4; G. Montègre, *La Rome des français au temps des Lumières: Capitale de l'antique et carrefour de l'Europe, 1769–1791* (Rome, 2011); B. Marc et al, eds, *L'Académie de France à Rome au XVIIIe siècle. Le palais Mancini: un foyer artistique dans l'Europe des Lumières (1725–1792)* (Rennes, 2016).

[34] M. Andrieux, *La vie quotidienne dans la Rome pontificale au XVIIIe siècle* (Paris, 1962), chs 1 and 6. On the reputation of French visitors, see inter alia R. Ridley, *Magick City: Travellers to Rome from the Middle Ages to 1900*, vol. 2 (London, 2020), pp. 20, 22; J. Goethe, *Italian Journey* [1786–1788], trans. W. Auden and E. Mayer (London, 1970), p. 150.

[35] See, for example, C. de Brosses, *Le président de Brosses en Italie: lettres familières écrites d'Italie en 1739 et 1740*, vol. 1 (Paris, 1869), p. 5; *CAFR*, vol. 8, p. 312; ibid., vol. 13, p. 396; ibid., vol. 15, p. 209; C. Dupaty, *Lettres sur l'Italie en 1785* [1788], vol. 2 (Paris, 1797), p. 10; ibid., vol. 3, pp. 20, 25.

[36] C. de Montesquieu, *Voyages de Montesquieu*, vol. 1 (Paris, 1894), p. 262; Jaucourt, 'Rome', p. 347; Dupaty, *Lettres sur l'Italie en 1785*, vol. 1, p. 157; ibid., vol. 2, pp. 10, 163.

[37] J.-B. Boyer d'Argens, *Lettres juives, ou correspondance philosophique, historique, et critique, entre un Juif voyageur à Paris & ses correspondans en divers endroits* (The Hague, 1738), vol. 1, pp. 153–60; ibid., vol. 2, p. 82.

[38] G. Montègre, 'François de Paule Latapie, un savant voyageur français au coeur de la Rome des Lumières', *Mélanges de l'École française de Rome. Italie et Méditerranée*, vol. 117, no. 1 (2005), p. 415. On perceived differences between ancient and modern Romans, see, for example: C. de Montesquieu, *Considérations sur les causes de la grandeur des Romains* (Paris, 1734), ch. 18; idem, *Voyages de Montesquieu*, vol. 1, p. 262; Boyer d'Argens, *Lettres juives*, vol. 1, pp. 169–74, 195–200; ibid., vol. 2, pp. 178–9.

THE MAKING OF A MISSIONARY OF ANTIQUITY, 1755–85   21

Quatremère rejected this dismal picture of Rome's decline painted by his anti-clerical compatriots. He sided with antiquarians and other international residents who praised the papacy's custodianship of antiquities and considered this 'magic city' the epicentre of the learned world.[39] Indeed, from his first voyage onwards he repeated his conviction that Rome was 'a sort of mappa mundi in relief', 'centre of all nations', and capital of art and knowledge.[40] His attitude partly stemmed from his religious devotion, but it also reflected optimism surrounding Pope Pius VI's efforts to stimulate the economy and recover antiquities for his Vatican temple to pagan gods, the Museo Pio-Clementino.[41] Quatremère insisted that, since the fifteenth century, the papacy had advanced knowledge and rescued ancient columns and arches from 'the injuries of time and barbary'.[42] However, he believed that this rediscovery accelerated under Pius VI: 'Never, in such a space of time, were more antique monuments brought to light…The pontifical government, aided by the…efforts…of artists and savants, helped carry the passion for antiquity to the highest level. Every day, the earth yielded some fragment from the ancient patrimony of the arts'.[43]

Quatremère was also unusually amenable to Roman culture. He wrote in Italian, listened to *opera buffa*, and embraced local customs. For instance, one Holy Wednesday he sat for hours in the Sistine chapel waiting for the Compline because, unlike in Paris, this service of sung prayers began late at night and continued into the early hours.[44] However, despite his hunger and exhaustion, he was inspired rather than embittered by this cultural misunderstanding; he cherished experiencing Michelangelo's frescos in this candlelit space whilst listening to liturgical music.[45]

Quatremère's interests evolved in Rome. He initially practised sculpture and started carving a marble bust of the Greek mythological figure Niobe—a subject whose pathos also appealed to David during the 1770s. Like other aspiring

---

[39] Favourable interpretations of papal Rome included J. Barthélemy, *Voyage en Italie de M. l'abbé Barthélemy* (Paris, 1802), pp. 29–30, and J. Lalande, *Voyage d'un françois en Italie, fait dans les années 1765 et 1766*, vol. 5 (Paris, 1786), 88–90. On the context, see M. Andrieux, *Les français à Rome* (Paris, 1968), p. 131; Montègre, *La Rome des français*, pp. 108, 110–11, 118; L. Norci Cagiano, 'La Rome de Caylus et "l'idea del bello"', in N. Cronk and K. Peeters, eds, *Le comte de Caylus: les arts et les lettres* (Leiden, 2004), pp. 111–24.

[40] Quatremère, *Letters*, p. 117; idem, 'Rome', *EMA*, vol. 3, p. 300.

[41] C. Todeschi, *Opere di monsignore Claudio Todeschi* (Rome, 1779), vol. 1, p. viii; J. Collins, *Papacy and Politics in Eighteenth-Century Rome: Pius VI and the Arts* (Cambridge, 2004), ch. 4; idem, 'Museo Pio-Clementino, Vatican City: Ideology and Aesthetics in the Age of the Grand Tour', in C. Paul, ed., *The First Modern Museum of Art: The Birth of an Institution in 18th- and Early-19th-Century Europe* (Los Angeles, 2012), pp. 113–44; S. Howard, 'An Antiquarian Handlist and the Beginnings of the Pio-Clementino', *Eighteenth-Century Studies*, vol. 7, no. 1 (1973), pp. 40–61.

[42] Quatremère, 'Antonine (Colonne)', *EMA*, vol. 1, pp. 54–5; 'Arc Triomphal', *EMA*, vol. 1, p. 90.

[43] Quatremère, *Le Jupiter olympien* (Paris, 1815), p. i. See also 'Appienne (la Voie)', *EMA*, vol. 1, pp. 63–4; 'Belveder', *EMA*, vol. 1, pp. 263–4; 'Porphyre', *EMA*, vol. 3, p. 172; 'Zabaglia', *EMA*, vol. 3, p. 653.

[44] É. Quatremère, 'Notice historique', pp. 661–2.

[45] Quatremère, *Considérations morales*, pp. 98–9.

22 QUATREMÈRE DE QUINCY

artists, Quatremère perhaps attended nude figure-drawing classes besides drawing real antiquities and casts from various collections.[46] However, he became disillusioned over the challenge that sculptors faced, blaming the lucrative market for copies and restorations of antiquities for disincentivizing original commissions.[47] In these conditions, he claimed, the only artists who excited his curiosity were the painters Anton Raphael Mengs and Pompeo Batoni and the engravers Giovanni Piranesi and Giovanni Volpato.

His disappointment with contemporary sculpture in Rome meant that he instead invested his energies in researching antiquity and its revival. He recalled how he 'contracted the habit of living only with the antique' and its greatest sixteenth- and seventeenth-century interpreters.[48] He immersed himself in antiquity through books and engravings. He read Johann Joachim Winckelmann and learned how this German art historian (who was Pope Clement XIII's prefect of antiquities, until his untimely death in 1768) interpreted antiquities according to their style rather than subsuming them into chronologies of reigns derived from ancient textual authorities.[49] Just as importantly, he imbibed Winckelmann's faith in the ideal in art, optimism that understanding antiquity could help living artists, and historical conclusion that ancient genius resulted less from freedom and more from sage patronage and fruitful religious beliefs.[50]

Quatremère also immersed himself in antiquity by studying in-situ ruins and monuments besides what he called 'marvels' in the Museo Pio-Clementino's 'sumptuous galleries'.[51] Whilst most travellers checked off highlights (namely, the Pantheon, the Forum and its temples, the Capitoline, the Colosseum, the Theatre of Marcellus, and ancient arches, columns, obelisks, and baths), Quatremère

---

[46] Jouin, *Quatremère*, p. 5, n. 2. Life classes were available in the French School, Accademia di San Luca, Accademia del Nudo (officially called the Accademia del Disgeno), Scuola Libera del Nudo, and the studios of Pompeo Batoni and other masters; see R. Cassanelli et al., eds, *Ruins of Ancient Rome: The Drawings of French Architects Who Won the Prix de Rome* (Los Angeles, 2002), pp. 27–8; L. Barroero, 'I primi anni della scuola del Nudo in Campidoglio', in D. Biagi Maino, ed., *Benedetto XIV e le arti del disegno* (Rome, 1998), pp. 367–76; E. Bowron, 'Academic Life Drawing in Rome, 1750–1790', in R. Campbell, ed., *Visions of Antiquity: Neoclassical Figure Drawings* (Los Angeles, 1993), pp. 78–9.

[47] Quatremère, 'Notice sur Canova, sur sa réputation, ses ouvrages et sa statue du Pugilateur', *Archives littéraires de l'Europe*, vol. 3 (1804), pp. 10–11.

[48] Quatremère, *Canova*, pp. 29–30.   [49] Quatremère, *Letters*, pp. 101–2.

[50] Quatremère read no German and therefore probably knew Winckelmann through his *Monumenti antichi inediti* (Rome, 1767–8) or the first French translation of *Geschichte der Kunst des Alterthums* [1764], *Histoire de l'art chez les anciens*, trans. G. Sellius (Paris, 1766). Quatremère's first library included later French translations, which he probably acquired in Paris: *Histoire de l'art chez les anciens*, trans. M. Huber (Amsterdam, 1781) and *Lettres familières*, trans. and ed. H. Jansen (Amsterdam, 1781). Important studies of Winckelmann and his reception include É. Pommier, *Winckelmann, inventeur de l'histoire de l'art* (Paris, 2003) and K. Harloe, *Winckelmann and the Invention of Antiquity: History and Aesthetics in the Age of Altertumswissenschaft* (Oxford, 2013).

[51] For Quatremère's opinion of the Museo Pio-Clementino, see 'Belveder', *EMA*, vol. 1, pp. 263–4; idem, *Letters*, p. 98. Quatremère's first library contained books printed in Rome that he probably acquired during these years in the city: G. Lauro's *Antiquae urbis splendor* (Rome, 1612); C. Blancus, *Pitture dipinte nella volta della Cappella Sistina nel Vaticano* (Rome, 1773); F. Franzini, *Roma antica e moderna* (Rome, 1668); E. Cabrale, *Delle ville e de' piu notabili monumenti antichi della citta, e del territorio di Tivoli* (Rome, 1779).

THE MAKING OF A MISSIONARY OF ANTIQUITY, 1755–85   23

considered ancient Rome a unified organism that one needed to understand holistic-ally. For him, the city yielded not just models of taste but examples of grandeur and spectacular engineering. His Rome was a metaphorical book, filled with clues for challenging dogmas and recovering the true nature of ancient architectural orders.[52]

Quatremère now fashioned himself as a 'missionary of antiquity'.[53] An anecdote that sounds apocryphal illustrates his reputation: according to the story, one evening in the church of Trinità dei Monti Quatremère became embroiled in a heated argument about antiquity that continued well into the night until his weary adversary coughed blood.[54] David's contemporaneous portrait captured this same proselytizing zeal. David depicted Quatremère holding an adjustable metal divider to the plan of an ancient temple, seated before a pared-down background enlivened with an archaic unfluted column on a stone plinth. Although David inscribed the painting with the words 'To my friend A. Quatremère de Quincy', few documents illuminate their relationship.[55] Certainly, however, both men stood out amidst their compatriots because they came from prosperous Parisian families and received classical educations before turning to sculpture and painting respectively.[56]

During the late 1770s, Quatremère began two antiquarian projects. In the first project, he planned to describe and illustrate lost ancient Greek masterpieces by combining his practical knowledge of sculpture with ancient material and textual evidence.[57] He intended his second project to recover the true Greek Doric order and correct how modern architects used it. This project followed his suspicion that the Doric order had degenerated at the hands of the Romans because famous Roman-era examples, such as the Colosseum's ground-level arcades, differed from spoliate columns found in early Christian churches, such as San Pietro in Vincoli.[58] Quatremère's underlying assumption for both projects was that a better understanding of ancient Greek art would clarify architectural rules and remind future generations that art should fill defined places and spiritual and social uses, even if future artists could never equal the ancient Greeks.

Quatremère left Rome in July 1779. Lacking the means to travel to Greece, he headed south to study what remained from Magna Graecia. He later reflected that

---

[52] Quatremère, *Le Jupiter olympien*, p. iv; 'Architrave', *EMA*, vol. 1, p. 131; 'Basilique', *EMA*, vol. 1, pp. 222–3; 'Dorique', *EMA*, vol. 2:1, p. 235.
[53] Quatremère, *Canova*, p. 30.   [54] É. Quatremère, 'Notice historique', p. 662.
[55] Körner and Piel, '"A mon ami A. Quatremère de Quincy": Ein unbeakanntes Werk Jacques-Louis David, aus dem Jahre 1779'. This oil on canvas portrait measuring 91 × 72 cm is in a private collection. It is reproduced in Quatremère, *Letters to Miranda and Canova* (Los Angeles, 2012), Figure 1.
[56] A. Schnapper and A. Sérullaz, *Jacques-Louis David, 1748–1825* (Paris, 1989).
[57] *Le Jupiter olympien* was the most famous fruit of this research.
[58] Quatremère, 'Dorique', *EMA*, vol. 2, p. 249.

24 QUATREMÈRE DE QUINCY

such 'far-away journeys' magnified his 'love of antiquity'.[59] He first visited Naples and the surrounding area with David and the sculptor François Suzanne.[60] Most foreigners enjoyed the coastal climate, natural beauty, plentiful entertainments, enlightened rule, and court culture in Naples, but Quatremère admired little besides Domenico Fontana's Fountain of Neptune and the gallery of antiquities containing what he described as 'the scattered riches of diverse collections'.[61]

Several other sites in Campania captured his attention. To the north of Naples, he visited Luigi Vanvitelli's Royal Palace of Caserta and its spectacular aqueduct. He found the Palace's design and execution in perfect unison despite its enormous scale: simple yet varied like the finest ancient architecture, the Palace was 'an ensemble from which one could neither subtract nor add anything'.[62] To the south, he explored several ancient sites. He found Herculaneum and Pompeii—towns buried under volcanic ash after the first-century eruption of Vesuvius until their respective rediscovery in 1738 and 1748—remarkable sources of Roman taste, construction, and decoration even if he disregarded excavated artefacts as models worth imitating.[63] Seeing the Museo Ercolanese in the Royal Palace of Portici convinced him that France should create museums for Gallo-Roman antiquities that could not remain in situ.[64]

Disappointed that sites in Baiae and Cumae remained unexcavated, Quatremère continued south to Paestum in the Gulf of Salerno (Fig. 1.1).[65] Slightly removed from the

---

[59] É. Quatremère, 'Notice historique', pp. 662–3; Quatremère, *Canova*, p. 29. Quatremère's exploration of southern sites demonstrates that he was not simply the 'armchair archaeologist' described by M. Greenhalgh in 'Quatremère de Quincy as a Popular Archaeologist', *Gazette des beaux-arts* (1968), vol. 71, no. 1191, pp. 249–56. Quatremère's nineteenth-century biographers provided cursory accounts of this southern voyage. See, for example, Guigniaut, 'Notice historique', pp. 366–7.

[60] P.-A. Coupin, 'Notice nécrologique sur Jacques-Louis David', *Revue encyclopédique*, vol. 34 (April 1827), p. 37, is the earliest claim in print that Quatremère and David travelled together. Vien's correspondence only contains references to David and Suzanne's journey, but he had no reason to mention Quatremère; *CAFR*, vol. 13, pp. 451, 454–5.

[61] Sweet, *Cities and the Grand Tour*, p. 165; Quatremère, *Histoire de la vie et des ouvrages des plus célèbres architectes*, vol. 2, pp. 79–80, 308; idem, *EMA*, vol. 2, pp. 741–2. On Naples as a hub for scholarship and cultural diplomacy, see C. Mattusch, ed., *Rediscovering the Ancient World on the Bay of Naples, 1710–1890* (New Haven, 2013); A. Fittipaldi, 'Museums, Safeguarding and Artistic Heritage in Naples in the Eighteenth Century: Some Reflections', *Journal of the History of Collections*, vol. 19, no. 11 (2007), pp. 191–202; and E. Dodero, *Ancient Marbles in Naples in the Eighteenth Century* (Leiden, 2019).

[62] Quatremère, *Histoire de la vie et des ouvrages des plus célèbres architectes*, vol. 2, pp. 301–3; 'Aqueduc', *EMA*, vol. 1, p. 69. His second library (*Bibliothèque*, p. 76) included Vanvitelli's *Dichiarazione dei disegni del Reale Palazzo di Caserta* (Naples, 1756).

[63] Quatremère's later descriptions suggest first-hand knowledge. See, for example, Quatremère, 'Pompeia', *EMA*, vol. 3, pp. 158–61, and 'Dissertation sur la mosaïque dite d'Alexandre à Arbèles', in F. Mazois, ed., *Les ruines de Pompéi*, vol. 4 (Paris, 1838), pp. 87–91. His first library included guidebooks for these towns: C.-N. Cochin and J.-C. Bellicard, *Observations sur les antiquités d'herculaneum* (Paris, 1757); P. Sarnelli, *La guida de' forestieri curiosi di vedere, e di riconoscere le cose più memorabili di Pozzuoli, Baia, Cuma, Miseno, Gaeta ed altri luoghi con vicini, Saverio Rossi* (Naples, 1768).

[64] Quatremère, 'Muséum', *EMA*, vol. 2, pp. 741–2; idem, *Journal des savants* (Oct. 1817), p. 597.

[65] Quatremère, 'Baies', *EMA*, vol. 1, pp. 117–18; and 'Cumae', *EMA*, vol. 2, p. 160; É. Quatremère, 'Notice historique', p. 662. On the rediscovery of Paestum, see S. Lang, 'The Early Publications of the Temples at Paestum', *Journal of the Warburg and Courtauld Institutes*, vol. 13, no. 1 (1950), pp. 48–64; R. Serra, ed., *Paestum and the Doric Revival, 1750–1830* (Florence, 1986); G. Ceserani, *Italy's Lost Greece: Magna Graecia and the Making of Modern Archaeology* (Oxford, 2012), ch. 1.

modern town, the rediscovery of ancient Paestum in the 1740s had inspired artists and scholars alike and provoked debate about the origins of architecture and the criteria of beauty in this art. Many visitors expressed shock upon seeing the expansive capitals and squat and baseless Doric columns of the Temples of Neptune and Ceres. In their eyes, these oddly formed, ill proportioned structures in rough materials contradicted received standards based on Roman examples and authorities.[66] To explain the strangeness of Paestum, some writers suggested that the Etruscans had imitated Egyptian architecture. Other writers theorized that these were indeed ancient Greek structures, only 'primitive sketches' using the 'squat proportion' that persisted in Magna Graecia's peripheries long after rules had been established on the Greek mainland.[67]

By contrast, Quatremère and David belonged to a new generation of visitors who saw Paestum with sympathetic eyes and rejected the idea that its ancient

Fig. 1.1 Thomas Major, 'Internal view of the pseudo dipteral Temple of Basilica, taken from the South' (detail), in *Les Ruines de Paestum, ou de Posidonie, dans la Grande Grèce, par T. Major, traduit de l'anglais* (London, 1768). BnF.

---

[66] S. de Jong, *Rediscovering Architecture: Paestum in Eighteenth-Century Architectural Experience and Theory* (New Haven, 2015).

[67] P. Paoli, *Rovine della città di Pesto, detto ancora Posidonia* (Rome, 1784); J.-D. Le Roy, *The Ruins of the Most Beautiful Monuments of Greece* [1770], trans. D. Britt (Los Angeles, 2004), p. 232; S. de Jong, 'Subjective Proportions: Eighteenth-Century Interpretations of Paestum's "Disproportion"', *Architectural Histories*, vol. 4, no. 1 (2016).

structures demonstrated the 'heavy and clumsy character' of art's infancy. For their generation, understanding such an unfamiliar style necessitated experiencing in person the site rather than simply reading descriptions and studying measurements and illustrations.[68] Quatremère thus later described his subjective impressions upon entering the 'vast and monstrous plain' and walking towards the wall enclosing the surviving ruins.[69] If his feelings convinced him immediately that Paestum's temples exemplified the true Greek Doric order, he henceforth wanted to prove his verdict with supporting scholarship and additional material evidence.[70] Following Quatremère's lead, David also discerned at Paestum the essence of heroic, massive, and virulent architecture. Just as David compared his journey south to an operation removing a cataract because it opened his eyes to the antique, Paestum's influence on his art is visible in the architectural settings and archaic linearity of his *Oath of the Horatii* (1785) and *Brutus* (1789).[71] Such was the transformation in French attitudes towards Paestum that, at the end of the century, one expert proposed that the French Republic should seize control to prevent the site's continued degradation under the Kingdom of Two Sicilies.[72]

In mid-August 1779, David and Suzanne returned to Rome and Quatremère sailed to Sicily. He remembered in his last years an incident from the four-day voyage, perhaps because it symbolized the role chance played in rediscovering the past: the sailors raised the anchor, he recalled, and inadvertently caught another, much older one, covered in coral.[73] Sicily was not part of his original plan and the poor road network and unreliability of maps and guidebooks meant that navigating the island remained difficult. However, his decision to visit Sicily coincided with growing artistic and scholarly interest in the island. This intriguing periphery of civilized Europe had a unique history and geography and was rich in volcanic specimens, flora and fauna, and natural history.[74] His interest lay in the 'numerous and important ruins' dating from when Sicily was part of Magna Grecia.[75]

---

[68] Goethe, *Italian Journey*, pp. 218–19. Goethe articulated in more emphatic terms the same sentiment as Quatremère: 'It is only by walking through and round [the structures at Paestum] that one can attune one's life to theirs and experience the emotional effect which the architect intended.'

[69] Quatremère, 'Paesdum', in *EMA*, vol. 3, p. 57.

[70] Quatremère, 'Basilique', *EMA*, vol. 1, pp. 222–3; 'Dorique', *EMA*, vol. 2, pp. 235–8; 'Paestum', *EMA*, vol. 3, p. 22; idem, 'Sur la restitution du temple de Jupiter Olympien à Agrigente', *Archives littéraires de l'Europe*, vol. 6 (1805), pp. 75, 86–7; Quatremère, 'Diminution', *EMA*, vol. 2:1, p. 217.

[71] H. Kohle, 'The Road from Rome to Paris: The Birth of a Modern Neoclassicism', in D. Johnson, ed., *Jacques-Louis David: New Perspectives* (Newark, 2006), p. 75.

[72] C. La Gardette, *Les ruines de Paestum ou Posidonia* (Paris, year VII [1799]), p. 4.

[73] É. Quatremère, 'Notice historique', p. 663.

[74] Goethe, *Italian Journey*, pp. 246, 220; C. Raymond, 'La découverte des antiquités de Sicile chez les voyageurs du XVIIIe siècle', *Bulletin de la société nationale des antiquaires de France* (1990), pp. 221–39; M. Pinault, *Houël. Voyage en Sicile (1776–1779)* (Paris, 1999); G. Ceserani, 'The Charm of the Siren: The Place of Sicily in Historiography', in C. Smith and J. Serrati, eds, *Ancient Sicily from Aeneas to Cicero* (Edinburgh, 2000), pp. 174–93; É. Nicolosi, *Les représentations de la Sicile au XVIIIe siècle chez les voyageurs français, britanniques et germaniques*, unpublished doctoral thesis: Université Laval (2020).

[75] É. Quatremère, 'Notice historique', pp. 662–3.

Quatremère's route around the island is undocumented, but references in his later writings suggest that he made his way to Agrigento and then crossed the south-west and south-east coasts before returning to the mainland.[76] He later recalled visiting in 1779 the 'ruins and precious debris of monuments' in the Valley of the Temples in Agrigento.[77] His striking descriptions conveyed the subjectivity of viewing artwork and captured how different ruins inspired particular emotions. For example, the Temple of Hera-Lacina provoked grief: after reading reports that it remained almost intact in 1700, he regretted that recent earthquakes and storms had overturned more than half its columns. Other temples chastened him: the remains of the Temple of Hercules resembled 'a mountain of blocks knocked over and piled up in a terrifying manner'; and the sight of the enormous remains of the colossal Temple of Jupiter forced him to 'stop in his tracks' before the prowess of the ancients.[78] By contrast, he found that the Temple of Concordia inspired pleasure. This Temple survived because the Bishop of Agrigento converted it into a church in the ninth century; its harmonious design and elegant proportions demonstrated how the Greeks combined good taste with baseless Doric columns. In Quatremère's eyes, therefore, most fragments at Agrigento were valuable as authentic artefacts that helped one reimagine the past. By contrast, however, he considered the well-preserved Temple of Concordia a timeless model for architects that should be 'restored' because its artistic value surpassed its use as a historical document.[79]

Quatremère next probably explored several places on the east coast, including Syracuse and Catania and perhaps other ancient sites such as Taormina.[80] Syracuse was the largest city on the island in ancient times, but in 1779 there was relatively little for him to see because important sites remained unexcavated. As elsewhere, he noted that many visible vestiges had survived thanks to Christians salvaging and repurposing materials, such as the Doric columns from the Temple of Minerva embedded in the cathedral. What impressed him most in Syracuse was the Christian catacombs, whose 'mysterious tranquillity' and scale, he reflected, alone indicated the city's ancient grandeur.[81] In Catania, Quatremère encountered Prince Ignazio Biscari, the royal intendant of antiquities. He considered

---

[76] Quatremère, 'Camerina', *EMA*, vol. 1, pp. 405–6.

[77] Quatremère, 'Agrigente', *EMA*, vol. 1, p. 15. On the importance of Agrigento for Quatremère, see J. Hoefer, ed., 'Quatremère', *Nouvelle biographie générale*, vol. 41 (Paris, 1862), p. 286; P. Bertoncini Sabatini, 'Da Agrigento verso Atene: il viaggio alla sorgente del genio ellenico di Quatremère de Quincy', in A. Carlino, ed., *La Sicilia e il Grand Tour: la riscoperta di Akragas. 1700–1800* (Rome, 2011), pp. 51–71.

[78] Quatremère, 'Agrigente', *EMA*, vol. 1, pp. 14–15; idem, 'Sur la restitution du temple de Jupiter olympien à Agrigente', p. 83; idem, 'Dorique', *EMA*, vol. 2, p. 232.

[79] Quatremère, 'Agrigente', *EMA*, vol. 1, pp. 14–15.

[80] Quatremère, 'Taurominium ou Taormine', *EMA*, vol. 3, p. 422.

[81] Quatremère, 'Amphithéâtre', *EMA*, vol. 1, p. 37; 'Catacombes', *EMA*, vol. 1, p. 548; 'Dorique', *EMA*, vol. 2, p. 234; 'Syracuse', *EMA*, vol. 3, pp. 421–4. Quatremère's visit predated Giuseppe Voza's excavations in in Syracuse.

28 QUATREMÈRE DE QUINCY

Biscari both a model custodian, because this prince had rescued the city's ancient theatre and other antiquities that disputes and disasters had almost obliviated, and an enlightened collector, because his 'large and magnificent museum' displayed 'all genres of antiquity with as much taste as knowledge'. The section of the museum that Biscari devoted to architectural features inspired Quatremère's vision for a museum of architecture in France.[82]

Quatremère left Sicily for Rome and then returned to Paris in 1780.[83] His Italian voyage had coincided with a relatively stable period in French political history, one characterized by ministerial continuity and cooperation between the restored parlements and Louis XVI. However, political affairs worsened while he was in Paris. Jacques Necker resigned as finance minister and his successor grappled with the cost of France's involvement in the War of American Independence.[84]

Quatremère was surely aware of these developments given their implications for his family's business, but, like other antiquarians, he cultivated an image of Stoic indifference towards transient events. Before 1789, he acquired very few books about politics.[85] In Paris, he instead tried to establish himself as an authority on architecture, reading widely and consulting ancient texts and modern scholarship to explain his findings in Italy. His library included books that he probably acquired at this time: recent writings by famous architects and architectural theorists such as Laugier, Le Camus de Mézières, Viel de Saint-Maux, and Patte; classic writings by Vitruvius, Delorme, Androuet du Cerceau, Palladio, Perrault, and d'Aviler; and several books on the history of ancient and modern architecture.

Since his social milieu mirrored his intellectual pursuits, he befriended architects such as Jacques Molinos, Jacques-Guillaume Legrand, and the latter's father-in-law, Charles-Louis Clérisseau, that 'faithful and savant draughtsman of the antique', as he put it, who wanted to publish drawings and descriptions of France's antiquities.[86] He perhaps also met Léon Dufourny, who shared his fascination with Italy's Greek Doric remains.[87] He joined the Thalie lodge in 1782 to meet

---

[82] Quatremère, 'Catania', *EMA*, vol. 1, pp. 556–7; idem, *Letters*, p. 97.

[83] Quatremère, *Canova*, p. 29.

[84] C. Jones, *The Great Nation: France from Louis XV to Napoleon* (London, 2003), pp. 301–24.

[85] L. Brockliss, *Calvet's Webb. Enlightenment and the Republic of Letters in Eighteenth-Century France* (Oxford, 2002), pp. 335–44. Quatremère's first library indicates his lack of interest in current political affairs, although it included works of political philosophy by Montesquieu and de Vattel besides overviews of French and English political history.

[86] É. Quatremère, 'Notice historique', p. 667. Citing Quatremère from 'Composée', *EMA*, vol. 2:2, p. 29. On Clérisseau's study of Gallo-Roman antiquities in southern France, see T. McCormick, *Charles-Louis Clerisseau and the Genesis of Neo-Classicism* (Cambridge, MA, 1990), pp. 135–40. Clérisseau only published the first of several planned volumes: *Antiquités de France: monuments de Nîmes* (Paris, 1778). Quatremère mentioned Clérisseau's project five times in *EMA*, vol. 1.

[87] Quatremère, 'Dorique', *EMA*, vol. 2, p. 232, acknowledged Duforny's contribution to the study of the Doric order and indicates that he knew the architect's unpublished work. He reiterated this opinion in *Recueil de notices historiques*, pp. 234–48.

architects and bolster his credentials as an authority on architecture.[88] Joining a lodge was unremarkable even for devout Catholics because Freemasonry was the most popular form of voluntary association in Paris: one in twenty adult men belonged to masonic orders, including many architects for whom membership presented opportunities for professional and intellectual advancement.[89] Although Freemasonry's Greco-Roman ethos dovetailed with his sensibilities, he ceased being a member in 1786 once he established his reputation as a savant.

He lived comfortably rather than extravagantly in Paris. His mother had bequeathed him 60 000 livres, which his father invested in municipal bonds to give him an annual fixed income of 3,000 livres. He received this income on 8 November 1782 for the first time and then returned to Rome.[90]

Quatremère's second Italian voyage lasted from late 1782 to spring 1785.[91] Inspired by Clérisseau's example, he perhaps stopped en route to visit several Gallo-Roman monuments in southern France. He later wrote about these monuments in terms that imply familiarity, questioning why his compatriots cherished antiquities in Italy when they neglected those in France, such as the arena in Arles that was 'jammed full of houses'.[92]

Quatremère arrived in Rome in early 1783 and remained until summer. His stay overlapped with David and Jean-Baptiste Rondelet, but he formed closer friendships with the sculptors Louis-Pierre Deseine (a Prix de Rome winner who later described Quatremère as 'my former *camarade* in Rome') and Canova.[93] He soon venerated Canova as a miraculous figure, singlehandedly responsible for resurrecting 'the style, system and the principles of antiquity'.[94] Yet, somewhat at odds with this verdict, he later drew attention to his own role as the artist's guide, claiming that he steered Canova towards the restrained classical *style of Theseus and the Minotaur* (1782) and away from the naturalism of *Daedalus and Icarus* (1779), and recalling how he persuaded Canova to make specific alterations, such as changing a figure in the *Monument to Pope Clement XIV*.[95] Whatever his real influence, they met frequently over the next months. Canova introduced Quatremère to English patrons and friends, such as

---

[88] A. Le Bihan, *Francs-maçons parisiens du Grand Orient de France (fin du XIIIe)* (Paris, 1966), p. 409.

[89] K. Loisselle, *Brotherly Love: Freemasonry and Male Friendship in Enlightenment France* (Ithaca, 2014), pp. 6–7, 198; A. Vidler, *The Writing on the Walls: Architectural Theory in the Late Enlightenment* (Princeton, 1987), pp. 92–3.

[90] E. Lemay, ed., *Dictionnaire des législateurs, 1791–1792*, vol. 1 (Paris, 2007), p. 619; Quatremère, *Canova*, p. 29.

[91] Ibid., pp. 20, 29.

[92] Quatremère, 'Arles', *EMA*, vol. 1, p. 135. See also *EMA*, vol. 1, pp. 65, 92, 94, 135, 178, 626; and vol. 3, pp. 16–18, 39, 586–7; Quatremère, *Letters*, p. 100.

[93] L.-P. Deseine, *Opinion sur les musées, où se trouvent retenus tous les objets d'arts qui sont la propriété des temples consacrés à la religion catholique* (Paris, 1803), p. iv.

[94] Quatremère, *Canova*, pp. 29–34.

[95] Ibid., p. 48; H. Honour, 'Canova's Studio Practice—I: The Early Years', *Burlington Magazine*, vol. 114, no. 828 (March 1972), pp. 146–59.

30 QUATREMÈRE DE QUINCY

the dealer Gavin Hamilton, and Quatremère introduced Canova to the sculptor Antoine-Henri Bertrand.[96]

In summer 1783, Canova left for the quarries of Carrara and Quatremère returned to Naples. Here, Quatremère met Dominique-Vivant Denon, the *chargé d'affaires* and an engraver and expert on medals and gems, who provided letters of introduction to facilitate his return to Sicily.[97] Quatremère arrived in Palermo in time for the July festival of Saint Rosalia.[98] Palermo was then as populous as Rome and he admired the city's cross-shaped plan, magnificent gates, monuments, fountains, and squares. Most memorable, however, was the shrine on Mount Pellegrino.[99] In the cold light of day, he noted, the shrine's polychromatic bronze and alabaster statue of Rosalia was unremarkable, but during the festival the statue exercised a transformative spiritual power over worshippers. Local people, he recalled, looked through 'silent tears of tender affection' at Rosalia in her dim and modest hermitage. They felt that they were in the presence of their saint, not a representation of her: 'all believed that they saw her, believed that they were speaking to her.' The power of artefacts thus lay in their surroundings as much as their objective quality.[100]

Quatremère remained in Sicily with Denon's assistance for around six months. Details of his second Sicilian voyage remain unclear, but his later descriptions of Segesta and Selinunte imply that he explored the west of the island.[101] In early 1784, he returned to Rome where he researched and penned two essays on ancient architecture. The first used his findings on the Doric order, but the second required research into ancient Egyptian architecture to answer the question announced in April by the Academy of Inscriptions for the Prix Caylus: 'What was the state of the architecture of the Egyptians, and what do the Greeks appear to have borrowed from it?'[102] Founded in 1663 to provide Latin verses that glorified the monarch, over the next century the Academy of Inscriptions was committed to understanding ancient and Middle Eastern languages and

---

[96] Schneider, *Quatremère*, p. 3; Quatremère, *Canova*, p. 25; *Carteggio*, p. 4.

[97] Artaud, 'Quatremère', *Biographie universel*, vol. 62, p. 339. Denon's motivation might have been to undermine Saint-Non's research on Sicily; see J. Nowinski, *Baron Dominique Vivant Denon (1747–1825): Hedonist and Scholar* (Cranbury, 1970), pp. 44–56. Until their relationship soured during the Consulate, Quatremère praised Denon as 'a connoisseur, an amateur and an artist, but above all a man of taste and a draftsman'; Quatremère, *EMA*, vol. 2:1, p. 284.

[98] É. Quatremère, 'Notice historique', p. 663, mentioned that his cousin was in Palermo for the festival. However, other circumstances suggest that Étienne was probably mistaken to claim that this happened in 1779 because it is doubtful that Antoine Quatremère was in Palermo that July. Moreover, in 1815 Antoine Quatremère mentioned seeing the statue 'more than thirty years' ago—a recollection that makes July 1782 more likely than July 1779; Quatremère, *Considérations morales*, p. 77.

[99] Quatremère, *De l'architecture égyptienne* (Paris, 1803), p. 110; idem, *EMA*, vol. 2:1, p. 342.

[100] Quatremère, *Considérations morales*, pp. 74–7.

[101] Quatremère, *EMA*, vol. 2, pp. 232, 246. He knew Segesta sufficiently well to correct Jean Houël's illustration in *Voyage pittoresque des isles de Sicile* (Paris, 1782); he also displayed his knowledge of the ruined temples at Selinute by providing measurements, and noting capitals and fluting patterns in small fragments.

[102] É. Quatremère, 'Notice historique', p. 662; Quatremère, *Canova*, p. 41.

interpreting monuments, medals, and inscriptions to uncover past morals and practices.[103] Its essay prize capitalized on the fashion for Egyptian-style decoration and theorizing about origins whilst also challenging competitors because Egyptian architecture remained mysterious.[104] Since visiting Egypt was dangerous and expensive, Quatremère turned to Egyptian artefacts in the Palazzo Borgia at Velletri, such as bas-reliefs from tombs in the grottos of Thebes.[105] He later recalled feigning interest in Cardinal Stefano Borgia's treasured Coptic inscriptions and Arabic coins when he really wanted to study Egyptian inscriptions, gems, and statues.[106]

Quatremère finished writing the essays during the first half of 1785. Before leaving Rome for Paris, he exchanged promises with Canova to 'write to each other as often as possible' and probably met Pierre-Paul Prud'hon, who arrived in January as the winner of the Dijon Prize.[107]

---

[103] D. Roche, *France in the Enlightenment*, trans. A. Goldhammer (Cambridge Mass., 1993), pp. 102–5; C. Grell, *Le dix-huitième siècle et l'antiquité en France 1680–1789*, vol. 1 (Oxford, 1995), pp. 110–16; M. Fumaroli, 'Le comte de Caylus et l'académie des inscriptions', *Comptes rendus des séances de l'Académie des inscriptions et belles-lettres*, vol. 139, no. 1 (1995), pp. 225–50.

[104] Archives de l'Institut, Prix caylus 1785—Académie des inscriptions et belles-lettres, D74. The same file contains a note added to Del Rosso's entry ('Richerche sul'archittetura egiziana', p. vii) that dispelled his claim that Quatremère had visited Egypt and explained that Quatremère had instead seen Borgia's collection.

[105] Quatremère, *EMA*, vol. 2, p. 295; idem, *EMA*, vol. 3, p. 309.

[106] É. Quatremère, 'Notice historique', pp. 664–5.

[107] *Carteggio*, pp. 3–4; E. Guffey, *Drawing an Elusive Line: The Art of Pierre-Paul Prud'hon* (Newark, DE, 2001), p. 51; Schneider, *Quatremère*, p. 63; Quatremère, *Recueil de notices historiques*, p. 283.

2

The Friend of the Arts, 1785–9

After returning to Paris, Quatremère established a reputation as an authority on architecture and a friend of the arts who shaped public opinion and official policy on cultural matters in the city. His first writings, published during these years, explored themes that reappeared in his later works in different forms. Even before 1789, when events compelled him to become involved in public affairs, he devised ideas about the arts that informed his conservative politics.

Quatremère's essays of 1784–5 should be read as two parts of a single endeavour. In both, he argued for the supremacy of ancient Greek architecture, sketched generative 'types' of construction, and theorized how architecture imitated nature. He wanted to defend Grecianist conventions against historical relativism and eclecticism, demonstrate his expertise on ancient architecture, and influence how living architects used classical orders. For Grecianists such as Quatremère, Greek art stood for a system of values—'noble simplicity and sedate grandeur', masculinity, and civic behaviour—that intersected with the new discourse of patriotism.[1]

For his first essay, his cousin recounted that he 'gathered the materials of a considerable work' on the Greek Doric order only to burn the manuscript after using its contents in other writings.[2] He perhaps feared that publishing the manuscript in its entirety would offend Le Roy; revealingly, his main writings on the Doric order appeared later, towards the end of Le Roy's life or after his death in 1803. Understanding Quatremère's destroyed essay thus requires cautiously reading his later publications on the Doric order—an exercise in reconstruction justified by the importance of the subject for his thinking about architecture and its relationship to society.[3] His essay originated from his realization that the proportions of Roman and Greek Doric remains sat uneasily with modern rules dictating use of the order. His impression in Paestum and Agrigento was that what remained of the temples exemplified the true Greek Doric order, but

---

[1] J. Winckelmann, *Reflections on the Painting and Sculpture of the Greeks with Instructions for the Connoisseur, and an Essay on Grace in Works of Art* [1755] (London, 1765), pp. 2, 34. On the language of patriotism, see D. Bell, *The Cult of the Nation in France: Inventing Nationalism, 1680–1800* (Cambridge, MA, 2009), chs. 2 and 4.

[2] É. Quatremère, 'Notice historique', p. 662.

[3] Most useful is 'Dorique', *EMA*, vol. 2:1, pp. 232–59. This entry was published in 1801 yet mostly written in the 1780s given that: his discussion of Agrigento ignored the restorations of 1786–7; and its content is consistent with cognate entries published in 1788 in *EMA*, vol. 1, such as 'Agrigente', 'Bois', 'Basilique', 'Cabane', 'Capital', 'Cannelés', and 'Caractère'.

Quatremère de Quincy: Art and Politics during the French Revolution. David Gilks, Oxford University Press.
© David Gilks 2024. DOI: 10.1093/oso/9780198745563.003.0003

he recognized that his verdict stemmed from a stylistic judgement and he therefore wanted to buttress his view by synthesizing ancient and modern discoveries 'under a single critical and comparative view'.[4]

For Quatremère, modern authorities had devised the proportions for the Doric order using ancient Roman ruins and Vitruvius' *De architectura* whilst dismissing as outliers ancient Greek monuments with different proportions.[5] Chief amongst them, Le Roy argued that the Doric order was short and inconsistent until the first century when, under the Romans, it became elongated and elegant. Le Roy therefore dismissed Greek temples in southern Italy as impoverished imitations, which merely demonstrated that the order degenerated abroad and that the Etruscans created a squat version of it.[6]

According to Quatremère, by contrast, the order originated with the Greeks' primitive wooden cabins. The Greeks, he imagined, experimented over several centuries with soft and plentiful wood until they perfected a design, which they imitated in scarce stone once they created towns. The resulting Doric temple was the fruit of the inherited weave of communal life, not the gift of nature or masterstroke of an individual genius. For Quatremère, this story of origins contained the 'principles of architecture': it demonstrated that perfection occurred gradually in response to need, and it revealed how architecture imitated nature at several removes.[7]

Quatremère reasoned that all ancient examples of the Doric order derived from the same inherited maxims, even if their measurements differed. Since the Romans corrupted this severe order (by stretching its proportions to resemble the Ionic and Corinthian orders, suiting their taste for 'luxury' and 'magnificence'), architects must now imitate correct examples of the true Greek Doric if they wished to convey 'strength and solidity'.[8] His reinterpretation of the order thus engendered prescriptions for architects: the parts and the whole must correspond perfectly; and columns must have strong proportions, simple entablatures, and capitals with several filets but no astragal. However, he insisted that this new knowledge provided architects with more, rather than less, freedom because it liberated them from academic rules, expanded their repertoire of options, and revealed that columns varied in shape, tapering, number of flutes, and use of a base. For instance, southern Italian examples could 'restore to the language or music of architecture its grave tone' by inspiring architects to reintroduce the order's baseless variant.[9] Correctly using the Doric order, he argued, required ending the fashion in Paris to 'prostitute' the order as a pseudo-archaic decorative caprice or to mix its features with Ionic and Corinthian proportions.

---

[4] Quatremère, 'Sur la restitution du temple de Jupiter Olympien à Agrigente', pp. 76–9.
[5] Ibid., pp. 72–7, 87.   [6] Le Roy, *The Ruins*, pp. 218–19, 312–19.
[7] Quatremère, 'Dorique', pp. 235–6.   [8] Ibid., pp. 247–9.
[9] Ibid., p. 255. Even before the Revolution, Quatremère considered architecture a language; see, for example, *EMA*, vol. 1, pp. 362, 477.

34 QUATREMÈRE DE QUINCY

Egregious recent examples littered the city, he lamented: Jacques-Denis Antoine's Hôpital de la Charité (reconstructed 1778–81), Charles de Wailly's Thêatre (1779–82), Alexandre-Théodore Brogniart's convent of the Capucins of the Chaussée-d'Antin (1780–3), and Charles-Nicolas Ledoux's barriers for the General Farmers' Wall (1785–8).[10]

Quatremère's Prix Caylus entry developed several ideas from his essay on the Doric order. The Academy of Inscriptions asked about Egyptian architecture and its influence on Greece just when fascination with ancient Egypt risked destabilizing the Greco-Roman foundations of taste. Caylus himself claimed that Egypt predated and influenced Greek art—a thesis that Piranesi adapted to relativize Greece's influence over the Italian peninsula and bolster his polemic for Etruscan genius and Roman eclecticism.[11] By contrast, leading figures in the Academy of Architecture, such as François Blondel and Le Roy, defended Greek supremacy, contrasting harmonious Greek architecture that pleased the mind to enormous Egyptian constructions that merely astonished the eyes.[12] Quatremère realized that the Academy of Inscriptions wanted competitors to reassert the Grecianist position, but his essay also articulated his thoughts on the origins and evolution of architecture and relationship between architecture, painting, and sculpture.

Throughout his essay, he insisted that Greece's debt to Egypt must have been insubstantial because Egyptian building and Greek architecture were incomparable. He first demonstrated their incomparable origins by theorizing how primitive societies built. He claimed that itinerant shepherds, such as in China, made tents; that hunters and fishermen lived in caves, which the Egyptians copied as stone structures; and that farming societies in Greece made huts using wood, which they perfected then fixed in stone to invent architecture.[13] The paradox of plenty lay at the heart of his theory of originating types and their subsequent development. In his schema, the Greeks escaped the tyranny of the hut because the scarcity of stone obliged them to experiment with wood. By contrast, the Egyptians mostly remained enslaved to the cave because superabundant stone

---

[10] Quatremère, 'Dorique', pp. 235–6, 245, 255; 'Barrières', *EMA*, vol. 1, p. 216.

[11] A. de Tubieres, Comte de Caylus, 'De l'architecture ancienne' [1749], *Mémoires de littérature, tirés des registres de l'Académie royale des inscriptions et belles-lettres*, vol. 23 (Paris, 1756), p. 300; G.-B. Piranesi, 'An apologetical essay in defence of the Egyptian and Tuscan architecture', in idem, *Divers manners of ornamenting chimneys* [1769], reproduced in J. Wilton-Ely, *Givovanni Battista Piranesi: The Polemical Works*, pp. 28–9; G.-B. Piranesi, *Observations on the Letter of Monsieur Mariette: With Opinions on Architecture*, trans. C. Beamish and D. Britt (Los Angeles, 2002). More generally, see R. Wittkower, 'Piranesi and Eighteenth-Century Egyptomania', in idem, *Studies in the Italian Baroque* (London, 1975), pp. 258–73.

[12] Le Roy, *The Ruins*, pp. 209–10, 228–9; K. Smentek, *Mariette and the Science of the Connoisseur in Eighteenth-Century Europe* (Cambridge, MA, 2014), p. 208.

[13] Archives de l'Académie des inscriptions et belles-lettres, Prix Caylus, 1785, MS D74, no. 1, pp. 1–8. (This writing is hereafter cited as Quatremère, Prix Caylus.)

stymied innovation and technical skill so that craftsmen never progressed beyond simple stonework for 'monstrous' and indestructible pyramids.[14]

If the Egyptians partly escaped the tyranny of the cave with temples whose polygonal columns were crude stone imitations of weak trees bound together, Quatremère dismissed suggestions that the Greeks copied these temples. Superficial similarities existed between all temples, he argued, but profound differences between Greek and Egyptian temples reflected their contrary purposes: Egypt's dogmatic religious institutions required monotonous designs whereas Greco-Roman religion permitted variety and evolution.[15]

Quatremère was equally dismissive of Egyptian ornamentation and decoration.[16] Under the Egyptians, he argued, painting and sculpture failed to enliven buildings because these media were enslaved to hieroglyphics and the need to communicate an unchanging belief system. If some Egyptian decorations on capitals imitated nature (craftsmen copied selections of plants, seeds, fruits, and human heads that had been arranged on temples), he insisted that this process involved little thought.[17]

He concluded that, since there was no architecture per se before the Greeks, the Greek debt to Egypt was limited to minor features such as caryatids and Corinthian capitals. Egyptian construction and Greek architecture originated from contrary primitive types and developed in different ways because of contrary religious institutions, patronage, and attitudes towards nudity. Whereas Greek social conventions perfected painting and sculpture, which in turn perfected proportions and principles for architecture, Egyptian conventions stymied painting and sculpture and left these arts unable to assist builders escape from the tyranny of the cave. Quatremère's reflections in this respect rehearsed Winckelmann's explanation that Greek art benefited from beautiful bodies, favourable mentalities and customs, religion, and patronage whereas Egyptian art suffered from the scarcity of opportunities to study bodies and represent anyone other than rulers and gods.[18]

Quatremère's entry was somewhat strategic: if his defence of the Grecian status quo appealed to Le Roy, he humoured the Egyptophile Gabriel Brottier by including modest examples of how Egypt influenced Greece.[19] The Academy

[14] Ibid., pp. 9–25, 40.   [15] Ibid., pp. 26–40.   [16] Ibid., pp. 41–53.

[17] P. Griener, 'De Dupuis à Quatremère de Quincy. Les enjeux du paradigme hiéroglyphique dans la théorie de l'art à la fin du XVIIIème siècle', in J. Pigeaud and J.-P. Barbe, eds, *La redécouverte de la Grèce et de l'Egypte au XVIIIe siècle et au début du XIXe siècle* (Nantes, 1997), pp. 131–42; Quatremère, Prix Caylus, p. 44.

[18] Ibid., pp. 54–65; Winckelmann, *History of the Art of Antiquity* [1764], trans. H. Mallgrave (Los Angeles, 2006), p. xii.

[19] Quatremère expunged these examples when he published his essay as *De l'architecture égyptienne considérée dans son origine, ses principes et son goût, et compare sous les memes rapports à l'architecture grecque. Dissertation qui a remporté, en 1785, le prix proposé par l'Académie des inscriptions et belles-lettres* (Paris, 1803). Differences between his original Prix Caylus essay, his entry 'Egyptienne' (*EMA*, vol. 2, pp. 282–321), and his 1803 book reveal both his willingness to adapt and his desire to rebut

36 QUATREMÈRE DE QUINCY

duly awarded him the 500 livres gold medal. The only other known contestant, Italian architect Giuseppe Del Rosso, repeated the Romanist argument that the Greeks copied Egyptian architecture.[20]

Several newspapers reported Quatremère's success, but he decided against publishing his essay immediately. He perhaps wanted to wait until more was known about Egypt, for instance through a royal expedition to Egypt, such as he called for at the end of his essay. However, a more likely explanation is that, by 1786, he was preoccupied after agreeing to 'edit and compose' two volumes on architecture for Charles Panckoucke's *Encyclopédie méthodique*.[21] Quatremère's willingness to work quickly for a token sum suited Panckoucke, even if architecture did not feature prominently in the original *Encyclopédie* (1751–72) that this powerful publisher wished to reorganize into thematic series.[22] Other authors working for the venture were far better known, but Quatremère was part of Panckoucke's inner circle of around twenty friends. He was in the right place at the right time when the publisher decided to commission new volumes to attract new subscribers who would compensate for losses resulting from delays and high print costs.[23]

Quatremère spent the next year gathering information from over two thousand books about the history, theory, and practice of architecture. He organized his research into several categories for different entries. Historical entries would include biographies, accounts of buildings across the world, and descriptions of cities and their classical monuments. 'Metaphysical' entries would provide concepts (such as order, symmetry, unity, variety, beauty, harmony, discordance, invention, genius, and imitation) that informed 'theoretical' entries about proportions and other maxims of taste. A larger number of practical entries would explain technical words, rules of the orders, optics, perspective, plans,

---

Denon's Egyptophile arguments. See V. Petridou, 'A. C. Quatremère de Quincy et son mémoire sur l'architecture égyptienne', in C. Grell, ed., *L'Egypte imaginaire de la Renaissance à Champollion* (Paris, 2001), pp. 178, 181–2.

[20] Archives de l'Académie des inscriptions et belles-lettres, Prix Caylus, 1785, MS D74, no. 2. Del Rosso's essay was written partly in Italian and submitted late; it was later published as *Richerche sul'architettura egiziana* (Florence, 1787). The Academy's archives contain just two essays, but the question also inspired J. Belgrano, *Dell'architettura egiziana: dissertazione* (Parma, 1786). The Academy could award no prize if the jury considered all entries unworthy.

[21] *Journal de Paris*, no. 318, 14 Nov. 1785, p. 1309; and *L'Esprit des journaux*, vol. 2, Feb. 1786, p. 295. When he finally published the essay in 1803, he distributed copies to members of the National Institute, savants, and artists; Institut de France, Archives de l'Académie des inscriptions et belles-lettres, Paris, E 305.

[22] Getty Institute Research Library MS 850209 is a retrospective, undated memorandum containing several incorrect dates but stating that the original contract paid 240 livres for 800 pages or 1,600 columns. Cited in Lavin, *Quatremère*, pp. 192–3.

[23] R. Darnton, *The Business of the Enlightenment: A Publishing History of the Encyclopédie, 1775–1800* (Cambridge, MA, 1979), pp. 74–5; S. Tucoo-Chala, *Charles-Joseph Panckoucke et la librairie française 1736–1798* (Paris, 1977), pp. 323–32, 343.

and elevations—those on ancient and modern construction he would outsource to Rondelet.[24]

Quatremère worked tirelessly to complete the manuscript for a first volume in June 1787. This was published the following year and dedicated to Guillaume-Chrétien de Lamoignon de Malesherbes for his efforts to liberalize censorship.[25] If many entries synthesized existing knowledge, the volume was nevertheless a landmark in the history of architectural theory.[26] We can summarize the volume under several rubrics that explain its originality and demonstrate that his thinking about art and architecture pre-dated the Revolution.

The first rubric is the history of architecture that Quatremère developed piecemeal over numerous entries. Despite aiming to provide a universal compendium, he focused on Greco-Roman classical style and its revival rather than other architectural traditions: for him, Gothic architecture was scarcely a subject for art history and Egyptian, Chinese, Persian, and Indian architectures were merely primitive counterpoints to the cosmopolitan classical style that transcended boundaries across Europe.[27] His chronology applied to the arts familiar early modern narratives about polite society: the Greeks thus invented architecture, the Romans copied them, taste declined in the sixth century when the Goths invaded Italy, but taste recovered after the fifteenth century because papal Rome created the conditions for the rediscovery of antiquities and Florence provided opportunities for Brunellesci's genius.[28]

The second rubric is his philosophical case for the antique, which he considered synonymous with beauty, perfection, and the genius of ancient Greece. Whereas

---

[24] Quatremère, *EMA*, vol. 1, pp. i–viii. M. Leoni, 'Quatremère de Quincy e il primo tomo (1788–1790) del Dizionario di architettura dell'Encyclopédie Méthodique', Unpublished PhD thesis, Polytechnic of Turin (2013), p. 144, notes that *EMA*, vol. 1, contained 117 entries on construction (13 per cent of the total) and 135 entries (15 per cent) on history, and that the proportion of entries on history declined in vols 2–3 (to just over 10 per cent).

[25] Panckoucke, 'Avis…aux souscripteurs' (14 May 1787), in A.-L.-M. Lepeletier, *Encyclopédie méthodique. Histoire naturelle*, vol. 3 (Paris, 1787), p. 4; Quatremère, *EMA*, vol. 1, covered 'Abajour' to 'Coloris des fleurs'. The next volumes were delayed because Quatremère stopped working on them between 1789 and 1795; Guigniaut, 'Notice historique', p. 51. The second volume appeared in two parts in 1801 and 1820; the third volume appeared in 1825. The completed work contained *c*.8,000 entries on 2,148 double-columned pages. An abridged version appeared with a new publisher as *Dictionnaire historique d'architecture* (Paris, 1832), 2 vols; S. Younes, ed., *The True, the Fictive, and the Real: The Historical Dictionary of Architecture of Quatremère de Quincy* (London, 1999), provides translations of select entries from the latter.

[26] L. Baridon, 'Le Dictionnaire d'architecture de Quatremère de Quincy: codifier le néoclassicisme', in C. Blanckaert and M. Porret, eds, *L'Encyclopédie méthodique (1782–1832). Des lumières au positivisme* (Geneva, 2006), p. 691. V. Farinati, 'Storia e fortune di un dizionario. Quatremère de Quincy in Italia', in V. Farinati and G. Teyssot, eds, *Dizionario storico de architettura* (Venice, 1985), pp. 43–80, notes Quatremère's reliance on Milizia, Hirshfield, Roland le Virloy, and d'Aviler for his more derivate entries. He cited Winckelmann, Piranesi, and Clérisseau repeatedly; *EMA*, vol. 1, pp. 11, 16, 25, 41, 49, 53, 57, 65, 146, 153, 186, 197, 199, 208, 236–7.

[27] Quatremère, *EMA*, vol. 1: 'Arabe', p. 71; 'Arabesques ou Moresques', p. 73; 'Arcades', p. 99; 'Asiatique architecture', pp. 146–51; 'Caractère', p. 495; 'Chinoise architecture', pp. 653–71; 'Chapiteau', pp. 607–9.

[28] Ibid., pp. iii–iv; 'Architecture', pp. 109–27; 'Bruneleschi', pp. 334–43; 'Buonaroti', pp. 367–8.

science advanced through experiments, the only way to improve architecture lay in recovering and classifying ancient examples because this scholarly endeavour would enrich the range of models that future architects could imitate. In this respect, he considered the antique a middle ground between, at one extreme, the servitude behind Egyptian architecture and, at the other extreme, the 'vicious' modern inventions and deviations from the antique that proliferated in Paris, such as pseudo-rustic bossage and 'bizarre, ridiculous and defective ornaments'.[29] The antique was thus no tyrant whose examples should be copied slavishly; instead, respecting its spirit allowed architects to 'breathe a fecund liberty' and adapt examples to suit society's needs.[30]

The third rubric is his argument for the primacy of architecture amongst the fine arts. He used the volume to attack the opinion that the architect was simply someone 'who undertook and led building' and that architecture served practical needs and was therefore unlike arts that provided pleasure by representing an idealized form of nature.[31] He countered that architecture, painting, and sculpture had a shared foundation in *dessin* ('drawing'), but that architecture was superior to its 'brothers'. This was partly because, as Vitruvius and Alberti had recognized, architects needed to be both intellectuals and artists, but above all because architecture imitated nature in a more sophisticated way.[32] Developing his earlier account of the origins and development of architecture, he hypothesized that the early Greeks were farmers who protected their property by making huts, which they perfected once the Greek mastery of painting and sculpture revealed rules for beauty and proportions. Once sufficiently urbanized and wealthy, he continued, the Greeks imitated in stone their perfect wooden structure to create the temple that embodied architecture. Architecture thus imitated nature, but it stood alongside music at the apex of the arts of imitation because its indirect imitation of nature freed it from the burden of representation.[33] Considered in a larger historical context, Quatremère argued in the tradition of the *paragone* and helped establish the modern system of the arts.[34]

The fourth and final rubric is his polemical use of the volume to influence policy and shape public opinion about urban improvements and contemporary architecture in Paris. This rubric is easily overlooked, but restoring the context of local action to the work helps identify a link joining his writings on the arts to his

---

[29] Ibid., pp. 14, 215–16, 279, 309.

[30] Ibid., 'Antique', pp. 47–53; 'Barbare', p. 209; 'Baroque', p. 210; 'Bizarrerie', p. 282.

[31] C. Batteux, *The Fine Arts Reduced to a Single Principle* [1746], ed. and trans. J. Young (Oxford, 2015); S. Parcell, *Four Historical Definitions of Architecture* (Montreal, 2012), pp. 200–1; M. Groult, 'De la science à l'esthétique. L'architecture dans l'Encyclopédie de Diderot et d'Alembert et la Méthodique de Quatremère de Quincy', *Dix-huitième siècle*, no. 31 (1999), p. 534; J.-F. Féraud, *Dictionnaire critique de la langue française*, vol. 1 (Paris, 1787–8), pp. 247, 254.

[32] Quatremère, 'Architecte', *EMA*, vol. 1, pp. 101–6.

[33] Quatremère, 'Caractère' and 'Architecture', *EMA*, vol. 1.

[34] O. Kristeller, 'The Modern System of the Arts: A Study in the History of Aesthetics', *Journal of the History of Ideas* (1952), vol. 13, no. 1, pp. 17–46.

sense of civic duty and, in turn, his politics. At various points, for example, his criticism of deficient and defective public facilities echoed warnings from administrators and urban theorists.[35] He thus complained that Paris lacked hygienic meat markets; its public baths compared poorly to those in Florence; and its water infrastructure was inferior to that in ancient Rome—writing during an acrimonious dispute over improving water supply, he noted that in Paris 'one would not dare to even think about such an expensive public convenience'. Elsewhere in the volume, he criticized the city's appearance and disregard for its heritage. He complained, for instance, that no worthy monuments had been erected during the last century, that the vogue for 'rejuvenating the exterior of edifices' damaged what had been spared from outright destruction by improvers and speculators, and that there was no purpose-built library to house the city's collections of books and manuscripts.[36]

Several lengthier entries provided detailed critiques of Paris architecture and urban development. His entry 'Cemetery', for instance, lamented the shortage of dignified burial places besides revealing his opinion that Catholicism and social hierarchy served the public good. He warned that the campaign to remove overcrowded cemeteries disregarded the Catholic faith and ignored the wishes of Parisians, who wished to remain close to deceased relatives, and artists, who made a living from funerary statues. The city could meet public demands, he argued, by imitating the Campo Santo, the remarkable Pisan cemetery that memorialized distinguished local figures, banished 'the vain pretext of equality', and inspired 'that soft and profound melancholy that accompanies the idea of death'.[37]

Quatremère's famous entry 'Character' was also a criticism of developments in Paris because he used it to attack architectural fashions, the proliferation of private mansions, and the scarcity of recent monuments created by the Crown. Architectural writers traditionally used the word *character* for the art of endowing a building with properties that suited its owner and purpose. However, he made the term more historical and civic.[38] According to Quatremère, some sorts of character were impervious to human agency because they stemmed from the climate, material environment, and deeply rooted social habits, but architects could alter 'relative character' (or '*convenance*') to imprint an edifice with the 'physiognomy' that communicated its nature and purpose.[39] To employ 'relative character', he argued, architects needed to distribute forms, structures, materials, attributes, decoration, and ornamentation in ways that mobilized a shared language that the public understood.[40] Yet, he complained, architects undermined this endeavour by disconnecting appearance from purpose, muddling

---

[35] B. Belhoste, *Paris Savant: Capital of Science in the Age of the Enlightenment*, trans. S. Emanuel (Oxford, 2018), pp. 169–94; Garrioch, *The Making of Revolutionary Paris*, pp. 207–37.

[36] Quatremère, *EMA*, vol. 1, pp. 65–6, 165, 190, 281, 286, 311, 346.   [37] Ibid., pp. 677–83.

[38] W. Szambien, *Symétrie, goût, caractère: théorie et terminologie de l'architecture à l'âge classique 1550–1800* (Paris, 1986), chs 8–9.

[39] Quatremère, 'Caractère', *EMA*, vol. 1, pp. 477–97.   [40] Ibid., pp. 498–521.

40 QUATREMÈRE DE QUINCY

language, and confusing the social order. When architects should have sought 'simplicity, modesty and...elegance without luxury', they instead deployed lavish materials, superfluous decoration, and ornamentation, thereby spreading 'unintelligible jargon' that corrupted the public.[41] In response, he proposed what amounted to sumptuary laws that rationed architecture's 'riches' for suitably civic purposes. Architects should, he argued, use the full range of columns, peristyles, orders, and ornaments in royal palaces and churches to express grandeur, power, and magnificence, but they should use these features sparingly for lesser public buildings and omit them altogether from private ones.[42] Quatremère thus rebutted the idea that architects should regulate designs, forms, and decorations according to what d'Aviler called the 'rank, dignity and opulence of the owner'. He instead extended Blondel's claim that *convenance* required the purpose and place of an edifice to determine its 'form and proportion'.[43]

Quatremère's first volume for Panckoucke thus contained subtle polemics that belie his reputation as an esoteric thinker. His willingness to intervene in Paris controversies was even more apparent in two short pieces that he wrote for periodicals whilst finishing the volume.

The first concerned the future of the Fountain of the Innocents during the demolition of the adjacent medieval church and cemetery. The Fountain (Fig. 2.1) was created by Pierre Lescot and Jean Goujon for Henri II's ceremonial entry in 1549. It was an ornate building on a rectangular plan at the corner of a block of houses at the north-east corner of the cemetery; water poured from lion-head taps on its base, which supported an upper-storey loggia with two exposed sides displaying Goujon's bas-reliefs. It became an iconic part of the cityscape despite its modest size, but expectations for fountains changed and eighteenth-century critics complained that it was neglected, poorly situated, and incorrectly designed; some critics even remarked that Goujon's celebrated sculptures failed to announce its purpose. By the mid-1780s, during the transformation of the cemetery and surrounding area into a vegetable market, this criticism of the Fountain lent plausibility to the rumoured plan to remove these sculptures and destroy their architectural frame.[44]

In 1787, Quatremère mobilized public opinion against this plan to 'dismember' the Fountain. In a letter to the *Journal de Paris* (owned by Panckoucke's brother-in-law, Jean-Baptiste Suard), he rallied fellow 'friends of the arts' against a 'barbarous attack, worthy of the Goths' and insisted that the authorities dismantle and reconstruct the Fountain 'in its entirety' because its architecture and sculpture

---

[41] Ibid., p. 508.   [42] Ibid., pp. 507–9.

[43] Cited in Szambien, *Symétrie, goût, caractère*, ch. 8.

[44] D. Gilks, 'The Fountain of the Innocents and its Place in the Paris Cityscape, 1549–1788', *Urban History*, vol. 45, no. 1 (2018), pp. 51–9.

Fig. 2.1 François-Victor Sabatier, *Fountain of the Innocents. Past and present views.* Engraved by Jean-Joseph Sulpis. 59.5 × 44.4 cm. Musée Carnavalet. The upper drawing shows how the Fountain was remade in 1788; the small drawing in the lower left illustrates the plan. The other small drawings depict the Founatin as it appeared before it was dismantled in 1787.

42   QUATREMÈRE DE QUINCY

were one unified whole.[45] He used the greater part of his letter, however, to rebut Blondel's criticism of the Fountain, thereby casting himself as the worthy successor to the authority who penned entries on architecture for the original *Encyclopédie*. Blondel judged that the Fountain lacked the 'character' of an aquatic building since it featured neither strong orders nor superabundant water. Quatremère countered that this critique ignored Lescot and Goujon's intention to create a temple of the nymphs (not a 'puerile' modern fountain that threw water for effect or featured carvings imitating icicles) and overlooked how, given the scarcity of water, they chose the Corinthian style to supplement nature with 'art and poetry' over the rustic or Doric orders that would have appeared monotonous.[46] Quatremère concluded his letter with a heritage argument to preserve the Fountain despite its flawed architecture: condemning monuments that fell short of present-day norms meant renewing the cityscape constantly, treating 'repositories of the genius of each century' like 'ephemeral products of fashion' rather than 'sacred' objects of 'public veneration'.[47]

The municipality responded to his letter by assuring the editors of the *Journal de Paris* that the Fountain would be saved.[48] Over the next months, a committee examined several plans to incorporate the Fountain into the market, finally accepting Quatremère's proposal to create a free-standing, four-sided structure using three original arcades and an additional replica. His proposal reflected urban-planning trends for locating fountains in the middle of markets and making iconic monuments more visible by relocating them or clearing surrounding structures, but the committee liked his proposal mostly as an economical means to create a symmetrical square and facilitate the circulation of people, goods, and traffic.[49] The architect Bernard Poyet oversaw the Fountain's recreation: he heeded Quatremère's suggestion to commission new sculptures in the manner of Goujon, but he added a monumental base and ornamental features that Quatremère regretted.[50]

Art historians interpret Quatremère's intervention to save the Fountain either as an example of his insistence that artwork remain in situ or as an isolated precursor to the notion of artistic patrimony that, according to conventional wisdom, started in earnest during the Revolution with the state response to

---

[45] Quatremère, 'ARTS. Aux auteur du Journal. Paris 31 January 1787', *Journal de Paris*, no. 42, 11 Feb. 1787, pp. 181–3; Gilks, 'The Fountain of the Innocents and its Place in the Paris Cityscape, 1549–1788', pp. 59–62.

[46] Quatremère's criticism of icicles probably alluded to Soufflot's Trahoir Fountain (1775).

[47] Quatremère, 'ARTS. Aux auteur du Journal', pp. 181–3.

[48] *Journal de Paris*, no. 42, 11 Feb. 1787, p. 183.   [49] Quatremère, *EMA*, vol. 3, pp. 475–7.

[50] Gilks, 'The Fountain of the Innocents and its Place in the Paris Cityscape, 1549–1788', pp. 61–9; Quatremère, *Dictionnaire historique d'architecture*, vol. 1, pp. 679–80. In 1787, Quatremère proposed adapting Goujon's 'female figures entirely in a comparable manner' by copying the sculptor's bas-reliefs that decorated the Old Louvre. Several years later, he repeated this suggestion for the sake of completing the decoration of the Louvre; idem, *Seconde suite aux Considérations sur les arts du dessin* (Paris, 1791), p. 90.

'vandalism'.[51] However, both interpretations overstate the originality of Quatremère's letter as a heritage intervention. Closer attention to what happened in Paris during the previous decades reveals that he and others followed in the footsteps of Louis Petit de Bachaumont's mid-century campaign to save the Medici Column. By the 1780s, many writers, artists, and architects feared that improvements and new construction threatened the city's historic identity.[52] One author regretted, for example, that whitening church interiors removed traces of age whilst another complained that Paris had 'become almost unknowable' and requested readers send information about monuments facing 'the destructive hammer'.[53] During Quatremère's travels in Italy, he had seen how historic monuments had been repurposed; he now joined his fellow Parisians when he expressed concern for the Fountain, questioned the destruction of Bullant's Hôtel Soissons, and asked why monuments such as the Porte Saint-Antoine had not been dismantled and reconstructed elsewhere.[54]

The real significance of Quatremère's intervention to save the Fountain lies in what it reveals about his attitude towards the authenticity of artworks and reusing monuments. Remaking the Fountain required restoring it to how, in his mind, Lescot and Goujon had intended it, or at least to how it ought to have been.[55] He later spelled out that an architect responsible for finishing and preserving a masterpiece needed to identify its 'essence' and, if necessary, impose 'unity' to ensure its appropriateness for its new purpose.[56] Far from being a dogmatic theorist of original context, on this and on later occasions he warned against leaving monuments in situ if they would invite 'more pity than esteem'. As an admirer of how Christians repurposed ancient monuments in Italy, he instead advocated transforming, displacing, repurposing, and adding to Paris monuments to make them 'useful to the public'.[57] One could thereby 'give a new existence to

---

[51] É. Pommier, 'Une intervention de Quatremère de Quincy', in M. Fleury and G.-M. Leproux, eds, *Les Saints-Innocents* (Paris, 1990), p. 145; idem, 'Quatremère de Quincy et le patrimoine', in G. Pavanello, ed., *Antonio Canova e il suo ambiente artistico fra Venezia, Roma e Parigi* (Venice, 2000), p. 475; J.-P. Babelon and A. Chastel, *La notion de patrimoine* (Paris, 1994); M.-A. Sire, *La France du patrimoine: les choix de la mémoire* (Paris, 2005), p. 14; N. Dubin, *Features and Ruins: Eighteenth-Century Paris and the Art of Hubert Robert* (Los Angeles, 2013), pp. 123–6; Poulot, 'The Cosmopolitanism of Masterpieces', pp. 4–5.

[52] *Mémoires secrets pour servir à l'histoire de la République des Lettres en France depuis 1762 jusqu'à nos jours*, vol. 11 (London, 1779), p. 233; A. Pingré, *Mémoire sur la colonne de la halle aux bleds et sur le cadran cylindrique que l'on construit au haut de cette colonne* (Paris, 1764); J.-B.-L Gresset, *Épître à monsieur de Tournehem...sur la colonne de l'hostel de Soissons* (Paris, 1752). On the contemporary perception that Paris was changing rapidly, see A. Potofosky, *Constructing Paris in the Age of Revolution* (Basingstoke, 2009), p. 24.

[53] L.-S. Mercier, *Le tableau de Paris*, vol. 7 (Amsterdam, 1783), pp. 73–4; *Journal de Paris*: no. 46, 15 Feb. 1787, p. 197; no. 50, 19 Feb. 1787, pp. 217–8.

[54] Quatremère, *EMA*, vol. 1, pp. 94, 286, 346, idem, 'ARTS. Aux auteur du Journal', p. 183.

[55] Quatremère, *EMA*, vol. 3, p. 476.

[56] Quatremère, *Rapport fait au Directoire du département de Paris, sur les travaux entrepris, continués ou achevés au Panthéon français depuis le dernier compte, rendu le 17 Novembre 1792* (Paris, 1793), p. 50.

[57] Quatremère, *EMA*, vol. 1, p. 346.

the wise debris' of the past.[58] This mentality informed how he wished to remake the Fountain as a free-standing monument in 1787 and how he transformed Soufflot's Sainte-Geneviève into the Panthéon in 1791–4.

Two years after Quatremère's letter about the Fountain, he was embroiled in the controversy surrounding the Théâtre de Monsieur. He defended this new theatre protected by Marie-Antoinette that offered all-year-round Italian comic opera in the Tuileries.[59] The Royal Academy of Music (known as the Paris Opera) and other traditional privileged theatres resented their new rival's financial support and luxurious stage-sets, but, rather than attacking the queen, they revived mid-century arguments branding comic opera unnatural and rebellious.[60] In response, Quatremère penned an article for Panckoucke's *Mercure de France* that, at first glance, reads like an impartial defence of comic opera in general.[61]

Quatremère urged the public to recognize that Italian and French opera reflected national differences: whilst French opera balanced music with poetry, Italy's harmonic language, climate, institutions, and schools meant that Italian comic opera prioritized music. Yet, he argued, Italian opera was superior, not just different, because in Italy the progress of musical instruments and singing reversed the ancient hierarchy, which placed declamation above music, meaning that in Italy music subsumed poetry and acting. In Italy, where pleasures were purer than in France, each genre pleased just one human faculty: ballet-pantomime thus pleased the eyes whilst opera pleased the soul. Since 'the unity of the soul' prevented one from enjoying multiple, simultaneous pleasures from different art forms, the genius of opera comic lay in the fact that other arts did not temper its music. Instead, opera comic's music imitated nature indirectly as 'a purely ideal art' imitating the silent soul, representing man in his potential state whilst drama represented man in his actual state.[62]

Music historians read Quatremère's defence of comic opera as a late contribution to the 'Querrelle des bouffons'. However, closer consideration of its polemical context suggests that he was deployed to write an article rebutting criticism of the Théâtre de Monsieur, which in return granted him free seats for life. This is not to say that this curious piece can be reduced to mere opportunism. Indeed, the article is especially revealing because he used it to develop a theory of

---

[58] Quatremère, *Recueil de notices historiques*, p. 352.

[59] Quatremère, 'De la nature des opéras des bouffons italiens, et de l'union de la comédie et de la musique dans ces poèmes', *Mercure de France*, no. 12, March 1789, pp. 124–48. Reprinted in *Archives littéraires de l'Europe*, vol. 16 (1807), pp. 1–39.

[60] A. Di Profio, *La révolution des Bouffons: l'opera italien au theatre de Monsieur 1789–1792* (Paris, 2003), pp. 21, 43, 76–9, 83.

[61] M. McClellan, 'The Italian Menace: Opera Bouffa in Revolutionary France', *Eighteenth-Century Music*, vol. 1, no. 2 (2004), pp. 249–63.

[62] Quatremère, 'De la nature des opéras des bouffons italiens, et de l'union de la comédie et de la musique dans ces poèmes', pp. 124–48.

imitation—according to which artists must never steal 'property' from other arts because each art had its own 'tribunal' and its own means to imitate nature—that in the second half of his life he wrote about at length.[63]

Little is known about Quatremère's life in Paris before the Revolution besides several fragments of information. Sometime before summer 1788, he moved from the central rue Sainte-Croix-de-la-Bretonnerie to the intersection of the Boulevard du Temple and rue de Ménilmontant, close to the city's north-east limit. In July 1788, he met John Campbell and Henry Tresham, antiquaries and friends of Canova.[64] His maternal grandfather, the *marchand mercier* Jacques Boujot, died on 29 December 1788.

Quatremère perhaps joined Panckoucke's gatherings in the Hôtel de Thon, rue des Poitevins, where Jacques Mallet du Pan and other members of Panckoucke's circle discussed the worsening financial, subsistence, and political crisis. Most of the circle opposed both censorship and the Crown declaring bankruptcy to solve its financial woes.[65] If Quatremère was exposed to discussions about current affairs, he avoided mentioning them in his letters to Canova; he instead toyed with returning to Rome before deciding to spend several months in England in spring 1789 when his fellow electors in Paris were preoccupied with the General Estates in Versailles.[66] Before his voyage, he acquired books on English history, architecture, and engineering.[67] His correspondence and later writings indicate that he saw Charles Townley's marble antiquities, socialized with Marchant, Tresham, and Campbell in London, and visited Greenwich, Oxford, and many stately houses.[68]

He formed an ambivalent opinion of England. His letter to Canova towards the end of his voyage smacked of Anglophobia: he complained about the 'humid and gloomy' climate, 'hard, frank, yet malicious and tiresome' national character; lack of 'beautiful art...and monuments' in London; and how England's private

---

[63] É. Quatremère, 'Notice historique', pp. 657–69. My interpretation supports M. Leoni, 'Art, morale et politique. Les écrits de Quatremère de Quincy sur le théâtre, à l'aube de la Révolution française', in C. Doria, ed., *La morale de l'homme politique* (Paris, 2015), pp. 17–33.

[64] I. Leroy-Jay Lemaistre, *Canova: Psyché ranimée par le baiser de l'Amour* (Paris, 2003), pp. 16, 62; *Carteggio*, p. 5.

[65] Tucoo-Chala, *Charles-Joseph Panckoucke*, pp. 183–6.

[66] *Carteggio*, pp. 12–13; É. Quatremère, 'Notice historique', p. 668. Misleading clues in Quatremère's *Canova et ses ouvrages, ou Mémoires historiques sur la vie et les travaux de ce célèbre artiste* (Paris, 1834), pp. 48–50, imply that he made a third voyage to Rome. However, there is no other evidence for such a voyage, and Quatremère was preoccupied at this time with the *Encyclopédie méthodique* and his English voyage.

[67] These books were C.-F.-X. Millot, *Élémens de l'histoire d'Angleterre* (Paris, 1781); R. Henry, *Histoire d'Angleterre* (Paris, 1789); J.-L. Delolme, *Constitution de l'Angleterre* (Geneva, 1787); *Parecbolae sive Excerpta e corpore statutorum Universitatis Oxoniensis* (Oxford, 1771); C. Labelye, *Description of Westminster Bridge* (London, 1751); B. Higgins, *Experiments and Observations Made with a View of Improving the Art of Composing and Applying Calcareous Cements* (London, 1787).

[68] *Carteggio* (letter dated 22 June 1789), pp. 9–11; Quatremère, *EMA*, vol. 2, pp. 563, 447.

collections of antiquities were scattered across the dull countryside.[69] However, his later writings praised the architecture of Inigo Jones, Wren and Gibbs, recommended the design and construction of bridges and prisons, and admired how London had been rebuilt after the Great Fire.[70] At the end of June, he left England for a more riotous and politicized Paris than the city he had left.

Quatremère was thirty-three years old when he returned to France on the eve of the Revolution. His socio-economic background did not determine his later hostility towards the Revolution, but his life before 1789—his education, artistic training, antiquarian studies, and web of acquaintances—puts into context how he navigated the revolutionary decade and exercised such influence. His pre-revolutionary writings brought his name to the attention of savants and artists whilst establishing his reputation as an authoritative commentator who stood apart from the academies. Moreover, the substance of these writings shows that his reflections on art and architecture had matured into fairly settled forms before 1789.[71] His belief in the inimitable supremacy of ancient Greece predated the Revolution. The Greeks, he argued as early as 1785, approximated God's hand when they devised intelligent and harmonious proportions and created 'true models of beauty' after grasping the ideal in nature, rather than copying individual manifestations of nature.[72] Equally, we can see that his theory of architectural types, his argument that architecture was a language and an art that imitated nature, and his attempt to negotiate absolute and relative beauty all predated 1789. Finally, years before the patrimonial upheavals of the revolutionary decade, he concluded that artworks affected viewers most powerfully if they were useful and created (or recreated) for public places and civic or religious purposes.

Quatremère's first writings provide few direct clues about his political opinions before 1789, but we can nevertheless discern in them the outlines of his preference for a certain kind of patriotic, civic-minded enlightened absolutism. In the context of the crisis of the late 1780s, for instance, he voiced opinions that were hardly politically neutral when he praised 'the magnificence and grandeur' of the arts under Louis XIV, defended Marie-Antoinette's Théâtre de Monsieur, stated that the Enlightenment resulted from the papacy's intellectual and moral leadership, and insisted that historic monuments deserved 'religious respect' and 'should be like titles of nobility for the nation' because they evoked its past glories.[73] His ideal form of rule appears to have been a revived Crown that still nurtured geniuses and

---

[69] *Carteggio* (letter dated 22 June 1789), pp. 9–11. This last complaint echoed Winckelmann, who regretted that 'many noteworthy pieces have been carried away [from Rome] to England, where they—as Pliny says—are exiled to remote country estates'; *History of the Art of Antiquity*, p. 77.

[70] Quatremère, *EMA*, vol. 2: pp. 2, 100, 126–8, 445–7, 486, 563; vol. 3: pp. 214, 532, 645–9, 595. His attitude towards England became more favourable over time—the decisive shift was in 1798–9 when he wanted to emigrate to London.

[71] Lavin, *Quatremère*, p. 149, makes the contrary argument that Quatremère incorporated 'the Revolutionary experience into his theory of architecture'.

[72] Quatremère, Prix Caylus, p. 64.   [73] Quatremère, *EMA*, vol. 1, pp. 69, 130, 288, 346.

commissioned ambitious artworks in the highest genres, but that also, to a greater extent than in recent decades, patronized the rediscovery of the past (by organizing a cultural expedition to Egypt and creating museums of newly excavated Gallo-Roman antiquities) and directed sensitive improvements in Paris, including acting on behalf of the *patrie* against private and corporate interests. In this last vein, he attacked luxurious private residences that stole the materials and the 'language' reserved for public buildings and railed against the 'barbaric...builders [*entrepreneurs*]' who threatened monuments belonging to the greatest centuries of the Crown.[74]

We can also discern in his pre-revolutionary writings a conception of art that prefigured his conservative politics. He defended the academic hierarchy of genres, primacy of the antique, and idea that artists must respect the 'property' of each medium. He favoured gradual evolution, praising how the Greeks developed the wooden hut over centuries whilst lamenting the modern rush to innovate. He poured scorn on the belief that artistic greatness depended on freedom, preferring a reading of art history that emphasized wise patronage to ensure artists created artworks for specific purposes and places in response to real needs. In a revealing passage dating from around 1786–7, he complained that, over the previous half century, 'political causes' had ruined the arts by encouraging a 'spirit of novelty'. This spirit killed the principle of the arts of genius, which was to follow the fixed laws provided by 'immutable and eternal' nature.[75]

---

[74] Quatremère, 'ARTS. Aux auteur du Journal', pp. 181–3.
[75] Quatremère, *EMA*: vol. 1, p. 31; vol. 2: pp. 235–6, 253.

3

Art in a Regenerated Nation, 1789–91

When Quatremère returned to Paris during the tumultuous month of July 1789, he found his family organizing charity relief in the parish of Saint-Germain-l'Auxerrois.[1] The atmosphere had changed during his absence, but the breakdown of the Crown's authority originated from its long-term failure to tax enough to pay for wars and service debt interest. If ministerial factionalism and divisions amongst elites stymied reform throughout the century, after 1786 Louis XVI faced several interlinked crises: a fiscal crisis caused by scheduled debt repayments; a political crisis caused by disputes over the form of a representative body to sanction taxes and reassure lenders; and a foreign-policy crisis caused by Prussian interference in the Dutch Republic. When the king finally agreed in 1788 to convoke the General Estates, the elections coincided with high bread prices that reduced demand for manufacturing and depressed tax revenue.[2] The six hundred propertied electors in Paris only chose representatives in May 1789, once pro-ceedings had already started in Versailles. However, soon after arriving, these Paris representatives inspired their fellow representatives of the Third Estate to declare themselves a national assembly. On 20 June, representatives of the Third Estate and their allies from the other Estates swore to remain united until they had written a constitution and restored public finances. After failing to dissolve the assembly, Louis XVI ordered remaining deputies to join it.[3]

However, the king's action hardly reassured Parisians, who feared that he planned to subjugate the assembly and its supporters. Insurgents attacked tollgates, searched for weapons, stormed the Bastille, and paraded heads of murdered officials. Louis XVI wished to avoid further bloodshed or a mutiny. He therefore declined to unleash the army and instead reluctantly accepted that the assembly was a sovereign body. The representatives of the General Estates then formed a National Constituent Assembly that worked with the king and his ministers. The representatives wanted to create a constitution that enshrined the joint rule of the monarch and representative legislative, and that upheld the ideals of the Declaration of the Rights of Man: government answerable to citizens, civil equality, property, and free expression. But the representatives

---

[1] Labat, *Vie de demoiselle Anne-Charlotte Bourjot*, p. 126.
[2] This summary draws upon T. Kaiser and D. Van Kley, eds, *From Deficit to Deluge: The Origins of the French Revolution* (Princeton, 2010).
[3] R. Blackman, *1789: The French Revolution Begins* (Cambridge, 2019), p. 82.

Quatremère de Quincy: Art and Politics during the French Revolution. David Gilks, Oxford University Press.
© David Gilks 2024. DOI: 10.1093/oso/9780198745563.003.0004

ART IN A REGENERATED NATION, 1789–91   49

also tried to restore law and order, by forming the National Guard and abolishing 'feudalism', and to repair national finance, by nationalizing and selling Church property. They had some cause for celebration on 14 July 1790 when they joined the royal family, national guardsmen, and a hundred thousand spectators at the Champ de Mars. This Festival of the Federation seemed like an exalted occasion symbolizing consensus and the end of revolution.[4]

These national developments in 1789–90 were accompanied by a municipal revolution that brought Quatremère into politics. In July 1789, the municipal government of Paris was enlarged and then reorganized into the Assembly of Representatives of the Commune of Paris, responsible for overseeing public works, police, order, passports, and supplies. The mathematician and national representative Jean-Sylvain Bailly was elected mayor and the city's sixty districts each elected two representatives for the Commune's general assembly in the City Hall.[5] The district Pères-de-Nazareth in the northern Marais elected Antoine Quatremère, and Saint-Opportune elected his cousin Marc-Étienne Quatremère.[6] Antoine Quatremère stood out in the Commune: although it included many lawyers and former members of the assembly of electors, there were few men of letters or artists and he was the only representative listed as an 'architect'.[7] His election illustrates how propertied citizens turned to a wealthy family that was untainted by its past and famous for its commitment to local affairs. A survey of representatives reassured the public that he was not a 'lawyer, procurer or an academician and therefore has no interest being an aristocrat'.[8]

The Commune provided Quatremère with his political apprenticeship over the eighteen months that he represented Pères-de-Nazareth and, when districts were replaced by sections in May 1790, the section Temple. His duties included purely administrative matters: he studied papers found in the Bastille; acted as secretary to the Commune; organized a ceremony honouring Lafayette, commander of the National Guard, for bravely defusing a riot; and helped select and procure uniforms for national guardsmen—an endeavour

---

[4] M. Ozouf, *La fête révolutionnaire, 1789–1799* (Paris, 1977), ch. 2; R. Taws, *The Politics of the Provisional: Art and Ephemera in Revolutionary France* (University Park, PA, 2013), ch. 3.

[5] H. Bourne, 'Improvising a Government in Paris in July, 1789', *American Historical Review*, vol. 10, no. 2 (1905), pp. 280–308; B. Shapiro, *Traumatic Politics: The Deputies and the King in the Early French Revolution* (University Park, PA, 2009), pp. 87–93; P. Robiquet, *Le personnel municipal de Paris pendant la Révolution* (Paris, 1890), p. 18. In September 1789, the number of representatives in the Commune increased from 120 to 300.

[6] S. Lacroix, ed., *Actes de la Commune de Paris pendant la Révolution*, first series (Paris, 1894–8), vol. 1, p. 4, and vol. 2, p. 681; Robiquet, *Le personnel*, pp. 147, 552. The election of two Quatremères to the Commune has caused confusion. For instance, Marc-Étienne's argument for municipal control over grain has been misattributed to his cousin; M.-É. Quatremère (fils), *Motion de M. Quatremère* (Paris, 1789), pp. 1–4.

[7] Robiquet, *Le personnel*, pp. 205, 207, 222; Lacroix, ed., *Actes de la Commune*, first series, vol. 1, pp. 4, 634–5.

[8] *Etrennes à la vérité, ou Almanach des aristocrates pour la présente année, seconde de la liberté, 1790* (Paris, n.d. [1790]), p. 57.

facilitated by his ties to the textile trade.[9] Other responsibilities required his expertise in architecture and the fine arts. For example, he worked with architects on municipal projects. In August 1789, he and Jacques Cellerier transformed the lieutenant general of police's *Hôtel* into the mayor's residence, which required adapting what remained from Robert de Cotte's early eighteenth-century design.[10] In September, he co-organized the benediction of the National Guard's flags, repurposing Notre-Dame cathedral for a religious and patriotic ceremony.[11] The following year he contributed to several plans, including those concerning the future of the Place de la Bastille and conversion of houses into barracks. One proposal reveals his devotion to Louis XVI: in March 1790, despite the democratic argument for using the vernacular, he sent Bailly a Latin composition to inscribe beneath a marble bust of the patriot king who 'carries the French nation in his breast'.[12]

However, Quatremère's most conspicuous contribution to the Commune concerned theatres rather than the fine arts. Drama and opera loomed large in the local economy and debates about state protection, censorship, and policing. (Since Paris playhouses could entertain 13 000 people every night, their combined weekly audience surpassed the number of visitors who saw the biennial Salon of painting and sculpture in August-September.) The Commune was concerned because it gained oversight of theatres after the Declaration of the Rights of Man raised questions about their organization and freedom. Could the new regime continue censoring performances and restricting the number of theatres? Could the Paris Opera, Comédie-Française, and Comédie-Italienne retain subsidies, monopolies over repertoires, and taxes from other theatres and performers?[13]

Quatremère and his fellow representatives became embroiled in a free-speech controversy when the Comédie-Française requested permission to stage Marie-Joseph Chénier's *Charles IX* (1788). Chénier insisted that his play was neither calumnious nor contrary to morals and that he had the right to criticize a bad king, but Bailly feared that the play invited spectators to note similarities between Saint Bartholomew's Day Massacre and Louis XVI's rumoured intention

---

[9] Lacroix, ed., *Actes de la Commune*, first series, vol. 1, pp. 264, 600, 606; Robiquet, *Le personnel*, pp. 155, 196; *Journal de Paris*, no. 320, 16 Nov. 1789, p. 1487; Lemay, ed., *Dictionnaire des législateurs*, vol. 2, p. 619.

[10] Lacroix, ed., *Actes de la Commune*, first series, vol. 1, p. 219; B. de Andia and al, eds, *Paris, lieux de pouvoir et de citoyenneté* (Paris, 2006), p. 174; R. Neuman, 'French Domestic Architecture in the Early 18th Century: The Town Houses of Robert de Cotte', *Journal of the Society of Architectural Historians*, vol. 39, no. 2 (1980), p. 142.

[11] Lacroix, ed., *Actes de la Commune*, first series, vol. 2, pp. 42, 681; Robiquet, *Le personnel*, p. 161.

[12] Lacroix, ed., *Actes de la Commune*, first series, vol. 2, pp. 84, 86, and vol. 4, p. 489.

[13] L. Clay, 'Patronage, Profits, and Public Theatres: Rethinking Cultural Unification in Ancien Régime France', *Journal of Modern History*, vol. 79, no. 4 (2007), pp. 738, 769; idem, *Stragestruck: The Business of Theatre in Eighteenth-Century France and Its Colonies* (Ithaca, 2013), p. 2; J. Ravel, *The Contested Parterre: Public Theater and French Political Culture, 1680–1791* (Ithaca, 1999), ch. 5.

to suppress patriots in July 1789.[14] The Commune therefore asked Quatremère and several other representatives to examine the script.[15] Quatremère favoured granting permission to perform the play because he shared Panckoucke's opposition to censorship in general, including how, before 1789, royal censors needed to pre-approve plays and reserved the authority to change and ban those already in production. For Quatremère and Panckoucke, the scandal caused by Beaumarchais's *Marriage of Figaro* (1778) showed that inept censorship could amplify implicit social critique. However, the Commune remained divided until the audience at the Comédie-Française interrupted the performance of another play to demand Chénier's controversial piece. Bailly subsequently sanctioned this fait accompli, but the affair blurred the line separating the desirable communication of opinions from undesirable 'abuses of this freedom'.[16]

The Commune was equally divided over the liberty of theatres.[17] The Crown had previously protected privileged theatres and required entrepreneurs and troupes of actors to obtain permission for new establishments. However, in summer 1789 the privileged theatres, fearing proposed changes, warned the Commune that unregulated competition would harm quality.[18] Bailly was sympathetic during the debate on a provisional decree for regulating theatres; he reasoned that theatres were public establishments that should be spread across Paris for economic reasons. His stance worried the Théâtre de Monsieur: it wanted to relocate to a purpose-designed theatre by Legrand and Molinos on the rue Feydeau (Fig. 3.1) after the royal family moved to the Tuileries palace, but the Comédie-Italienne performed in the nearby Salle Favert and wanted its competitor banished to the rue de Vaugirard.

This was the context in which Quatremère spoke out against concessions to privileged theatres that would harm the Théâtre de Monsieur.[19] His rhetorical opposition to 'despotism' and the 'violation of liberty' has tricked modern scholars

---

[14] M.-J. Chénier, *Adresse de M.J. de Chénier, auteur de la Tragédie de Charles IX, aux soixante districts de Paris* [1790] (Paris, 1795), pp. 1–4.

[15] Lacroix, ed., *Actes de la Commune*, first series, vol. 1, p. 321.

[16] S. Maslam, *Revolutionary Acts: Theatre, Democracy, and the French Revolution* (Baltimore, 2005), pp. 39–57; 'Declaration of the Rights of Man and Citizen' (27 Aug. 1789), in J. Stewart, ed., *A Documentary Survey of the French Revolution* (New York, 1951), pp. 113–15. As Charles Walton shows, the line between free speech and its abuse became clearer in August 1791 once fear that press freedom encouraged violence led to a decree enabling the prosecution of writers who provoked disobedience to the law; C. Walton, *Policing Public Opinion in the French Revolution: The Culture of Calumny and the Problem of Free Speech* (Oxford, 2009), p. 163. By this time, Quatremère was also concerned about the danger of calumny; Quatremère, *Seconde suite aux Considérations sur les arts du dessin, ou Projet de règlement pour l'École publique des arts du dessin* (Paris, 1791), p. 75.

[17] On the liberty of theatres, see M. Pouradier, 'Le débat sur la liberté des théâtres: le répertoire en question', in M. Poirson, ed., *Le théâtre sous la Révolution: politique du répertoire (1789–1799)* (Paris, 2008), ch. 1; and M. Darlow, *Staging the French Revolution: Cultural Politics and the Paris Opera, 1789* (Cambridge, 2012), ch. 3.

[18] Anon., *Observations sur les spectacles de Paris*; cited in Darlow, *Staging the French Revolution*, p. 102.

[19] Quatemère, unnamed article in *Moniteur universel*, no. 53, 22 Feb. 1790, pp. 212–3.

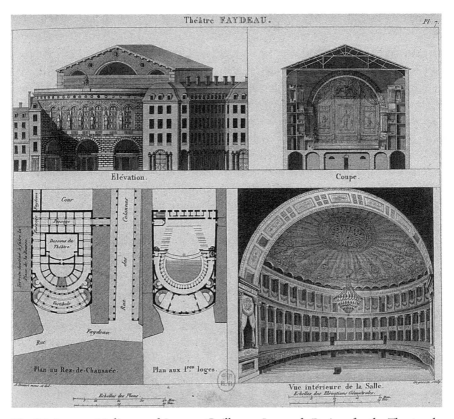

Fig. 3.1 Jacques Molinos and Jacques-Guillaume Legrand, *Designs for the Theatre de Monsieur on the rue de Feydeau*, 1788–91. Printed in Alexis Donnet and Giovanni Giacomo Ogiazzi, *Architectonographie des théâtres de Paris, ou Parallèle historique et critique de ces édifices considérés sous le rapport de l'architecture et de la décoration* (Paris, 1821), plate 7. BnF, département Littérature et art, V-22085.

into treating his intervention as 'the first principled repudiation of theatrical privilege'.[20] However, closer study shows that he used his position in the Commune to lobby for Marie-Antoinette's theatre at the expense of the Comédie-Italienne. To advance his aim, he opposed municipal interference on the grounds that the Commune lacked the means and the rationale to limit the number of theatres or determine their repertoires and locations. Like Fréron and Robespierre, he insisted that theatres should choose 'the quarter that suits them'. The public alone should determine the success or failure of theatres, Quatremère concluded, because it was 'the only competent judge'.[21]

[20] Darlow, *Staging the French Revolution*, p. 102.
[21] Ibid., p. 103; P. McPhee, *Robespierre: A Revolutionary Life* (New Haven, 2012), p. 89; Quatremère, *Moniteur universel*, no. 53, 22 Feb. 1790, pp. 212–3.

In February 1790, the Commune decided to oversee theatres in Paris whilst awaiting a report on their future. However, the subsequent report reflected contradictory demands and failed to provide answers. On the one hand, it singled out for assistance the financially beleaguered Paris Opera, arguing that this venerable institution should return to the centre of Paris (a fire forced it to relocate several years earlier) besides retaining royalties from other performers and its monopoly over French opera in the city. On the other hand, the report proposed radically reforming the theatrical landscape by making the public the owner of all theatre buildings, which the Commune would then lease to eight theatre enterprises who would pay performers from their profits.[22]

In early April, the Commune debated the report.[23] Whilst some critics wanted more regulation because they envisaged theatres having a didactic civic role, others wanted theatres to be run their own theatres. By contrast, Quatremère called upon the Constituent Assembly to create a free market and reiterated his argument that regulation was 'feudal barbarity'.[24] Since Italian cities had multiple thriving theatres, he asked, why should the Commune cap their number in Paris? Did forcing some theatres to undesirable locations not effectively seize their property by reducing their future earnings? The report's iniquity, he emphasized, was apparent when one contrasted the fortunes of two theatres. The Théâtre de Monsieur had spent four months finding a home only to be forced outside Paris whilst the Paris Opera would receive generous support, even though audiences would never pay from their own pockets for 'such an expensive and pompous opera'. Evoking the concept of moral hazard, he insisted that the Commune allow uneconomical theatres to fail 'as a lesson' to others. He rejected outright treating playhouses as public property. In a striking instance of bad faith, he urged representatives to apply the same free market ethos that had fuelled the Paris construction boom—a boom that he previously lamented for destroying the city's historic identity. Such a free market, he reassured his audience, need not rule out censoring immorality and funding the best theatres. He proposed creating an expert jury to censor and award theatres, which, copying ancient Greek practice, would sit amongst audiences to ensure transparency.[25]

Quatremère's speech was applauded and printed.[26] His arguments against regulation were fruitless in the widest sense: just as the Commune continued subsidizing the Opera and limiting the number of theatres, the revolutionary state ultimately wanted theatres to 'purify morals, give lessons in civic virtue, and

---

[22] Darlow, *Staging the French Revolution*, p. 105. The Opera moved next to the Porte Saint-Martin after the Grande Salle du Palais-Royal burnt down in 1781.

[23] Maslam, *Revolutionary Acts*, p. 38; Lacroix, ed., *Actes de la Commune*, first series, vol. 4, pp. 395–9.

[24] Quatremère, *Discours prononcé à l'assemblée des représentants de la commune, le 2 avril 1790, sur la liberté des théâtres, et le rapport des commissaires* (Paris, 1790).

[25] Ibid., pp. 1–26.   [26] Arnault, ed., 'Quatremère', p. 167.

become a school for patriotism'.[27] However, he achieved his immediate aim because the Commune allowed the Théâtre de Monsieur to perform on the rue de Feydeau. Moreover, partly as a result of his intervention, the Constituent Assembly abolished monopolies over repertoires and restrictive licenses for new theatres. His efforts to liberate theatres also made him appear an enlightened and authoritative spokesperson for performers, writers, and artists. Ironically, lobbying for the Théâtre de Monsieur thus earned him an ill-deserved reputation as the enemy of 'despotic' cultural institutions.

Quatremère's thoughts on national politics during his time with the Commune are undocumented. Given his comments on other occasions, he perhaps feared popular violence and supported restoring law and order. In February 1790, his cousin Jean-Nicolas Quatremère-Roissy was pressured, as presiding judge, into condemning Thomas de Mahy, Marquis de Favras, to death for his role in a purported royalist plot.[28] Despite optimism surrounding the Festival of the Federation in July, perceptive observers feared the growth of Paris clubs and provincial violence besides the potential consequences of nationalizing Church property and insisting the clergy swear the Civic Oath.

Quatremère resigned from the Commune in October 1790 and spent several weeks outside Paris before returning in mid-November. He tried selling engravings of Canova's sculptures to Pierre-François Basan, a dealer on the rue Serpente, only to find that recent events had destroyed the market. As he complained to his friend, 'no one any longer speaks about the arts'. He pondered joining the emigration in Rome, but he remained in Paris because he became, as he told Canova in summer 1791, 'preoccupied in our affairs and doing what I can to serve the arts'.[29]

He served the arts above all by defending from outright abolition the Academy of Painting and Sculpture and the Academy of Architecture. His writings on the academies applied his earlier reflections on the arts, but they also demonstrate his ability to think strategically and influence policy. Although modern scholars have interpreted these writings as esoteric contributions to art theory or as critiques of the academies, closer attention to their substance and context reveals that they consisted mostly of practical suggestions to preserve the status quo by implementing limited reforms.[30]

---

[27] Le Chapelier, cited in Darlow, *Staging the French Revolution*, pp. 119–20.

[28] *Journal de Paris*, no. 51, 20 Feb. 1790, pp. 202–3; B. Shapiro, *Revolutionary Justice in Paris, 1789–1790* (Cambridge, 1993), pp. 163–8, confuses Antoine Quatremère with his cousin.

[29] *Carteggio* (letter dated 16 Nov. 1790), pp. 12–13; ibid. (letter dated 7 June 1791), pp. 13–14.

[30] Schneider, *Quatremère*, p. 151; A. Potts, 'Political Attitudes and the Rise of Historicism in Art Theory', *Art History*, vol. 1, no. 2 (1978), pp. 191–213; P. Bordes, *Le serment du jeu de paume de Jacques-Louis David: le peintre, son milieu et son temps, de 1789 à 1792* (Paris, 1983), p. 52; Pommier, *L'art de la liberté*, pp. 59–91; Lavin, *Quatremère*, p. 129.

The academies in question were created in the seventeenth century to glorify the king and provide patronage, but after the mid-eighteenth century they were tasked with glorifying the *patrie* and advancing knowledge. In the century before the Revolution, public opinion was divided on their worth and whether they liberated genius or buttressed tyranny.[31]

The Academy of Painting and Sculpture had a distinctive place in this story.[32] Founded in 1648 when artists employed by the Crown sought independence from the medieval Academy of Saint Luke, its members—most of them painters— considered themselves cerebral practitioners of the liberal arts in pursuit of truth, not craftsmen seeking profit and pleasure. To reinforce this image, members gave lectures and displayed in the Academy's rooms finished masterpieces that appeared works of the mind rather than the hand. Members enjoyed privileges, including accommodation and studios in the Louvre, a monopoly over Crown commissions, the right to teach using nude male models, and the right to publicly display their work indoors, which meant that they alone exhibited at the Salon.[33] Despite the Academy's attempts to distinguish itself from the Academy of Saint Luke, its hierarchy resembled a traditional guild.[34] Junior artists were accepted to the rank of *agréé* after presenting their work; 'received' members (*reçu*) benefited from privileges after executing another specified work that met senior academicians' unanimous approval; and professors and senior figures (*officiers*) took decisions.[35] Like the guilds, the Academy tried to train aspiring artists. Students copied drawings by masters and drew from casts of antiquities and nude male models, but, in practice, instruction provided by the Academy was laclustre: since life classes were overcrowded and professors were unenthusiastic, the Academy left masters to teach technical skills in their studios.[36]

The Academy monopolized Crown patronage, but during the first half of eighteenth century its hold over taste weakened because wealthy private patrons preferred variety and grace to academic formality. In response, the Academy

---

[31] P. Burke, *The Fabrication of Louis XIV* (New Haven, 1994), pp. 50, 58; R. Briggs, *Early Modern France* (Oxford, 1998), p. 83; C. Jones, *The Great Nation: France from Louis XV to Napoleon* (London, 2003), p. 179. For examples of attitudes towards the academies, contrast J. d'Alembert, 'Académie', *Encyclopédie*, vol. 1, p. 52, and L.-S. Mercier, *Paris Delineated*, vol. 2 (London, 1802), p. 58.

[32] There is an extensive literature on the Academy of Painting and Sculpture. My account draws upon L. Vitet, *L'Académie royale de peinture et de sculpture: étude historique* (Paris, 1861); C. Michel, *Académie royale de peinture et de sculpture (1648–1793): la naissance de l'Ecole française* (Geneva, 2012); C. Guichard, 'Arts libéraux et arts libres à Paris au XVIIIe siècle: peintres et sculpteurs entre corporation et Académie royale', *Revue d'histoire moderne et contemporaine*, vol. 49, no. 3 (2002/3), pp. 54–68.

[33] Michel, *Académie royale*, p. 29; J. Lichtenstein and C. Michel, eds, *Conférences de l'Académie royale de peinture et de sculpture*, 6 vols (Paris, 2006–15); R. Berger, ed., *Public Access to Art in Paris: A Documentary History from the Middle Ages to 1800* (University Park, PA, 1999), ch. 9.

[34] On the guilds, see S. Kaplan, *La fin des corporations* (Paris, 2001).

[35] Michel, *Académie royale*, ch. 6.

[36] R. Benhamou, *Public and Private Art Education in France 1648–1793* (Oxford, 1993), pp. 46–89.

56 QUATREMÈRE DE QUINCY

revived its status in Europe by reimposing discipline, investing in the highest genres of painting and sculpture, and capitalizing on the rediscovery of antiquity and appetite for 'Grecian' style.[37] However, reforms intended to improve the Academy caused internal divisions. Above all, some members complained that the reformed statutes of 1777 handed excessive power to the director general of royal buildings and a handful of senior academicians.[38]

The Academy of Architecture had a different history, structure, and remit that explains why its members remained relatively united during the early Revolution. Created by Colbert in 1671 to assist the Crown, its original members wanted to distinguish themselves from stonemasons by cultivating their image as intellectuals who formulated rules from a classical architectural language. Throughout the eighteenth century, the Academy remained under the control of the director general of royal buildings and its members helped the Crown construct and conserve buildings. It was both more exclusive and more egalitarian than its counterpart for painting and sculpture because its membership was limited to thirty-two yet every member could vote. Although it provided teaching, many talented students came from private studios independent of its school.[39]

Criticism of the academies predated 1789, but the Revolution's promise to abolish privilege threatened their existence. The clamour for reform started in September when some members of the Academy of Painting and Sculpture penned *The Will of the Artists*. Inspired by the Third Estate in Versailles, the authors took aim at the Academy's royal character. They demanded that the leader of the Academy should be elected by members rather than appointed by the king, and therefore requested an immediate election to replace the comte d'Angiviller, director general of royal buildings. The pamphlet's authors also challenged the Academy's hierarchy of artists: by demanding that the Salon include paintings by Jean-Germain Drouais (David's gifted student, who died before reaching the rank of *reçu*), they implied that all artists, irrespective of rank or membership, should be able to exhibit their work.[40]

The pamphlet provoked heated debate after the Academy's leaders rejected these demands. Some members criticized restrictions on speaking and voting in the Academy's assemblies and suggested that more democratic forums should steer reform. Whilst the engraver Simon-Charles Miger proposed 'a general assembly' of academicians and a report on leadership abuses, the painter

---

[37] Goethe, *Italian Journey*, p. 381.

[38] R. Benhamou, *Regulating the Académie: Art, Rules and Power in Ancien Régime France* (Oxford, 2009), p. 41.

[39] H. Lemonnier, 'Cinquante années de l'Académie royale d'architecture (1671–1726)', *Journal des savants*, Oct. 1915, pp. 445–60; idem, 'Introduction', in *Procès-verbaux de l'Académie royale d'architecture, 1671–1793*, vol. 9 (Paris, 1926), pp. xxiv–vii; A. Gerbino, 'Architectural Theory in the Service of the Crown: the Foundation of the Académie royale d'architecture', in M. Swenarton et al., eds, *The Politics of Making* (Abington, 2007), ch. 8.

[40] *Voeu des artistes* (Paris, 1789), pp. 1–4.

Jean-Bernard Restout called for the abolition of ranks.[41] The task of calming the quarrel fell upon the septuagenarian Vien, first painter to the king and director of the Academy. Dissidents hoped that this doyen of the Grecian revival would embrace reform, but Vien instead complained to d'Angiviller that 'foolish hot heads' stoked discord.[42] If Vien and other leaders of the Academy accepted that some changes were needed, they wanted to control discussions about reform by creating separate assemblies for each rank.

Quatremère avoided commenting on the dispute, although in mid-September he voiced support for Vien whilst reviewing a catalogue of the Uffizi Gallery and Pitti Palace in Florence.[43] In an uncharacteristically jingoistic passage, he enthused that the catalogue was a 'monument of national glory' that epitomized the triumph of the French school over Italy—a triumph led by Vien, that 'faithful guardian of antique traditions' who had 'preserved...good taste during the shameless dissolution of painting'.[44]

During winter 1789–90, most members of the Academy also rallied behind Vien.[45] Dissidents responded by taking their grievances to the Commune with a memorandum—signed by thirty-three artists, including Jean-Baptiste Robin and David—declaring the Academy incompatible with liberty and equality, insisting that all members were 'equal in rights', and demanding that members have their say reforming the Academy's 'monstruous statutes'.[46] Several months later, the dissidents contrived controversy by addressing the Constituent Assembly directly on the future of Martin Desjardins's *Monument to Louis XIV* (1686). In the context of the dispute over the Academy's future, what the dissidents said about this sculpture group on the Places des Victoires mattered less than how they presented themselves as the Academy's official delegation, despite lacking any authorization from Vien and d'Angiviller. Shortly afterwards, David told national representatives that the Academy was incompatible with the new regime.[47]

The dissidents' strategy obliged all academies to explain to the Constituent Assembly their reform plans. Whilst some national representatives asked why the state still financed the academies given 'reclamations against their despotism',

---

[41] S.-C. Miger, *Lettre à M. Vien, chevalier de l'ordre du Roi, premier peintre et directeur de l'Académie royale de peinture et de sculpture* (Paris, [20 Nov.] 1789); J. Restout, *Discours prononce dans l'Académie royale de peinture et sculpture, samedi 19 decembre 1789* (Paris, 1790).

[42] T. Gaehtgens and J. Lugand, *Joseph-Marie Vien: peintre du Roi (1716–1809)* (Paris, 1988), p. 40.

[43] Quatremère, 'Tableaux, bas-reliefs, statues et pierres gravées de la Galerie de Florence et du Palais Pitti', *Mercure de France*, no. 38 (19 Sept. 1789), pp. 62–8. The volume reviewed was J.-B. Wicar and A. Mongez, *Tableaux, statues, bas-reliefs et camées, de la Galérie de Florence et du Palais Pitti*, vol. 1 (Paris, 1789).

[44] Quatremère, 'Tableaux, bas-reliefs, statues et pierres gravées de la Galerie de Florence et du Palais Pitti', p. 63.

[45] Benhamou, *Regulating the Académie*, pp. 61–3.

[46] *Chronique de Paris*, no. 37, 12 Feb. 1790, pp. 146–7.

[47] S. Lacroix, ed., *Actes de la Commune de Paris*, second series, vol. 4 (Paris, 1905), pp. 604–6; Benhamou, *Regulating the Académie*, pp. 61–3; J. Jules David, ed., *Le peintre Louis David*, vol. 1 (Paris, 1880), pp. 82–7.

58 QUATREMÈRE DE QUINCY

others asked why the Crown controlled the selection of academicians given that the nation was sovereign. Although the Abbé Grégoire and other representatives defended the academies, the Assembly asked its Constitutional Committee to gather memoranda and report on their reform.[48]

The Assembly's move hardened divisions by encouraging rival factions inside and outside the Academy of Painting and Sculpture to write competing memoranda.[49] Antoine Renou, permanent secretary of the Academy, led the conservative faction dominated by the *officiers*.[50] Renou insisted that the Academy had already been reformed by Louis XVI and that it flourished thanks to its privileges and statutes. He therefore dismissed demands to remake the Academy in the image of the Revolution: if the demand for equality ran counter to the inequality of talent central to an elite institution, the demand for liberty ignored how the Academy already encouraged competition, liberated artists from the guild, and allowed an unlimited number to join its ranks.[51]

Julien and other artists from the conservative faction presented a more conciliatory position. Although they opposed substantial changes being proposed (such as allowing more female members, creating a single institution for the fine arts, and holding competitions for state-funded commissions), they feigned enthusiasm for introducing more equality by moderating discipline, promoting members through majority vote (rather than unanimity), and abolishing the rank of *agrée*—a sleight of hand intended to remove young artists from any future general assembly.[52]

The so-called 'majority', dominated by middle-ranking 'received' academicians, shared the conservative's desire to preserve the Academy's hierarchy and monopoly over the Salon, but it also advocated significant reforms.[53] It proposed: a single 'Central Academy' for painting, sculpture, engraving, and architecture; voting rights for all members (including an unlimited number of women); fairer tests for *agrées* to become full members; elections for senior appointments; and improving teaching by offering students a library and museum, more professors and lessons, and prizes for neglected genres and media.[54] Most members of the

---

[48] *AP*, vol. 18, 20 Aug. 1790, pp. 174–82; C. Gillispie, *Science and Polity: The Revolutionary and Napoleonic Years* (Princeton, 2004), pp. 186–8; B. Plongeron, *L'abbé Grégoire et la république des savants* (Paris, 2001), p. 44.

[49] Gaehtgens and Lugand, *Vien*, p. 41.

[50] H. Jouin, *Antoine Renou premier secrétaire perpetuel de l'École nationale des beaux-arts (1793–1806)* (Paris, 1905), p. 22.

[51] A. Renou, *Esprit des statuts et réglemens de l'Académie royale de peinture et de sculpture, pour servir de réponse aux détracteurs de son régime* (Paris, 1790), pp. 3, 5, 17–18.

[52] Benhamou, *Regulating the Académie*, pp. 167–72; *Adresse à l'Assemblée Nationale par la presque totalité des officiers* (Paris, 1790), pp. 1–36.

[53] The 'majority' included several *officiers* and many *agrées*. Their relationship with Vien remained sufficiently warm for some of them to reconcile with him when he fell sick; L. Auricchio, *Adélaïde Labille-Guiard: Artist in the Age of Revolution* (Los Angeles, 2009), p. 71.

[54] *AP*, vol. 19, 21 Sept. 1790, pp. 122–33; Benhamou, *Regulating the Académie*, appendix 8; the 'majority' expressed its view between September 1790 and May 1791 in several documents reproduced in this volume.

Academy of Architecture agreed with this 'majority' position. On behalf of the Academy of Architecture, Charles-Axel Guillaumot thus proposed retaining most statutes whilst allowing academicians to elect new members and presidents without Crown interference.[55]

Whereas the *officiers*, 'majority', and Academy of Architecture proposed modest reforms, several new bodies demanded far-reaching changes. For example, Restout lobbied on behalf of the Commune of the Arts (formed in September 1790) for an open Salon and open competitions for state commissions.[56] This last issue came to the fore in December 1790 when the Constituent Assembly wanted a statue of Rousseau. Houdon produced a terracotta model expecting that he would receive the commission because he owned Rousseau's death mask and was a leading academician, but, despite his credentials, the Commune of the Arts and Paris Commune demanded a competition as a matter of principle.[57]

Quatremère followed these debates during his time in the Paris Commune and even attended meetings of the Commune of the Arts to understand what was at stake.[58] Did the Academy of Painting and Sculpture speak for all artists? Should the Crown, National Assembly, some or all academicians control the academies? Did Salons, commissions, and teaching require reform? In response to the Constituent Assembly's request for memoranda addressing such issues, he presented himself as an honest broker.

Between August 1790 and January 1791, Quatremère researched and wrote his first reform plan: *Considerations on the Arts of Drawing in France; Followed by a Plan for the Academy or the Public School, and a Plan for a System of Encouragements*.[59] He wanted to advise the Constituent Assembly on education and the academies. Despite arguing that theatres fend for themselves in an open market, he insisted that the state should fund painting, sculpture, and architecture—the three arts based on drawing that imitated nature.[60]

---

[55] Lemonnier, ed., *Procès-verbaux de l'Academie royale d'architecture*, vol. 9, pp. 362–7.

[56] Pommier, *L'art de la liberté*, pp. 20–3.

[57] *AP*, vol. 16, pp. 619–20, 721; A. Poulet et al., *Jean-Antoine Houdon: Sculptor of the Enlightenment* (Chicago, 2005), p. 170; J.-A. Houdon, *Réflexions sur les concours en général et sur celui de la statue de J.-J. Rousseau en particulier* (Paris, 1791).

[58] Quatremère, *Seconde suite*, p. 8. The Commune of the Arts started as a loose-knit gathering in the Academy's meeting rooms. Julien co-signed the memorandum creating it—AN, ADVIII, dossier 2, paper 5. It drew together more than half the artists in Paris. However, it later became more radical and favoured abolishing the academies. See A. Jourdan, 'Les concours de l'An II. En quête d'un art républicain', in M. Lapied and C. Peyrard, eds, *La Révolution française au carrefour des recherches* (Aix-en-Provence, 2003), pp. 265–9; and H. Lapauze, ed., *Procès-verbaux de la Commune générale des arts de peinture, sculpture, architecture et gravure et de la Société populaire et républicaine des arts* (Paris, 1903).

[59] Quatremère, *Considérations sur les arts du dessin en France, suivies d'un plan d'Académie, ou d'École publique, et d'un système d'encouragemens* (Paris, 1791). This work appeared in print sometime before being mentioned in *Moniteur universel*, no. 27, 27 Jan. 1791, supplement.

[60] Quatremère, *Considérations sur les arts*, pp. v–vi.

60 QUATREMÈRE DE QUINCY

In the first part of the *Considerations on the Arts of Drawing*, Quatremère explained that the state must pay for an academy. Although enemies of the arts considered them frivolous at best and harmful at worst, he countered that the arts benefited the economy and could improve citizens if placed in wise legislators' hands.[61] He warned, however, that freedom alone would not regenerate the arts despite optimistic comparisons between ancient Greece and revolutionary France.[62] Nature and convention favoured the arts in Greece, but in France artists were condemned to depict figures in fashionable clothes, rather than nude, and often to create artworks for private dwellings, rather than public spaces. Just as foreign fruits required greenhouses, the arts in France required financial encouragements and opportunities to fulfil social needs.[63] Such support, he added, could no longer come from the Church, hitherto the greatest source of artistic inspiration and patronage. Since the state had sequestered Church property, the state needed to pay for the arts as well as the clergy.[64]

Quatremère developed the implications of this conclusion in the second part of the *Considerations*. He argued that reformers should recognize that the arts had thrived under Louis XIV and Louis XVI and therefore improve what already existed. He then proposed reforming the structure of the academies, their pedagogy, and how artwork was commissioned.[65]

The structural reforms that he suggested were intended to reassure the *officiers* by confronting false ideas about equality. He proposed that merging the two academies of the arts into a single 'academy of the arts of drawing' would both save money and improve education by encouraging students to draw rather than over-specialize prematurely.[66] Since this new academy, he continued, would exist simply to teach, it would require just seventy-two members and no honorific positions. His proposal looks radical at first glance, but in practice it would have required abolishing the rank of *reçu* whilst retaining *all* full members. His underlying intention was quite apparent from how he proposed new members should be elected: only full academicians, he insisted, had suitable expertise, so electing new members must remain their prerogative.[67]

Quatremère's critics grasped that his proposed academy was more exclusive than what currently existed. However, he tried to cast this proposal in a favourable light by arguing that having fewer academicians meant that a larger number of talented artists would work independently of the institution, thereby counterbalancing its authority.[68] Since these talented artists would only accept their exclusion if the Salon and state commissions were open to everyone, he argued with a

---

[61] Ibid., pp. 1–87.   [62] Ibid., pp. 52–69.   [63] Ibid., pp. 49–50.

[64] Ibid., pp. 15–52.   [65] Ibid., pp. 70–87.   [66] Ibid., pp. 91–5.

[67] Ibid., pp. 95–101, 106–19. Quatremère ignored the fact that the Academy of Painting and Sculpture and Academy of Architecture had a combined membership greater than seventy-two.

[68] A. Renou, *Réfutation de la seconde suite aux Considérations sur les arts de dessin par M. Quatremère de Quincy* (Paris, [20 June] 1791), p. 4. Quatremère clarified his position in *Seconde suite*, pp. 40–1.

disingenuous rhetorical flourish that the Academy of Painting and Sculpture must surrender its 'vicious' monopoly and allow every artist to submit work to 'the tribunal of public opinion'. Quatremère's ostensibly radical argument for open Salons and competitions thus originated from his conservative strategy to secure an exclusive academy by surrendering indefensible privileges that were already on the cusp of being abolished.[69]

Similarly, his proposal for teaching feigned enthusiasm for reform. After repeating familiar criticism of the Academy of Painting and Sculpture, his ideas for improving teaching were modest and traditional. First, he suggested abolishing most prizes whilst increasing spending on elite winners of the Rome Prize.[70] Second, he argued that teaching should refocus on drawing: to teach students to distinguish between the individual specimen and the ideal, life classes should employ more male and even female models, and classes for drawing antiquities and architectural ornaments should use improved collections of casts and previously 'scattered and neglected' originals.[71] Third, to appease the 'majority', he added that the reformed academy could offer other classes (on optics, mathematics, geometry, perspective, anatomy, history, and historic clothing and customs), but he insisted that students must retain 'the greatest liberty' attending them.[72]

Quatremère also proposed reforming how the state commissioned artwork. On closer scrutiny, his proposal would have ensured that elite artists dominated funding.[73] For him, Louis XVI's success reviving the arts through a programme of commissions proved that future encouragements must respect the spirit of reforms introduced after 1774. In practical terms, the state should thus allocate 100 000 livres per annum to commission new artworks and, to a lesser extent, acquire historic artworks.[74] At a time when d'Angiviller was under pressure to economize, in effect Quatremère proposed ringfencing spending and transforming discretionary royal generosity into a statutory budget.[75] He argued that this funding should give some artists more freedom and others less. On the one hand, leading masters should receive generous commissions, enjoy liberty choosing their subjects, and benefit from the state purchasing and displaying their finest efforts in Paris. On the other hand, lesser artists should produce civic artworks:

---

[69] Quatremère, *Considérations sur les arts*, pp. 98–106. Quatremère later clarified in *Seconde suite*, pp. 75–6, that his reformed academy should control the Salon.

[70] Quatremère, *Considérations sur les arts*, pp. 135–7.

[71] Ibid., pp. 122–31. On the academic theories underpinning Quatremère's proposals on teaching, see M. Barasch, *Theories of Art: From Plato to Winckelmann* (London, 2000), pp. 310–49.

[72] Quatremère, *Considérations sur les arts*, pp. 132–6; idem, *Seconde suite*, pp. 61–8, 121.

[73] Quatremère, *Considérations sur les arts*, pp. 138–58.

[74] Ibid., pp. 86–7, 146. Quatremère clarified this proposal several months later in *Seconde suite*, p. 78, when he claimed that the Crown had spent 60 000 livres per annum on commissions and works of encouragement. His figure was broadly correct: between 1775 and 1790, the director general of royal buildings spent an average of 100 000 livres per annum on acquisitions and commissions. Quatremère thus proposed matching this sum but prioritizing commissions.

[75] AN, O1 1147, fol. 143 (d'Angiviller to Suvée, 3 June 1790).

these artists should depict designated 'national subjects' from the distant past; and they should execute these works in prescribed sizes that were suitable for city halls and squares in departmental capitals. Distributing artwork across the nation, he argued, would help justify state spending and enlighten provincial taste, inspire talent, and stimulate demand for the arts besides inspiring 'virtue and glory'—for instance, a painting depicting the siege of Calais in 1346–7 would stoke anti-English sentiment if displayed in the Pas-de-Calais.[76] Quatremère's critics understood that he proposed treating subaltern artists like artisans, but he balanced this reactionary part of his plan by ostensibly embracing reform elsewhere. Unlike conservative *officiers*, he understood that open competitions for state-funded commissions were inevitable. Rather than fight a losing battle, he thus proposed that an Academy-appointed jury should award funding to artists. Although this funding should, in theory, be open to all artists irrespective of their status, he suggested that, in practice, the jury should base its decisions above all on artists' reputations—a ploy that would ensure leading academicians still dominated funding.[77]

Several newspapers praised Quatremère's *Considerations on the Arts of Drawing*. One noted his 'impartiality' whilst another enthused that he 'speaks of the arts as an artist, antiquity as a scholar, and liberty as a citizen; he thinks like a philosopher and writes like a man of letters'. Readers recognized that his opposition to 'equality' and desire to 'preserve...instruction in the arts of drawing' supported the academies.[78] The *officiers* therefore saw no need to criticize his intervention at this moment.

Perhaps unwittingly, however, Quatremère widened the debate beyond the question of how to make academies compatible with the abolition of privileges.[79] Over the next months, different factions therefore offered their positions on the Salon, education, funding, museums, and conservation of monuments and artworks.

In March 1791, the 'majority', supported by the Academy of Architecture, presented a more detailed reform project. The 'majority' also supported open competitions and Salons, but, unlike Quatremère, it proposed that the reformed academy should be a large institution of equal members who included engravers and other artists of less prestigious media.[80] This attempt by the 'majority' to revise the statutes infuriated conservatives such as d'Angiviller, Renou, and Deseine;

[76] Quatremère, *Considérations sur les arts*, pp. 145–50, 153, 158–66; idem, *Seconde suite*, pp. 79–81, 84. During the Restoration, Quatremère returned to this idea that commissioned paintings should represent the history of France; Schneider, *Quatremère*, p. 80.

[77] Quatremère, *Considérations sur les arts*, pp. 140–57; idem, *Seconde suite*, p. 86.

[78] *Chronique de Paris*, no. 26, 26 Jan. 1791, pp. 101–2; *Journal des savants*, April 1791, no. 136, pp. 244–5.

[79] *AP*, vol. 22, p. 581.

[80] AN, F17 1310 (document dated 21 March 1791); Benhamou, *Regulating the Académie*, pp. 75, 80, and appendix 8.

ART IN A REGENERATED NATION, 1789–91   63

Vien's poor health and family affairs left him unable to moderate their intransigent response.[81]

At the other extreme, some artists wanted radical organizations to replace the Academy. In April, Restout argued that the Commune of the Arts should control the national museum and oversee the conservation of artistic monuments. Like many artists, Restout idealized the potential of museums to liberate students from despotic masters by providing them with unmediated lessons.[82] Similarly, Robin proposed that his Society of the Arts of Drawing should replace the academies whilst Jean-François Garneray from the Society of Artists complained that the Academy and ministerial power enslaved artists.[83]

Once the debate evolved, demands to abolish the academies intensified and d'Angiviller's authority collapsed. Quatremère therefore revised his original proposals in response what he called 'debates and divisions in the academic brawl'.[84] In the first half of April, he quickly penned the first of two supplements to the *Considerations on the Arts of Drawing*.[85] This new work attacked the plan of the 'majority' and took umbrage at its proposal to include engravers. His underlying argument was that masters of different media and genres were unequal, and that the Academy must respect how its seventeenth-century founders differentiated between the arts of genius and mechanical arts.[86] He feared that the 'majority' served the 'jealous mediocrity' that wanted to improve its fortunes at the expense of academic tradition.[87] The 'majority' plan, he complained, would make the current Academy worse by perpetuating its problems, contradicting its founding purpose, and reintroducing sources of corruption eliminated under Louis XVI.[88] The 'majority', he claimed, would concentrate excessive power in one institution and abuses would become common if, as suggested, that institution remained an honorific body.[89] Whilst the 'majority' wanted an inclusive institution with

---

[81] A. Renou et al., *A Messieurs du comité de constitution par les officiers de l'Académie royale de peinture et de sculpture en apportant leur nouveau plan de statuts* (Paris, 1791), pp. 1–4; idem., *Précis motivé, par les officiers de l'Académie royale de peinture et de sculpture* (Paris, 1791); L.-P. Deseine, *Réfutation d'un projet de statuts et règlements, pour l'Académie centrale de peinture, sculpture, gravure et architecture* (Paris, 1791); idem, *Considérations sur les Académies, et particulièrement sur celles de peinture, sculpture et architecture* (Paris, 1791); idem, *Réponse au mémoire sur l'Académie royale de peinture et sculpture* (Paris, 1791); Anon. ['M. le Cte'], *Lettre anonyme contre le graveur Miger, au sujet de sa Lettre à J. Vien* (n.d., n.p.). On Vien's circumstances, see Gaehtgens and Lugand, *Vien*, p. 42.

[82] Pommier, *L'art de la liberté*, pp. 25, 93–4, 332; Poulot, *Musée, nation, patrimoine*, p. 196.

[83] J.-B. Robin, 'Plan pour la formation d'une société des arts du dessin a Paris', *Extrait du tribut de la société nationale des neuf soeurs. 14 avril 1791* (n.p. [Paris], n.d. [1791]), pp. 1–16; J.-F. Garneray et al., *Mémoire et plan relatifs à l'organisation d'une École nationale des beaux-arts qui ont le dessin pour base; par une société d'artistes* (Paris, 1791).

[84] Quatremère, *Considérations sur les arts*, pp. 166–8; idem, *Suite aux considérations sur les arts du dessin en France, ou Réflexions critiques sur le projet de statuts et règlement de la majorité de l'Académie de peinture et de sculpture* (Paris, 1791), p. i.

[85] *Moniteur universel*, no. 102, 12 April 1791, p. 422, mentioned the recent publication of Quatremère's *Suite aux considérations*.

[86] Quatremère, *Considerations sur les arts*, pp. ix–x, 148; idem, *Suite aux considérations*, pp. 37–43.

[87] Ibid., p. 27.   [88] Ibid., p. 4.   [89] Ibid., pp. 21–5.

equality for unequal talents, he insisted that only the best artists should teach and deliberate.[90] He also rebutted its plan to reform teaching. Whilst history showed that the greatest artists had been instructed above all in drawing, the 'majority' wanted excessive instruction for every genre and medium—an expensive and counterproductive idea that would perpetuate bad habits, stifle 'liberty', and encourage over-specialization. In his view, the state should simply fund instruction in drawing and award Rome Prizes for painters, sculptors, and architects rather than engravers.[91]

Quatremère's attack on the 'majority' enhanced his standing as the author of 'excellent works on the fine arts' and convinced the Directory of the Department of Paris to appoint him to its first Committee of Public Instruction alongside Talleyrand (the chair), lawyer Pierre-Louis de Lacretelle, writer Jean Gallois, and savant Charles-François Dupuis.[92] Whilst working on his next supplement to the *Considerations on the Arts of Drawing*, as a committee member he examined plans to transform the Louvre into a museum, reported on the state of colleges and houses of public education, and recommended punishing rebellious students in the college Mazarin to prevent indiscipline spreading to Louis-le-Grand.[93]

He published his final reflections on reforming the academies in the second half of May.[94] He elucidated his original plan and rebutted critics seeking to abolish the Academy of Painting and Sculpture. The 'reign of liberty', he announced, provided an opportunity to change the social role of the arts for the better, but seizing that opportunity required enacting his plan for an academy of permanent members that would ensure pedagogical consistency, organize the Salon, and distribute funding.[95] He acknowledged that zealous 'friends of liberty' disliked his proposal for permanent members, but he dismissed as unworkable their plan to hand the Academy's responsibilities to a temporary body elected by a general assembly of artists.[96] As a concession to his critics, however, Quatremère proposed a more democratic, if slightly smaller, institution to the one he described in January. He now proposed a reformed academy with just sixty members who could all vote in a general assembly. Forty permanent and unpaid members would take decisions and prevent 'accidental innovations', and the remaining twenty

---

[90] Ibid., pp. 15–28.   [91] Ibid., pp. 9–15, 28–47, 49.

[92] *Journal de Paris*, no. 118, 28 April 1791, p. 476; Lacroix, ed., *Actes de la Commune de Paris*, second series, vol. 4 (Paris, 1905), pp. 97–8.

[93] BHVP: MA-NA-191, fols 161 and 492; Lacroix, ed., *Actes de la Commune de Paris*, second series, vol. 4, pp. 291–4.

[94] *Chronique de Paris*, no. 138, 18 May 1791, pp. 349–50, reviewed the work. Quatremère claimed that he wrote this second supplement earlier (*Suite*, p. i), but its contents reveal that he wrote some or most of it in May.

[95] Quatremère, *Seconde suite*, pp. 1–11. Quatremère claimed that his proposed academy would cost under 100 000 livres per annum whereas the one proposed by the 'majority' would cost more than 180 000 livres (ibid., p. 99).

[96] Ibid., pp. 12–41.

members would be salaried teachers elected for two-year terms.[97] He also defended refocusing teaching on drawing as the best way to ensure that geniuses flourished, and criticized rival plans that would either neglect or stifle students.[98]

In two other respects, Quatremère used this second sequel to change tack more fundamentally. His first change of direction concerned membership. To appease those who wanted drastic reforms, he dismissed his earlier 'reprehensible' insistence that only current academicians could elect new members and suggested handing this task to a jury of six artists. Although he pitched this change as a radical concession, in practice the jury would have produced similar outcomes: to ensure academicians retained control, he suggested that they should handpick suitable artists (from both inside and outside the Academy's ranks) who should then elect representatives.[99] His second change of direction concerned the Louvre. In January, he had criticized the project to transform this royal palace into a museum displaying incongruous artefacts.[100] Now, in May, he rallied behind the Crown's long-term plan to create a royal museum that displayed its historic collection alongside recently purchased artworks.[101] Indeed, he urged the Crown to go further, describing his vision to transform the Louvre into a 'temple of science' containing a 'National Institute' of all academies and a museum that unified 'veritable national property' amongst Old Master paintings and drawings, antiquities, statues, prints, and other precious objects.[102] This temple, he suggested, should advance knowledge, satisfy public curiosity, educate students, and inspire artists to dream about displaying their paintings in the Grand Gallery dedicated to French masterpieces.[103] He changed his mind about the Louvre for several reasons. The explanation lies partly in the heritage context because over the first half of 1791 museums could help mitigate the threat of destruction to cultural property. However, Quatremère also realized the rhetorical value of symbolically appropriating the palace as a means to appease radical reformers. Only the nation, he declared disingenuously, could rescue from fickle monarchs this great yet unfinished and neglected monument.[104]

If Quatremère's reform plans evolved over the first half of 1791, two themes remained constant in his approach to the debate. First, he always favoured compromise and wanted to reform the academies to prevent their abolition. He therefore tried to appeal to different artists: nationalizing the Louvre and holding

---

[97] Ibid., p. 52. Curiously, his revised plan for an academy included six savants; he also proposed that salaried teachers could be re-elected, the first time without any interval.

[98] Ibid., pp. 42–9.   [99] Ibid., pp. 40–1.

[100] Quatremère, *Considérations sur les arts*, pp. 78, 159–62.

[101] Berger, ed., *Public Access to Art in Paris*, pp. 81–90, 137–40, 247; J. Connelly, 'The Grand Gallery of the Louvre and the Museum Project: Architectural Problems', *Journal of the Society of Architectural Historians*, vol. 31, no. 2 (1972), pp. 120–32.

[102] Quatremère, *Seconde suite*, pp. 24–5, 57–9, 62–3, 87–93.   [103] Ibid., pp. 67, 87–93.

[104] Quatremère, *Seconde suite*, pp. 91–3. Quatremère's discourse drew upon a critique of the Crown that emerged in the mid-century according to R. Wittmann, *Architecture, Print Culture, and the Public Sphere in Eighteenth-Century France* (London, 2007), p. 84.

66   QUATREMÈRE DE QUINCY

open Salons and competitions appealed to reform-minded artists; respecting the educational role of private studios and allowing elite artists to choose their own subjects appeased David; and excluding engravers appealed to conservative *officiers*.[105] Second, he always mobilized the language of reform by paying lip service to 'freedom of expression', the 'tribunal of public opinion', the 'new national will', and a 'republic in which all artists would be fellow citizens' who triumphed over 'despotism', 'censorship', and 'vicious privileges'.[106] Yet, beneath this language, his thinking remained traditional. He wanted to preserve generous state support for elite artists and hand the Academy more control over funding, the Salon, and the museum. He rejected the revolutionary dogmas that liberty would regenerate the arts and that artists should record recent events. Contrary to the spirit of the times, he defended the hierarchy of genres, valorized painting, sculpture and architecture over less noble arts, and scorned Jean-Jacques Bachelier's 'parasitic' Free Drawing School for promoting 'mechanical arts'.[107] Moreover, if he refrained from commenting on the tense relations in 1791 between Louis XVI and the Constituent Assembly, his repeated praise for the king and his rejection of demands to apply the elective principle to public positions were far from politically neutral. With the benefit of hindsight, we can see that these interventions prefigured his politics as a national representative in the Legislative Assembly.

Quatremère's readers from across the spectrum of the debate grasped that he wanted to preserve the Academy of Painting and Sculpture. Whilst Renou and conservative *officiers* recognized that he shared their opposition to 'equality', engravers recognized that his support for the hierarchy of media and genres ran counter to their interests.[108] However, during the second half of 1791, Quatremère gained an undeserved reputation as 'the greatest enemy of the Academy' after one facet of his plan was seized upon without reference to his overall scheme. The key moment occurred in summer 1791 when the idea that the Salon would, just as before, honour the king and exclude non-academicians appeared anachronistic. After Louis XVI tried to escape with his family in June and d'Angiviller's post was abolished, artists petitioned the Constituent Assembly to demand a reformed Salon. Bertrand Barère supported their cause and paraphrased Quatremère to

---

[105] Quatremère returned to the subject of engravers in the second half of 1791; *Réflexions nouvelles sur la gravure* (Paris, n.d. [1791]), pp. 1–8.

[106] Quatremère, *Considération sur les arts*, pp. 98, 102.

[107] Quatremère previously supported Bachelier's school, but it now ran counter to his idea for a reformed academy; see U. Leben, 'New Light on the École Royale Gratuite de Dessin: The Years 1766–1815', *Studies in the Decorative Arts*, vol. 1, no. 1 (1993), p. 113.

[108] *Chronique de Paris*, no. 16, 26 Jan. 1791, pp. 101–2, and no. 138, 18 May 1791, p. 549; *Journal des savants*, no. 136, April 1791, pp. 244–5; C.-É. Gaucher, *Lettre à M. Quatremère de Quinci, sur la gravure* (n.d., n.p.); R. Portalis and H. Draibel, *Charles-Étienne Gaucher, graveur. Notice et catalogue* (Paris, 1879), pp. 47–52.

explain that 'the Salon is the press for painting'.[109] Once the Assembly voted on 21 August for an open Salon, Quatremère's name was henceforth synonymous with this triumph, even though, ironically, his original proposal in January was part of his scheme to make the Academy more exclusive.[110]

Quatremère's association with the open Salon of 1791 was reinforced when he was asked to co-organize the exhibition with David and other artists.[111] David and Quatremère's friendship and shared responsibility played into false rumours that they coordinated all their efforts, whether designing the composition of David's *Tennis Court Oath* or conspiring against the Academy.[112] Renou resented Quatremère's real and imagined influence and resorted to calumny. From June onwards, Renou dismissed him as a failed artist, called him an 'intruder' seeking fame by destroying the Academy, and, not unreasonably, accused him of covering himself in 'the cloak of democracy and liberty' to further his ambitions. Renou had initially ignored Quatremère's reform plans, but he now attacked them for personal reasons: Quatremère, he argued, falsely accused the Academy of neglecting teaching and exercising tyranny whilst proposing impractical and expensive reforms that would force leading academicians to boycott teaching, commissions, and Salons.[113] Renou later resorted to more underhand methods. In November 1791, he warned the president of the Legislative Assembly that Quatremère was a threat to the arts:

> Monsieur Quatremer [sic], who knows [David] and is prouder than him, flattered David's ambition to support his own. This Monsieur Quatremer aspires to be at the head of the arts in France, which would be the greatest misfortune the arts could experience. To achieve his goals, he plotted to be named a deputy. He made a plan that, if adopted, would force the greatest artists to flee, because it turns them into retained masters.

In this same spirit, in January 1792 Renou wrote another letter calling Quatremère an 'enemy' of the arts.[114] Renou's attacks ceased when Quatremère lost favour in

---

[109] *AP*, vol. 29, pp. 611–14. Barère alluded to Quatremère, *Considérations sur les arts*, p. 102: the means to counterbalance the influence of a reformed academy 'will in the republic of the arts be what liberty of the press is in a state. It is the free public exhibition in the same place accorded without distinction to all artists.'

[110] *AP*, vol. 29, pp. 305–6; AN, C76, no. 749 (the Constitutional Committee received three petions for an open Salon, including one from the Commune of the Arts in early August).

[111] Jules David, *Le peintre Louis David*, vol. 1, p. 95.

[112] Bordes, *Le serment*, p. 76. Quatremère and David's friendship survived their contrary attitudes towards the Academy. For instance, a letter from Pierre Seriziat to David, his brother-in-law, in October 1791 called Quatremère their 'friend in common' and sought Quatremère's support obtaining a judicial appointment; AN, DIII 384, no. 492.

[113] A. Renou, *Refutation de la seconde suite aux Considérations sur les arts de dessin par M. Quatremère de Quincy* (Paris, 1791), p. 1–8.

[114] AN, F17 1065, no. 25; Schneider, *Quatremère*, pp. 158, 163.

68 QUATREMÈRE DE QUINCY

the Commune of the Arts, but during the Restoration several dissatisfied former members of the Academy resumed his discourse. Their writings cemented the myth that Quatremère was 'the greatest enemy of the Academy during the Revolution'.[115]

Despite Quatremère's intentions, he thus earned a reputation as David's ally, the *vainqueur* of the academic Bastille, and theoretician of the Commune of the Arts. The misunderstanding reveals the extent to which shifting circumstances created unstable interpretations and perceptions of texts and authors. Yet, however misunderstood, his reflections on reform had other consequences truer to his intentions. For instance, he helped convince deputies to preserve the academies and, in the form of the Beauharnais law of 17 September, create a system for state-funded art commissions.[116] Similarly, his proposal to house academies in the Louvre resurfaced in Talleyrand's plan for an elite national institute complete with laboratories, libraries, and museums.[117] His reflections also reached a wider audience than his previous writings and helped make him the authoritative voice on the arts. *The Chronique de Paris* thus called him 'the student of Vitruvius and Winckelmann, one of our best writers and most excellent patriots', and the Constituent Assembly considered him—besides Condorcet, Dacier, Lacépède, Monge, Malesherbes, and Necker—as a potential governor to the king's children.[118]

Quatremère's reputation led Talleyrand to hand him two responsibilities in 1791. The first was to report on transforming the church of Sainte-Geneviève (Fig. 3.2) into an eternal resting place for the nation's 'great men'. The Committee of Public Instruction handed him this brief after he defended the Constituent Assembly's controversial decree to convert Soufflot's church.[119] As we will see in the following chapter, his report, written in May and presented and published over the summer, explained how suppressions and additions to transform the structure into a 'Monument of Great Men' would cost less than finishing it as a church.[120] The Directory of the Department approved and appointed him to lead the project.[121]

---

[115] L.-P. Deseine, *Notices historiques sur les anciennes académies royales* (Paris, 1814), pp. 56–7, 177–8; J.-P. Paroy, *Précis historique de l'origine de l'Académie royale de peinture, sculpture et gravure* (Paris, 1816), pp. 15–18; idem, *Mémoires du comte de Paroy: souvenirs d'un défenseur de la famille royale* (Paris, 1895), pp. 263–5.

[116] *AP*, vol. 31, p. 58.

[117] C.-M. Talleyrand-Périgord, *Rapport sur l'instruction publique, fait au nom du Comité de Constitution à l'Assemblée nationale* (Paris, 1791).

[118] *Chronique de Paris*, no. 217, 5 Aug. 1791, p. 375; P. Buchez, *Histoire de l'Assemblée Constituente*, vol. 5 (Paris, 1846), p. 372.

[119] Quatremère, *Moniteur universel*, no. 103, 13 April 1791, p. 423.

[120] Quatremère, *Rapport sur l'édifice dit de Sainte-Geneviève, fait au Directoire du Departement de Paris* (Paris, 1791), pp. 1–43.

[121] Lacroix, ed., *Actes de la Commune*, second series, vol. 4, p. 294; A. Tuetey, ed., *Répertoire général des sources manuscrites de l'histoire de Paris*, vol. 3 (Paris, 1894), no. 2318, p. 220.

Fig. 3.2 Jean-Jacques Lequeu, *Inclytis J. G. Soufflot regii architecti manubis*, 1781. Engraving. 41.5 × 33.8 cm. BnF, département des Estampes et photographie, RESERVE FOL-QB-201 (113). Lequeu's view represented Soufflot's vision rather than how the church of Sainte-Geneviève appeared.

His second responsibility was to co-organize the Salon. Under Talleyrand's chairmanship, he joined a committee consisting of David, Vincent, Pajou, Legrand, and Bervic that reckoned with the logistical challenge of an open Salon in which an unprecedented number of artists submitted works. The Salon eventually displayed nine hundred artworks, double the number shown in the Salon of 1789, and used the Galerie d'Apollon because the Salon Carré was too small.[122] Quatremère invited electors to the preview in September. Over the next months, the exhibition broke the record for visitor numbers with roughly one in ten Parisians visiting.[123] However, responses were mixed. Some critics complained that few artworks spoke to events since 1789. Their observation was hardly misplaced because the only works that alluded to the Revolution were portraits of deputies, and the most admired piece, Julien's *Amalthea*, had been commissioned in 1785 for the queen's Rambouillet dairy.[124] Other critics lamented the range of talent in a Salon that enabled around one hundred and fifty artists to display work for the first time.[125] If first-timers such as Jean-Pierre Saint-Ours and François-Xavier Fabre distinguished themselves, *Le père Duchesne* cursed the 'scribbling of bloody imbeciles who believe themselves painters and who are only good for making beer signs'.[126] Quatremère probably agreed: although he had supported the right to exhibit, he later expressed aversion to seeing an abundance of mixed efforts displayed in one place.[127]

Quatremère's experience in the Commune, role in the Salon, and report on Sainte-Geneviève magnified his pre-revolutionary reputation as a missionary of antiquity and friend of the arts in ways that help explain why he was elected to the incoming Legislative Assembly.[128] The national elections in summer 1791 placed a premium on reputation because electors (chosen from a relatively small number of citizens, who paid ten-days tax per year, by a larger number of tax-paying adult men) elected representatives without candidate lists.[129] Motivated electors could therefore organize themselves to select representatives like Quatremère irrespective of whether he enjoyed majority support. Quatremère benefited from two groups of electors. The first group consisted of those who feared a social revolution. He cultivated ties with them by joining the National Guard's second company of the battalion of Pères-de-Nazareth and co-founding the Sainte-Chapelle

---

[122] C. Caubisens-Lasfargues, 'Le Salon de Peinture pendant la Révolution', *Annales historique de la Révolution française*, vol. 22, no. 164 (April 1961), p. 204.

[123] Bibliothèque de l'Institut, Paris, MS 2555, dossier 4, no. 43; U. van de Sandt, 'Institutions et concours', in R. Michel and P. Bordes, eds, *Aux armes et aux arts! Les arts de la Révolution, 1789–1799* (Paris, 1988), pp. 140–4.

[124] Worley, *Pierre Julien*, pp. 87–91.

[125] Caubisens-Lasfargues, 'Le Salon de Peinture pendant la Révolution', p. 204; R. Michel, 'Salon de 1791', in Michel and Bordes, eds, *Aux armes et aux arts*, pp. 26–38.

[126] Cited in M. Poniatowski, *Talleyrand: les années occultées 1789–92* (Paris, 1995), p. 361.

[127] Quatremère, Letter to Lemonnier (April 1828), reproduced in 'Une lettre de Quatremère de Quincy', *Archives de l'art français, nouvelle série*, vol. 1 (1907), pp. 189–92.

[128] É. Charavay, ed., *Assemblée électorale de Paris, 26 août 1791–12 août, 1792: procès-verbaux de l'élection des députés à l'assemblée législative, des hauts jurés, des administrateurs, du procureur général syndic* (Paris, 1894), p. xxxix. Quatremère was chosen as an elector by section Temple in June, then elected as a representative for Paris in September after winning 366 votes from 719 electors.

[129] M. Crook, *Elections in the French Revolution: An Apprenticeship in Democracy, 1789–1799* (Cambridge, 1996), pp. 69–70.

club, which supported the election of conservative figures and opposed radicals such as Condorcet and Brissot.[130] The second group of electors was small yet cohesive, consisting of writers, actors, and artists who believed that, as a national representative, he could advance their interests.

Quatremère certainly believed in his mandate to serve the arts. In his address to the electoral assembly of the Department of Paris, he delivered the standard proclamation of loyalty to the *patrie*, law, and Constitution and then thanked electors for choosing him to defend the arts, those 'children of pleasure and necessity, fathers of wealth and national prosperity'. The president of the electoral assembly, Claude-Emmanuel de Pastoret, duly commended Quatremère for liberating the arts: 'Everyone must enjoy [the arts] and find in them ... a living lesson of patriotism and virtue. All true friends of the arts will assist your efforts, which will be supported by that illustrious painter [David] who is our colleague and your friend.'[131]

Quatremère thus became a significant public figure during the early Revolution: in 1789 he was a relatively obscure missionary of antiquity, but by September 1791 he was the leading spokesperson for artists, actors, and writers and a national representative. Throughout these years, he paid lip service to the Revolution whilst also praising Louis XVI's reforms and patronage. Privately, he considered joining the emigration and feared that the Revolution undermined the arts.

---

[130] Charavay, ed.. *Assemblée électorale de Paris*, p. 30; J. Robinet, *Condorcet: sa vie, son œuvre, 1743–1794* (Geneva, 1968), pp. 132–3; A. Challemel, *Les clubs contre-révolutionnaires* (Paris, 1895), pp. 447, 450, 465–6. The Sainte-Chapelle club had around four hundred members, including one of Quatremère's relatives, Pécoul (David's father-in-law), and many members of the Feuillant club.

[131] Lemay, ed., *Dictionnaire des législateurs*, vol. 2, p. 619.

4
The Nation's Temple, 1791

Quatremère's transformation of Soufflot's church of Sainte-Geneviève might suggest that he embraced the Revolution and even that he was guilty of dechristianization and vandalism. This interpretation originated with Quatremère himself, who used his work at the Panthéon between August 1792 and spring 1794 to demonstrate his civism, and was revived in the early nineteenth century when his enemies smeared his reputation by republishing excerpts from his reports on the transformation.[1] In recent decades, scholars have reinforced this interpretation by projecting the Panthéon's present-day status as the paradigmatic republican monument backward onto its origins.[2] However, closer examination of Quatremère's reports and other documents reveals that formed a pragmatic vision by May 1791, the month before the Flight to Varennes spread republican sentiment, to adapt Soufflot's masterpiece and spare it from destruction.

Reinterpreting the Panthéon's early history can clarify the relationship between Quatremère's art and politics, but the subject has wider implications given this monument's art-historical importance and symbolic freight as part of the modern French Republic's identity.[3] If the church of Sainte-Geneviève is central to the art history of Enlightenment France, the Panthéon is a rare example of a large-scale architectural project during the revolutionary decade—a period better known for destruction and utopian designs besides innovation in visual ephemera, graphic art, and portraiture.[4] In modern times, the Panthéon

---

[1] J.-P. Paroy, *Opinions religieuses, royalistes et politiques de M. Antoine Quatremère de Quincy* (Paris, 1810).

[2] See, for example, Lavin, *Quatremère*, pp. 168–74.

[3] Scholarship on Sainte-Geneviève/Panthéon includes G. Vauthier, 'Le Panthéon français sous la Révolution', *Annales révolutionnaires*, vol. 3, no. 3 (1910), pp. 395–416; P. Chevallier and D. Rabreau, *Le Panthéon* (Paris, 1977); M.-L. Biver, *Le Panthéon à l'époque révolutionnaire* (Paris, 1982); M. Ozouf, 'Le Panthéon. L'École normale des morts', in P. Nora, ed., *Les lieux de mémoire*, vol. 1 (Paris, 1984), pp. 129–66; B. Bergdoll, ed., *Le Panthéon symbole des révolutions. De l'église de la nation au temple des grands hommes* (Paris, 1989); R. Etlin, *Symbolic Space: French Enlightenment Architecture* (Chicago, 1994), pp. 101–6, 115–20; Middleton and Baudouin-Matuszek, *Rondelet*, chs. 2, 5–6, 9; Potofosky, *Constructing Paris*, ch. 3; A. Jourdan, *Les monuments de la Révolution 1770–1804. Une histoire de représentation* (Paris, 1997), pp. 154–8, 237–41.

[4] For scholarship characterizing the art history of the Revolution in these terms, see inter alia Michel and Bordes, eds, *Aux armes et aux arts*; J. Leith, *Space and Revolution: Projects for Monuments, Squares, and Public Buildings in France 1789–1799* (Montreal, 1991); R. Taws, *The Politics of the Provisional: Art and Ephemera in Revolutionary France* (University Park, PA, 2013); A. Freund, *Portraiture and Politics in Revolutionary France* (University Park, PA, 2014).

Quatremère de Quincy: Art and Politics during the French Revolution. David Gilks, Oxford University Press.
© David Gilks 2024. DOI: 10.1093/oso/9780198745563.003.0005

THE NATION'S TEMPLE, 1791   73

has become the republican site of memory par excellence, an 'impossible monument' that represents the entire nation in theory whilst commemorating 'men of the left' in practice.[5] Yet the Panthéon's modern status obscures what Quatremère was doing in 1791. We therefore need to explain the Constituent Assembly's decision to repurpose Sainte-Geneviève before re-examining his proposals and direction of the project.

The idea for the Panthéon originated in the eighteenth-century cult of illustrious men. Just as the Crown celebrated heroic lives to encourage patriotic loyalty and emulation, secularized elites imagined that their pathway to immortality required deeds rather than devotion.[6] The proliferation of portrait busts, waxworks, printed eulogies, and books about national heroes both reflected this new cult and helped establish a canon of great lives.[7] Some writers such as Rousseau even thought that public sculptures depicting virtuous and talented men, rather than kings, could regenerate morals.[8]

When French writers travelled abroad, however, they noticed that France lacked a temple for national heroes. Voltaire noted that the Englishman 'raises the Admiration of the Spectator' through monuments in Westminster abbey, 'which the Gratitude of the Nation erected, to perpetuate the Memory of those illustrious Men who contributed to its Glory'.[9] Similarly, visitors to Italy could admire Raphael's tomb in the Pantheon in Rome and the de facto shrine for great Tuscans in Santa Croce in Florence.[10] By comparison, the Crown in France was hamstrung by fear that the cult of illustrious men elevated talent above loyalty, and genius above the monarch. Efforts to commemorate great men thus appeared laclustre, despite the Crown commissioning portrait busts and representing the king as a benevolent father of the nation who helped

---

[5] P. Higonnet, *Paris: Capital of the World*, trans. A. Goldhammer (Cambridge, MA, 2002), p. 159.

[6] J.-C. Bonnet, *Naissance du Panthéon: essai sur le culte des grandes hommes* (Paris, 1998), p. 10; Bell, *The Cult of the Nation*, ch. 4.

[7] F. Dowley, 'D'Angivillier's Grands Hommes and the Significant Moment', *Art Bulletin*, vol. 39, no. 3 (1957), pp. 527–35; J. McManners, *Death and the Enlightenment: Changing Attitudes to Death among Christians and Unbelievers in Eighteenth-Century France* (Oxford, 1981), pp. 332–3; J. Hargrove, *Les statues de Paris. La représentation des grands hommes dans les rues et sur les places de Paris*, trans. M.-T. Barrett (Paris, 1989); D. Poulot, 'Pantheonisations in Eighteenth-Century France: Temple, Museum, Pyramid', in M. Craske, ed., *Pantheons: Transformations of a Monumental Idea* (Aldershot, 2004), ch. 6; A. Lilti, *Figures publiques: l'invention de la célébrité, 1750–1850* (Paris, 2014), p. 89.

[8] J.-J. Rousseau, 'Discourse on the Sciences and Arts [1750]', in *Rousseau: The Discourses and Other Early Political Writings*, ed. and trans. V. Gourevitch (Cambridge, 1997), pp. 23–4. See also A.-R. Mopinot de La Chapotte, *Proposition d'un monument à élever dans la capitale de la France* (Paris, 1790), pp. 10–11.

[9] Voltaire, *Letters Concerning the English Nation* [1734] (Oxford, 2009), p. 113.

[10] S. Pasquali, 'From the Pantheon of Artists to the Pantheon of Illustrious Men: Raphael's Tomb and its Legacy', in Craske, ed., *Pantheons*, pp. 38–9; idem, 'Neoclassical Remodelling and Reconception', in T. Marder and M. Jones, eds, *The Pantheon: From Antiquity to the Present* (Cambridge, 2015), pp. 330–53.

Fig. 4.1 Alexandre Duplessis, *The Apotheosis of Voltaire led by Truth and crowned by Glory*, 1791 (after the c.1775 oil painting by Duplessis). Etching on ivory laid paper. Image with text and vignette. 49.7 × 60.4 cm. The Art Institute of Chicago. Reference number 2013.528.

genius flourish.[11] Several figures therefore urged bolder forms of commemoration. As early as 1765, one author argued that creating a Christian Elysium in Sainte-Geneviève would demonstrate the 'nation's respect' for 'savants, poets, orators [and] famous artists' who 'enlightened France and the universe'. The 'remains of great men', hitherto condemned to 'gothic tombs...amid the crowd of the dead', should instead 'receive...the ultimate tribute that man can render virtue'.[12] In the same vein, Duplessis's painting *The Apotheosis of Voltaire Led by Truth and Crowned by Glory* showed the philosophe entering a temple that resembled Sainte-Geneviève (Fig. 4.1).

This idea of using Soufflot's church as a national temple reflected its reputation as the greatest example of modern architecture in France. The circumstances surrounding its creation are well known. In 1744, Louis XV recovered from illness

---

[11] A. McClellan, 'D'Angiviller's "Great Men" of France and the Politics of the Parlements', *Art History*, vol. 13, no. 2 (1990), pp. 174–91; G. Scherf, 'La galerie des "grand hommes" au Cœur des salles consacrées à la sculpture française du XVIIIe siècle', *Revue du Louvre et des musées de France*, vol. 5, no. 6 (1993), pp. 58–67; T. Gaehtgens, 'Du Parnasse au Panthéon: la représentation des hommes illustres et des grands hommes dans la France du XVIIIe siècle', in T. Gaehtgens and G. Wedekind, eds, *Le culte des grands hommes, 1750–1850* (Paris, 2010), pp. 144–5.

[12] [M. Reb...], 'Essai sur les tombeau des grands hommes dans les sciences, les lettres et les arts', *Mercure de France*, vol. 1, art. 1, Jan. 1765, pp. 17–20.

and vowed to dedicate a new church to the popular fifth-century patron saint of Paris.[13] The Crown appointed Soufflot to design a monumental structure on the Montagne Sainte-Geneviève that replaced the medieval abbey and asserted the power of Gallicanism. Soufflot wanted to combine Gothic lightness with ancient Greek purity besides surpassing in scale the largest churches in London and Rome. By designating the crypt as a mausoleum for the genofavians who guarded the saint's relics, Soufflot unintentionally created a convenient future home for both his own remains and those of pantheonized heroes. Responses to his ambitious design only increased its fame: although Pierre Patte and Mercier criticized the ornamental details and structural integrity of the dome, Le Roy judged Soufflot's masterpiece 'the perfect culmination in the evolution of the design of the Christian church'. Unfinished when Soufflot died in 1780, one of his eulogizers nevertheless referred to the church as 'the Temple of the Nation' and Hubert Robert gave it pride of place in his capriccio of Parisian monuments.[14]

The idea of using the church of Sainte-Geneviève as a national temple thus predated 1789, but developments during the early Revolution made it possible. The decree of 2 November 1789 placed ecclesiastical property 'at the disposition of the nation', leading to the sale and destruction of much religious architecture besides the possibility of repurposing unfinished churches in Paris, such as those dedicated to Sainte-Geneviève and Sainte-Marie-Madeleine (started in 1763).[15] Nationalizing church property also caused the marquis Charles de Villette to fear for the tomb of his late friend Voltaire once the abbey of Scellières and its grounds in Champagne were sold. Villette argued that the church of Sainte-Geneviève should be renamed the 'French Pantheon' and filled with the portraits and remains of great men such as Voltaire.

The Constituent Assembly initially shied away from a proposal that risked offending Catholics, but the deaths of Benjamin Franklin and Mirabeau demonstrated that Paris lacked a venue for mourning these apostles of liberty.[16] The national representatives resorted to using the main grain store for Franklin's service in July 1790, but Mirabeau's sudden passing in April 1791 prompted them to come up with a better solution.[17] La Rochefoucauld d'Enville argued that the death of the Assembly's famous orator was an opportunity to revive ancient practices for commemorating heroes. Most of his fellow representatives preferred the church of Sainte-Geneviève over other

---

[13] H. Williams, 'Saint Geneviève's Miracles: Art and Religion in Eighteenth-Century Paris', *French History*, vol. 30, no. 3 (2016), p. 342.

[14] Mercier, *Tableau de Paris*, vol. 7, pp. 93, 200–1; Abbé Lacroix, *Éloge historique de Soufflot* [1785], reprinted in *L'oeuvre de Soufflot à Lyon: études et documents* (Lyon, 1982); Etlin, *Symbolic Space*, pp. 101–5. Hubert Robert's painting *The Monuments of Paris* (1789) is reproduced in G. Faroult, ed., *Hubert Robert (1733–1808): un peintre visionnaire* (Paris, 2016) and on the cover of the present work.

[15] Leith, *Space and Revolution*, pp. 138–9.

[16] C.-M. de Villette, *Lettres choisies de Charles Villette sur les principaux événements de la Révolution* (Paris, 1792), pp. 62–8; *Journal de Paris*, no. 315, 11 Nov. 1790, p. 1282; *Chronique de Paris*, no. 327, 23 Nov. 1790, p. 1305.

[17] M. Deming, *La halle au blé, 1762–1815* (Paris, 1984), p. 97.

options such as the royal necropolis of Saint-Denis and the Altar of the Patrie on the Champ de Mars.[18] After a commemorative service in the church of Saint-Eustache, a procession carried an urn containing Mirabeau's heart to Sainte-Geneviève. The next week, the Assembly decreed that this church would 'receive the remains of great men' and instructed the Directory of the Department of Paris to adapt the edifice and engrave on the west front words proposed by the comte de Pastoret, the Department's attorney general: 'To great men, a grateful *patrie*'.[19]

The Constituent Assembly's decision resulted from the combined efforts of three former nobles: Villette, Pastoret, and La Rochefoucauld-Liancourt. However, its decree was immediately attacked. The archbishop of Paris, the former abbé of Sainte-Geneviève, and the national representative Jean-François Lambert complained that the Assembly deprived Parisians of their finest church and their saint's shrine.[20] Several writers criticized storing corpses in a church as a retrograde and architects argued that the church of Sainte-Geneviève was too luxurious and elegant because a national mausoleum should be raw, simple, 'masculine, grand and wise'.[21] They doubted that simple alterations could transform the existing structure. Antoine Vaudoyer thus warned against merely placing 'a name on a monument to give it the character that one desires'.[22] Criticism of the Assembly's decision was accompanied by alternative proposals. For example, some critics suggested creating an open-air, tree-lined cemetery on the edge of Paris, taking after Rousseau's burial site in Ermenonville on an island surrounded with poplars.[23] Similarly, some commentators suggested moving Mirabeau's remains to the western outskirts of Paris, where the Champ de Mars might provide a 'passage of honour' for 'zealous servants of the *patrie*'.[24]

Villette conceded that many 'philosophical writers regret the decree', but he and other supporters of the Assembly's decision answered criticism.[25] They argued that the church of Sainte-Geneviève was the most economical option, because it could be finished and adapted with national funding earmarked for public

---

[18] Bonnet, *Naissance du Panthéon*, p. 266.

[19] *AP*, vol. 24, pp. 536–8, 543–4, 554, 697, 709. AN, F13 1935 contains documents recording how Mirabeau's remains were placed beneath the cloister of the former Abbey of Sainte-Geneviève and then on 13 Dec. 1791 moved to the Panthéon crypt.

[20] AN, F13 1925; M. Sluhovsky, *Patroness of Paris: Rituals of Devotion in Early Modern France* (Leiden, 1998), p. 205.

[21] L. Héron, *Représentations d'un citoyen à la nation* (Paris, [May] 1791), pp. 1–10.

[22] A.-L. Vaudoyer, *Idée d'un citoyen françois sur le lieu destiné à la sépulture des hommes illustres de France* (Paris, [5 April] 1791), p. 2.

[23] S. Hoisman, 'Le culte des grands hommes dans les jardins paysagers: le tombeau de Jean-Jacques Rousseau sur l'Île des Peupliers à Ermenonville', in Gaehtgens and Wedekind, eds, *Le culte des grands hommes*, pp. 180–7.

[24] Prudhomme, *Révolutions de Paris*, no. 91, 9 April 1791, p. 643; Vaudoyer, *Idée d'un citoyen*, p. 4.

[25] Villette, *Lettres choisies*, p. 138.

workshops to create jobs, whereas the alternatives required buying land and financing construction. They added that the church was ideally located because it was visible across Paris, carried rich historical associations, and provided both a left-bank terminus for processions and a symmetrical counterweight to the proposed Temple of the Law on the right bank. Finally, defenders of the Assembly's decree suggested that the church actually belonged to the Revolution: Soufflot's radical design, they argued, resulted from the revolution in ideas that had paved the way for 1789. Even Soufflot's iconographic scheme, Villette insisted, precluded the Revolution because displaying side-by-side the branches of Judeo-Christian faith announced 'universal tolerance'.[26]

Quatremère remained silent until April 1791 when he published a newspaper article defending the Assembly's decision. Repeating his strategy in the quarrel over reforming the academies, he positioned himself as a mediator and an impartial pragmatist. Part of his argument evoked public opinion: just as widespread support for the decree meant that one must respect the Assembly's wish, the popular response to Mirabeau's death proved that the public wanted to gather the remains of 'the authors of good deeds' and 'perpetuate their memory'.[27] The other part of his argument reassured readers that the church could be adapted: he accepted that the church was imperfect for its new purpose, but insisted that wise changes would give it a mournful character whilst preserving the edifice's stylistic unity and ensuring that ther interior resembled neither a catacomb nor a disorderly repository of funeral monuments. Although Quatremère's support perhaps stemmed from his desire to influence the project, the opinion that he expressed was consistent with his preference for preserving monuments by adapting and repurposing them.

Quatremère also used this article to urge representatives to allow the Directory of the Department of Paris to spend national funds on cemeteries. The debate over a national temple, he argued, highlighted the scarcity of burial places as a result of the earlier tragic decision to banish the dead. The lack of cemeteries, he noted, prevented Parisians from mourning their relatives and virtuous local figures, and deprived the city of sculpted memorials that offered reminders of the past and consolations for life's brevity. He concluded by reprinting an abridged entry from the *Encyclopédie méthodique: architecture* describing Italian cemeteries to imitate.[28]

Quatremère joined the Directory of the Department's Committee of Public Instruction a fortnight later and in May was tasked with reporting on work to finish the church of Sainte-Geneviève. Over the next weeks, he gathered information from administrators, contractors, and site-supervisors, worked with

---

[26] M. Deming, 'Le Panthéon révolutionnaire', in Bergdoll, ed., *Le Panthéon symbole des révolutions*, pp. 101–4.

[27] Quatremère, *Moniteur universel*, no. 103, 13 April 1791, p. 423.

[28] Ibid. Quatremère reproduced his entry 'Cemeteries' from *EMA*, vol. 1, but he now added an opportunistic reference to Voltaire.

78 QUATREMÈRE DE QUINCY

the Directory, and colluded with La Rochefoucauld-Liancourt to provide the Constituent Assembly with identical estimates for completing Sainte-Geneviève as a national temple.[29] Upon discovering the recent history of delays, inflated costs, and misused funds, he blamed anarchic administration and mutinous labour relations since the municipality assumed control 1789.[30] 'Workers... regard their work as their property and the building as a republic in which they are co-citizens; as a result, they believe that it is for them to name their leaders and inspectors and to arbitrarily distribute work.'[31]

Quatremère finished his report in May, although he only formally presented it to the Directory on 4 July.[32] He first provided an overview of Soufflot's design besides the history of the building's administration and construction.[33] He then described structural work required to complete the edifice, irrespective of its function, and 'additions and suppressions' to transform it into a national temple.[34] He insisted that his plan cost almost 1 million livres less than finishing the edifice as a church because he proposed: making mostly decorative, rather than structural, changes; creating a future-proof iconography that conveyed general maxims, rather than illustrating recent events and dogma; removing more than adding; and ending anarchy on the site.[35] He concluded with recommendations for reforming the administration and a budget and timeline for realizing his proposed changes.[36]

He insisted throughout the report that executing the Directory's wish meant that the structure must function solely as a monument 'to great men'. He therefore ruled out the possibility that the structure could simultaneously function as a Christian church and proposed renaming it 'Mausoleum of great men', 'National monument', 'Basilica', 'Cenotaph', or 'Pantheon'.[37]

---

[29] AN: F13 1138 and O1 1702. In May–June 1791, Quatremère corresponded with Cuviller, *premier commis des bâtiments* about costs, accounts, and building masters; he also exchanged letters with Soufflot le Romain, inspector of works, and Poncet, the contractor responsible for masonry. Cuviller's unpublished 'Notice sur Ste-Geneviève' (AN, O1 1702, 8 June 1791) provides the fullest description of church's state.

[30] Quatremère, *Rapport sur l'édifice dit de Sainte-Geneviève, fait au Directoire du Département de Paris* (Paris, 1791), pp. 16, 18–21. For convenience, this source is hereafter referenced as *Rapport* (1791).

[31] *Rapport* (1791), p. 20. Villette also criticized labour relations; *Lettres choisies*, p. 134.

[32] Tuetey refers in *Répertoire générale*, vol. 3, no. 2302, p. 219, to Quatremère's original manuscript, which is no longer traceable. In 1792, Quatremère published an abridged version whose title indicates that he completed the original report in May: *Extrait du premier rapport présente au Directoire dans le mois de mai 1791, sur les mesures propres à transformer l'église de Sainte-Geneviève en Panthéon français* (Paris, 1792).

[33] Quatremère, *Rapport* (1791), pp. 3–22.   [34] Ibid., pp. 22–35.

[35] Ibid., pp. 43–6. Quatremère claimed that completing the edifice as a temple of the nation would cost 1.76 million livres compared to 2.65 million to complete it as a church.

[36] Ibid., pp. 35–50.   [37] Ibid., pp. 24–5.

What, then, was Quatremère's vision in Spring 1791? Since he believed that the temple's function must determine every measure, he envisaged an edifice that embodied the Constituent Assembly's decision to create an eternal resting place for great men that expressed the gratitude of the *patrie*.

Quatremère's plan to transform the surrounding area was oddly ambitious. Soufflot wanted before the western front a semi-circular esplanade where the faithful could gather. Schools for law (1771–4) and theology would, Soufflot envisaged, frame the esplanade whilst roads running west and south would connect the church to the city.[38] However, most of Soufflot's scheme remained unrealized at the start of the Revolution; the area remained irregular and houses on the rue Saint-Étienne encumbered the church's north transept (Fig. 4.2).[39]

Quatremère therefore seized the opportunity to describe a far-reaching scheme to transform the entire surrounding area. He envisaged creating a 'national Elysium', a tree-lined walled enclosure that imitated the ancient *temenos*—an area the Greeks reserved for worshipping gods. This 'sacred wood' would, in his view: display monuments to virtuous men; provide a new cemetery for Paris; reinforce 'religious sentiment' and reflection amidst the 'spectacle of nature';

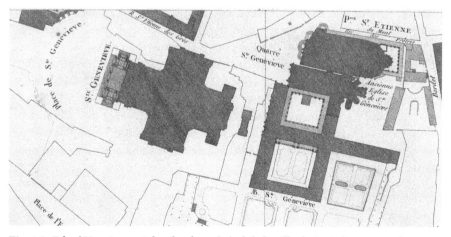

Fig. 4.2 Edmé Verniquet, *Atlas du plan général de la ville de Paris* (Paris, 1795), no. 53 (detail). BnF, département Philosophie, histoire, sciences de l'homme, GR FOL-LK7-6043. Produced between 1780 and 1790, Verniquet's map shows that, at the start of the Revolution, the area around Sainte-Geneviève remained irregular.

---

[38] AN, CP N III Seine 213 and 882 show Soufflot's 1757 plan for the area.
[39] E. Verniquet, *Atlas du plan général de la ville de Paris* (Paris, year IV [1795]), no. 53.

80 QUATREMÈRE DE QUINCY

frame the temple to ennoble its qualities; and, contrary to Soufflot's plan, separate the temple from the tumultuous city.[40] Yet creating this Elysium required not only completing Soufflot's esplanade to the west but also demolishing houses and the Collège de Montaigu to the south, and garden of the abbey of Sainte-Geneviève to the east.[41] The cost of acquisitions and demolitions suggests that Quatremère's Elysium was a utopian ploy of sorts. He perhaps intended to appease critics of the Assembly's decree who favoured an open-air national mausoleum, or to offer a moderate alternative to more ambitious demands for an even larger enclosure, which would make the temple seem smaller and require destroying the abbey and church of Saint-Étienne-du-Mont.[42]

In stark contrast to these ambitious plans for the surrounding area, Quatremère proposed modest structural changes to the building itself. Namely, to suppress the planned sacristy, the lantern tower on the dome, and the eastern bell towers. Removing these towers, he insisted, would actually 'repair' the building because Soufflot added them against his will due to the 'prejudices of his time'.[43] However, despite his respect for the architect, Quatremère also envisaged an inexpensive yet far-reaching change that opposed the spirit of Soufflot's design. Whereas Soufflot wanted to create a luminous structure inspired by late Gothic architecture, Quatremère wanted to imitate the archaic solidity and sombre interiors of Greek Doric temples. Just as he previously argued that minimizing 'punctures and openings' gave temples an appropriate character, he now proposed infilling the thirty-nine large windows and the portals flanking the central door. These suppressions would darken the interior and outside create vast uninterrupted walls that would provide a unified receptacle to support the dome.[44]

Quatremère's vision required removing and replacing external sculptures. Since he found Soufflot's ornamental patterns and shapes a deadening distraction that 'prevents the soul feeling great sentiments', he envisaged suppressing the rolling pattern beneath the pediment, garlands beneath the architrave, elaborate frames beneath the peristyle, and ornaments beneath the gallery of the dome's circular colonnade. However, he accepted Soufflot's use of the Corinthian order and

---

[40] Quatremère, *Rapport* (1791), pp. 32–3; Quatremère, *Rapport fait au Directoire du Département de Paris, le 13 novembre 1792* (Paris, 1792), pp. 18–19. This second report is hereafter referenced as *Rapport* (1792). During the Empire, Quatremère described a similar cemetery; 'Rapport fait au conseil municipal de Paris...sur les concessions de terrains dans les cimetières' [19 April 1805] in AN, F2 (I) 123, pp. 6–7.

[41] Quatremère, *Rapport* (1791), pp. 32–3. Mention of the Abbey's garden indicates the extent of his plan, which is consistent with drawings in Musée Carnavalet, D.3630.

[42] AN, F 13 333, no. 302: Quatremère's letter to the Directory of the Department of Paris, April 1793, dovetails with the vision he outlined in *Rapport* (1791).

[43] Quatremère, *Rapport* (1791), pp. 26–7; idem, *Rapport* (1792), pp. 13–16. Villette also proposed removing the towers; *Chronique de Paris*, no. 123, 3 May 1791, p. 490.

[44] Quatremère, 'Caractère', *EMA*, vol. 1.

warned that purging all ornamental details risked creating unanticipated problems, such as making the exterior monotonous.[45]

Given that few architectural changes were possible, Quatremère envisaged that his ability to announce the temple's function lay above all with the 'figurative language' of allegorical sculpture. He therefore planned an ambitious iconographical programme that would teach citizens to obey the law and make sacrifices for the 'new divinity' that was the *patrie*. All artworks, he insisted, must communicate how the *patrie* protected rights, freedom, and property, and thereby nourished geniuses who repaid their debt when their renown honoured the *patrie*.[46] This iconographical programme resulted from recent events, he later acknowledged, but he wanted it to celebrate values that transcended the Revolution.[47]

Quatremère was most concerned with sculptures on the west front, which he considered the face that revealed the temple's body and soul.[48] Villette favoured adapting Soufflot's scheme, but Quatremère did not hesitate on artistic or heritage grounds to suppress the original bas-reliefs: in his opinion, those located beneath the peristyle depicted incongruous scenes from the lives of Geneviève, Peter, and Paul whilst the tympanum relief depicting the *Celebration of the Sacrifice of the Mass* was an 'insipid mass of clouds, angels, and rays' that Coustou handed to his students to execute.[49]

By summer 1791, Quatremère had determined what should replace these subjects. He mused that the tympanum provided an opportunity to revive the ancient art of bas-relief in a large triangular recess. For this space, he devised a female personification of the *patrie* ('a woman clothed in a long dress accompanied by symbols characterizing France') who would crown two figures of Genius (shown as a restless winged male figure) and Virtue (an imperturbable female figure), flanked by symbolic representations of stricken vices and passions.[50] Quatremère favoured replacing the five bas-reliefs beneath the tympanum with a single continuous sculpture in the manner of ancient Greek friezes and Ledoux's design for Chaux, but structural factors forced him to retain the original dimensions.[51] In his scheme, the central relief should depict an allegory of the

---

[45] Quatremère, *Rapport* (1792), pp. 8–9, 19–23, 25–8. He described these changes in detail in 1792, but his overall vision was clear by summer 1791.

[46] Ibid., pp. 23–7.

[47] Quatremère, *Rapport fait au Directoire du département de Paris: sur les travaux entrepris, continués ou achevés au Panthéon français depuis le compte-rendu le 17 novembre 1792 & sur l'état actuel du monument, le deuxième jour du second mois de l'an 2 de la République française, une & indivisible* (Paris, 1793), p. 73. This third report is hereafter cited as *Rapport* (1793).

[48] Quatremère, *Rapport* (1793), p. 3.

[49] Quatremère, *Rapport* (1791), pp. 5, 25–6; *Rapport* (1792), p. 24. On the original sculptures, see I. Leroy-Jay Lemaistre, 'De Sainte-Geneviève au Panthéon, les différents programmes de sculpture, à la lumière des récentes découvertes', in Bergdoll, ed., *Le Panthéon symbole des révolutions*, pp. 234–5; and É. Portet, 'Les collections du Panthéon. Étude, inventaire et perspectives scientifiques', *In situ. Revue des patrimoines*, no. 29 (2016).

[50] Quatremère, *Rapport* (1791), pp. 25–6; *Rapport* (1792), p. 25.

[51] Quatremère, *Rapport* (1793), p. 8.

Declaration of the Rights of Man: 'Nature…supported by Equality and Liberty', accompanied by symbols of 'the happiness of the countryside, wealth of cities and tranquillity of the empire'. To one side of this central relief, he imagined works depicting what the *patrie* did for man with education and law; and, to the other side, he imagined works depicting what man owed the *patrie*. Text on the west front would reinforce the didactic character of these bas-reliefs. The Constituent Assembly had already demanded 'To great men, a grateful *patrie*', which he planned to spell out on the frieze with bronze letters, but he envisaged using additional text, such as an inscription above the entrance stating the temple's name (such as 'National Basilica') and tablets either side of the entrance listing constitutional rights and duties.[52] Quatremère included text because, like many contemporary architects, he wanted architecture to speak but struggled to do so without words.[53]

Quatremère planned an audacious final allegorical sculpture for the exterior in the form of a freestanding figure crowning the dome. At pains to justify the cost, he argued that this colossus would restore the spirit of Soufflot's design because the architect intended to place an effigy of Sainte-Geneviève on the dome. To update Soufflot's idea, Quatremère proposed replacing the patron saint of Paris with an allegorical Renown, depicted as a winged female figure sounding a trumpet.[54]

Quatremère proposed altering the interior as well. To create a sombre space that encouraged visitors to respect the 'religious silence' and behave as worshippers rather than art connoisseurs, he envisaged infilling all windows except small inlets in the upper parts of the church and dome. This change reflected his understanding of Greek temples, but also imitated Mirabeau's funeral ceremony in which black cloths had covered the windows in Saint-Eustache.

He envisaged further simplifying the interior by eliminating ornaments whose richness contradicted the sobriety required for a temple of the nation. Whilst he conceded the practical case for completing fluting on columns, he favoured suppressing other half-finished details, such as fleur de lys, chiffres, medallions of kings, palms, flowers, cherub heads, and angels.[55]

The same mindset determined his plan to create decorative artwork inside the temple. Soufflot's scheme told the story of the Judaeo-Christian faith, with each side of the church recounting the histories of ancient Jewish rites, Greek orthodoxy, and the Latin and Gallican churches. Whilst some commentators in 1791

[52] Quatremère, *Rapport* (1791), p. 26.

[53] Wittman describes architects' dilemma in *Architecture, Print Culture and the Public Sphere*, p. 211.

[54] Quatremère, *Rapport* (1791), p. 27. Soufflot's plans for a colossal figure are clear in *Plan général de l'église de Sainte-Geneviève, de la place & de la rüe au devant, suivant le dernier projet présenté au Roy par Mr le Marquis de Marigny, approuvé par Sa Majesté le 2 mars 1757, inventé et dessiné par J. G. Soufflot* (Paris, 1757), plate 3.

[55] Quatremère, *Rapport* (1792), pp. 22–3.

recommended finishing Soufflot's scheme by filling remaining spaces with symbols from other cults, Quatremère insisted that this 'philosophical pantheon' must serve only the 'truly universal' religion of '*la morale*'. He therefore rejected mixing emblems and instead proposed creating new bas-reliefs, displaying the virtues and the fruits of genius, for inside the twenty internal pendentives (i.e. the triangular segments of spheres) that supported the vaults in the nave, transepts, and dome.[56] The reliefs in the west vault, nearest the entrance, would depict allegories of ethics, legislation, politics, and history to convey moral and philosophical virtues. Reliefs in the east vault would contain allegorical representations of strength, justice, impartiality, and devotion to convey patriotic virtues. The vault in the north transept would contain allegories of astronomy, geometry, physics, and agriculture to show how genius enriched knowledge whilst the vault in the south transept would contain allegories of painting and sculpture, architecture and music, poetry and eloquence, and navigation and commerce to demonstrate how genius enriched the arts.[57] Alongside these new bas-reliefs, Quatremère wanted to create new features and artworks for the area directly beneath the central dome, which would henceforth receive a solitary spotlight that would draw worshippers towards it. He proposed a simple and versatile altar of the *patrie*, consisting of a platform with three granite steps.[58] As one approached the altar and looked up, he imagined, one would admire the large pendentives of the dome, each displaying an allegorical subject that summarized iconography from the adjacent nave or transept. He envisaged above these large bas-reliefs a spectacular painting on the underside of the cupola depicting 'the apotheosis of genius and virtue'. Since he never followed through with this planned painting (the only instance when he considered using this medium in his decorative scheme), he perhaps included it initially simply as an offer to David, whom he alluded to in his report without naming.[59]

Over spring 1791, Quatremère thus devised a clear vision for the temple and its surrounding area. Curiously, although he insisted that all changes reflect the edifice's new function, his report also recognized that its form and uses would evolve. Indeed, he understood that the temple served two different, if related, functions: first, to inspire emulation by sustaining the memory of great men; and, second, to house the remains of these great men.[60] This duality led him to preserve the crypt and upper church as distinct spaces, rather than joining them by making a circular hole beneath the dome in the manner advocated by Viel de Saint-Maux.[61] He admired the crypt and judged that its heavy primitive character was already

---

[56] Quatremère, *Rapport* (1791), p. 29; Quatremère wrote short descriptions for convenience in this first report, but he implied that he had already devised in full his programme.
[57] Quatremère, *Rapport* (1792), p. 30.   [58] Quatremère, *Rapport* (1791), p. 34.
[59] Ibid., pp. 28–30, 7.   [60] Quatremère, *Rapport* (1793), p. 71.
[61] Deming, 'Le Panthéon révolutionnaire', p. 116.

84 QUATREMÈRE DE QUINCY

perfectly suited to receive the remains of great men.[62] Using the crypt this way allowed him, he argued, to commemorate great men in the upper church without this space becoming a macabre catacomb. He envisaged that the upper church would eventually display around three hundred monuments, thereby providing work for sculptors and forming a sentimental museum like the Campo Santo. Far from wanting a sparse interior punctuated by isolated allegorical bas-reliefs, he wanted to display a range of monuments: freestanding and attached to the walls, allegorical and representative, portrait busts and urns on columns, bas-reliefs, sculpted sarcophagi crowned by effigies of great men, and tablets inscribed with epigraphs. This part of his plan had currency at the time, as indicated by a print showing the interior of the temple with a sculpture of Louis XVI surrounded by busts and medallions of great men.[63] However, Quatremère feared recreating the sundry confusion inside Saint-Denis and Westminster abbey and therefore wished to coordinate the colours and sizes of monuments.[64] He proposed inscribing monuments for men whose remains were below in the crypt with the words '*Hic iacet*' ('Here lies'), but he imagined that the upper church and the Elysium could also display monuments to men whose remains had not been transferred.

Quatremère realized that a temple used funerals alone would attract few visitors. To democratize the space, encourage citizens to serve the *patrie*, and justify the project's cost, he therefore suggested that the temple should hold other civic ceremonies, such as annual awards for virtue, patriotism, and devotion to the public good.[65] Moreover, although the temple was intended to commemorate exceptional individuals, he suggested that it could also celebrate banal good deeds that everyone could undertake. Charles Chaisneau took up this idea in 1792 when he proposed columns and pyramids dedicated to virtuous citizens.[66]

After the Directory of the Department received Quatremère's report, La Rochefoucauld-Liancourt sent it to the minister of the interior with a request for the Imprimerie Royale to print 1,500 copies for national representatives and provincial departments. The minister agreed and noted that Quatremère had already expressed his desire to publish the report without delay.[67]

When the report finally appeared in print in mid-July, however, recent events meant that the Constituent Assembly's earlier decree to transform the church of Sainte-Geneviève took on ideological connotations that Quatremère had never

---

[62] Quatremère, *Rapport* (1793), p. 32; *Rapport* (1791), p. 32.

[63] Anon., 'Galerie des célèbres patriotes', BnF, reproduced in Deming, 'Le Panthéon révolutionnaire', p. 117.

[64] Quatremère, *Rapport* (1791), pp. 30–2.   [65] Quatremère, *Rapport* (1791), pp. 33–5.

[66] C. Chaisneau, *Le Panthéon français, ou Discours sur les honneurs publics décernés par la nation à la mémoire des grands hommes* (Dijon, 1792), p. 9.

[67] AN, F17 1084: see the extract of deliberations of the Directory of the Department of Paris and letters dated 4–5 July 1791.

Fig. 4.3 Unknown artist, *Transfer of the remains of Voltaire to the Panthéon*, 1791. 8 × 14.5 cm. Printed in *Révolutions de France et de Brabant*. BnF, département Estampes et photographie, RESERVE QB-370 (24)-FT 4.

imagined. The crucial shift occurred during June and July 1791 after Villette finally convinced the Assembly to transfer Voltaire's remains. Preparations were underway when, on 20–1 June, the royal family escaped and fled east, only to be stopped in Varennes near the Austrian border. Their flight led to calls for a republic and encouraged radical commentators to contrast the glorious return of Voltaire to the shameful return of 'an imbecile king'.[68] Voltaire's pantheonization bolstered and distorted his posthumous reputation, so that this one-time friend of Frederick the Great and apologist for the Maupeou coup became 'Saint Voltaire, the enemy of tyranny'.[69] The ceremony, more abstract and antique than Mirabeau's, was the first secular revolutionary festival.[70] It cost almost 36 000 livres and culminated with the entry of Voltaire's remains on a horse-drawn pseudo-antique carriage (Fig. 4.3).[71] Camille Desmoulins observed that 'no saint of the old calendar could boast of having made as brilliant an entrance into heaven as the new arrival'.[72] Revealingly, the way that

---

[68] R. Reichardt and H. Kohle, *Visualizing the French Revolution: Politics and the Pictorial Arts in Late Eighteenth-Century France* (London, 2008), pp. 13–15.
[69] I. Davidson, *Voltaire: A Life* (London, 2012), ch. 32; R. Pearson, *Voltaire Almighty. A Life in Pursuit of Freedom* (London, 2005), pp. 410–17.
[70] Jourdan, *Les monuments de la Révolution française*, p. 159.
[71] AN, F13 1136, file labelled 'translation of Voltaire to the Panthéon'. No documents in this file indicate that Quatremère assisted with the ceremony; the evidence instead shows that the carriage Schneider attributed to him was actually designed by Jacques Cellerier and created by Nicolas Lhuillier.
[72] C. Desmoulins, *Révolutions de France et de Brabant*, no. 85, July 1791, p. 291.

86   QUATREMÈRE DE QUINCY

radicals adopted Voltaire encouraged Marc-Étienne Quatremère to organize an unsuccessful campaign against his pantheonization.[73]

Voltaire's pantheonization raised expectations in some quarters for transforming the church of Sainte-Geneviève in ways that were at odds with Quatremère's vision. However, the debate about how to use the temple of the nation was not yet monopolized by radical voices. Moderate and conservative writers tried to reclaim the temple by demanding the pantheonization of figures such as Charles-Michel de l'Épée and even Henri IV.[74]

It was in the context of this contestation that, on 19 July 1791, the Directory of the Department handed Quatremère responsibility for the project, giving him the official title 'commissioner of the administration and general direction of works'. Influential figures such as Sieyès, Pastoret, and La Rochefoucauld-Liancourt supported his appointment despite his ignorance of building sites.[75] However, he was given this role above all because his vision was economical, he could work without a salary, he understood municipal politics, and he was an authority on architecture. The Directory also shared his desire to reorganize the project's administration whilst keeping the Crown's experts, instead of replacing them with civil engineers employed by the Paris municipality.[76] For all his criticism of the administration in the report, Quatremère ultimately retained key personnel: Rondelet and Soufflot le Romain (the architect's nephew) had together managed the site since Soufflot's death, and under Quatremère they remained inspectors of construction and ornamentation respectively.[77] Similarly, Bourbon remained surveyor and Poncet and Bouillette remained the main contractors for masonry and carpentry.[78]

Quatremère's appointment divided opinion. Some newspapers noted his credentials and praised his willingness to follow the Assembly's decree by creating a 'purely civic building'.[79] However, he also endured 'envious murmurs' and Soufflot le Romain criticized him for mischaracterizing the site's management and proposing administrative improvements and physical changes that had already been implemented or suggested.[80]

---

[73] M.-E. Quatremer [sic], *Pétition à l'Assemblée nationale, relative au transport de Voltaire* (Paris, 1791). Marc-Étienne gathered 163 signatures and presented this petition to the Constituent Assembly. The petition opposed Voltaire's transfer to 'this new temple where everything will be God except God himself'.

[74] *Révolutions de Paris*, no. 136, 11–18 Feb. 1792, pp. 309–13.

[75] Bibliothèque de l'Institut de France, MS 2555, file 4, no. 42. AN, 284 AP/9, dossier 5—Quatremère letter to Sieyes, 16 Jan. 1794. Quatremère thanked Sieyès: 'I never forget that it was under the auspices of Citizen Sieyès that I commenced work on the Panthéon.'

[76] Potofosky, *Constructing Paris*, p. 114.   [77] AN, F13 1138 (table of employees, 1791).

[78] Tuetey, ed., *Répertoire générale*, vol. 3, no. 2318, p. 220. Bourbon, Poncet, and Bouillette each received 3,600 livres per annum; administrative officers received between 1,200 and 4,000 livres.

[79] *Chronique de Paris*, no. 217, 5 Aug. 1791, pp. 875–6; *Moniteur universel*, no. 220, 8 Aug. 1791, p. 910.

[80] Quatremère, *Rapport* (1792).

We can draw several conclusions about Quatremère's vision. Most significantly, his iconographic choices anticipate his conservative politics as a representative in the Legislative Assembly. Heeding Winckelmann's advice that allegories should be clear and graceful, he avoided the 'reign of abstractions and the subtleties of metaphysics' and instead devised what he considered a timeless sculpture programme that mobilized familiar subjects, such as allegories of Renown and the *patrie* and the theme of the union between law and liberty. His omission of negative representations of aristocracy and monarchy, and positive allusions to revolutionary journées, was hardly an apolitical choice when these subjects were common elsewhere.[81] Quatremère's iconography therefore soon appeared outdated once the *bonnet rouge*, pike, Hercules (as an allegory of the people), and symbols of equality dominated the semiotic landscape.[82]

However, Quatremère's vision also reveals his pragmatism as much as his commitment to a political ideal or an architectural theory. If elements of his vision reflected his experience of Coustou's studio, Italian voyages and thoughts about ancient architecture, the Campo Santo and Westminster abbey, for the greater part he responded to the Constituent Assembly's decree and worked within budgetary and structural constraints.[83] Given the contexts in which he devised his vision for transforming the church, it is anachronistic to make comparisons with the reuse in 1793 of Notre-Dame cathedral as a Temple of Reason. Quatremère's vision in 1791 also underlines the extent to which he was no dogmatic theorist. In theory, his 'art of characterizing' required approaching a monument as an indivisible thought, but, on this occasion, he argued that minor alterations could recharacterize a Catholic church as a temple of the nation. The basic division in his sculpture programme (i.e. allegorical sculptures for fixed decorations and figurative sculptures for moveable decorations) was similarly practical, suggesting that he anticipated a future in which some individuals might be commemorated one moment and rejected the next.[84]

Finally, we can conclude that Quatremère's vision reveals the extent to which he wanted to preserve Soufflot's masterpiece. He later reflected that Soufflot's design was indulgent, even as a church, but that this architect nevertheless created 'the greatest monument of the eighteenth century'.[85] Quatremère therefore followed the same implicit rules for reusing masterpieces that he had recommended

---

[81] Leith, *Space and Revolution*, p. 49; B. Bergdoll, *European Architecture, 1750–1890* (Oxford, 2000), p. 116.

[82] Jourdan, *Les monuments de la Révolution française*, pp. 236, 243–4; R. Wrigley, 'Transformations of a Revolutionary Emblem', *French History*, vol. 11, no. 2 (1997), p. 152.

[83] Deming, 'Le Panthéon révolutionnaire', pp. 97–150. For a different interpretation that credits Quatremère with more originality and agency, see J. Clarke, *Commemorating the Dead in Revolutionary France: Revolution and Remembrance 1789–1799* (Cambridge, 2009), p. 132.

[84] Quatremère, *Rapport* (1793), p. 49.

[85] Quatremère, *Histoire de la vie et des ouvrages des plus célèbres architectes*, vol. 2, p. 341.

88 QUATREMÈRE DE QUINCY

in 1787 for remaking the Fountain of the Innocents. In both instances, he favoured repurposing monuments to ensure their survival and usefulness. He reasoned that any changes must respect the essence of the original design, or restore what the original creator had intended, but he warned that architects came unstuck if they tried to innovate when finishing old buildings. In 1791, he therefore limited his vision to changes that made the edifice appropriate for its new purpose besides changes that purified the building according to taste and merit. He feared that more drastic intervention would allow 'the dangerous... mania for novelty' to introduce a new style.[86]

---

[86] Quatremère, *Rapport* (1793), pp. 61–5.

5
Devoted to the King, 1791–2

Mallet du Pan considered Quatremère 'wholly and gratuitously devoted to the king' as a national representative in the Legislative Assembly.[1] Yet historians have either dismissed his role as 'insignificant', 'diffuse and colourless', or overlooked it entirely because he wrote no surviving personal letters or memoirs documenting this period in his life.[2] This chapter will therefore paint a fuller portrait of him as a representative by scrutinizing his reports and writings, relevant legislative records and newspapers, and references to him and his circle in memoirs, and by identifying the political nature of his contributions to festivals, theatre reform, artistic patronage, national heritage, and museum policy. Modern scholarship on the Legislative Assembly provides the background for reinterpreting this evidence.[3]

Quatremère entered the Manège—the former riding school where the Assembly convened—on 2 October 1791 and swore allegiance to the Constitution several days later.[4] He resembled the other representatives in some respects: all 745 were sufficiently wealthy to hold office and most were in their thirties and had served in local politics and administration.[5] But he nevertheless stood out amongst the multitude of provincial lawyers because of his 'prodigiously loud voice', familiarity with Paris, and knowledge of the arts.[6]

Quatremère sat in the Assembly amongst the right-wing caucus affiliated with the Feuillant club; he voted with it and was one of its principal spokesmen.[7]

---

[1] Mallet du Pan, *Mémoires*, vol. 2, p. 299. The citation comes from Mallet du Pan's letter to the Comte de Sainte-Aldegonde, 19 April 1797: 'Quatremère de Quincy m'est particulièrement connu: c'est un homme plein de courage, de verve, d'inflexibilité et de talent. Il fut le plus ardent dans l'Assemblée législative à combattre la Gironde et la république; il était tout au roi et gratis.' I have followed the translation in *Memoirs and Correspondence of Mallet du Pan, Illustrative of the History of the French Revolution*, ed. A. Sayous, vol. 2 (London, 1852), p. 309.

[2] F.-A. Aulard, *Les orateurs de la Législative et de la Convention*, vol. 1 (Paris, 1885), pp. 83, 136–7.

[3] C. Mitchell, 'Political Divisions within the Legislative Assembly of 1791', *French Historical Studies*, vol. 13, no. 3 (1984), pp. 356–89; idem, *The French Legislative Assembly* (Leiden, 1988); T. Tackett, 'Les députés de l'Assemblée législative, 1791–1792', in C. Le Bozec and É. Wauters, eds, *Pour la Révolution française: recueil d'études en hommage à Claude Mazauric* (Rouen, 1998), pp. 139–44; E. Lemay, 'Les législateurs de la France révolutionnaire (1791–1792)', *Annales historiques de la Révolution française*, vol. 347, no. 1 (2007), pp. 3–28; idem, ed., *Dictionnaire des législateurs*.

[4] *AP*, vol. 34, p. 49.

[5] M. Edelstein, *The French Revolution and the Birth of Electoral Democracy* (Ashgate, 2014), p. 139.

[6] *Journal de Paris*, no. 285, 12 Oct. 1791, p. 1160; Mitchell, *The French Legislative Assembly*, p. 105; Tackett, *The Coming of the Terror in the French Revolution* (Cambridge, MA, 2005), pp. 148–9.

[7] M. Vovelle, *The Fall of the French Monarchy 1787–1792*, trans. S. Burke (Cambridge, 1984), p. 211; Mitchell, *The French Legislative Assembly*, pp. 377–8, 382–6. This caucus numbered between 150 and 264 representatives, depending on when and how one counts.

Quatremère de Quincy: Art and Politics during the French Revolution. David Gilks, Oxford University Press.
© David Gilks 2024. DOI: 10.1093/oso/9780198745563.003.0006

However, this caucus was no party with formally agreed policies, so understanding his politics requires examining his ideals, allegiances, and ties to other royalists.[8]

Quatremère admired Louis XVI as a reformer and an enlightened patron of the arts and wanted a stronger, more centralized Bourbon monarchy, unshackled by the 'ancient constitution' and the parlements.[9] However, his vision for reformed absolutism placed him at odds with leading figures in the Feuillant club that he joined sometime between mid-July and early October 1791. Within the club, he rejected most Monarchiens' preference for English-style monarchy, opposed Barnave's enthusiasm for destroying the Old Regime, and made no effort to help restore Lafayette's popularity after the Champ de Mars massacre.[10] Inside the Assembly, he found that many Feuillant deputies, such as Mathieu Dumas, were moderate 'constitutionalists' and a few, such as Louis-Stanislas Girardin, wanted the duc d'Orléans to be king.[11] His main ally, Vincent-Marie Viénot-Vaublanc, never joined the club and was to the right of most Feuillants in the Assembly. Vaublanc was a nobleman-cultivator, minor military officer turned defender of colonial slavery, and de facto leader of what he called the 'royalist-constitutional party'. Vaublanc claimed that Quatremère 'supported the principles that I had developed', namely, to defend Louis XVI and his ministry and to oppose the Jacobins, the 'anarchy of factions', and legislation against émigrés and refractory priests.[12] Radical journalists often named Vaublanc and Quatremère in the same sentence. For instance, Louis-Marie Prudhomme reflected that they were the only royalist legislators with the 'courage to fulfil their mandates'.[13] Both men were ultra-royalist politicians after 1815, but in 1791–2 they moderated their private

---

[8] I take my cue from Munro Price's sage advice that, in the absence of any firm party organization, to understand high politics one must examine the careers of individual monarchists; M. Price, 'Le Centre perdu: Malouet et les 'monarchiens' dans la Révolution française. By Robert Griffiths', *Historical Journal*, vol. 32, no. 2 (1989), p. 504.

[9] Quatremère, *Opinion sur les dénonciations faites contre M. Duport* (Paris, 1792); idem, *Considerations sur les arts*, pp. 86–7; idem, Letter to Mallet du Pan, 18 Aug. 1799, in Mallet du Pan, *Mémoires*, vol. 2, pp. 414–5; M. de Bombelles, *Journal*, ed. J. Charon-Bordas vol. 7 (Geneva, 2002), p. 180.

[10] J.-P. Bois, *Lafayette* (Paris, 2015), p. 185.

[11] A. Challamel, *Les clubs contre-révolutionnaires: cercles, comités, sociétés, salons, réunions, cafés, restaurants et librairies* (Paris, 1895), p. 316, shows that Quatremère joined the Feuillant club by October at the latest. Mitchell, *The French Legislative Assembly*, pp. 377–8, suggests that there were around 100 Feuillant national representatives in October 1791 and 264 by December. Scholarship on Feuillant politics includes: G. Michon, *Adrien Duport et le parti Feuillant* (Paris, 1924); R. Griffiths, *Le centre perdu. Malouet et les 'monarchiens' dans la Révolution française* (Grenoble, 1988); J. Egret, *La révolution des notables: Mounier et les Monarchiens* (Paris, 1950); F. Dendena, *I nostri maledetti scranni!: il movimento fogliante tra la fuga di Varennes e la caduta della monarchia (1791–1792)* (Milan, 2013); idem, 'L'expérience révolutionnaire dans les mémoires des leaders feuillants', in O. Ferret and A.-M. Mercier-Faivre, eds, *Biographie & politique* (Lyon, 2014), pp. 183–98; idem, 'La haine des honnêtes gens. Stratégies éditoriales de la presse feuillante et construction des identités collectives', *Annales historiques de la Révolution française*, vol. 384, no. 2 (2016), pp. 83–108; J. Hardman, *Barnave: the Revolutionary who Lost his Head for Marie Antoinette* (New Haven, 2023).

[12] Aulard, *Les orateurs*, pp. 97–105; Challamel, *Les clubs contre-révolutionnaires*, p. 320; V.-M. Viénot Vaublanc, *Mémoires sur la révolution de France et recherches sur les causes qui ont amené la Révolution de 1789 et celles qui l'ont suivie* (Paris, 1833), vol. 1, pp. 349, 376, 426, 483; vol. 2: pp. 44, 47, 65.

[13] L.-M. Prudhomme, *Histoire générale et impartiale des erreurs, des fautes et des crimes commis pendant la Révolution française*, vol. 4 (Paris, 1797), p. 113.

convictions to avoid harming the king.[14] Quatremère understood the need to mend relations between 'constitutionalists' at home and intransigent counter-revolutionaries abroad and therefore followed Feuillant friends who publicly supported the Constitution, such as Duport-Dutertre, the justice minister, and Pastoret, the first president of the Legislative Assembly.

Vaublanc claimed in his memoirs that impersonal forces doomed the Legislative Assembly to failure. Certainly, the Assembly faced challenges because representatives were divided over the Constitution, especially the powers that it gave the monarch to suspend legislation, choose ministers, and conduct foreign policy. The representatives also inherited intractable dilemmas from the Constituent Assembly, such as how to end 'feudalism', reorganize education, supervise worship, and instigate popular sovereignty and freedom of opinion.[15] However, Vaublanc's retrospective judgement was clouded by his eagerness to excuse his heroic failure and demonstrate his virtuous consistency.[16] His pessimistic account obscures the prevailing optimism during the last months of 1791 when the king and queen, conservative deputies, Feuillant club, and 'triumvirate' of Lameth, Barave, and Duport formed a relatively unified royalist alliance that helped maintain relations between the executive and legislative.[17] During this period, by publicly supporting the Constitution and demanding that émigrés return, Louis XVI persuaded uncommitted centrist representatives to cooperate with the executive. Convinced that constitutional monarchy had triumphed and the Constitution would bring 'peace' and 'happiness', the right-wing press adopted a conciliatory tone designed to assure public opinion that the Revolution was over.[18]

During the first months of the Legislative Assembly, Quatremère criticized Brissotinist attempts to mobilize Parisians and destabilize the government. He first addressed the subject of ecclesiastics who refused to swear the oath of allegiance to the Constitution. Rumours that these refractory priests conspired against the Revolution prompted some local officials and Jacobin representatives to demand punishments such as withholding pay or banishment. Quatremère condemned such 'intolerant' demands, criticized representatives who tried to halt

---

[14] H. Jouin, *David d'Angers: sa vie, son œuvre, ses écrits et ses contemporains*, vol. 1 (Paris, 1878), p. 164; C. Lacretelle, *Histoire de la révolution française*, vol. 3 (Paris, 1825), pp. 4–5.

[15] M. Fitzsimmons, 'Sovereignty and Constitutional Power', in D. Andress, ed., *The Oxford Handbook of the French Revolution* (Oxford, 2015); 'The Constitution of 1791', in Stewart, ed., *A Documentary Survey*, pp. 240–5, 248–9, 253.

[16] V.-M. Viénot Vaublanc, *Mémoires de M. le comte de Vaublanc* (Paris, 1857), p. 181. Vaublanc conformed to the pattern of several Feuillant memoirists who published accounts in the 1820s that Dendena analyses in 'L'expérience révolutionnaire dans les mémoires des leaders feuillants'.

[17] J. Hardman, *Marie-Antoinette: The Making of a French Queen* (New Haven, 2021), pp. 245–6.

[18] Dendena, 'La haine des honnêtes gens. Stratégies éditoriales de la presse feuillante et construction des identités collectives', pp. 86–7.

debates about the mistreatment of non-jurors, and reminded the Assembly that the Constitution guaranteed clerical salaries and religious freedom.[19]

The second subject that Quatremère addressed was the royal veto. He urged his fellow representatives to reject a petition that attacked Louis XVI for vetoing legislation against refractory priests. He argued that radical Parisian journalists and clubs had written this petition and passed it around the provinces to create the illusion that it represented the 'national will'. Yet some representatives, he complained, supported this seditious petition with 'shameful mentions and...incendiary addresses' that threatened the Constitution and royal veto.[20] Radical deputies such as Delacroix and Brissot responded by calling him a spokesperson for the Feuillant club who insulted honest petitioners.[21]

The third subject concerned how the Assembly convened. In October, he immediately asked to verify the election results because he hoped to discredit Jacobin representatives by finding irregularities. Instead of delegating this task to a committee, he insisted that deputies from every department check through the documentation.[22] Over the next months, he then tried to reduce public interference by changing the Assembly's regulations and modifying the Manège's layout. Feuillant deputies feared that Parisians, who had already blighted the Constituent Assembly and electoral assemblies, would interrupt proceedings because the Legislative Assembly had fewer representatives than its predecessor and therefore more seats for spectators. In this context, technical and aesthetic issues about the room became politically contentious.[23] Technical and aesthetic issues about the room became politically contentious in this context. Whereas Jacobins such as Georges Couthon demanded more seats in the tribunes, Quatremère wanted to create a calm environment by reducing space for spectators and passing a code of conduct that stipulated 'respect for the law', 'decent dress', and discipline. He urged deputies to learn from the respectful nature of England's House of Commons and set an example of how to behave by upholding the law, defending the Constitution, and shunning 'burlesque pantomimes of patriotism'.[24] He later proposed other changes to create a more pensive atmosphere. Representatives should devote Sundays to reading rather than meetings, he suggested, and they should meet in a more suitable environment because there were 'more connections than one might think between the space occupied by an assembly and the sprit animating its

---

[19] J. Byrnes, *Priests of the French Revolution: Saints and Renegades in a New Political Era* (University Park, PA, 2014), pp. 49–59; G. Lallement, ed., *Choix de rapports, opinions et discours prononcés à la tribune nationale depuis 1789 jusqu'à ce jour*, vol. 8 (Paris, 1822), p. 76; *AP*, vol. 34, p. 423; *AP*, vol. 35, pp. 108–12; *Moniteur universel*, no. 322, 18 Nov. 1791, p. 1343.

[20] *AP*, vol. 36, p. 24.

[21] P.-J.-B. Buchez and P.-C. Roux, eds, *Histoire parlementaire de la révolution française*, vol. 3 (Paris, 1834), pp. 193–4.

[22] *AP*, vol. 34, pp. 30–1.

[23] Edelstein, *The French Revolution*, p. 138; Mitchell, *The French Legislative Assembly*, pp. 106–8.

[24] *AP*, vol. 38, p. 138.

members'.[25] This meant making the Salle du Manège smaller because this former riding school, twenty metres wide and sixty meters long, resembled 'an arena of gladiators' or 'a large street' in which deputies could neither see nor hear most of their peers. A smaller hall naturally meant fewer public seats.[26] Although Quatremère failed to change the protocols or the dimensions of Salle du Manège, his efforts to minimize public participation led to him being asked to gather complaints about the public's behaviour, to liaise with the architect of the Manège, and to report on designs for a new assembly hall and statue of Rousseau.[27]

Quatremère worked fastidiously in the last quarter of 1791 for the Legislative Assembly's secretariat and committees for regulations, printing and the architecture of the Manège, but over the winter of 1791–2 he devoted most time to the Committee of Public Instruction.[28] This important Committee was responsible for devising the free and universal 'system of public instruction' promised by the Constitution besides assessing state support for colleges, specialist institutions, and provincial academies and for improving education in the widest sense by protecting the arts and sciences.[29] The sheer range of its responsibilities obliged the Committee to create several sub-committees: one worked on the general system of instruction whilst others oversaw existing establishments, gathered correspondence about libraries and monuments, replied to petitions, and reported on memoranda.

Although the Feuillant representatives dominated proceedings in the Assembly in autumn 1791, they were a minority on the twenty-four-strong Committee of Public Instruction.[30] Quatremère was therefore unable to prevent Condorcet, bête noire of royalists, becoming president and proposing a democratic education plan at odds with his opinion that there were 'barely three points in France

---

[25] *AP*, vol. 39, p. 630.

[26] *AP*, vol. 39, pp. 168–9. *Journal de Paris*, no. 285, 12 Oct. 1791, pp. 1159–60, summarized Quatremère's intervention, but the author added that he preferred a circular or an elliptical room. Later accounts, such as A. Brette, *Histoire des édifices où ont siégé les assemblées parlementaires de la Révolution française et de la première République*, vol. 1 (Paris, 1902), pp. 205–6 and P. Brassart, *Paroles de la Révolution. Les assemblées parlementaires, 1789–1794* (Paris, 1988), misattributed this last idea to Quatremère, who favoured modest adaptations over reconstructions; see, for example, *AP*, vol. 38, p. 110. On the Manège, see J.-P. Heurtin, *L'espace public parlementaire: essai sur les raisons du législateur* (Rennes, 1999), p. 72; Mitchell, *The French Legislative Assembly*, pp. 9–12.

[27] Tuetey, ed., *Répertoire général*, p. 6; Mitchell, *The French Legislative Assembly*, p. 108; *PVCIP*, pp. 48, 119, 279.

[28] Lemay, ed., *Dictionnaire des Législateurs*, vol. 2, p. 619; *AP*, vol. 39, p. 394.

[29] 'The Constitution of 1791', p. 232. On the importance attached to education, see esp. D. Julia, 'Instruction publique/éducation nationale', in A. Soboul, ed., *Dictionnaire historique de la Révolution française* (Paris, 1989), pp. 575–81; B. Backzo, ed., 'Instruction publique', in F. Furet and M. Ozouf, eds, *Dictionnaire critique de la Révolution française*, vol. 3 (Paris, 1992), pp. 275–97; M. Ozouf, *L'École de la France: essais sur la Révolution, l'utopie et l'enseignement* (Paris, 1984); and the special issue 'Pédagogies, utopies et révolutions (1789–1848)', for *La Révolution française: Cahiers de l'Institut d'histoire de la Révolution française*, no. 4 (2013).

[30] *PVCIP*, pp. xvii–xviii; R. Palmer, *The Improvement of Humanity: Education and the French Revolution* (Princeton, 1985), p. 104.

94   QUATREMÈRE DE QUINCY

where...*lycées* could have any success'.[31] He initially held some sway over the arts and cultural heritage because the committee included few distinguished men of letters, but even in these domains he was ultimately frustrated.

Quatremère's first task was to settle a dispute over the Salon jury. Legislation authored by Alexandre Beauharnais in the Constituent Assembly allocated 100 000 livres to encourage painting, sculpture, and engraving by awarding artists who displayed work in the biennial Salon. The decree earmarked 70 000 livres for history painters and sculptors and 30 000 livres for engravers and painters of genre and architectural scenes, including 10 000 livres for representations of French ports. Beauharnais envisaged a jury consisting of all one hundred and fifty or so members of the Royal Academy of Painting and Sculpture, four jurors from other Royal Academies plus twenty non-academic artists chosen by exhibitors.[32] However, many artists feared that a jury dominated by the Academy would favour academicians over outsiders.[33] A deputation of non-academic artists therefore asked the new Legislative Assembly to reform the jury (by excluding non-exhibiting members of the Academy and ensuring that half the jurors came from outside the Academy) and allow a general assembly of exhibiting artists to scrutinize its decisions.[34]

Quatremère proposed compromises in October 1791 to defuse criticism whilst preserving the Academy's dominance of the jury and protecting funding for the highest genres. He feigned support for the deputation and argued for a new jury, consisting of twenty judges chosen by academicians and a further twenty chosen by exhibitors from outside the Academy. He thought that this jury would alter the distribution of awards for lesser genres whilst preserving funding for the highest genres.[35] Quatremère failed to convince the Assembly, but the newly formed Committee of Public Instruction asked him to draft revised legislation to settle the dispute.[36] In early November, he repeated his idea for a reformed jury, ignoring committee members who suggested drastic measures, but over the next week the defiant refusal of conservative academicians to participate in any jury selection undermined his attempted compromise. His report argued that for this Salon alone there should be an equal number of judges from inside and outside the Academy, meaning that non-academicians must not select academicians and vice versa—a measure that would, in fact, have prevented non-academicians from choosing radical academicians. He followed the report with a vague

---

[31] Lemay, ed., *Dictionnaire des Législateurs*, vol. 1, p. x; *PVCIP*, p. 119. W. Murray, *The Right-Wing Press in the French Revolution, 1789–92* (Woodbridge, 1986), pp. 215–6, and Vaublanc, *Mémoires sur la révolution*, vol. 1, p. 70, describe royalist hatred of Condorcet.

[32] *AP*, vol. 31, p. 58.   [33] *AP*, vol. 34, pp. 265, 281–2; Tuetey, ed., *Répertoire général*, pp. 269–70.

[34] *AP*, vol. 34, pp. 281–2.

[35] Ibid., pp. 282–3. Quatremère thus abandoned the views on juries that he expressed earlier that year; *Considérations sur les arts*, pp. 140–57, and *Seconde suite*, p. 86.

[36] *AP*, vol. 34, pp. 283–4.

decree proposal designed to hand decisions to the Directory of the Department.[37] To appear reform-minded, Quatremère perhaps colluded with Jean-Baptiste Huet de Froberville by asking his ally to publicly complain that his proposal was 'humiliating for the Academy'.[38] However, Quatremère received little support in the Assembly because the right feared harming the Academy and the left mistrusted his intentions given how the quarrel had escalated.[39]

After the Assembly postponed debating Quatremère's proposal, the Committee of Public Instruction handed Charles-Gilbert Romme the responsibility for reforming the jury. In December, Romme convinced his fellow legislators with his decree proposal that an assembly of exhibitors should elect any twenty academicians and twenty non-academicians from amongst the artists who exhibited in the Salon.[40] Although Quatremère played a marginal role in Romme's decree, he influenced the new jury: appointed by the Directory of the Department as one of four non-voting commissioners, in spring 1792 he ensured that prizes went to his friends and sculptors employed at the Panthéon.[41]

Despite Quatremère's failure to reform the jury, until spring 1792 he remained the Committee of Public Instruction's unofficial spokesperson for the arts. For instance, he helped organize its contribution to documenting and preserving books, manuscripts, scientific artefacts, artworks, and historic monuments. The Committee's conservation work came at a formative moment in the history of safeguarding national heritage—one borne out of the rise of a more expansive conception of patrimony and the fear, especially after the nationalization of Church property, that artefacts and monuments of historic, scientific, or artistic interest would be sold abroad, neglected, or destroyed.[42]

---

[37] *AP*, vol. 35, pp. 60–1; Quatremère, *Rapport et projet de décret présentes à l'Assemble Nationale, Par M. Quatremère, au nom du Comite d'Instruction publique, le 14 novembre 1791, Sur les réclamations des artistes qui ont exposé au Salon du Louvre* [Paris, 1791], pp. 1–9.

[38] *AP*, vol. 35, pp. 61–2. Huet was Permanent Secretary of the Orléans Royal society of Physics, Natural History and the Arts; his views on the academies were consistent with Quatremère and Pastoret's; see, Tuetey, *Répertoire général*, vol. 6, p. 277; *AP*, vol. 35, p. 555; J.-B. Huet, *Opinion ... sur le rapport du Comité d'instruction publique, & sur la pétition des artistes concernant la nomination des juges pour les prix d'encouragement accordés aux arts, par l'Assemblée-nationale-constituante* (Paris, 1792).

[39] *PVCIP*, pp. 2, 11–12, 15–16; *AP*, vol. 34, p. 641; *AP*, vol. 35, p. 355; Tuetey, *Répertoire général*, vol. 6, pp. 268–9, 272–3; *Journal de Paris*, no. 310, 6 Nov. 1791, p. 1259.

[40] *AP*, vol. 35, pp. 87, 391, 451–2, 554–6; *PVCIP*, p. 40; Tuetey, *Répertoire général*, vol. 6, p. 275. Romme initially proposed retaining four judges from other academies, but later agreed to replace them with non-voting commissioners appointed by the Directory of the Department. A. Galante Garrone, *Gilbert Romme. Histoire d'un revolutionaire, 1750–1795* (Paris, 1975) makes the case for Romme's originality as a thinker.

[41] M. Furcy-Raynaud, ed., *Procès-verbaux des assemblées du jury: élu par les artistes exposants au salon de 1791 pour la distribution des prix d'encouragement* (Paris, 1906), pp. 1, 24, 26, 30, 55, 64, 72, 75.

[42] D. Poulot, *Surveiller et s'instruire: la Révolution française et l'intelligence de l'héritage historique* (Oxford, 1996), part 1; Pommier, *L'art de la liberté*, chs 1–3.

Other organizations had already started to address this last concern. In 1789–90, the Committees of Ecclesiastical Administration and Alienation of National Lands helped classify and restore artefacts and monuments and asked departmental administrators to gather library catalogues, create repositories in cities, and preserve 'monuments, churches and houses that form part of the national domain'. In the same spirit, the Commission of Monuments (established in November 1790) proposed reusing churches in Paris as local repositories and creating 'superb museums' in Nantes, Lyons, and Bordeaux 'from the spoils of our suppressed churches and monasteries'.[43]

Quatremère clearly understood these heritage concerns when he joined the Committee of Public Instruction because he had previously proposed creating both a museum that centralized Gallo-Roman antiquities and a 'temple of the arts' in the Louvre.[44] In late 1791, he joined the sub-committee tasked with gathering information on libraries and monuments and assumed responsibility for liaising with scholars and administrators in the Gard, Seine-Inférieure, and Paris.[45] In this capacity, he urged the Commission of Monuments to secure 120 000 volumes from Saint-Germain-des-Prés, the Collège Mazarin, and Sorbonne and asked the Assembly to acquire private collections to prevent their sale abroad.[46] For example, he persuaded representatives to accept Jacques Charles's offer of three hundred machines and scientific instruments, for which the collector merely wanted in return a suitable home for these objects because their existing showroom at the Place des Victoires no longer sufficed. He warned that the Assembly must act quickly because the king of Spain had already tried to buy 'this precious and rare repository'.[47]

Quatremère admired enlightened private collectors such as Charles, but he loathed what he called the 'mania' for collecting and therefore attacked Alexandre Lenoir's opportunistic hoarding.[48] He encountered Lenoir, a painter turned art administrator, in 1792 when the Commission of Monuments asked the Committee of Public Instruction to investigate the Petits-Augustins repository.

---

[43] Y. Cantarel-Besson, ed., *La naissance du Musée du Louvre: la politique muséologique sous la Révolution d'après les archives des musées nationaux* (Paris, 1991), vol. 1, p. xx; Tuetey, *Répertoire général*, p. 127; L. Tuetey, ed., *Procès-verbaux de la Commission des Monuments (1790–1794)*, vol. 1 (Paris, 1902), pp. 16–17, 38, 265–7; F.-M. Puthod de la Maisonrouge, *Les monuments ou le pèlerinage historique* (Paris, 1790), Prospectus, pp. 2–3.

[44] Quatremère, *EMA*, vol. 1, p. 557; idem, *Considérations sur les arts*, p. 129; idem, *Seconde Suite*, pp. 88–9, 91–2.

[45] *PVCIP*, pp. 19, 22.

[46] *PVCIP*, pp. 83–4; Tuetey, ed., *Répertoire général*, p. 124; S. Belayé, 'Les enrichissements de la Bibliothèque nationale', in A. Fierro, ed., *Patrimoine parisien 1789–1799: destructions, créations, mutations* (Paris, 1989), pp. 65–7.

[47] *Journal des débats*, vol. 28, 8 Jan. 1792, pp. 187–8; T. Hankins and R. Silverman, *Instruments and the Imagination* (Princeton, 1999), pp. 61–3; B. Belhoste, *Paris Savant: Capital of Science in the Age of the Enlightenment*, trans. S. Emanuel (Oxford, 2018), pp. 134–5; *Collection générale des décrets rendus par l'Assemblée Nationale*, vol. 25, pp. 77–9.

[48] Quatremère's first printed attack on Lenoir was an anonymous piece several years later in *Journal littéraire*, no. 11, 16 Oct. 1796, pp. 361–7.

As the repository's guardian Lenoir was responsible simply for storing statues from Parisian religious establishments, but his ambition to create a permanent collection led him to accumulate superabundant paintings and other objects. Quatremère recommended selling all artefacts that would never be suitable to send to the national museum in the Louvre, but Lenoir continued his project and published a catalogue the following year for the 256 artefacts exhibited in the repository.[49]

Quatremère also tried using his position as a member of the Committee of Public Instruction to advance the status of savants and artists. For instance, in February 1792 he argued that the Assembly should demonstrate its respect for scholars by asking national representatives to attend the funeral of Athanase Auger, the distinguished Hellenist, translator, and rhetorician who provided the Committee with 'excellent writings on education'.[50] He tried on another occasion to protect living artists by exempting them from émigré laws intended to sequester property from individuals living abroad. He argued that artists, including six hundred or so French artists in Italy alone, must be free to travel, make discoveries, and bestow glory upon the nation. Only exempting artists with formal training would discriminate against talented artists such as Louis-François Cassas: this distinguished topographical draughtsman was in Rome creating prints using sketches made during his Ottoman travels, but since he had trained as an engineer rather than artist then the proposed law would brand him an émigré.[51] (Quatremère prudently ignored that Cassas had worked for Choiseul-Gouffier, the reactionary ambassador to Constantinople whom the Legislative Assembly was trying to remove.) Quatremère convinced most representatives, but Jean-Pascal Rouyer recognized that émigrés could declare themselves artists to exploit such an exemption.[52]

Quatremère also served the arts by imploring the Assembly to honour cultural institutions and contracts that predated the Revolution. For instance, he argued that the state should pay masters from the Royal School of Singing because they

---

[49] *PVCIP*, p. 331; Tuetey, ed., *Procès-verbaux de la Commission des Monuments (1790–1794)*, vol. 1, pp. xxx–xviii 49, 55–60, 98, 100; A. Lenoir, *Notice succincte des objets de sculpture et architecture: réunis au dépôt provisoire national* (Paris, 1793). The fullest account of Lenoir and his Museum is G. Bresc-Bautier et al., *Un musée révolutionnaire. Le musée des monuments français d'Alexandre Lenoir* (Paris, 2016).

[50] *AP*, vol. 38, p. 263. Quatremère alluded to Auger's *Projet d'éducation générale pour le royaume* (Paris, 1789).

[51] *AP*, vol. 39, pp. 479–81. Cassas's work appeared several years later in his *Voyage pittoresque de la Syrie, Phenicie, Palestine et de la Basse-Egypte* (Paris, 1799). Scholarship on Cassas and his patron includes L. Pingaud, *Choiseul-Gouffier: la France en Orient sous Louis XVI*, vol. 2, esp. pp. 248–51; and E. Fraser, *Mediterranean Encounters Artists between Europe and the Ottoman Empire, 1774–1839* (University Park, PA, 2017), ch. 2.

[52] *AP*, vol. 39, p. 481. Mitchell, *The Legislative Assembly*, pp. 48–9, describes the émigré controversy.

served the national interest and encouraged emulation.[53] In the same vein, he insisted that the state should honour its contract with Auguste-Louis de Rossel de Cercy for paintings depicting maritime battles from the American War of Independence and even engrave them at its expense. These paintings by a talented artist and naval officer represented the nation's first battles 'under the banner of liberty', he argued, even if they were commissioned under 'despotism'.[54] Although he convinced some representatives with an interest in the navy and the arts, such as Armand de Kersaint and Louis-Claude Chéron de La Bruyère, tense relations between the navy and Assembly meant that few representatives wanted to support an aristocratic former naval officer.[55]

For all Quatremère's efforts concerning the fine arts and scholarship, his most prominent interventions as a member of the Committee of Public Instruction were on behalf of dramatists. During the first months of 1792, he made a spirited case for extending dramatists' right to profit from their own writings when most legislators instead wanted these writings to serve the public good through state ownership.[56]

His intervention should be understood in the context of a long-running dispute between authors, theatres, and publishers. The Crown used censorship, patronage, and privileges to control authors, but during the second half of the eighteenth century authors wanted to benefit from the rise of a reading public and therefore claimed that they owned their writings.[57] The Crown enabled some authors to exploit their writings commercially and reclaim their manuscripts from publishers after ten years, but authors continued to complain that publishers exploited their property.[58] Dramatists were especially aggrieved because they suffered at the hands of theatres as well as publishers; they complained that privileged Parisian theatres acquired their plays and treated them as their exclusive property whilst

---

[53] *AP*, vol. 44, pp. 11–12; *PVCIP*, pp. 68, 106–7, 128. Quatremère ignored the fact that Louis XVI had intended the School to improve singing in the Royal Chapel by training students 'in the taste of the conservatories of Italy; AN: O1 618, piece 43, Breteuil to Calonne.

[54] *PVCIP*, pp. 63, 172–6; *AP*, vol. 42, pp. 404–5.

[55] *AP*, vol. 43, pp. 32–3, 526–7; W. Cormack, *Revolution and Political Conflict in the French Navy 1789–1794* (Cambridge, 2004), pp. 109–42; A.-L. de Rossel de Cercy, *Mémoire pour M. de Rossel* (Paris, 1792), p. 13.

[56] Scholarship on intellectual property debates during the Revolution includes Anon., 'Fragments d'histoire de la protection littéraire: la lutte entre les auteurs dramatiques et les directeurs de théâtre sous l'Assemblée législative française (1791–1792)', *Le droit d'auteur: organe officiel du Bureau de l'Union internationale pour la protection des œuvres littéraires et artistiques*, no. 10 (15 Oct. 1890), pp. 105–10; and C. Hesse, 'Enlightenment Epistemology and the Laws of Authorship in Revolutionary France, 1777–1793', *Representations*, vol. 30 (1990), pp. 109–37; K. Scott, 'Art and Industry: Intellectual Property and the French Revolution', in idem, *Becoming Property: Art, Theory and Law in Early Modern France* (New Haven, 2019), ch. 5; R. Geoffroy-Schwinden, *From Servant to Savant Musical Privilege, Property, and the French Revolution* (Oxford, 2022).

[57] T. Blanning, *The Pursuit of Glory: Europe, 1648–1815* (London, 2008), p. 523; G. Turnovsky, *The Literary Market: Authorship and Modernity in the Old Regime* (University Park, PA, 2010), p. 16.

[58] J. Ginsberg, 'A Tale of Two Copyrights: Literary Property in Revolutionary France and America', *Tulane Law Review*, vol. 64, no. 5 (1990), p. 996.

new provincial theatres staged plays without permission or after paying a derisory sum upfront.[59]

The Revolution complicated the dispute because the idea of individual property rights clashed with public-good arguments and because in practice the abolition of earlier patents suited printers at the expense of writers.[60] In these circumstances, dramatists such as Beaumarchais, Nicolas Dalayrac, and Nicolas-Étienne Framery petitioned the Constituent Assembly in 1790 to demand legal recognition that their writings were their property, and an end to the monopoly enjoyed by the Comédie-Française.[61] Isaac Le Chapelier responded on behalf of the Assembly, authoring legislation in early 1791 that was intended to placate dramatists. Le Chapelier argued that liberalizing the theatres by allowing anyone to establish a theatre and stage plays would benefit dramatists by increasing the number of theatres and therefore demand for plays, but he rejected the idea that dramatists should own their work indefinitely. Dramatists should, he suggested, 'draw an honourable salary from their glorious work' for the duration of their lives and their families should then receive posthumous royalties for five years, but the state should thereafter resume ownership of their work.[62] However, Le Chapelier's law satisfied no one. Theatre directors benefited from the state's inability to enforce the law, which they nevertheless asked the new Legislative Assembly to overturn. They argued that it prevented theatres from recuperating sunk costs and encouraged dramatists to form an illegal corporation that sold the same work to printers and theatres.[63]

The Committee of Public Instruction asked Quatremère to gather memoranda from directors, composers, and playwrights and report on a new decree. Quatremère favoured individual author copyright, but he was obliged to revise his draft decree because Condorcet favoured public ownership. In the Committee's discussions he therefore conceded a transition period during which theatres could continue performing their existing plays for five years since the first staging.[64]

In his report, Quatremère nevertheless argued boldly for dramatists' rights, reiterated that theatres must obtain permission to stage plays, and proposed a transition period of just one year.[65] Responding to the public-ownership argument, he distinguished between the 'metaphysical' quality of writing, which was

---

[59] L. Clay, *Stagestruck: The Business of Theater in Eighteenth-Century France and Its Colonies* (Ithaca, 2011), n. 92.

[60] *Declaration of the Rights of Man and the Citizen*, articles 11 and 17, in Stewart, ed., *A Documentary Survey*, pp. 113–14; Ginsberg, 'A Tale of Two Copyrights', p. 1016.

[61] E. Lunel, *Le théâtre and la Révolution* (Paris, 1910), pp. 64–5.   [62] *AP*, vol. 22, pp. 209–14.

[63] *AP*, vol. 28, pp. 441–2; M. Carlson, *Theatre of the French Revolution* (Ithaca, 1970), p. 72.

[64] *PVCIP*, pp. 47–8, 62–3, 66. For Romme and Condorcet's stance, see *AP*, vol. 49, pp. 107–8 and *PVCIP*, pp. 62, 93–4; and Condorcet, *Fragments sur la liberté de la presse* (Paris, 1776).

[65] Quatremère, *Rapport approuvé par le Comité d'instruction publique de l'Assemblée législative, sur les réclamations des directeurs de théâtre, & la propriété des auteurs dramatiques* (Paris, 1792), pp. 30–1, 13. The note on the first page reveals that Quatremère printed his *Rapport* much later and independently of the Assembly when Romme proposed contrary legislation.

authors' gift to society when their work was printed or staged, and its commercial quality, which should belong to authors in perpetuity. Eager to use the language of the moment to demonstrate his reformist credentials, he argued that new legislation must behove a revolution that liberated dramatists after 'despotism' had 'misunderstood, usurped and violated' the fruits of genius, that 'most incontestable and personal of all property'.[66] In response to theatre directors who criticized Le Chapelier's law, he argued that the act of printing and the act of staging created distinct products, that theatres were not required to pay dramatists for performances pre-dating 1791, and that a transitional period for staging plays would minimize financial risk for established theatres.[67]

The Assembly rejected Quatremère's solution, however, because his report sat uneasily with his decree proposal and many representatives feared ruining theatres in their home departments. His failure enabled Romme to draft pro-theatre legislation, which enabled provincial theatres to stafe any plays printed, sold, or performed before 13 January 1791 and reduced dramatists' exclusive right over new plays to just ten years.[68]

This episode concerning dramatists reminds us that the Revolution was no glorious dawn for author copyright. Le Chapelier in 1791, Romme in 1792, and Lakanal in 1793 feared that treating author-copyright as a natural right would hamper knowledge, ruin provincial theatres, and allow authors and publishers to behave like corporations. Although Quatremère considered authors owners rather than workers, most national representatives wanted writers to only receive enough remuneration to be motivated to write.[69] Quatremère perhaps adopted such an outspoken position to assist Panckoucke in his battle against counterfeiter publishers, but his efforts were consistent with his belief that artwork should remain the property of its creator and that property acquired through inheritance, labour, and investment was sacrosanct.[70]

Quatremère undertook other responsibilities for the Committee of Public Instruction in 1792, such as serving its sub-committee for financing educational establishments, proposing tutors for the dauphin and soliciting reports on educational, theatrical, and scientific subjects.[71] However, his influence in the Committee diminished after he failed to pass legislation on the Salon jury and theatres. He was henceforth preoccupied with the political crisis

---

[66] Ibid., pp. 4–13.   [67] Ibid., pp. 16–28.   [68] *AP*, vol. 48, pp. 107–8.

[69] Kennedy, *A Cultural History of the French Revolution*, p. 184; Ginsberg, 'Tale of Two Copyrights', p. 1016; Hesse, 'Enlightenment Epistemology', pp. 109–37.

[70] Quatremère, *Seconde suite*, pp. 53–4; idem, *Rapport*, p. 22; D. Kulstein, 'The Ideas of Charles-Joseph Panckoucke, Publisher of the *Moniteur Universel*, on the French Revolution', *French Historical Studies*, vol. 4, no. 3 (1966), pp. 304–19.

[71] *PVCIP*, pp. 291–2, 340–1.

that engulfed the Assembly and undermined cooperation between the legislative and executive.[72]

Quatremère lived up to his reputation in the first months of 1792 as a leading voice on the Feuillant right of the Assembly when he intervened in two affairs. The first concerned the minister of the navy, Bertrand de Molleville, whom the Naval Committee accused of helping officers emigrate.[73] Quatremère urged the Assembly to have faith in the minister and instead ask why the Naval Committee overstepped its authority given that the Constitution permitted only the judiciary to accuse ministers.[74] The Naval Committee, he lamented, believed that its role was simply to register the verdict of 'public opinion', which had apparently already condemned the minister. Its behaviour thereby created the precedent for the populist 'political excommunication' of the entire executive: 'Would posterity imagine', he asked, 'that in these deliberations the most imposing judicial act had been dragged through this indecent prostitution of applause, whistling, booing and threats?'[75] His speech infuriated Maxim Isnard, a rising star of the Brissotin left, who demanded that Quatremère defend the minister rather than attack the public, but it helped prevent impeachment. Vaublanc claimed that Quatremère 'spoke with...power and eloquence...against the tribunes' whilst Bertrand de Molleville reflected that 'an honest man, whom I knew only through his reputation, finally came to my defence'.[76]

The second affair concerned the Marquis de Pelleport. The municipal authority of Stenay in the Meuse Department had arrested Pelleport and his brother, who were heading to Germany on a secret mission for the foreign minister. Radical national representatives demanded details concerning his purported mission because Pelleport had been at the Coblenz émigré camp in June during Louis XVI's attempted escape; they also tried to exploit the affair to get suspicious agents classified as émigrés and claim power for the Assembly over diplomatic appointments. Quatremère countered with a speech in which he argued that diplomacy required secrecy, that Pelleport must resume his mission, and that foreign policy was the monarch's constitutional prerogative. However, murmurs and laughter in the Assembly prevented him from being heard. Although the Assembly ultimately found no case against Pelleport, the affair emboldened radical representatives to attack the executive and demand legislative oversight over foreign policy.[77]

---

[72] Hardman, *Marie-Antoinette*, pp. 245–6.

[73] Mitchell, *The French Legislative Assembly*, ch. 12; Cormack, *Revolution and Political Conflict in the French Navy*, ch. 5.

[74] *AP*, vol. 37, p. 368; *AP*, vol. 38, p. 89.

[75] Ibid., pp. 88–9. On the wider context, see G. Glénard, *L'exécutif et la constitution de 1791* (Rennes, 2009), p. 469.

[76] *AP*, vol. 38, pp. 88–9; Buchez and Roux, eds, *Histoire parlementaire*, vol. 6, p. 15;Vaublanc, *Mémoires sur la révolution*, vol. 1, p. 349; A.-F. Bertrand de Moleville, *Histoire de la révolution de France*, vol. 7 (Paris, 1802), pp. 58–62.

[77] *AP*, vol. 38, p. 589; *Moniteur universel*, no. 49, 18 Feb. 1792, p. 199.

Such interventions helped Quatremère's election as one of the six secretaries to the president of the Assembly between 20 February and 20 March. This nominally administrative role placed him at the centre of the Assembly's day-to-day affairs and allowed him to determine which petitions and subjects to supress and which to send the Assembly or its committees. Like other Feuillant secretaries, Quatremère abused the role to block Jacobin deputies as part of a new hostile strategy that dovetailed with the Feuillant press adopting an aggressive anti-Jacobin stance. André Chenier led the way in late February with an article in *Journal de Paris* proclaiming that the 'destruction [of the Jacobin club] is the only remedy to the evils facing France'.[78] The Feuillant struggle against the Jacobins came to the forefront during Quatremère's time as secretary in response to the rehabilitation of the Châteauvieux regiment. This regiment had been sentenced to the galleys after the Nancy mutiny in August 1790, but the Legislative Assembly pardoned the soldiers in December 1791 and radical representatives then proposed inviting them to the Assembly as guests of honour whilst the Jacobins planned a festival in their name in Paris. The Feuillant press reacted violently in March–April 1792, urging national guardsmen to ignore the festival and asking 'honest men' to take up arms against this 'crime'.[79]

The rehabilitation of the Châteauvieux regiment reflected the extent of the royalist crisis in spring 1792 after the Feuillant representatives lost control in the Assembly and deprived Louis XVI of the cooperative legislative that had briefly enabled constitutional monarchy to function. The crisis was exacerbated by many factors, including the Court's indecisiveness, the Feuillant club's failure to establish provincial branches and sustain membership levels, and the growing number of uncommitted centrist representatives who feared that the government was failing to address anxieties about émigrés and non-jurors in their home departments.[80] However, the crisis resulted above all from foreign-policy miscalculations.

In late 1791, Feuillant leaders naively imagined that the spectre of an armed congress of foreign powers against France might bolster the illusion that the king supported the Constitution.[81] Marguerite-Louis-François Duport-Dutertre, the minister of justice and most influential figure in the ministry, thus hatched a plan to create the impression that France was prepared to threaten war: France would publicly demand that the Elector of Trier disband émigré camps or face war, but Louis XVI would privately send a mission to the Elector to prevent war.

---

[78] *AP*, vol. 38, p. 689; *AP*, vol. 39, pp. 47, 114, 190–1; Mitchell, *The French Legislative Assembly*, pp. 29–32; Dendena, 'La haine des honnêtes gens. Stratégies éditoriales de la presse feuillante et construction des identités collectives', p. 91.

[79] Dendena, 'La haine des honnêtes gens. Stratégies éditoriales de la presse feuillante et construction des identités collectives', pp. 97–100.

[80] Mitchell, *The French Legislative Assembly*, pp. 78, 86–7.

[81] F. Dendena, 'A New Look at Feuillantism: The Triumvirate and the Movement for War in 1791', *French History*, vol. 26, no. 1 (2012), pp. 6–33.

However, Duport-Dutertre's plan backfired because putting war on the agenda strengthened the position of hawks such as the national representative and journalist Jacques-Pierre Brissot, who wanted France to attack the 'coalition of despots' to expose treason at home. The war minister, Narbonne, succeeded Duport-Dutertre as the de facto chief minister and gambled in early 1792 on a policy of restoring cooperation between the ministry and Assembly through a limited war and a tactical alliance with the Girondins. Unfortunately, Narbonne miscalculated, alienated other ministers and turned Austria's foreign minister, Kaunitz, against France.[82] The Girondins welcomed the fallout with Austria only to suffer embarrassment when their hoped-for alliance with Prussia was scuppered in February by the defensive pact between the central European rivals. Ironically, a pact that undermined Girondin diplomacy removed a brake on Girondin warmongering because it made the 1756 Franco-Austrian Treaty of Versailles obsolete.

The death of Emperor Leopold II in March removed another obstacle to conflict and the war lobby became wider if more divided. In mid-March, Louis XVI threw caution to the wind by replacing his 'honourable' Feuillant ministry with one filled by men whose struggles would, he hoped, reflect badly on the Girondins. When this Girondin ministry recommended war against Austria, Louis XVI acquiesced and the Assembly voted overwhelmingly in favour on 20 April.[83] Feuillants such as Dumas, Beugnot, and Becquey voted against war and warned that it might harm the king and rally Europe against France.[84] Quatremère never explained publicly why he voted for war, but he perhaps agreed with the vast majority of his other Feuillant allies that Austria was a credible threat, that war might restore national unity and support for Louis XVI, or simply that a successful campaign would empower Louis XVI whilst an unsuccessful one might result in a restoration.[85]

There would be no short and victorious war, however, and France's dilapidated armies were routed in the Austrian Netherlands. Commanders on the eastern front advised entering peace negotiations, but the Girondin ministry and Legislative Assembly wanted the government to seize control of military order, form armaments commissions, and mobilize popular support by punishing émigrés and non-jurors. Feuillant leaders and national representatives responded by obstructing measures intended to fight war effectively. Although Feuillant ministers and national representatives played their part in the origins of the war, by May they privately pinned their hopes on an invasion or a domestic crisis ending the Revolution whilst publicly masking their reactionary defeatism beneath

---

[82] Mitchell, *The French Legislative Assembly*, pp. 155–8; Hardman, *Marie-Antoinette*, pp. 245–6.
[83] J. Hardman, *The Life of Louis XVI* (New Haven, 2016), p. 414.
[84] T. Kaiser, 'La fin du renversement des alliances: la France, l'Autriche et la déclaration de guerre du 20 avril 1792', *Annales historiques de la Révolution française*, vol. 1, no. 351 (2008), pp. 77–98.
[85] Mitchell, *The French Legislative Assembly*, pp. 79–80.

104 QUATREMÈRE DE QUINCY

their devotion to a constitution that disallowed legislative interference in foreign and military affairs. Quatremère joined Feuillant attempts to obstruct unconstitutional measures that he said would lead to what he and other 'honest men' called, months before August, a 'second revolution'.[86] For instance, he rejected making foreigners declare residency, dismissing this measure as the result of false rumours of counter-revolutionary plotting when the Assembly should instead investigate the Surveillance Committee that threatened liberty and undermined trust.[87]

Quatremère was amongst the Feuillants during these difficult months who defended Duport-Dutertre against accusations that he had conspired against the state as justice minister.[88] Quatremère insisted that his 'pure and patriotic friend of twenty-five years' had demonstrated his commitment to the Revolution by dismantling the Old Regime's archaic, decentralized, and anti-commercial legal framework and replacing it with principles that harmonized 'scattered and often disparate materials'.[89] Did Duport-Dutertre's accusers, he asked, really want the restoration of archaic parlements in which lawyers wore ceremonial red robes? For Quatremère, there was no case against Duport-Dutertre: like all ministers, Duport-Dutertre had made mistakes and applied unpopular laws, but he had never endangered the state or undermined the Constitution.[90] Quatremère concluded with an antagonistic proposal against the likes of Jean-Paul Marat: given that Duport-Dutertre's accusers had acted in bad faith or ignorance, he suggested that in future denouncers should forfeit a deposit if found guilty of defamation.[91] In the same spirit, Quatremère defended royalist newspapers, defended former ministers Bertrand de Moleville and Armand Marc Montmorin against the accusation that they belonged to the queen's 'Austrian Committee', and defended Justice of the Peace Pierre Henry-Larivière when he was attacked for arresting several national representatives who were members of the Cordelier club. The Commune of the Arts duly expelled Quatremère because it could no longer tolerate such unambiguous expressions of his royalist politics.[92]

---

[86] Dendena, 'La haine des honnêtes gens. Stratégies éditoriales de la presse feuillante et construction des identités collectives', p. 106.

[87] AP, vol. 43, pp. 424, 540–1, 549–50. On this Surveillance Committee dominated by radical representatives, see M. Eude, 'Le comité de surveillance de l'Assemblée Législative (1791–1792)', Annales historiques de la Révolution française, vol. 36, no. 176 (1964), pp. 129–48.

[88] AP, vol. 41, pp. 184–201, 470. His speech was reported in Journal de Paris, no. 155, 3 June 1792, p. 624. Other Feuillants also defended the former minister. See, for example, J.-C Beugnot, Opinion sur les denonciations portees contre M. Duport [Paris, 1792], p. 4; British Library, Bibliothèques historique de la revolution, vol. 118, no. 4.

[89] Quatremère, Opinion sur les dénonciations faites contre M. Duport, ci devant ministre de la justice (Paris, 1792); abridged in AP, vol. 41, p. 473.

[90] AP, vol. 41, pp. 472–4, 476–7.   [91] AP, vol. 49, pp. 469–77.

[92] Mitchell, The French Legislative Assembly, p. 114; AP, vol. 42, p. 713; AP, vol. 43, p. 541; Journal de Paris, no. 142, 21 May 1792, p. 572.

DEVOTED TO THE KING, 1791–2   105

Quatremère spent May organizing the Festival of the Law. Although this was the most remarkable festival under the Legislative Assembly, the scholarship on festivals overlooks its distinctive character.[93] By revisiting the origins, organization and iconography of the Festival of the Law, we can explain how Quatremère used the event to defend the Constitution, depict the triumph of legitimate state force over illegitimate popular violence, and reoccupy public space in Paris from the Jacobins and other popular clubs. On closer inspection, Quatremère's organization of the Festival was therefore an attempt—one that dovetailed with the efforts of editors and contributors to Feuillant newspapers—to give the royalist movement a collective identity personified by the propertied 'honest man' who upheld law and order and wanted to thwart a second revolution.[94]

The Festival of the Law was held in Paris on 3 June 1792 to commemorate Jacques-Guillaume Simonneau, mayor of Étampes, who had been murdered during a grain riot in early March. Simonneau's posthumous heroization by royalists had not been straightforward because radical national representatives at first claimed him for their own cause.[95] Initially, radicals had argued that the murder of this courageous Jacobin mayor by a 'numerous and cowardly aristocracy' demonstrated that the Assembly should arm the people and they lobbied for three days of mourning, Simonneau's pantheonization, and a pyramid on the murder site. Although in early March the *Journal de Paris* also called for his pantheonization, the Feuillant press and representatives soon understood the meaning of this nascent cult of Simmoneau and tried to ensure that the public forgot this former mayor.[96] Quatremère thus proposed hiding any national commemoration within a generic ceremony for all 'victims of patriotism'.[97] However, over the next weeks, local initiatives, including several

[93] J. Ehard and P. Viallaneix, eds, *Les fêtes de la révolution* [1974] (Paris, 2012); M. Ozouf, *Festivals and the French Revolution* [1976], trans A. Sheridan (Cambridge, MA, 1991); R. Sanson, *Les 14 juillet, fête et conscience nationale, 1789–1975* (Paris, 1976); J. Guilhaumou, 'Nous/vous/tous: la fête de l'union du 10 aout 1793', *Mots. Les langages du politique*, vol. 10 (1985), pp. 91–108; V. Jouffre and B. de Andia et al., *Fêtes et révolutions* (Paris, 1989); P. Dupuy, ed., *La fête de la fédération* (Rouen, 2012); G. Mazeau, 'La Révolution, les fêtes et leurs images: spectacles publics et représentation politique (Paris, 1789–1799)', *Images Re-vues*, hors-série 6 (2018).

[94] Vovelle, *The Fall of the French Monarchy*, p. 161; Dendena, 'La haine des honnêtes gens. Stratégies éditoriales de la presse feuillante et construction des identités collectives', p. 100. My reinterpretation nuances Vovelle's verdict that the Festival was the response of bourgeois supporters of the Feuillants to Voltaire's pantheonization and the celebration of the Châteauvieux regiment. In what follows, I agree with Dendena on the creation of a collective identity in the Feuillant press, but suggest that Feuillant deputies such as Quatremère were collaborators rather than passive followers of that press.

[95] J.-C. Bonnet, 'La mort de Simonneau', in J. Nicolas, ed., *Mouvements populaires et conscience sociale, 16e-19e siècles* (Paris, 1987), pp. 671–6; J. Gélis, 'Émeute de marché et pouvoir local: le cas Simonneau, 1792', in *L'Essonne, l'Ancien Régime et la Révolution* (Saint-Georges-de-Luzençon, 1991), pp. 145–54; M. Dorigny, 'La mort de Simonneau: un révélateur des conflits politiques au printemps de 1792', in *L'Essonne*, pp. 155–61; S. Sanyal, 'The 1792 Food Riot at Etampes and the French Revolution', *Studies in History*, vol. 18, no. 1 (2002), pp. 23–50.

[96] *Journal de Paris*, no. 73, 13 March 1792, p. 297.

[97] *Moniteur universel*, no. 67, 7 March 1792, and no. 69, 9 March 1792; F.-A. Aulard, ed., *La société des Jacobins: recueil de documents pour l'histoire du club des Jacobins de Paris*, vol. 3 (Paris, 1892),

106 QUATREMÈRE DE QUINCY

provincial ceremonies and a play at the Théâtre du Marais about Simmoneau's life and death, increased pressure for a national festival in his name.[98] Ironically, by April radicals changed tack and disowned Simonneau once they became convinced that the mayor had, in fact, inflated the price of grain and given the order to fire on protestors in the fateful riot that led to his death.[99]

This about-turn created the possibility for Feuillant representatives to adopt Simmoneau as the courageous defender of the law. They belatedly decided to honour the mayor after the Paris Commune held the Festival of Liberty on 15 April. David's organization of the Festival of Liberty marked the decisive radical shift in his politics and the end of his friendship with André Chenier.[100] The festival included the usual secular hymns, pseudo-antique costumes, and figurative and allegorical visual props, but David and the Commune caused controversy by covering statues of kings and celebrating the Châteauvieux regiment.[101] Radical representatives and journalists praised the festival's spontaneous, democratic, and participatory character. By contrast, critics called it a 'festival of assassins' and described a 'crapulous orgy, impious and sacrilegious festival' that undermined sovereignty by implying that the people made the law. Adding insult to injury, critics exclaimed, this festival, in a brazen act of symbolic reappropriation, received the mutineers on the Field of the Federation at precisely the spot where Lieutenant André Désilles had been commemorated for sacrificing his life supressing the mutiny.[102]

National guards from prosperous sections reacted by petitioning the Assembly to honour defenders of the law such as Désilles and Simonneau.

---

p. 431; J. Debry, *Rapport sur les honneurs à rendre à la mémoire de J.-G. Simonneau, maire d'Étampes, au nom du comite d'instruction publique... et decret du 28 mars 1792* (n.d.), pp. 1–6; Tuetey, ed., *Répertoire général*, vol. 4, pp. 66–8; *AP*, vol. 39, p. 464; *AP*, vol. 40, p. 101.

[98] L. Marquis, *Les rues d'Étampes et ses monuments* (Étampes, 1881), ch. 2; P. Baillot, *Récit de la mort de Guillaume Simonneau* (Dijon, 1792), p. 9; H. Grégoire, *Discours prononcé dans l'église cathédrale de Blois* (Rennes, 1792); E. Gosse, *La Mort de Simonneau* (Paris, 1792); P. Doliver, *Pétition de quarante citoyens des communes de Mauchamp, Saint-Sulpice-de-Favières, Breuillet, Saint-Yon, Chauffour et Breux, voisines d'Étampes et qui ont eu le bonheur de ne tremper en rien dans la malheureuse affaire arrivée dans cette ville, communiquée le 27 avril à la Société des amis de la Constitution, séante aux Jacobins, et présentée le 1er mai à l'Assemblée nationale* (n.p., 1792), pp. 1–20.

[99] D. Hunt, 'The People and Pierre Dolivier: Popular Uprisings in the Seine-et-Oise Department (1791–1792)', *French Historical Studies*, vol. 11, no. 2 (1979), pp. 210–13; S. Wahnich, 'Un avocat sensible dans l'émotion de l'événement: le curé Dolivier face au meurtre du maire d'Etampes, printemps 1792', *Nuevo Mundos* (2006): http://journals.openedition.org/nuevomundo/1984; McPhee, *Robespierre*, pp. 120–1.

[100] P. Bordes, *Le Serment du Jeu de Paume de Jacques-Louis David: le peintre, son milieu et son temps, de 1789 à 1792* (Paris, 1983), p. 81.

[101] *Révolutions de Paris*, no. 145, 14–21 April 1792, p. 96; L. Vardi, *The Physiocrats and the World of the Enlightenment* (Cambridge, 2012), pp. 262–4; Ozouf, *Festivals*, pp. 72–3.

[102] M. Biver, *Fêtes révolutionnaires à Paris* (Paris, 1979), pp. 47–52; Dowd, *Pageant-Master*, pp. 55–77; L. Vardi, *The Physiocrats and the World of the Enlightenment* (Cambridge, 2012), pp. 262–4; Ozouf, *Festivals*, pp. 72–3; Dendena, 'La haine des honnêtes gens. Stratégies éditoriales de la presse feuillante et construction des identités collectives', p. 100.

Feuillant representatives took up their cause.[103] Quatremère ensured that the Assembly handed petitions to the Committee of Public Instruction, which asked him to draft a decree for a national festival. Quatremère quickly drafted a short proposal that he read to the Assembly several days later.[104] His proposed festival was unique for its political message, but he shared the widespread opinion that visual and auditory stimuli were 'the strongest instruments that one can deploy on the soul'. The festival must, he said, express the 'nation's outrage' at Simonneau's murder but also use this tragedy to demonstrate the Assembly's mandate 'to calm the downpour of disorder' and remind citizens to 'respect the law'. He requested 10 000 livres for a festival that, he explained, would honour public servants and conclude with a service in the Panthéon during which Simonneau's mayoral sash would be suspended from the vaults.[105]

Radical deputies such as Louis Albitte complained that Quatremère wished to evoke 'martial law' or the Old Regime hierarchy of corporations.[106] However, the Assembly voted for Quatremère's proposal with only minor amendments and entrusted the festival to the Directory of the Department of Paris, which immediately asked Quatremère to organize the iconography, decorations, and procession.

During the second half of May, Quatremère planned a festival that used Simonneau to personify how 'free men are slaves of the Law'. He devised ways to involve Marie Olympe de Gouges, who asked him to include women, and Pierre-François Palloy, who offered him a model miniature Bastille, and solicited contributions from distinguished artists. François-Joseph Gossec composed scores and Antoine Roucher wrote sung verses. Roland used plaster and cloth to create an ephemeral allegorical female figure of the Law, whom he depicted as a seated colossus holding a regal sceptre and resting on a tablet of the laws—an effort that resembled his bas-relief for the Panthéon because both were based on classical sculptures of Ceres, Roman goddess of agriculture and grain.[107] David perhaps created the grisaille depicting Simonneau's death.[108]

---

[103] Tuetey, ed., *Répertoire général*, vol. 4, pp. 68–9; *AP*, vol. 43, pp. 51–2; AN, F17 1692 contains nineteen petitions.

[104] *PVCIP*, pp. 273, 280, 284–6. Quatremère's report covered in *Journal de Paris*, no. 134, 13 May 1792, pp. 539–42.

[105] Quatremère, *Décret sur les honneurs a rendre a la mémoire de Jacques-Guillaume Simonneau, maire d'Etampes, précédé du rapport fait au nom du Comite d'instruction publique* (Paris, 1792), pp. 1–4; *AP*, vol. 43, pp. 268–9.

[106] Ibid., pp. 269–71.

[107] Quatremère, *Recueil de notices historiques*, p. 109; idem., *Rapport fait au directoire du département de Paris* (Paris, 1792), pp. 13–14.

[108] L.-G. Pitra, 'Lettre de M. Pitra, électeur de 1789, in M. Tourneux, ed., *Correspondance littéraire, philosophique et critique*, vol. 17 (Paris, 1882), pp. 139–45; *Courrier des LXXXIII départements*, vol. 9, 9 June 1792, p. 133. David denied his involvement once he grasped what the Festival of the Law meant.

The Festival of the Law went according to plan on 3 June.[109] Ten thousand participants gathered at the Place de la Bastille at eight in the morning.[110] Palloy offered Simonneau's widow an engraved stone from the fortress and an orderly procession marched west across the *grands boulevards*, via the church of Sainte-Marie-Madeleine (Fig 5.1), to the Place Louis XV and across the Pont Louis XVI to the left bank, where it continued to the Field of the Federation.[111] The procession

Fig. 5.1 Jean-Louis Prieur, *Funeral Procession in Honour of Simoneau, Mayor of Etampes, 3 June 1792*. Engraved by Pierre-Gabriel Berthault and printed in *Tableaux historiques de la Révolution française* (Paris, 1804), no. 61. 30.3 × 45.4 cm. Musée Carnavalet. Inventory no. G.28461.

---

[109] *Détails de la cérémonie arête par le directoire du département de Paris pour la fête décrète par l'assemblée nationale* (Paris, 1792), pp. 1–8; Tuetey, ed., *Répertoire général*, vol. 4, p. 70.

[110] *Discours prononcé... par Palloy, le patriote, accompagne de ses apôtres, lorsque le cortège de la fête célèbre... a la mémoire de Jacques-Guillaume Simonneau... s'est présente sur l'emplacement de la Bastille* (Paris, n.d.), pp. 1–2.

[111] My description combines information from: *Details de la cérémonie*; J.-A. Roucher, 'Variétés', in *Journal de Paris*, no. 157, 5 June 1792, pp. 633–4; *Révolutions de Paris*, no. 147, p. 216; Pitra, 'Lettre de M. Pitra, électeur de 1789'; A.-J. Gorsas, 'Paris. Pompe funèbre de Simonneau', in *Le courrier des LXXXIII départements*, vol. 9, 4 June 1792, pp. 53–63. It also draws upon prints by Jean-Louis Prieur for *Révolutions de Paris* and Jean Duplessis-Bertaux for *Tableaux historiques de la Révolution française*. Although their prints took liberties with the procession order, they captured the martial orderliness and approximate form of symbolic artefacts.

had a martial air because the first section consisted mostly of soldiers playing marching music and carrying weapons (Fig. 5.2). Participants in the second section carried flags, symbols, and banners representing national unity. The third section included police commissioners, judges of the peace, and members of the judicial and commercial tribunals, who marched behind a symbol of the law carried on a sacred table. In the fourth section, Simonneau's family, friends, and fellow municipal officers from Etampes and Paris carried François Masson's scarred sculpted bust of Simonneau, a pyramid embellished with bas-reliefs depicting Simonneau, his mayoral sash, and his wife's letter declining a state pension.[112] The fifth section carried the book and tablets of the law, a statue of Minerva, and Roland's figure of Law, carried by men in Persian dress whom critics interpreted as slaves. At the tail of the procession, national representatives and men and women held banners explaining the passage of the law from legislators to adults to children.

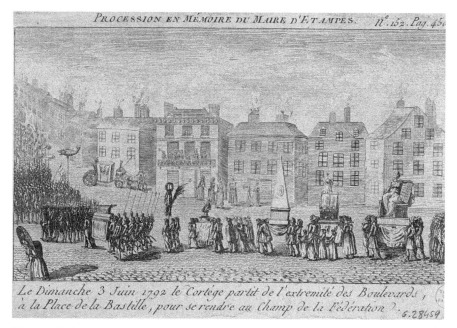

Fig. 5.2 Unknown artist, *Procession in Memory of the Mayor of Etampes*. Printed in *Révolutions de Paris*, 2–9 June 1792, no. 152, p. 450. 12.2 × 18.3 cm. Musée Carnavalet. Inventory no. G.28459.

---

[112] Dulaire, *Thermomèter du jour*, 5 June 1792; *Courrier des LXXXIII départements*, vol. 9, 9 June 1792, p. 133. Keen to capitalize on Simonneau's posthumous fame, Masson advertised plaster copies of the sculpted bust for forty livres plus postage—*Moniteur universel*, no. 220, 7 Aug. 1792, p. 926.

The procession arrived in the afternoon at the Field of the Federation, which Legrand and Molins had arranged to make artefacts and delegations visible to the 200 000 spectators. The architects suspended Simonneau's sash and portrait from a palm tree placed at the Altar of the Patrie that was surrounded by national representatives and elected magistrates. Below the Altar, national guards and soldiers arranged their flags to evoke the earlier ceremony honouring Désilles.[113]

François-Alexandre Tardiveau, the Assembly's president, started the ceremony when he climbed the Altar to the sound of Gossec's *Funeral Hymn* and delivered a eulogy quoting Simonneau's purported last words: 'You can kill me, but you will never make me break the law.' Tardiveau then placed a civic oak crown on Simonneau's portrait and the crowd cried '*Vive la loi!*' during an inundation that, according to a sympathetic observer, transformed collective sadness into euphoria. Tardiveau embraced Simonneau's sons and wept tears of 'religious pain' whilst heralds proclaimed the Assembly's decrees.[114] Roucher's ode was sung to Gossec's sombre *The Triumph of the Law*: an indicative line stated that 'Law rules... through love and... instilling fear'.[115] At the end, incense was burnt, the book of the law was raised, cannon sounded thrice, and the national guard presented their weapons.[116]

Reactions to the Festival of the Law were polarized along predictable lines. Royalists described 'the triumph of good citizens' and an orderly event 'applauded' by 'honest men'.[117] By contrast, radical commentators described an undemocratic festival featuring 'bayonets, swords and uniforms' and complained that battalions arranged flags to evoke the 17 July massacre or the ceremony honouring Désilles. They criticized the regal sceptre carried by Roland's figure and complained that Quatremère's pompous 'lesson to the people' was incomprehensible to most spectators, who could neither read Latin nor distinguish the flag of the law from a Chinese shark on a pike. Hostility towards Simonneau conditioned such critical reactions. One national guard thus recalled how 'agitators' convinced other guards from Saint-Marcel that Simonneau had been 'a traitor, a hoarder, an aristocrat, and that his conduct had the goal of starving the people'.[118]

If reactions were polarized, everyone understood equally well that the Festival of the Law made an explicit political argument (that the national executive and legislative enforced and created the law) and issued a thinly veiled threat (that the constituted authorities could strike against the Jacobin club).

---

[113] *Journal de Paris*, no. 157, 5 June 1792, pp. 633–4.   [114] Pitra, 'Lettre de M. Pitra'.

[115] C. Role, 'Roucher, Gossec, Simonneau ou le triomphe de la loi', *Études Héraultaises* (2005), pp. 1–4.

[116] *Journal de Paris*, 7 June 1792, no. 159, pp. 641–2.

[117] Vaublanc, *Mémoires sur la révolution*, vol. 1, p. 416; J. Godechot, ed., 'Fragments des mémoires de Charles-Alexis Alexandre sur les journées révolutionnaires de 1791 et 1792', *Annales historiques de la Révolution française*, vol. 24, no. 126 (1952), p. 164.

[118] Ozouf, *Festivals*, pp. 72–3; *Courrier des LXXXIII départements*, vol. 9, 9 June 1792, p. 133.

The playwright and poet Gamas captured this spirit with the lines '*Redoublez encor d'énergie / En combattant les factieux*' ('Redouble your energy once again / In fighting the fractious').[119]

The Festival of the Law was thus unique despite superficial resemblances between revolutionary festivals.[120] Its true counterpart was the Panthéon, which Quatremère also conceived as a 'figurative catechism of the obligations of men in society'.[121] The festival and Panthéon both espoused strength and sacrifice for the law and they both combined allegory, biography, and text to transform glorious deeds into sources of emulation. For both projects, Quatremère shunned allusions to events and the opportunity to forge a language particular to the Revolution; he instead adapted an antiquarian visual repertoire that reflected the pre-revolutionary cult of the nation's great men. Many contemporaries naturally found both the festival and the Panthéon tediously didactic, and Quatremère later admitted that his 'emblematic sermon' did 'not have a great moral effect on minds'.[122]

The Feuillants intended the Festival of the Law to convince 'honest men' to act against the Jacobins, but over the summer the Feuillants faced a much larger crisis. Military setbacks and fears that enemies were trying to manipulate the currency, force up food prices, and encourage desertion and civil war undermined faith in constitutional monarchy.[123]

Tension intensified after demonstrators entered the Tuileries on 20 June. Louis XVI had prompted the resignation of his Girondin ministry when he vetoed legislation to deport refractory priests and mobilize national guards to defend Paris, but the Gobelins section demanded the ministry's reinstatement and national guards. Citizens from Saint-Marcel and Saint-Antoine forced their way into the palace. Louis XVI's courage helped defuse the danger to the royal family until Pétion, the mayor of Paris, arrived, but the invasion of the Tuileries provoked a hostile backlash in which Feuillant deputies and the right-wing press vilified the Jacobins for seducing the populace.[124] Quatremère demanded justice, attacked the Jacobins and demanded the indefinite suspension of Pétion and Manuel, the capital's procurer, for dereliction of duty, violating the Constitution, compromising public safety, disobeying the Directory of the Department's order, and

---

[119] Gamas, 'Sur la mort de Simonneau, maire d'Étampes, qui a péri en voulant faire exécuter la loi', printed later in *Almanach des Muses de 1793, ou Choix des poésies fugitives de 1792* (Paris, 1793), pp. 43–4.

[120] For a contrary interpretation, see Mona Ozouf, *Festivals*, pp. 61–2.

[121] Quatremère, *Rapport* (1791), p. 29.

[122] Quatremère, *Recueil de notices historiques*, pp. 108–9.

[123] McPhee, *Liberty or Death*, pp. 153–6.

[124] Murray, *The Right-Wing Press*, pp. 178–81; Dendena, 'La haine des honnêtes gens. Stratégies éditoriales de la presse feuillante et construction des identités collectives', pp. 84–5.

legitimizing a banned event by asking crowds to march under the national guard's banner.[125]

Quatremère identified the choice facing the Assembly: on the one hand, it could condemn the events of 20 June, uphold justice, punish 'blasphemes against the law', and demonstrate that 'the king is free and the nation will be free because its representatives are just'; on the other hand, it could set a dangerous example by allowing the Paris Commune to reinstate Pétion and Manuel, thereby demonstrating its powerlessness to uphold the law and Constitution. Quoting Seneca, he reminded deputies that 'he who does not prevent a crime when he can, encourages it'. Inaction, he warned, would undermine the administrative hierarchy by showing local representatives that they could disobey higher authorities and cause 'perpetual conflict' and then despotism. If the Assembly reinstated Pétion when he had encouraged sedition, he concluded, it should revoke honours given to Simonneau for opposing sedition.[126]

Several days later, Lafayette returned from the warfront to denounce the invasion of the Tuileries, threaten the Jacobins, and present a petition demanding an enquiry into what happened on 20 June. Radical representatives accused Lafayette of asking Nicolas Luckner to march on Paris and raged that this 'general of the Feuillants' wanted to establish a dictatorship and repeat last summer's massacre, but Feuillant representatives exonerated him and helped defeat the motion to ask the war minister whether Lafayette had obtained leave from his post.[127]

In the aftermath of this episode, the royalists were hampered by internal divisions, Marie-Antoinette's animus towards Lafayette, and Louis XVI's indecisiveness. Lafayette awaited a stronger pretext to justify marching on Paris because he doubted the loyalty of his soldiers, but, in the meantime, the city's clubs, sections, and provincial military units rallied against the threat he posed. Some Feuillant newspapers favoured suspending the Assembly whilst the king negotiated peace, and Feuillant representatives in the Assembly found themselves isolated after the new Feuillant ministry failed to win the confidence of a majority.[128] In these circumstances, Quatremère complained that seven or eight men surrounded him in the Manège to prevent him from speaking.

Like other Feuillants, Quatremère tried to undermine the war effort in July. For instance, he opposed declaring 'the country in danger' because the justification hinged on a fictitious conspiracy that, left unchecked, would lead to a 'new

---

[125] AP, vol. 45, 21 June, p. 445; Vaublanc, Mémoires sur la révolution, vol. 1, p. 483, vol. 2, p. 44; Quatremère, Opinion de M. Quatremère, député du département de Paris, qui n'a pu être prononcé dans la séance du 13 juillet, sur la suspension de MM. Pétion et Manuel, maire et procureur de la commune de Paris (Paris, n.d. [1792]), pp. 1–20. Quatremère was unable to read his speech, which was instead printed.

[126] Ibid., p. 20; AP, vol. 46, pp. 469–73.

[127] Mitchell, The French Legislative Assembly, pp. 92–100; Murray, The Right-Wing Press, p. 181.

[128] Ibid., p. 190.

revolution' or 'counter revolution' against the Constitution, the permanent session of Paris sections, a new Chief of Staff for the Paris national guard, and a camp of provincial national guards outside the capital.[129] Critics dismissed his concern as a distraction from the real conspiracy against the nation.[130]

Ironically, Quatremère defended Lafayette—the man tasked with preventing France's invasion—in a pamphlet that he drafted sometime in late July or early August before the report by the commission tasked with investigating Lafayette's purported conspiracy with Luckner.[131] He wrote when Prussian forces crossed the Rhine, the commander of the Austrian-Prussian army threatened to destroy Paris and the capital's sections, and clubs demanded that the king abdicate. His draft pamphlet reveals his arguments to convince Feuillants that Lafayette, 'emulator of Washington', could alone save 'liberty and the constitution' against 'illegal and arbitrary power'. Lafayette's response to the invasion of the Tuileries, he argued, was legal because there were no laws against generals petitioning the Assembly or leaving their armies under their officers, because the alleged conversation between Lafayette and military figures simply repeated Lafayette's legitimate view, and because Luckner denied the so-called 'Luckner memorandum'. He urged the Assembly to follow Lafayette's sensible demands to restore order, reprimand the Jacobins, and punish the organizers of 20 June. Lafayette's accusers, he concluded, revealed that their motive was to expose generals and replace them with appointments loyal to the 'Jacobin court': they accused Lafayette of petitioning when he had deliberated, making laws when he had demanded their enforcement, denouncing the Assembly when he had denounced factions, wanting to suppress clubs when he opposed their abuses, entering Paris with an army when he had arrived alone, and being a Cromwell when he supported the separation of powers.[132]

After drafting this pamphlet, Quatremère helped Vaublanc convince centrist representatives to oppose the decree accusing Lafayette, which was defeated on 8 August by 406 to 224 votes.[133] However, Lafayette's acquittal proved what Dumas called 'a last and deceitful ray of hope' since 'tumultuous crowds...surrounded the hall' and assaulted royalist deputies. Quatremère sought refuge in the Tuileries guardhouse before fleeing.[134] Fearing a 'Saint Bartholomew's Day massacre of royalists', he was amongst the nineteen representatives who remonstrated to the Assembly: 'After swearing to preserve the Constitution, I should fail in my duty

---

[129] *AP*, vol. 44, p. 71.   [130] *Moniteur universel*, no. 186, 4 July 1792, p. 774.
[131] Quatremère, *Opinion...sur les dénonciations dirigées contre M. Lafayette* (Paris, 1792). The British Library contains the only known copy of this pamphlet, suggesting that it was never widely distributed. Quatremère mentioned events between 28 June and 21 July, showing that he wrote during the last weeks of July or first weeks of August. The Imprimerie national printed the British Library version on thin paper as a twelve-page pamphlet, but circumstances changed by the time that Quatremère returned the proof. An editorial pen on the copy stated: 'One suspends printing until the order of M. Quatremère.' Another note stated that this was 'useless'.
[132] Quatremère, *Opinion*, pp. 1–12.   [133] Vaublanc, *Mémoires sur la révolution*, vol. 2, p. 202.
[134] M. Dumas, *Souvenirs du lieutenant général comte Mathieu Dumas de 1770 a 1836*, ed. C. Dumas, vol. 2 (Paris, 1839), p. 451.

if I did not denounce... yesterday's outrages.... I must tell the Assembly that I was... insulted, threatened and unable to find protection'. The Assembly must, he insisted, 'guarantee the personal safety of representatives... and the freedom of their opinions'.[135]

However, the danger deterred Quatremère and other royalists from attending the Assembly. After Lafayette surrendered to the Austrian camp, an insurrectionary committee mobilized crowds and provincial national guards to seize the City Hall and Tuileries. The 'second revolution' on 20 August led to the suspension of monarchy, imprisonment of the royal family, and creation of a provisional ministry that governed France with the Paris Commune and remaining legislators. This de facto government ordered democratic elections, and, while awaiting the results, closed royalist newspapers, passed laws against refractory priests, dissolved religious orders, introduced military service, and increased taxation. France's military fortunes improved during the second half of September when the new National Convention convened and declared the Republic. Victories removed the invasion threat and allowed France's armies to advance into the Rhineland, Savoy, and Low Countries, raising questions about the treatment of foreign peoples. The revolutionary state's war aims were now unclear because neither the Legislative Assembly (that had declared war) nor the Constitution (that the Assembly had insisted the 'King of Bohemia' recognize) existed any longer.[136]

Quatremère lay low in August and September because his reputation as a royalist legislator and the authoritarian director of the Panthéon endangered him. His correspondence suggests that he mostly remained in Paris even if he spent some time with other royalists in Cernay.[137] Laws against émigrés, loyalty to the Panthéon project, his father and uncle's age and health, and fear of forfeiting his inheritance perhaps convinced him to remain. In any case, he fared better than other prominent Feuillants and royalist national representatives until a warrant for his arrest in 1793: for instance, Barnave, Le Chapelier, and Bailly were executed; Jaucourt was imprisoned in August and then left for Switzerland; Pastoret returned to Provence then fled to Savoy; Dumas went to England and briefly returned to Paris before leaving for Switzerland; Duport and Lameth fled abroad; and Vaublanc initially hid in Paris and then travelled around France to avoid arrest. Several factors might explain why Quatremère avoided their plight. He perhaps benefited from the protection of Danton, the justice minister.[138]

---

[135] *AP*, vol. 47, p. 601; Arnault et al., *Dictionnaire historique et raisonné*, vol. 17, p. 167; *Moniteur universel*, no. 224, 11 Aug. 1792, p. 939.

[136] Blanning, *The Pursuit of Glory*, p. 626.

[137] F. Barrière, 'M. Quatremère de Quincy', *Revue de Paris*, vol. 5 (May 1850), p. 288. AN: F13 325 and F13 1935 show that Quatremère received letters as director of the Panthéon throughout summer and resumed writing letters in late October when the Department of Paris confirmed his appointment.

[138] Wallon, *Quatremère*, p. 550. Quatremère recalled Danton's help specifically in 1793–4 rather than 1792.

No documents incriminated him because he remained silent after 9 August and was not amongst the royalists who planned to accompany Louis XVI if he escaped Paris.[139] Finally, he was indispensable to the Department of Paris as director of the Panthéon; he therefore used this role to demonstrate his civism and depict himself as a non-political friend of the arts.

[139] Mitchell, *The French Legislative Assembly*, p. 386.

6

Republicanizing the Panthéon, 1792–4

Quatremère juggled his responsibilities in the Legislative Assembly with his work directing the transformation of Sainte-Geneviève. Practical considerations and new opportunities led him to revise parts of his original vision, but, by August 1792, he had already executed or agreed designs for most changes that he had envisaged in spring 1791. Although the Panthéon (as the former church was soon called) later became the paradigmatic monument of the Republic, this chapter will argue that in 1791–2 Quatremère instigated a decorative scheme that spelled out the optimistic Feuillant view: namely, that a peaceful and constitutional age had succeeded the tumultuous Revolution. As we will see, he continued to direct the project until his incarceration in 1794. Rather than treating his role at the Panthéon in 1792–4 as a sign of his support for the National Convention, the second half of the chapter argues that he introduced superficial changes to his original vision to prove his patriotism, complete the project, and protect sculptors working under him.

Quatremère was appointed to lead the 'direction and administration of the monument' in July 1791 and during his first year in this role he oversaw many changes that he had recommended in his initial report. His first challenge was to reform the Panthéon's finances and workforce. He immediately suspended work until August to reorganize the Panthéon's administration and eliminate inefficiency, confusion, and corruption. Quatremère and Lefevre, responsible for the Panthéon's accounts and archives, also overhauled how the office managed finances to avoid handling money directly by issuing vouchers that the Directory of the Department redeemed, and to improve accountability by verifying expenses, reporting spending more regularly and improving registers.[1] However, Quatremère and Lefevre were powerless in the face of the greater problem that the Legislative Assembly and then the Convention provided promised funds late and irregularly.[2]

---

[1] Quatremère, *Rapport* (1792), pp. 32–3, 42, 44, 51; A.-D. Laffon, *Rapport fait a l'Assemblée nationale, sur l'achèvement du Panthéon français au nom du comité de l'ordonnance des finances, le 24 décembre 1791* (Paris, 1791); AN, F13 333: file 'Minutes and letters for accounts'.

[2] Quatremère, *Rapport* (1791), p. 48; *AP*, vol. 36, 24 Dec. 1791, pp. 365–6; *AP*, vol. 37, 18 Feb. 1792, p. 643. In December, the Legislative Assembly made available just 50 000 livres; in February 1792, it finally earmarked 1.5 million livres that it planned to provide as monthly 50 000-livres tranches, but in practice funding remained irregular.

Quatremère de Quincy: Art and Politics during the French Revolution. David Gilks, Oxford University Press.
© David Gilks 2024. DOI: 10.1093/oso/9780198745563.003.0007

To ensure that day-to-day work continued, Quatremère retained talented figures familiar with the building, removed incapable individuals, and resisted political appointments.[3] In the office in the Collège des Quatre-Nations, twenty minutes' walk from the site, Quatremère therefore employed alongside Lefevre two other salaried experts: Saussine, who measured distances, and the architect Françin, who produced drawings, inspected the site, and liaised with him (Fig. 6.1).[4]

Fig. 6.1 Unknown artist, *Façade of the French Panthéon*. Undated (1794?). Drawing with ink wash. 47.5 × 44.5 cm. BnF, département estampes et photographie, RESERVE QB-370 (24)-FT 4. This drawing of the west front depicts the decorative sculpture programme and in-filling of large windows that Quatremère's described in reports and other writings. The balustrade figures were planned in 1793 but never executed.

---

[3] Potofosky, *Constructing Paris*, p. 114.
[4] Quatremère, *Rapport* (1792), pp. 35–8. Lefevre was paid 4,000 livres per annum and Saussine and Françin each received 1,500 livres. Surviving correspondence shows that the office was in the Collège des Quatre-Nations until summer 1792; see, for example BHVP, ms. 814, fol. 430 (Quatremère to Rondelet, 29 Aug. 1791); and AN, F13 1935 (14 April 1792).

118   QUATREMÈRE DE QUINCY

Other salaried experts were based at the site. Rondelet and Soufflot le Romain oversaw construction and ornamental sculpture respectively, but Bourdon, employed to gather accounts from contractors and write estimates and receipts, now assisted them with paperwork.[5] Quatremère ordered Rondelet and Soufflot in summer 1791 to reduce their reliance on entrepreneurs (or middlemen) who took a tenth of overall spending for their services and, he complained, were the enemy of 'good order, subordination, good execution and responsibility'. Rondelet continued to rely on Pincent for masonry and Boillette for carpentry, but he limited outsourced work to simple matters such as stonecutting and brought in-house complex construction such as spherical and elliptical vaults.[6] At Quatremère's request, Soufflot also introduced a new system in which he asked Quatremère to approve drawings for ornamental sculptures that he then passed to Lanoye (who recorded what everyone on site had done) and Liger (who traced the drawings onto stone, created models to copy, and supervised a hundred or so '*compagnon*' sculptors by working alongside them and perfecting their stonework).[7] Quatremère sent Soufflot and Lanoye lists of approved ornamental sculptors in an attempt to retain order and exclude troublemakers.[8]

Since Quatremère was preoccupied with his work as a legislator and member of the Committee of Public Instruction, he was grateful that this reformed administration worked effectively. He paid Rondelet's rent in September from his own pocket because he appreciated the help that he received from this honest and talented mathematician and engineer.[9] Quatremère's trust in the administration allowed him to limit his active role at the Panthéon to liaising with the Directory of the Department of the Seine and determining the programme of decorative sculptures.

The reformed administration made tangible progress after work on site resumed in August 1791. The Panthéon's appearance was soon transformed. The houses attached to its north transept were demolished and the large windows and smaller side doors on the west front were walled-up.[10] Scaffolding was erected outside and inside the structure to facilitate enable the fluting of unfinished columns and the removal of the lantern tower and decorative sculptures.[11]

---

[5] Quatremère, *Rapport* (1792), pp. 34–5. Rondelet, Soufflot, and Bourdon were each paid 3,600 livres.

[6] Ibid., pp. 47–8, 51.

[7] Ibid., pp. 39–42; AN, F13 333, Soufflot file: Quatremère to Soufflot (27 Aug. 1791). See also AN, F13 333, Delanoye file, for examples of Quatremère and Lanoye corresponding about prices, patterns, and suppressing ornaments.

[8] See, for example, AN, F13 333, Soufflot file: letters of 10, 17, 24 March 1792. Ornamental sculptors continued petitioning for work; see numerous examples in AN, F13 1938.

[9] Quatremère, *Journal de Savants*, 1818, p. 365; BHVP, ms. 814, fol. 432: Quatremère letter dated 29 Sept. 1791.

[10] AN, F13 333: see the letter of the Panthéon administration to Rondelet, 16 May 1792, and Quatremère's report of 30 June 1792 on reusing glass from the windows.

[11] Quatremère, *Rapport* (1792), p. 16; BHVP, ms. 814, fol. 434; AN, F13 333, Rondelet file: letters from Quatremère to Rondelet, 30 June 1792 (ordering scaffolding for the demolition of the lantern) and 21 Dec. 1792 (ordering the demolition of the towers).

Other work during Quatremère's first year as director was not immediately visible. For example, his administration ordered marble to pave inside the Panthéon and cast-metal letters to attach on the west front that spelled out 'French Panthéon, year III of liberty' and 'To great men, a grateful *patrie*'. (These letters were designed in late 1791, cast in bronze in the Périer brothers' Chaillot studio in early 1792, and stored until the pediment was ready.)[12] During his first year, Quatremère also settled on a more economical plan for the area. He had previously wanted to create a large sanctuary, but in 1791–2 he learned more about the cost of compensating landowners and settled on a more modest scheme that spared Saint-Étienne-du-Mont and the garden of the former abbey of Sainte-Geneviève.[13]

Quatremère invested most effort during his first year in the Panthéon's decorative sculptures, which he ultimately co-created because he selected artists, determined subjects, influenced styles, compositions, and execution methods. Although he was willing to allow artists to incorporate the recent emblems of the pike and Phrygian cap, his overall programme in 1791–2 articulated the confident Feuillant vision of the triumph of constitutional monarchy that culminated in the Declaration of the Rights of Man and celebrated the transition from upheaval to constitutionalism and rule of law.[14] Since Quatremère admired Moitte as a draftsman, the design style of the external bas-reliefs reflected this sculptor's influence as an unofficial leader in the Panthéon studio. Taking after Moitte's style, most other sculptors created angular, severe figures and highly legible if lifeless compositions that could be understood from afar.[15]

Designs for almost all exterior sculptures were commissioned and produced during Quatremère's first year. He chose artists without holding competitions because he wanted to assemble a team of hands-on sculptors who were prepared to adapt their styles and compositions and willing to coordinate their sketches and models. He therefore employed his friends and acquaintances from Coustou's studio or his Italian voyages whilst excluding celebrated academicians such as Pajou, Clodion, and Houdon. This approach left him exposed to criticism but

---

[12] AN: F13 325 (see letters dated 10 and 16 Nov. 1791 and 28 Jan. 1792 from Richard, the Périer brothers' secretary, to Françin on the cost); and F13 1936 (see letters dated 1 and 10 Dec. 1791 in which the brothers invited Quatremère to witness the casting, and a report dated 25 June 1792 that noted the thirty-seven letters with 144 studs cost 1,823 livres).

[13] AN: F13 1935 and F 13 333 contain memoranda and letters to Quatremère on the cost of acquiring property. See especially F13 1935, 'R' file: letters dated 10, 13, and 17 Jan. 1792 for Quatremère's correspondence with Roederer and the Directory of the Department reporting deeds and acquisitions. Quatremère concluded in a letter to the procurer syndic, dated 15 April 1793 (F13 333, no. 302) that a large square 'will be extremely expensive' and 'would absorb the building of the Abbey'. A variation on his revised plan was realized decades later.

[14] The best study of this Feuillant vision is Dendena, *I nostri maledetti scranni*.

[15] Quatremère, *Institut de France. Funérailles de M. Moitte, le 3 mai 1810* (Paris, 1810), pp. 1–6; G. Grammacini, 'Moitte, Quatremère de Quincy, l'architecture et la sculpture historique au Panthéon', in *L'art et les révolutions: XXVIIe congrès international d'histoire de l'art* (Strasbourg, 1992), p. 165; idem, *Jean-Guillaume Moitte (1746–1810): Leben und Werk* (Berlin, 1993).

120 QUATREMÈRE DE QUINCY

allowed him to treat the sculptures and architecture as one indivisible artwork.[16] Quatremère supported his preferred sculptors with funds, materials, and studios in the abbey of Sainte-Geneviève, where they created and up-scaled models before executing designs in stone or metal.[17]

Their work is scarcely appreciable today when one stands before the Panthéon because only two exterior sculptures installed during the Revolution survived later changes. Visualizing Quatremère's exterior decorative programme therefore requires gathering and interpreting sketches, plaster models, textual descriptions, financial records, and artists' representations.

The most ambitious part of the programme was the free-standing sculpture for the dome. Quatremère assigned Dejoux the task of creating an allegorical figure of Renown. Quatremère had envisaged a stone statue smaller than the lantern, but in 1792 he asked for a much larger, thirty-foot figure that Dejoux and other artists convinced him to cast in metal.[18] Dejoux created a model by summer and requested a studio where he could scale-up and cast the figure.[19] His design showed a winged female figure with a fanfare, palm branches, and a laurel-leaf crown, stepping across the dome to honour great men entering the Panthéon.[20] Quatremère admired Dejoux's stoic refusal to allow outside events to impinge upon his work: Dejoux, he later recalled, imagined that he was working for ancient Rhodes or Corinth rather than the Revolution.[21] If Dejoux's design resembled Moitte's bas-relief of the same subject for the Hôtel de Salm, it was nevertheless striking as the first of many planned colossal statues for Paris.

Quatremère attached special importance to the west front bas-reliefs, which several artists designed during the first half of 1792.[22] Moitte's bas-relief for the pediment was the largest and most expensive.[23] In the first months of 1792, Moitte produced a highly-finished drawing for 'The *Patrie* crowning Virtue and Genius' by adapting the pediment sculpture for the Athenian Parthenon that he knew through Jacques Carrey's drawing. Moitte emphasized the bond between France and the Crown by placing at the centre of his composition a female figure symbolizing the *patrie*, who stood beside a regal throne and shield bearing Bourbon fleur-de-lys. He showed this

---

[16] Quatremère, *Rapport* (1793), p. 79; AN, F13 325A: see Milot's letter to Quatremère demanding he apply the law of competition (7 Oct. 1793).

[17] BHVP, ms. CP 3435, fol. 129.

[18] Quatremère, *Rapport* (1792), p. 18; idem, *Rapport* (1793), p. 19.

[19] AN, F13 333A, no. 152, letter detailing studio (3 March 1793).

[20] R. Lingée after Dejoux, *La Renommée*, reproduced in C.-P. Landon, *Annales du musée et de l'école moderne des beaux-arts: Salon de 1808*, vol. 2 (Paris, 1808), plate 35.

[21] Quatremère, *Recueil de notices historiques*, pp. 81–2.

[22] AN, F13 333: Rondelet file, letter from Quatremère to Rondelet dated July 1792. A drawing by an unknown artist (labelled 'The architecture, by J. Rondelet; the fronton, by Moitte 1792') shows how the decorative scheme for the west front was devised in 1792 when additional architectural and ornamental changes were still being considered.

[23] AN, F13 1935: letter dated 28 Feb. 1792. Moitte was paid 28 000 livres.

female figure accompanied to one side by Genius, a winged male figure who carried a Herculean club and snatched a laurel crown. Beyond him was a child Genius whose torch of enlightenment halted griffins, fantastical creatures symbolizing error that pulled a chariot containing attributes of vice and passion. On the other side, the *patrie* was accompanied by the patient female figure of Virtue, who stood before a triumphant lion-drawn chariot carrying symbols of cardinal virtues and a flying female figure holding a figurine representing France. Beyond this procession, Moitte drew a semi-nude reclining male figure who represented Vice defeated and shamed.[24]

Quatremère asked different sculptors to create the five pronaos bas-reliefs, although Moitte influenced their compositions.[25] In response to calls for open competitions, Quatremère tried to create the illusion of a fair selection process by organizing his preferred sculptors to petition the Directory of the Department with requests that it divide commissions between them.[26] Guillaume Boichot created 'Nature accompanied by Liberty and Equality' for the central piece.[27] This showed Renown crowning Bountiful Nature (represented as a woman carrying a cornucopia) who presented France (signified by a Gallic cockerel and Bourbon fleur-de-lys) with the Declaration of the Rights of Man, which rested on a statue of the ancient fertility goddess Diana of Ephesus. Accompanying Nature were the sisterly figures Liberty (who held the scales of justice to emphasize that freedom required respect for the law) and Equality (who resembled Minerva but carried a Phrygian cap on her spear). If Boichot's erudite symbolism was perhaps incomprehensible to many viewers, learned circles understood the visual language that he borrowed from earlier prints and drawings.[28] Boichot's composition imitated the apotheosis scene from the Column of Antoninus Pius and Moitte's drawing 'The response of Louis XVI to La Fayette', but

---

[24] Grammacini, 'Moitte, Quatremère de Quincy, l'architecture et la sculpture historique au Panthéon', pp. 162, 165.

[25] Deming, 'Le Panthéon révolutionnaire', p. 131, reproduces sketches, seemingly in Moitte's hand, that were designs for Chaudet and Lesueur's bas-reliefs.

[26] AN: F13 1935 contains the petition (dated 4 April 1792) and Department's decision to commission these artists (17 May).

[27] Boichot's drawing *La nature offrant à la France la Déclaration des droits de l'Homme* (1791–2) (Musée de Chalon-sur-Saone) shows his design. Several sources confirm that Boichot realized this design in stone; see J.-B. Hilair, *Panthéon Français* (1794–5), BnF, département Estampes et photographie, Destailleur Paris, vol. 6, no. 1045; and the view of the Panthéon by an unidentified artist (BnF, De Vinck, no. 4186). Fragments of a plaster model constituting about three-quarters of the original composition demonstrate that Boichot's relief was deeper than Quatremère's instructions suggest; photograph reproduced in Portet, 'Les collections du Panthéon. Étude, inventaire et perspectives scientifiques', p. 13.

[28] See, for example, Anon., *Louis XVI signe la constitution* (Paris, n.d. [1791?])—Musée Carnavalet, Paris, G27084. This print depicted France as a woman surrounded by attributes that reappeared in the Panthéon, such as a Gallic cockerel, fleurs-de-lys, Genius, Fame, a cornucopia, and other symbols of abundance.

122 QUATREMÈRE DE QUINCY

his animated and interlinked female figures betrayed his admiration for the style of the Fontainebleau school.[29]

In Quatremère's scheme, the bas-reliefs flanking Boichot's composition illustrated what the *patrie* did for man and what man owed the *patrie*. For the left side, he therefore asked Jacques-Philippe Lesueur to depict the *patrie* presenting Education (represented as a benevolent figure whom children embraced as their second mother) to parents and Philippe-Laurent Roland to depict the *patrie*, under the gaze of Civil and Criminal Jurisprudence, showing Innocence the jury and statue of Justice. For the right side, Augustin-Felix Fortin created the 'Empire of the Law' in which he depicted a regal *patrie* teaching obeisance of the law before an old man and soldier who pledged to uphold and defend the law.[30] For the final relief, Chaudet created 'Devotion to the *Patrie*' in which Glory and Strength helped a dying warrior place his sword on the Altar of the *Patrie*.[31]

These bas-reliefs on the west front were part of Quatremère's original vision in May 1791, but in spring 1792 he seized the opportunity to embellish the portico with additional sculptures. He convinced Salon prize-winners to use their awards to create thirteen-foot-high allegorical figures that echoed subjects depicted in the bas-reliefs. He intended four of these figures for the area beneath the pronaos: Chaudet's 'Philosophy', Roland's 'Law' (the design of which was used for the Festival of the Law), Boichot's 'Strength', and Masson's 'Soldier dying in the arms of Motherland'. He planned to display two additional figures, Lorta's 'Liberty' and Jean Lucas de Montigny's 'Equality', before the peristyle.[32] Boichot alerted Quatremère to the challenges of working on this scale, but by 1794 clay models of most figures were in place.[33]

During Quatremère's first year, he also made progress redecorating inside the Panthéon. He designated subjects for the pendentive bas-reliefs and selected sculptors in May 1792 to create designs over the summer.[34] Since he realized that removing windows and superfluous ornamentation risked making the interior monotonous, he was eager: to complete cenotaphs for Mirabeau

---

[29] Jean-Guillaume Moitte, *Réponse de Louis XVI à la Fayette* (1790), Lille, Palais des Beaux-Arts. PL.1570; Lemaistre, 'Les différentes programmes de sculpture', pp. 238–9.

[30] Quatremère, *Rapport* (1792), pp. 10–11.

[31] Fortin and Chaudet's models were finished by early August at the latest, since Quatremère mentioned them in his correspondence: AN, F13 1138, letters dated 6–7 Aug. 1792. The bas-reliefs by Lesueur and Chaudet are still in situ on the west front.

[32] Quatremère, *Rapport* (1793), pp. 13–14. Quatremère's correspondence details these commissions and their cost and shows that subjects were decided over spring 1792. See, for example, correspondence from artists in April 1792 (AN, F13 333A, nos. 168–74). Lorta worked for free because he did not win a Salon prize.

[33] AN, F13 333A: Boichot letter to Quatremère (21 April 1792).

[34] AN, F13 1935: documents dated 8 May and 24 Nov. 1792 show how Quatremère asked sculptors to petition the Directory of the Department.

and Voltaire; to display Simonneau's mayoral sash, the chariot used for Voltaire's pantheonization, and a new portrait of Rousseau by Houdon; and to create an elaborate Altar of the *Patrie* that included allegorical representations of the departments and a seated colossal female allegorical figure of the *Patrie*, inspired by ancient polychromatic representations of deities.[35] Yet his original ambition in 1791 to populate the upper church with portraits and small monuments advanced slowly despite the support of writers such as Chaisneau, who called for columns and obelisks that listed worthy citizens and enabled everyone to aspire to eternal civic fame.[36]

Although Quatremère's vision for the Panthéon became more detailed during his first year, he remained wedded to his overall scheme and to using decorative sculptures to articulate the Feuillant discourse of constitutionalism, duties, legality, order, and the unity of Crown, *patrie*, and France. If his programme was sufficiently anodyne and allegorical to escape criticism before the second revolution, he was nevertheless attacked for his authoritarian management of the site. This tension should be seen in the wider context of difficult labour relations in Paris after the Le Chapelier law banned worker associations, but several issues were specific to the Panthéon.[37] For instance, the Commune of the Arts attacked how Quatremère commissioned artworks without competitions and as early as October 1791 the justice of the peace for the local section took up labourers' case after Quatremère stopped using the site as a work-creation scheme and cut the workforce by a fifth.[38] In this troubled environment, the entrepreneur Poncet accused masons of forming illegal alliances and masons responded with accusations of embezzlement.[39] Construction workers, ornamental sculptors, and a concierge called Baran requested work, but Quatremère insisted that he could not grant favours and the Directory of the Department urged him to mitigate strife by employing locals ahead of outsiders.[40]

---

[35] AN, F13 1933: Quatremère to Cellerier (11 Oct. 1791); BHVP, ms. 814, fol. 436: Quatremère to Rondelet; Quatremère resisted demands to surrender the chariot but was obliged to lend it for the Festival of Liberty (AN, F13 333: letters dated 1 Feb. 1792, 23 and 26 April 1792). Houdon's Rousseau progressed during 1791–2, but lost momentum after August 1792 and was never completed; see L. Réau, *Houdon: sa vie et son oeuvre*, vol. 1 (Paris, 1964), p. 424. Quatremère, *Rapport* (1792), p. 31. Quatremère first mentioned this colossal *Patrie* in writing in November 1792, but he described what he claimed was an earlier drawing depicting the subject.

[36] C. Chaisneau, *Le Panthéon français, ou discours sur les honneurs publics décernés par la nation à la mémoire des grands hommes* (Dijon, 1792), pp. 9–10.

[37] S. Kaplan, *La fin des corporations* (Paris, 2001), ch. 15; Potofosky, *Constructing Paris*, ch. 2.

[38] *PVCIP*, pp. 281–4; AN, F13 333: Quatremère's secretary to Durouseau (11 Oct. 1791); AN, F13 1938 documents the numbers of workers employed and shows that between July 1791 and early 1792 Quatremère reduced the number of masons by more than two-thirds.

[39] AN, F13 1137: Pierre Poncet file contains Quatremère's memorandum (20 Sept. 1791); AN, F7 4884 79: Pierre Poncet file documents how denunciations by workers led to Poncet's arrest.

[40] AN: F13 325 and F13 333, files for recommendations and complaints. In 1792, many ornamental sculptors requested work. Some demands reached the Legislative Assembly—*AP*, vol. 36, p. 279. Even Quatremère's father wrote on 23 March 1792 to recommend a sculptor called Moret. Quatremère had a list of one hundred sculptors to rehire if work became available.

124 QUATREMÈRE DE QUINCY

Complaints about his management and on-site injuries escalated after spring 1792 when politics became more partisan. Radical national representatives spotted an opportunity to undermine the relatively conservative Directory of the Department by attacking the Panthéon administration.[41] The national representative François-Valentin Mulot, a former librarian in the abbey of Saint-Victor turned cheerleader for the constitutional clergy, thus took up the cause of a sacked ornamental sculptor called Guibert, who complained about corruption and explained that Quatremère was 'more of a literary man than a builder'.[42] Several months later in July, Mulot widened his attack to demand that work cease until the Commune of the Arts had reported. Mulot also criticized costs, the selection of sculptors, and lack of independent oversight. Quatremère responded angrily, arguing that twenty years studying and ten years travelling to 'understand, research and compare the most beautiful monuments of antiquity and of Europe' should inspire confidence in his ability to determine matters of art and taste. He justified measures that he had already taken, such as suppressing the lantern tower and removing 'miserable puerilities' from inside the building.[43] Only reactionaries objected to his efforts, he insisted with a disingenuous rhetorical flourish; they were saddened to lose an edifice created for Catholic worship and allow him to complete a monument 'synonymous with the revolution'.[44]

Quatremère went into hiding and temporarily withdrew from his role at the Panthéon during the overthrow of the monarchy. He was therefore lying low during the decree to destroy 'all monuments containing traces of feudalism ... that remain in churches or other public places', the election of the Convention, and the declaration of the Republic.[45] However, despite facing dangers, in October he resumed work and returned to the administration's new office on 253 rue de Bac.[46] Over the next eighteen months, he used his role to feign support for the Republic whilst secretly joining Pastoret and André Chénier on an illegal counter-revolutionary committee.[47]

---

[41] AN, F13 333.

[42] AN: F13 1137, 'Memoire pour Joseph Guibert'; and F13 1138, which contains reclamations and Quatremère's responses. Guibert's complaints reached the Assembly in March 1792—AP, vol. 39, p. 380. Mulot wrote to the Directory of the Department on 13 June and Quatremère responded on 16 June (F13 1137). On Mulot, see M. Tourneaux, 'Notice préliminaire', in 'Journal intime de l'abbé Mulot, bibliothécaire et grand-prieur de l'abbaye de Saint-Victor (1777–1782)', Mémoires de la Société de l'histoire de Paris et de l'Ile-de-France, vol. 29 (1902), pp. 19–36.

[43] AN, F13 1935: letter to Roederer dated 1 Aug. 1792.

[44] AN: F13 333A: 'R' file, Quatremère to Roederer, no. 172, undated letter; F13 325A: Roederer to Quatremère (29 July 1792).

[45] AP, vol. 48, pp. 115–16.

[46] AN, F13 335: letter dated 12 July 1792. This letter shows that the office relocated after Quatremère asked for more funding and resisted sharing the Collège des Quatre-Nations with colleagues from the Committee of Public Instruction.

[47] Pierre-Jean David d'Angers noted Pastoret recalling how in 1794 he 'burnt all papers that could have compromised our committee's members'. Cited in La Province d'Anjou, vol. 4 (1929), p. 31. See also H. Jouin, David d'Angers: sa vie, son oeuvre, ses écrits et ses contemporains, vol. 1 (Paris, 1878), p. 380.

No evidence survives that sheds light on Quatremère's hopes and fears during this turbulent period. The Girondin faction initially dominated the Convention, which banished émigrés, tried Louis XVI, imposed the death penalty for advocating monarchy and threatening the Republic, and promised to help foreign peoples overthrow tyrants. However, the Girondins were discredited after they equivocated over the king's fate and introduced repressive measures in response to military defeats, defections, and civil war. They were finally overthrown in June when their attempt to weaken the Parisian popular movement sparked uprisings and the arrest of thirty-one of their deputies and ministers. The Montagnards, left-wing deputies occupying benches at the top of the Salle du Manège, then dominated the Convention and saved the Republic by expanding state power, mobilizing resources, creating the revolutionary army, concentrating power in the Committee of Public Safety and Committee of General Security, and placating popular demands by restricting prices and arresting suspects.[48]

Quatremère's situation worsened in September 1793 when David and other members of the Committee of General Security issued an arrest warrant. Their motive is unclear, but his political reputation and record dealing with labour disputes aroused suspicion.[49] The timing suggests that the warrant was connected to the declining influence of Danton, his 'protector extraordinaire'.[50] On 10 September, Claude-Louis Bonefant, police commissioner for the section Fontaine-de-Grenelle, and several of his men entered Quatremère's first-floor apartment on the rue du Bac. They carried a warrant to take him to Sainte-Pélagie house of arrest and search his property. However, Quatremère cited a law allowing civil servants to remain under house arrest at their own expense and the police uncovered no incriminating evidence. After undertaking the 'most exact examination', seizing papers from a desk and small glazed wardrobe in the library and searching through a cabinet on the ground floor between the court and garden, Bonenfant reported finding 'letters and memoranda concerning the sciences and arts' rather than any suspicious documents.[51]

Quatremère lived under surveillance during the crisis months that followed, when it seemed that foreign invasion and the federalist revolt would destroy the Republic. Prominent figures from the early Revolution, such as Bailly and Barnave, were executed. The Quatremère family's wealth attracted attention in this political climate. In January 1794, the Revolutionary Tribunal found Marc-Étienne Quatremère guilty

---

[48] Tackett, *The Coming of the Terror*, pp. 245–79.

[49] Earlier biographies suggest that the warrant resulted from denunciations by Quatremère's brother and Marat (Jouin, *Quatremère*, p. 29), but his brother remained incarcerated in the Hague and Marat was assassinated in July.

[50] Cited in Jouin, *Quatremère*, pp. 26–7. Quatremère used these words when recounting to Leclère how he turned to Danton when Leclère's mother was arrested.

[51] Archives de Paris: D10U1 3, dossier labelled 'Septembre 1793, an 2'. On Bonenfant, see A. Soboul and R. Monnier, *Répertoire du personnel sectionnaire parisien en l'an II* (Paris, 1985), p. 432.

126 QUATREMÈRE DE QUINCY

of 'complicity with unfaithful suppliers'. Despite his argument that he opposed tyranny, behaved charitably, and used the family textile business to clothe military volunteers at a fair price, the Tribunal concluded that his ownership of a large shop enabled him to finance enemies of the Revolution and that his charitable acts merely satisfied his 'fanaticism'.[52] Marc-Étienne was guillotined on 21 January and his widow was barred from inheriting his property.[53]

These circumstances help explain Quatremère's outward acquiescence with the Revolution as the administrator of the Panthéon. He adopted the revolutionary calendar in correspondence, agreed to use broken-up religious statues to pave around the Panthéon, and helped the ornamental sculptor La Salle 'destroy the signs of feudality' from the nearby Saint-Étienne-du-Mont.[54]

However, despite pressure to conform to Robespierre's republic of virtue and David's symbolic language, Quatremère stuck to his earlier vision in most respects. Structural work continued as planned: the towers and lantern were demolished; newly quarried stone paved the nave; and the interior became more sombre by removing ornaments and reducing light entering the remaining windows, whose glass was made less translucent.[55] Similarly, his plan for the surrounding area remained that of 1792. In April 1793, he simply repeated this idea when he wrote that the area should be sufficiently large to frame the Panthéon but not so large that it reduced the impression of the structure's size.[56]

He also remained wedded to his sculptural programme and used his role to help sculptors execute their earlier designs. For instance, in 1793 he oversaw the execution and installation of bas-reliefs for the west front.[57] He remained committed to Dejoux's *Renown*: this colossus was delayed by wartime shortages and attacked by the Paris Commune as a 'ridiculous work' that 'showed neither genius nor talent', but Quatremère acquired a studio for upscaling and casting the model. He argued that the finished work would be larger and cheaper than statues of kings and that the Academy of Sciences could use its pedestal as an observatory.[58]

---

[52] Barthélemy-Saint-Hilaire, 'Notice sur Étienne Quatremère', pp. 709–10; trial extracts appeared in *Pétition de la section des Marchés... à la Convention nationale, le 21 ventôse 3e année républicaine, tendante principalement à rétablir honorablement la mémoire du citoyen Quatremère, marchand de draps, rue Denis, assassiné au tribunal révolutionnaire* (Paris, 1795), p. 3.

[53] AN, T 1662, no. 1.   [54] AN: F13 333, 20 Sept. 1793; F13 325A, 18 Sept. 1793.

[55] Quatremère, *Rapport* (1793), pp. 15–16, 40–4.

[56] AN, F13 333, no. 302. In this memorandum, Quatremère presented options to the Directory of the Department and argued in favour of a medium-sized area around the Panthéon. His correspondence with Camus and Mitte shows his concern with demolishing neighbouring houses (F13 333: 1 and 16 Sept. 1793 and 18 Sept. 1793). During his imprisonment, his successors at the Panthéon briefly revived the idea of a large wooden area—'Rapport sur le Panthéon', 21 May 1794, BHVP, ms. 814, no. 129.

[57] Quatremère, *Rapport* (1793), p. 9. Boichot was paid 7,000 livres and his peers were paid 4,000 livres.

[58] M. Guillaume, ed., *Procès-verbaux du Comité d'instruction publique de la Convention nationale*, vol. 3 (Paris, 1897), p. 6; AN: F13 1935: Quatremère's report to the Directory of the Department (30 May 1793); F13 333; BHVP, ms. 814, doc. 442, 10 April 1793, and ms. CP 3435, fol. 129: 'Rapport sur le Panthéon'; Quatremère, *Rapport* (1793), pp. 16–19.

Even most parts of the decorative programme finalized *after* the second revolution generally conformed to his earlier vision. For instance, the freestanding sculptures that stood before the Panthéon corresponded to the bas-reliefs behind them and therefore alluded to an earlier moment.[59] On closer reflection, even Boichot's 'Strength', represented as a pensive Hercules, could not have been intended as a radical republican statement. Boichot rehearsed an earlier Gallic 'eloquent Hercules' who served the people; he did not anticipate the terrifying colossus that David later planned for the Île de la Cité in which Hercules became a symbol of the sovereign people crushing federalism.[60] The outmodedness of Boichot's Hercules was not lost on viewers by 1794. One observer asked why Boichot had represented 'the French people' with an aged Hercules and suggested that a standing, adolescent Hercules suited a people 'rejuvenated by liberty'.[61]

In the same vein, Quatremère retained his scheme for the internal triangular pendentive bas-reliefs in which he wanted to provide 'a sustained course in the essential virtues of man and the citizen' and to show how Philosophy gave rise to the Sciences and Arts that collectively triumphed in Patriotism.[62] Although these pendentives were designed and executed under the Republic, just three of the twenty displayed discernibly republican imagery, here in the form of ruined crowns and sceptres, a beehive, and allusions to the revolutionary calendar. The greater part of the scheme for the pendentives instead reflected the fact that Quatremère formed his vision in 1791 and, before August 1792, assigned his sculptors allegorical subjects that reiterated themes and symbols that were already used elsewhere in the Panthéon.[63] Entering the west nave, visitors could admire reliefs dedicated to 'Philosophy': Jean-Baptiste Stouf represented 'History' through Clio; Louis Auger represented 'Political science' with Force and Wisdom; Pierre-Nicolas Beavallet illustrated 'Morality' by depicting a woman teaching a young man; and, to represent 'Legislation', Antoine Léonard du Pasquier showed a scene adapted from Plutarch that showed Lycurgus of Sparta displaying his legal code before a beehive.

---

[59] Quatremère, *Rapport* (1792), pp. 14–15; idem, *Rapport* (1793), pp. 13–14, stated that five bas-reliefs were finished.

[60] Boichot later produced a scaled-down bronze version, *Seated Hercules* (1795). On the meaning of Hercules, see L. Hunt, *Politics, Culture and Class in the French Revolution* (Los Angeles, 1984), pp. 94–117; J.-C. Benzaken, 'Hercule dans la Révolution française (1789–1799) ou les "Nouveaux travaux d'Hercule"', in M. Vovelle, ed., *Les images de la Révolution française* (Paris, 1989), pp. 203–14; R. Reichardt, 'The Heroic Deeds of the New Hercules', in I. Germani and R. Swales, eds, *Symbols, Myths and Images of the French Revolution* (Regina, 1998), pp. 37–45.

[61] BHVP, ms. 814, no. 132.

[62] Quatremère made a similar argument in his *Letters on the Plan to Abduct the Monuments of Art from Italy* (1796), but in this later writing he described how the Arts and Sciences combined to create cosmopolitan 'civilization' rather than French patriotism.

[63] None of these pendentive reliefs survived in situ and only Pasquier and Beauvallet's works are visible in N.-M. Chapu, *Vues de l'église Sainte-Geneviève* (1826). However, one can gloss some sense of their style from Claude Ramey's plaster model (Musée Carnavalet, S3351) and from minor decorative works representing winged animals, which remain in situ around the west nave elliptical dome.

128 QUATREMÈRE DE QUINCY

If visitors turned left into the north nave, they could next admire subjects illustrating the Sciences: Louis Antoine Baccarit depicted 'Physics' as a woman unveiling Nature; Lucas showed the '*Patrie* crowning Agriculture'; François Marie Suzanne showed 'Geometry' mapping France with the help of Theory; and Francois-Nicolas Delaistre depicted 'Astronomy' showing Chronology the September equinox marking the new era. If visitors crossed into the south nave they could then admire reliefs symbolizing the Arts: Sebastien Chardin's 'Poetry and Eloquence'; Barthelemy Balise's 'Navigation and Commerce'; Ramey's 'Music and Architecture'; and Pierre Petitot's 'Painting and Sculpture', showing allegories of the arts holding hands over the fertility goddess.[64]

Finally, in the eastern nave, visitors could look up for representations of Patriotism, conceptualized as the ultimate fruit of Philosophy, the Sciences, and Arts: Pierre Cartellier represented 'Strength' with Hercules accompanied by Prudence; Jean-Joseph Foucou represented the subject of 'Trust and Fraternity'; François Masson echoed Chaudet's peristyle bas-relief in his 'Patriotic devotion', which showed a citizen expiring in the Patrie's arms; and Jean François Lorta represented 'Self-Sacrifice' through his depiction of women donating jewellery (a reference to Madame Moitte leading artists' wives and daughters in 1789 to donate jewellery to the state).[65] Exactly as Quatremère had envisaged in 1791, the four large pendentives beneath the cupola encapsulated themes from the naves: for these spaces, the sculptors Auger, Pasquier, Ramey, and Baccarit created wooden models of winged Geniuses of Philosophy, Science, Art, and Virtue. These models were installed by spring 1794 with the expectation that cast lead versions would eventually replace them.[66]

Quatremère thus continued directing the Panthéon much as before and was quick to explain that the project simply followed instructions he had received in 1791 to create a temple dedicated 'to great men'.[67] However, these real and rhetorical continuities should not blind us to the ways that he adapted after August 1792 to demonstrate that the Panthéon was in 'perfect accordance with all the progress of the revolution'.[68]

Multiple examples show, for instance, how he prudently heeded administrative and political demands. Facing financial constraints that reduced the project's monthly expenditure to under 50 000 livres, he sold discarded glass, resisted the army's demand for unused iron that he could reuse later, and abandoned

---

[64] Quatremère, *Rapport* (1793), pp. 28–35.

[65] N. Pellegrin, 'Les femmes et le don patriotique: les offrandes d'artistes de septembre 1789', in M.-F. Brive, ed., *Les femmes et la Révolution française*, vol. 2 (Toulouse, 1990), pp. 361–80.

[66] Quatremère, *Rapport* (1793), p. 39; AN, F13 325A, 4 Jan. 1794 (president of the Department of Paris approves the choice of artists); BHVP, ms. 814, no. 129: Commission des travaux publics, 'Rapport sur le Panthéon' (1794), refers to wooden models of the large pendentives. Claude Michallon was later tasked with Baccarit's work.

[67] Jourdan, *Les monuments*, pp. 162, 170.   [68] Quatremère, *Rapport* (1792), pp. 10–11.

the monumental painting on the underside of the cupola.[69] He also agreed to prepare the Panthéon for public viewings, festivals, exercises that encouraged 'good deeds...and instruction', and the honours bestowed upon Louis-Michel Lepeletier.[70] The pantheonization of this former nobleman and radical conventionnel cost 1667 livres and was attended by the Convention en masse. If Quatremère felt little sympathy for this regicide assassinated in January 1793, he nevertheless ensured that his tomb was decorated like Mirabeau's for the sake of consistency.[71] (Fortunately for Quatremère, during his time as director the Convention lacked the means to carry out other pantheonization honours granted to revolutionary heroes).[72] The new political context also forced Quatremère to adopt a more democratic approach to labour relations. He thus reemployed Guibert, indemnified injured and exhausted workers, cut fewer jobs over winters, and stopped defending Poncet.[73] He also tried to feign the impression that he commissioned sculptures democratically. For instance, in November 1792 he described an open competition for a colossal sculpture group and in 1793 he organized an internal competition for the large pendentives.[74]

Quatremère also modified some language that he used to describe his decorative programme after August 1792 to simulate republican values. For instance, he quietly altered his description of the pediment bas-relief so that 'Patrie' became 'Republic' and the vanquished male figure became 'aristocracy subjugated'.[75] Similarly, he argued that Dejoux's colossus embodied 'the revolution's victory over religious fanaticism' and pretended that his order to remove royal symbols predated the fall of the monarchy.[76]

---

[69] AN: F13 1935; F13 325, no. 479, 26 Feb. 1793 and June 1793; BHVP, ms. CP 3435, fol. 129: 'Rapport sur le Panthéon.'

[70] AN: F13 333A, no. 157: letters from Committee of Public Instruction (11 and 26 March 1793).

[71] BHVP, ms. CP 3435, fols 126–7, and ms. 814, letter 25 Jan. 1793 from Quatremère to Rondelet; AN, F13 333, 24 May instructions. L'Huillier was paid for Lepeletier's tomb (see the Panthéon administration letter to L'Huillier, 25 May 1794 in AN, F13 207).

[72] On the cult of revolutionary heroes, see R. Monnier, 'Le culte de Bara en l'an II', *Annales historiques de la révolution française*, vol. 52, no. 241 (1980), pp. 321–44; M. Vovelle, 'Agricol Viala ou le héros malheureux', *Annales historiques de la révolution française*, vol. 52, no. 241 (1980), pp. 345–64; M. Biard, *La liberté ou la mort. Mourir en député, 1792–1795* (Paris, 2015), pp. 223–30. The Convention declared honours for General Beaurepaire, Chalier, Gasparin, Fabre l'Hérault, Lepeletier, Marat, Bara, and Viala.

[73] See, for example, AN, F13 333: no. 187, Directory of Department to Quatremère (12 Oct. 1792); and Quatremère's letters blaming Poncet for accidents (4 July and 6 Dec. 1793).

[74] AN, F13 1936: Quatremère letter to sixteen sculptors (2 Oct. 1793). See also how he declared a competition in Quatremère, *Rapport* (1792), p. 31.

[75] Ibid., p. 25. In his printed *Rapport* of 1793, Quatremère reverted to calling this figure *Patrie*, probably accidentally but perhaps to distinguish it from representations of the Republic inside the Panthéon.

[76] AN, F13 1935: Quatremère's report to the Directory of the Department (30 May 1793). Quatremère always planned to remove sculpted medallions of kings and fleur-de-lys, but he only instructed Rondelet expunge them several weeks *after* 10 August. See AN, F13 333, Rondelet file, no. 178, Quatremère to Rondelet (29 and 30 Aug. 1792).

Quatremère also introduced small but significant material changes to his original conception. He abandoned most of the now defunct text that in 1791 he had wished to inscribe on the Panthéon's west front.[77] He participated in the wider drive to modify and rename statues by overseeing modest changes to several sculptures that updated their contents without altering their compositions.[78] For example, under Quatremère's direction, Lesueur added fasces (a symbol of fraternal unity borrowed from the ancient Roman Republic) to a shield whilst Moitte omitted from his design for the pediment relief the Bourbon fleur-de-lys that he had included in the model in June 1792.[79] Moitte perhaps also proposed modifying other designs. This was surely why he produced his highly finished pen and ink drawing showing 'Nature accompanied by Liberty and Equality', the subject of Boichot's central bas-relief on the west front. Boichot depicted France as a joyful young woman receiving the Declaration of the Rights of Man, but Moitte proposed replacing France with another female figure who symbolized despotism, wore a Bastille crown and expressed consternation. The fact that Moitte only created this alternative design in 1796 hints at the limits to Quatremère's willingness to modify designs to suit political circumstances.[80]

Under the Republic, Quatremère also commissioned and designed new sculptures and decorative features, although few were installed. One idea in early 1793 was broadly consistent with his original vision in 1791: namely, to commission thirty-two figures representing the virtues of great men to crown the colonnade around the dome.[81] However, over the next year, his subsequent proposals reflected his willingness to appease the Montagnards. For instance, he abandoned his earlier idea for an altar featuring eighty-three figures representing the departments, which now smacked of federalism and risked raising the awkward question of how to represent rebellious departments. In its place, he humoured David's proposal for a column honouring patriotic soldiers.[82] (Quatremère later derided this column, but he accepted the idea in the first half of 1794 because David was exceptionally powerful as a national representative, a member

---

[77] Quatremère, *Rapport* (1793), p. 12.   [78] Leith, *Space and Revolution*, p. 120.

[79] Quatremère, *Rapport* (1792), p. 25; AN, F13 1936: Quatremère to Lefebvre (4 June 1792). Compare Louis-Pierre Baltard's 1821 drawing of the model with Edme Gaulle's 1827 drawing of the stone pediment. Digitized reproductions can be viewed in the Jacques de Caso Visual Archive: NEG-428-029, -030 and -032 and NEG-434-052 and -054.

[80] Grammacini, 'Moitte, Quatremère de Quincy, l'architecture et la sculpture historique au Panthéon', notes that the reverse side of the drawing in the BnF is signed and dated 1796.

[81] Quatremère, *Rapport* (1793), pp. 19–21. BHVP, ms. 814, nos. 438 and 440 show Quatremère wrote to Rondelet in February 1793 after visiting the dome and proposed adding these sculptures during a discussion about cleaning. He later asked Rondelet whether the colonnade would support stone statues, 8–9 feet high (BHVP, 6 March 1793, ms. CP 3435, fol. 128). Rondelet replied (AN, F13 333A: 26 Aug. 1793) that the weight would not pose a risk. In 1794, temporary wooden sculptures were installed.

[82] J.-L. David, *Rapport fait à la Convention nationale* (Paris, 1793). The competition for the column is addressed by W. Szambien, *Les projets de l'an II, concours d'architecture de la période révolutionnaire* (Paris, 1986).

of the Committee of General Security, and the dominant voice for the arts.)[83] In the same spirit, in spring 1794 he commissioned designs for faux-bronze doors decorated with low-reliefs depicting topical subjects that were intended to complement David's planned festival honouring the child soldiers Bara and Viala.[84] Contrary to his earlier policy of avoiding allusions to events, he also oversaw designs for bas-reliefs that demonstrated adherence to the Republic. For example, sketches for bas-reliefs under the small east-nave oval vault represented the history of the Revolution since 10 August 1792 and included subjects such as the 'fall of the tyrant' and 'establishment of the Republic'.[85]

Quatremère's most remarkable idea for republicanizing the Panthéon was to create a colossal sculpture group celebrating the new deity that was the Republic. Our main source for his idea is an engraving with additional pen and ink that displayed his name as the artist and engraver (Fig. 6.2).

His design shows a colossal enthroned female figure, described beneath as 'The French Republic' and yet clearly inspired by ancient representations of Athena.[86] She holds a rod of justice above a female figure symbolizing Liberty and a triangular level above a male figure symbolizing Equality. These figures already existed in the Panthéon's iconographical programme, but Quatremère here demonstrated his mastery of the new visual language formed after the downfall of the Girondins in June 1793. He thus depicted Equality as a young and destructive Hercules, and Liberty as a chaste female holding a miniature Bastille (the emblem of both despotism and freedom) and a pike capped with a Phrygian bonnet (the emblems of the sans-culottes).[87] His design was innovative because he applied his original understanding of ancient Greek colossal polychromatic sculptures and therefore intended, his report reveals, to place the sculpture group on a pedestal flanked by candelabra and decorated with bas-reliefs. Rondelet used ephemeral materials to create a scale model to display in the east nave, although Quatremère hoped that he could eventually create the group using the coloured materials that he believed the ancient Greeks had used in sculptures of their deities.[88]

---

[83] BHVP, ms. CP 3435, fol. 129: 'Rapport sur le Panthéon'.

[84] Lesueur sketched subjects—Musée Carnavalet, D 7793; reproduced in Deming, 'Le Panthéon revolutionnaire', p. 292. However, Lesueur never executed his designs because the doors were cancelled after the fall of Robespierre.

[85] Quatremère, *Rapport* (1793), p. 35; these reliefs were never created, but Bocquet was selected to create them after Moitte's drawings (Musée Carnavalet; reproduced in Deming, 'Le Panthéon revolutionnaire', p. 132).

[86] Quatremère, 'La république Française', BnF, undated [June 1793–March 1794?]. The design corresponded to the description in *Rapport* (1793), pp. 36–7, but he reverted to calling this sculpture *Patrie*, as in *Rapport* (1792), p. 31, and referred to the figure as carrying a palm (rather than a rod). His design resembled his later depictions of Juno and Minerva in *Le Jupiter Olympien* (Paris, 1815), plates 8 and 20.

[87] H.-J. Lüsebrink and R. Reichardt, *The Bastille: A History of a Symbol of Despotism and Freedom* (Chapel Hill, 1997), ch. 3; M. Sonenscher, *Sans-culottes: An Eighteenth-Century Emblem in the French Revolution* (Princeton, 2008), pp. 338–41.

[88] Quatremère, *Rapport* (1793), pp. 36–7.

Fig. 6.2 Antoine Quatremère de Quincy, *Proposed Group to Execute inside the French Panthéon*. Engraving with ink wash, undated (1793–4?) 39.5 × 28 cm. BnF, département estampes et photographie, RESERVE QB-370 (44)-FT 4.

The Convention continued to suspect Quatremère despite such attempts to demonstrate his commitment to the Republic and despite his appeals to protectors such as Sieyès.[89] He defended his work at the Panthéon in his final report in November 1793, which argued that the 'republic of the arts' rather than the political authorities of the moment should judge his efforts.[90] However, Quatremère was imprisoned in March 1794 once his work neared completion and Robespierre turned against Danton.[91]

During the previous eighteen months, Quatremère had republicanized the Panthéon with conspicuous yet limited changes to his original vision. His critics during the Restoration accused him of being a turncoat and cited against him his willingness to use recycled stone from religious statues and his decision to remove decorations and ornaments from the former church.[92] Yet such choices need to be seen in context. His decision to remove royal and religious symbols predated the Republic and he simply followed the instructions that he received to create a secular temple. Far from being an exponent of 'vandalism', he wanted to adapt Soufflot's masterpiece for its new purpose and to prevent it being destroyed or radically altered. If he rejected the idealistic view that he could complete the edifice by following Soufflot's designs, he believed that the Panthéon must nevertheless remain synonymous with Soufflot.[93] In this spirit, he insisted that it must remain 'the edifice [Soufflot] created', warned against making further changes, and asked for Soufflot's tomb to be relocated to the crypt.[94]

Quatremère's legacy at the Panthéon is most visible in his enduring architectural and structural changes. However, his decorative programme was also consequential despite being largely replaced in the nineteenth century. Its significance lies partly in the method he devised for appointing sculptors, which provided an alternative to using one master's studio or holding endless competitions.[95] Although considered undemocratic by his critics, his system encouraged coordination, emulation, and completion. The sculptors who worked at the Panthéon thus respected 'the enlightened administrator who directed us' and later Imperial

---

[89] AN: 284AP/9: Quatremère to Sieyes (16 Jan. 1794).   [90] Quatremère, *Rapport* (1793), p. iii.

[91] Quatremère described the monument as 'not finished but at least very close to being so' (AN: F13 207: report, 7 March 1794). He then summarized remaining obstacles (F13 325A, 8 March 1794).

[92] J.-P. Paroy, *Opinions religieuses, royalistes et politiques de M. Antoine Quatremère de Quincy* (Paris, 1816); idem, *Précis historique de l'origine de l'Académie royale* (Paris, 1816), p. 18; Quatremère, *Rapport* (1793), p. 1.

[93] AN: F13 333A, Brebion letter (6 Sept. 1791); and F13 325A, Delassus letter (19 Oct. 1791).

[94] Quatremère, *Rapport* (1793), p. 80. He asked the Directory of the Department to relocate Soufflot's tomb from the former Abbey (AN, F13 325A, letter of 2 Jan. 1794). He got his way in 1829.

[95] Middleton and Baudouin-Matuszek, *Rondelet*, p. 137.

134 QUATREMÈRE DE QUINCY

administrators copied his system.[96] His programme is also important in the wider history of patriotic symbolism because his choice of allegories paved the way for the unifying figure of Marianne. His iconographic scheme ensured that sculptures on and inside the most prominent buildings in Paris made the strong, fecund female figure synonymous with the nation.[97]

[96] Schneider, *Quatremère*, p. 45; AN, F13 325, no. 182: Boichot letter (21 June 1793) and Chaudet letter (27 June 1793); J. Lebreton, *Notice historique sur la vie et les ouvrages de M. Moitte* (Paris, 1812), pp. 4–5.

[97] M. Agulhon, *Marianne into Battle: Republican Imagery and Symbolism in France, 1789–1880*, trans J. Lloyd (Cambridge, 1981); L. Hunt, 'Hercules and the Radical Image in the French Revolution', *Representations*, vol. 2 (1983), pp. 95–117.

7

Standing for the Counter-Revolution, 1794–6

On 2 March 1794, the Committee of General Security ordered Bonenfant to detain Quatremère and place his documents under seal.[1] Bonenfant and his men found Quatremère asleep when they visited the rue du Bac on 10 March. They searched his apartment and seized eight personal documents, scholarly notes, letters in Italian, and a work on architecture translated from Italian. Despite finding no incriminating evidence, they took Quatremère to the Madelonettes prison on the rue des Fontaines near the Temple.[2]

This former convent held around two hundred people when it opened as a prison in 1793, but when he arrived twice as many were crowded inside. Common prisoners occupied large ground-floor cells on the north wing whilst 'suspects' such as Quatremère who were detained pending investigation lived in smaller cells on the three upper floors. Inmates later recalled the vermin, poor ventilation, stench of communal latrines, and bland fare served in the refractory, mostly white beans and occasionally potatoes. However, wealthier detainees tempered hardship by paying for privileges such as books and larger cells. Convinced that they were about to die, they distracted themselves through exercising in the courtyard, conversing, writing letters and memoirs, and helping impoverished prisoners. They relied on guards and recent arrivals for information about current affairs because they had no access to newspapers.[3]

Quatremère busied himself with art. He was escorted to the Panthéon's office at least once. He also sculpted using clay found under a pile of rocks in the

---

[1] Bibliothèque de l'Institut, ms. 2555, dossier 4, no. 44.   [2] Archives de Paris, D10U1 3.
[3] O. Blanc, ed., *Last Letters: Prisons and Prisoners of the French Revolution, 1793–1794*, trans. A. Sheridan (New York, 1987), p. xii; A. de Maricourt, *Prisonniers et prisons de Paris pendant la terreur* (Paris, 1924), p. 156; R. Cobb, *The Police and the People: French Popular Protest, 1789–1820* (Oxford, 1993), p. 8. Graphic representations of the prison include: J.-P. Mariaval, *L'artiste dans sa prison: plan du 1er et 2e étage de la prison des Madelonnettes sous la tyrannie de Robespierre, l'an 1794 et la vue intérieure de sa chambre* (1795), Musée Carnavalet (Inv. D 09217); L. Boilly, *La Prison des Madelonnettes* (c.1805), Musée Carnavalet (Inv. P1310). Memoirs describing conditions include: L.-A. Champagneaux, 'Notice de l'éditeur, sur quelques circonstances de sa détention dans les années 1793 et 1794, pour servir de supplément aux Notices historiques de J. M. Ph. Roland', in idem, ed., *Œuvrés de J. M. Ph. Roland, femme de l'ex-ministre d'intérieur*, vol. 2 (Paris, year VIII [1800]), pp. 432–7; A.-J. Fleury, *Mémoires de Fleury de la Comédie française*, vol. 2 (Paris, 1844), pp. 173–212; and P.-E. Coissin, *Tableau des prisons de Paris, sous le règne de Robespierre* (Paris, year III [1795]), pp. 21–55.

Quatremère de Quincy: Art and Politics during the French Revolution. David Gilks, Oxford University Press.
© David Gilks 2024. DOI: 10.1093/oso/9780198745563.003.0008

136 QUATREMÈRE DE QUINCY

courtyard, modelling a pair of game players and an allegorical *L'Amour et l'Hymen* that he gifted to a newly wedded companion. After he created a figure of *Liberty*, he suggested a competition for composing the plinth inscription. Poisson de La Chabeaussière's stanza took first prize—one wonders whether Quatremère later appreciated the irony when the Directory selected this same companion's *Catéchisme français*, also written in prison around this time, as an official text for primary schools.[4] Unfortunately, few documents shed light on who he met inside. He arrived when the prison housed the former War Minister Jean-Frédéric de La Tour-du-Pin and the more cordial Louis Thiroux de Crosne, former lieutenant general of police, but these men were guillotined six weeks later and there is no evidence that he socialized with them.[5] However, he befriended the prison's kind concierge, Jean-Claude Vaubertrand, and in mid-July struck a rapport with two former Girondins who arrived from La Force prison.[6] One was Luc-Antoine Champagneux, a lawyer from Bourgoin had worked for Jean-Marie Roland when he was interior minister.[7] Champagneux recalled listening 'with pleasure to [Quatremère's] conversation that was strewed with the striking traits and curious anecdotes with which his mind and memory furnished him'. However, Champagneux found his companion untrustworthy, opinionated, and ambitious:

> This architect-sculptor [was] more amateur than artist; he had brought back from his travels in Italy an originality in taste rather than perfecting his art: few monuments were to his liking. Even Saint-Peter's of Rome was not graceful in his eyes, still less our Panthéon that he ceaselessly scraped away at for the time it was at his disposal and that, had he been in charge, he would perhaps have torn down. Quatremère had the same destructive ideas in politics. Devoured by ambition for high places, he threw himself into all avenues that might lead him there.[8]

The other man was Francisco de Miranda. This Venezuelan revolutionary had served the Spanish army during the War of American Independence and

---

[4] Tuetey, ed., *Répertoire général*, vol. 10, p. 439; F. Vaubertrand, *L'humanité pendant la terreur, récit en vers, avec des notes historiques* (Paris, 1861), p. 45; Jouin, *Quatremère*, pp. 28–9. According to Jouin, Quatremère later cast some of these clay models and displayed the bronze statues in his apartment as souvenirs of his imprisonment. He inscribed on one plinth his name and the year in the old style, 'QUATR. DE QUINCY. F. 1794'. On the *Catéchisme français, ou Principes de philosophie, de morale et de politique républicaine, à l'usage des écoles primaires* (Paris, year IV [1795]), its author and its remarkable success in print, see J.-C. Buttier, 'Les trois vies du Catéchisme républicain, philosophique et moral de La Chabeaussière', *Annales historiques de la Révolution française*, no. 364 (2011), pp. 163–92.
[5] S. Perry, *The Argus; Or, General Observer: A Political Miscellaney* (London, 1796), p. 365.
[6] Vaubertrand, *L'humanité pendant la terreur*, pp. 5, 25–7, 45–6.
[7] P. Feuga, *Luc-Antoine Champagneux ou le destin d'un Rolandin fidèle* (Lyon, 1991).
[8] Champagneaux, 'Notice de l'éditeur', p. 433.

commanded a French army under Dumouriez until his failure to take Maastricht led to his arrest in 1793.[9] Quatremère shared Miranda's love of fine objects and he was perhaps drawn to his charismatic personality and fascinated by his travels around the world and encounters with famous individuals. However, their friendship was not based on shared ideals. Quatremère was devoted to the Crown and altar and later opposed plundering artworks whereas Miranda was an anti-clerical 'disciple of Brissot' (in Mallet du Pan's words) who had looted artefacts from Belgium.[10] Instead, their friendship was founded on mutual self-interest because each man hoped the other might prove useful. Whilst Quatremère sought military allies and intelligence sources for the royalist cause, Miranda wanted guns and money for liberating Latin America and formed alliances accordingly.[11]

In June and July 1794, around 1,500 individuals were guillotined in Paris. Quatremère and his companions could only gauge what was happening by the rapid turnover of provincial suspects held in the Madelonettes on their way to the Revolutionary Tribunal. Dramatic events at the end of July gave inmates hope. The Republic's victory over Austria at Fleurus in late June had ended the invasion threat and encouraged opposition to state repression. Robespierre withdrew from public life for several weeks, only to threaten to purge the Convention when he reappeared on 26 July. Fearing Robespierre's next move, the following day left-wing Montagnards ambushed him in the Convention and ordered his arrest, but the Paris Commune offered him and his allies refuge. By the late evening of 27 July, some 3,400 National Guards and sectional artillerymen assembled on the Place de Grève before the City Hall. However, their commitment to Robespierre proved illusory and, amidst general confusion, they abandoned their posts and left the way for an armed force raised by Barras and loyal to the Convention to storm the City Hall.[12] Those detained in the Madelonnettes remained ignorant of events because security was doubled on 26–7 July, but over the next days they received newspapers recounting the arrest, trial, and execution of Robespierre and his accomplices. Quatremère was amongst the 3,500 or so individuals freed from the capital's prisons over the next month.

---

[9] K. Racine, *Francisco de Miranda: A Transatlantic Life in the Age of Revolution* (Wilmington, DE, 2003), chs 1–4.

[10] W. Robertson, *The Life of Miranda*, vol. 1 (Chapel Hill, 1929), p. 68; J. de Cazotte, *Miranda, 1750–1816. Histoire d'un séducteur* (Paris, 2000), pp. 23, 152, 105–6; J. Mallet du Pan, *Correspondance inédite de Mallet du Pan avec la cour de Vienne (1794–1798)*, ed. A. Michel, vol. 1 (Paris, 1884), p. 257.

[11] *Archivo del General Francisco Miranda*, vol. 4 (Caracas, 1929), pp. 204–6; Robertson, *The Life of Miranda*, vol. 1, pp. 68–72, 147; J. Rodriguez de Alonso, *Le siècle des lumières conté par Francisco de Miranda* (Paris, 1974), pp. 191, 205, 210; Cazotte, *Miranda*, pp. 25–7; M. Benisovich, 'Le Général Francisco de Miranda et ses amis Parisiens (1792–1798)', *Gazette des beaux-arts*, vol. 6 (1962), pp. 345–52; C. Parra-Pérez, *Miranda et la Révolution française* (Paris, 1926), p. 387; Champagneaux, 'Notice de l'éditeur', pp. 403–7.

[12] M. Lyons, 'The 9 Thermidor: Motives and Effects', *European Studies Review*, vol. 5, no. 2 (1975), pp. 123–46; C. Jones, 'The Overthrow of Maximilien Robespierre and the "Indifference" of the People', *American Historical Review*, vol. 119, no. 3 (2014), esp. pp. 698–708.

138 QUATREMÈRE DE QUINCY

Their subsequent accounts helped form the Thermidorian narrative that legitimized hatred of Robespierre's 'system of terror'.[13]

Quatremère was freed in early August after spending almost five months in the Madelonnettes. He requested the removal of seals from his rue de Bac apartment and moved to a nearby address on the rue Saint-Dominique-Saint-Germain.[14] His family was embroiled in property disputes with the state following the death of his uncle in September 1794, and he also now quarrelled with his ardently republican elder brother, Denis-Bernard Quatremère-Dijonval. In December 1792, Antoine Quatremère had tried to exclude Quatremère-Disjonval from their father's will by obtaining a notary's deed proving that his brother was an émigré who had fled France and refused to return. However, once released from prison in Utrecht in January 1795, Denis-Bernard accused Antoine and their father of paying the Stadhouder to prolong his incarceration.[15] Such familial annoyances during the year after Antoine Quatremère's release did not prevent him from spotting opportunities to unravel the legacy of the terror and undermine the Republic. He and other royalists argued that the Convention remained just as illegal, anti-clerical, and regicidal as before. These royalists rejected the Thermidorians' discourse that disturbances such as had occurred during the year II could be avoided in the future by improving the populace. They exploited press freedom to turn public opinion against the perpetrators, institutions, and controls of the terror. They rejoiced at the defeat of the popular movement in Paris and, once the Jacobins were purged, seized the opportunity to dominate sectional assemblies.[16]

In this political climate, Marc-Étienne Quatremère was posthumously rehabilitated and Antoine Quatremère returned to royalist politics in September 1794 as president of the primary assembly of the prosperous La Fontaine-de-Grenelle section.[17] Quatremère also discerned a way to unravel the legacy of the year II by depoliticizing David's competition for funding the arts, which the latter devised in 1793

---

[13] B. Baczko, *Ending the Terror: The French Revolution after Robespierre*, trans. M. Petheram (Cambridge, 1994), pp. 136–84.

[14] Archives de Paris, D10U1 3.

[15] Archives de Paris, DQ10 1447, dossier 3193 (files labelled 'Quatremer fils condamne' and 'Bureau du domaine nationaux, 13 messidor an 4 [1 July 1795]'); D.-B. Quatremère-Disjonval, *Lettre du citoyen Quatremère Disjonval, adjudant-général batave, au Cen. Cochon, ministre de la Police générale, de la République française* (n.p, n.d. [1796]), pp. 1–43.

[16] On the wider context of these aspects Thermidorian politics, see F. Gendron, *La jeunesse dorée: épisodes de la révolution française* (Montreal, 1979), p. 174; L. Chavanette, *Quatre-vingt-quinze: la terreur en procès* (Paris, 2017); Jones, 'The Overthrow of Maximilien Robespierre and the "Indifference" of the People', pp. 708–10; idem, '9 Thermidor: Cinderella among Revolutionary Journées', *French Historical Studies*, vol. 38, no. 1 (2015), p. 16.

[17] *Pétition de la section des Marchés en masse à la Convention nationale, le 21 ventôse, 3e année républicaine, tenante, principalement, à rétablir honorablement la mémoire du citoyen Quatremère, marchand des draps, rue Denis* (Paris, n.d. [1795]), pp. 1–6; S. R., 'Quatremère de Quincy', in *Nouvelle biographie générale*, ed. F. Hoefer, vol. 41 (Paris, 1862), p. 286.

after abolishing the academies.[18] Quatremère' naturally prescribed subjects that served the republic of virtue, such as architectural designs for a 'Temple of Equality', sketches for paintings depicting 'The Most Glorious Epochs of the Revolution', and models for colossal statues of 'Nature Regenerated' and 'The People Crushing Despotism, Fanaticism and Federalism'. Even David's choice of banal architectural subjects—such as tribunals, prisons, and baths—chimed with the ideological imperative to survey and cleanse society.[19] David packed the competition jury with political allies—including Charles-Philippe Ronsin, Hébert, several actors, a gardener, and shoemaker—whose ignorance would favour artists devoted to the Republic.[20]

Yet Robespierre fell from power shortly after artists submitted their entries. Once David was imprisoned and attacked as a 'tyrant of the arts', the Convention was compelled to allow disgruntled competitors to elect a more suitable jury.[21] Competitors duly chose artists, including Quatremère—named as a 'sculptor' in the jury's records.[22] During the first half of 1795, the jury examined around 480 entries in twenty-five categories, sometimes convening for several hours several times a week in the Louvre's Salle du Laocoon, where the Academy of Painting and Sculpture formerly gathered.[23]

---

[18] Dowd, *Pageant Master*, pp. 78–142; A. Schnapper, *David témoin de son temps* (Paris, 1980), 146–9; R. Michel, ed., *David contre David: actes du colloque organisé au musée du Louvre par le service culturel du 6 au 10 décembre 1989*, 2 vols (Paris, 1993), esp. vol. 1, pp. 319–456; P. Stein, ed., *Jacques Louis David: Radical Draftsman* (New York, 2022), pp. 173–215.

[19] *Moniteur universel*: no. 236, 15 May 1794, p. 960; no. 243, 22 May 1794, p. 988; no. 261, 9 June 1794, pp. 1063–4. Studies of the competition include J. Renouvier, *Histoire de l'art pendant la Révolution 1789–1804* (Geneva, [1863] 1996), pp. 17–22; Jourdan, *Les monuments de la Révolution*, pp. 174–8; idem, 'Les concours de l'An II. En quête d'un art républicain', in M. Lapied and C. Peyrard, eds, *La révolution française au carrefour des recherches* (Aix-en-Provence, 2003), pp. 263–78.

[20] J.-L. David, *Rapport fait au nom du Comité d'instruction publique par David, sur la nomination des cinquante membres du jury qui doit juger le concours des prix de peinture, sculpture et architecture* (Paris, n.d. [1793]), pp. 1–6. David proposed twenty-two judges who were not artists.

[21] E. Lajer-Burcharth, *Necklines: The Art of Jacques-Louis David after the Terror* (New Haven, 1999), pp. 8, 74; J. Lebrun et al., *Essai sur les moyens d'encourager la peinture, la sculpture, l'architecture et la gravure* (Paris, year III [1794–5]); AN: F7A 1307A ('Propositions des artistes réunis en Société au Museum'—petition signed by thirty-eight artists); Eynard and Tardieu, *Considérations sur l'état actuel des arts sur les concours de peinture, sculpture, architecture et gravure, et sur le mode de jugement; publiées par la Société républicaine des arts et présentées à la Convention nationale* (n.p., n.d. [Paris, 1794]), pp. 1–12; *Moniteur universel*, no. 72, 2 Dec. 1794, pp. 304–5.

[22] AN, F17 1280 ('Assemblée des artistes réunis au Museum pour la formation d'un jury des arts'). Girault received seventy votes, Julien received sixty-nine, Fragonard received sixty-six, and Vien and Quatremère each received fifty-nine votes.

[23] Quatremère replaced Vien as president sometime after 20 Jan. 1795, when a jury document was signed 'Vien president'; J. Lugand, 'Biographie', in T. Gaehtgens and J. Lugand, *Joseph-Marie Vien, peintre du Roi (1716–1809)* (Paris, 1988), p. 44. Dufourny served as secretary and meetings are documented in AN, F17 1057, 'Extrait des procès-verbaux du jury des arts, ou rapport fait au comité d'instruction publique sur les prix que le jury a décernes aux ouvrages de peinture, sculpture et architecture soumis a son jugement en vertu de la loi du 9 Frimaire de l'an 3e de la République française une et indivisible', pp. 39–43, and BnF, Collection Deloynes, 'Extrait de la séance du juri des arts au sujet du concours' (2 Jan. 1795), p. 272.

140 QUATREMÈRE DE QUINCY

Quatremère was powerful as the jury's president and part of the delegation reporting to the Committee of Public Instruction. He humoured the spirit of the competition to ensure funding for artists, but under his leadership the jury undermined David's ideological plans in several ways.[24] The jury abandoned highly politized categories such as the column intended for the Panthéon, arguing that David's 'unintelligible' specifications stifled artists' freedom and resulted in mediocre entries.[25] In this vein, the jury wanted geniuses to be free to choose their own subjects and therefore for certain prizes reversed David's preference for state-determined subjects. The jury also moved away from David's colossal allegorical statues and instead favoured portraits of great men, redolent of d'Angiviller's commissions before the Revolution. For example, the jury recommended that prize-winning sculptors create 'busts of famous persons of the French Nation or great men of other countries, illustrious for their virtues and love for liberty'. Consistent with this approach, the jury deemed that the strongest category was for a portrait of Rousseau to embellish the Champs-Élysées. It therefore advised the Committee of Public Instruction to pay Moitte for a bronze version of his winning sketch, showing 'Rousseau as Emile with a child taking his first steps'.[26] Quatremère considered Moitte's work 'entirely appropriate to the destination' for which it was designed. On the back of Moitte's success, he persuaded the Convention to create another competition for a statue of Rousseau as legislator, destined for the Panthéon that in October 1794 had received the Citizen of Geneva's remains.[27]

Quatremère also changed how the jury operated. Eager to appear democratic after David's purported tyranny, the jury increased the number of prizes (so that almost one in four entries received remuneration and sculptors and architects had more chance of winning than before) whilst preserving the small number of lucrative prizes.[28] Consistent with Quatremère's earlier recommendation, the jury also proposed sending second-place entries to the provinces

[24] AN, F17 1057, 'Extrait des procès-verbaux du jury des arts', pp. 9, 36.

[25] Ibid., pp. 13–15, 23, 33.

[26] Ibid., p. 21; Gramaccini, *Moitte*, vol. 1, pp. 115–23. Moitte's design was considered the best of twenty-seven entries, but he never executed the work because planned changes to the Champs-Élysées made the commission redundant.

[27] AN, F17 1307A, dossier 3, no. 7955 ('Lettre d'Antoine Quatremère, président du jury des arts, au sujet du jugement de la statue de J. J. Rousseau'); L. Portiez, *Rapport fait au nom du Comité d'instruction publique, sur les concours de sculpture, peinture et architecture, ouverts par les décrets de la Convention nationale* (n.p, n.d. [Paris, 1795]), pp. 7–15; AN, F17 1057, 'Extrait des procès-verbaux du jury des arts', pp. 6–9, 14, 25.

[28] Ibid., p. 39, shows that 108 prizes were awarded from 470 entries in twenty-five categories. Portiez, *Rapport*, pp. 7–15, listed prizes. See also sheets headed *Jury des arts* (Paris, n.d. [1795]), signed by Quatremère and Dufourny, which conform to the mss. in AN, F17 1057, 'Extrait des procès-verbaux du jury des arts', pp. 19–20, 27–9, 34–5. Several architectural partnerships won multiple prizes for designing utilitarian structures: for example, the jury awarded Durand and Thibault 43 000 livres and Percier and Fontaine 11 000 livres. The jury still awarded painters more funding than sculptors or architects, but painters submitted more entries and the tables only included immediate funding rather than funding for the cost of creating award-winning designs in permanent materials.

and creating a museum in Paris for award-winning architectural drawings and models.[29]

Quatremère's jury was a success by several measures. In the short term, the jury persuaded a sceptical Committee of Public Instruction to fund a tainted competition by removing its associations with the terror and convincing the Thermidorean Convention that the Revolution had hitherto deprived artists of work.[30] Louis Portiez thus repeated the jury's argument when he reported to the Convention that artists had suffered 'six years of sterility'.[31] In the long term, the jury trialled a new system for distributing funding that rolled back state interference and recognized that leading artists and experts were better judges than politicians, scientists, and artisans.[32] Such was the effectiveness of the jury that in summer 1795 the Convention asked a subcommittee from it to review earlier commissions whose funding had been eroded by inflation. Quatremère immediately recommended additional resources for Dejoux's *Renown* given its novelty for sculpture 'in France and even Europe'.[33]

Quatremère thus walked a tightrope with the jury to expunge certain ideological components from David's programme whilst humouring the political elites of the Thermidorian Republic. He adopted a similar strategy in his *Précis pour Miranda* in which he used the Thermidorian lexicon obligingly whilst confronting the Republic's foreign policy. He penned this peculiar writing because Miranda, rumoured to be a foreign agent, remained imprisoned after August 1794. Quatremère initially ignored Miranda's plight, but at the end of 1794 royalists wanted allies opposed to annexing neighbouring territories. He therefore belatedly joined Miranda's friends demanding his release. 'I shall enjoy not enjoy happiness, pleasure or liberty', he reassured Miranda, 'until I can share them with our dear general, whom I cordially embrace'.[34] He helped with his *Précis*, a disingenuous pamphlet that appeared anonymously for good reason when Miranda's friend Barrois l'aîné printed a small number of copies in December.[35] The pamphlet is, however, rightly attributed to Quatremère: it fits his circumstances

---

[29] AN, F17 1057, dossier 3, p. 32. Quatremère wanted to create a museum of architecture after seeing Biscari's museum in Catania (*EMA*, vol. 1, p. 557). However, the idea for such a museum had more general currency; Szambien, *Le musée de l'architecture*, esp. p. 35.

[30] AN, F17 1307A, pp. 40–1.   [31] Portiez, *Rapport*, pp. 1–5.

[32] AN, F17 1057, 'Extrait des procès-verbaux du jury des arts', p. 2.

[33] AN: F13 325A, 'Extrait du procès-verbal du jury des arts. Séance du 21 messidor de l'an 3ieme [9 July 1795]'; F17 1057, 'Extrait des procès-verbaux du jury des arts', p. 21; F13 1135, citing the minutes from the committee created to report on Dejoux's sculpture, dated 4 Thermidor year III, signed Quatremère, Vien, Legrand, Pajou, and Dufourney.

[34] Parra-Pérez, *Miranda*, pp. 290–3; Cazotte, *Miranda*, p. 141; Robertson, *The Life of Miranda*, vol. 1, pp. 147–8.

[35] [Quatremère], *Précis pour Miranda* (n.p, n.d. [Paris, Dec. 1794]), p. 1. Miranda was imprisoned in July 1793 and Quatremère mentioned that Miranda had spent seventeen months in prison. There is no evidence that the pamphlet was circulated; it was not mentioned in contemporary journals and other printed sources and the only version that I have traced is in the BnF.

and correspondence, reflects his willingness to adopt republican terminology, and contains telltale expressions (such as the 'contagion' of ideas and the 'resurrection' of 'civilization' over 'barbarism') that he reused over the next years.

Superficially, Quatremère's pamphlet eulogized Miranda, disarmed his critics, and attacked the 'conspiracy against the human race' that had led to his imprisonment in 1793. It thus compared Miranda to the heroes of American independence, praising him as a man of action and a thinker, a patriot and an enlightened citizen of the world, and a friend of humanity and an enemy of tyrants. Miranda's biography, the pamphlet insisted, explained his loyalty to France because his birth in Spain's Latin-American empire, service to the Spanish Crown, and numerous voyages taught him to understand tyranny and love liberty. Miranda, the pamphlet enthused, was French because he was a genius and geniuses belonged to the land of liberty.[36]

More substantively, Quatremère used the pamphlet to advance his own argument against the Republic occupying or annexing western Europe. His argument was not based on specific foreign-policy considerations; he instead mobilized against the post-Thermidor Republic the very same discourse that its supporters deployed to distinguish the regime from its terroristic predecessor. According to this discourse, the Republic in the year II committed 'vandalism', burnt books, persecuted artists and savants, and 'paralysed education' whereas the post-Robespierre Republic nurtured the arts and sciences, protected knowledge, and provided patronage for artists and savants.[37] Quatremère mimicked this discourse only to imply that military expansion abroad would undermine these efforts to revive 'the sciences and the arts' after the reign of 'ignorance and barbarism'. His pamphlet thus noted how Miranda learned during his voyages that powers must value 'civilization' over population size and landmass or else suffer the fate of the Ottoman Empire, whose decline illustrated what happened when a power embraced tyrannical expansion and sowed the seeds of ignorance.[38] Quatremère concluded that, to escape the ex nihilo mentality of the year II, France must revive respect for the past instead of wasting resources on annexations: 'only the history of peoples, monuments, and the arts of antiquity', he insisted, 'can expand the philosopher's horizon and transform into a complete theory the fleeting observations that the brevity of human life otherwise condemns us to make'.[39]

The former Girondin Jean Pelet de la Lozère repeated several of Quatremère's arguments in the Convention, perhaps contributing towards Miranda's release in January 1795.[40] Miranda enjoyed his liberty and cultivated an ostentatious image

---

[36] Ibid., pp. 1–11.

[37] Grégoire and Fourcroy, cited in J. Popkin, *A New World Begins: The History of the French Revolution* (New York, 2020), p. 424.

[38] [Quatremère], *Précis pour Miranda*, pp. 1–11.   [39] Ibid., p. 5.

[40] *Moniteur universel*, no. 118, 17 Jan. 1795, p. 482.

that stood out during this exceptionally fraught period when living standards collapsed in Paris. Mysterious contributions from foreign governments and loans from the English merchant John Hurford Stone bankrolled his lifestyle.[41] He first lived near the Place des Victoires and then rented from Legrand and Molinos a luxurious apartment at 667 rue Florentin that these architects had decorated in neo-Grecian style. Visitors described how he furnished his apartment 'like a satrap', filling it with artworks and books procured by artist friends to the point that it was 'entirely adorned in the Muses and Graces'. He wined and dined an eclectic range of visitors: military guests included Jean-Charles Pichegru and Napoleon Bonaparte, but he also entertained the jurist Jean-Étienne-Marie Portalis, the diplomat François Barthélemy, and the influential centrist politician François-Antoine Boissy d'Anglas. His opportunistic approach to French politics kept everyone guessing because his ultimate objective was to liberate Latin America; he therefore avoided committing himself and allowed his name to be put forward for different posts and in numerous intrigues.[42]

In early summer 1795, he published a pamphlet called the *Opinion of General Miranda on the Current Situation of France*. His reflections reveal his ambitions and indicate where his agenda intersected with Quatremère's. Whilst Miranda repeated Thermidorian commonplaces about Robespierre, he criticized the current Convention on two matters.[43] The first was the constitution. Miranda concurred with Boissy d'Anglas and the committee drafting the constitution that the disunity of royalists and defeat of the popular movement provided an opportunity to stabilize the Republic. He thus tacitly agreed with plans to ban petitions, clubs, and demonstrations and create a government of proprietors chosen by an electoral college. However, Miranda disagreed over the executive: the committee wanted an executive chosen by the legislators, but he favoured a stronger executive consisting of one or two wise men elected directly by the electorate—a measure that would doubtless pave the way for dynamic military men such as himself.[44]

The second matter was foreign policy. The revolutionaries had renounced war in 1789, declared war in April 1792, proclaimed their intention to export freedom in November 1792, fought a desperate war of survival in 1793, and yet, since summer 1794, the Republic's armies had behaved as conquerors rather than liberators in occupied neighbouring territories. Politicians and generals debated

---

[41] Cazotte, *Miranda*, pp. 101, 106.

[42] *Archivo del General Francisco Miranda*, vol. 13, p. 102, and vol. 14, pp. 203–5; Parra-Pérez, *Miranda*, pp. 295–6, 325, 328; Cazotte, *Miranda*, p. 153; Robertson, *The Life of Miranda*, vol. 1, p. 149; Benisovich, 'Le Général Francisco de Miranda et ses amis Parisiens (1792–1798)', pp. 345–52.

[43] F. Miranda, *Opinion du général Miranda sur la situation actuelle de la France, et sur les remèdes convenables à ses maux* (Paris, 1795). Miranda finished writing on 2 July (p. 23).

[44] Ibid., pp. 8–12. M. Ackroyd, *The French Debate: Constitution and Revolution, 1795–1800* (London, 2022), ch. 2, surveys the debate on the Constitution.

144 QUATREMÈRE DE QUINCY

annexations but generally favoured cynical statecraft over teacherly idealism.[45] Treaties with Prussia and the Dutch Republic in 1795 therefore paved the way for military cooperation and wealth extraction. Victories, Boissy d'Anglas recognized, should lead to a glorious peace and 'an equilibrium that will maintain public tranquillity' at home.[46] Miranda opposed this dominant opinion and warned that 'vain...conquests' would, on the contrary, undermine stability and incite foreign powers. Since the ancient 'glory of conquest' was 'unworthy of a Republic founded on respect for the rights of man and sublime maxims of philosophy', he insisted that France should seek peace immediately in Europe, accept her past frontiers, and restore normal diplomacy. Yet Miranda's reasoning set him apart from Quatremère and other royalists: he wanted France to avoid further conflict with Austria to free up resources for destroying Spain's Latin American empire. Policy recommendations in his *Opinion* therefore focused on his vision for France's Caribbean colonies and negotiating with Spain.[47]

Quatremère humoured the Thermidorian Republic in public when a Bourbon restoration seemed possible. However, over summer 1795 royalist hopes dissipated: the collapse of the First Coalition removed the possibility that an armed congress might abolish the Republic; the death of Louis XVII deprived royalists of a unifying figurehead; the Quiberon Bay fiasco undermined the case for amphibious operations; and the Convention countered the royalist threat in cities by releasing former 'terrorists'. Worst of all, royalist hopes for electoral success in the new legislative councils were also undermined. The Law of Two Thirds ensured that conventionnels would retain control of two in three seats and that, in subsequent elections, just one in three seats would be renewed. According to its critics, the referendum on this controversial law was illegitimate given the low turnout, confusion, miscounting, and opposition in Paris.[48] In this context, Quatremère joined a league of writers and politicians that adopted the tactic of attacking the outgoing Convention whilst maintaining a prudent silence on Louis XVIII and the restoration. This league included former

[45] S. Schama, *Patriots and Liberators: Revolution in the Netherlands 1780–1813* (New York, 1977), pp. 192–244; T. Blanning, *Reform and Revolution in Mainz 1743–1803* (Cambridge, 1974), pp. 322–34; idem, *The French Revolution in Germany: Occupation and Resistance in the Rhineland, 1792–1802* (Oxford, 1983), pp. 74–6, 86–98; M. Rapport, 'Belgium under French Occupation: Between Collaboration and Resistance, July 1794 to October 1795', *French History*, vol. 16, no. 1 (2002), pp. 53–82; R. Kubben, *Regeneration and Hegemony: Franco-Batavian Relations in the Revolutionary Era, 1795–1803* (Leiden, 2011), pp. 227–49; E. Kolla, *Sovereignty, International Law, and the French Revolution* (Cambridge, 2017), ch. 3, pp. 84–120.
[46] J. Hayworth, *Revolutionary France's War of Conquest in the Rhineland* (Cambridge, 2019), pp. 179–80.
[47] Miranda, *Opinion*, pp. 13–19. The wider quarrel between exponents of 'immediate peace' and 'glorious peace' is expertly described in M. Bélissa, *Repenser l'ordre européen (1795–1802): de la société des rois aux droits des nations* (Paris, 2006), pp. 71–84.
[48] M. Crook, *Elections in the French Revolution: An Apprenticeship in Democracy, 1789–1799* (Cambridge, 2002), p. 126; Popkin, *A New World Begins*, pp. 452–7.

STANDING FOR THE COUNTER-REVOLUTION, 1794–6 145

Feuillant legislators (such as Pierre-Samuel Dupont de Nemours, Pastoret, and Vaublanc), literary figures (including André Morellet, Suard, and Jean-François de La Harpe) and publicists and polemicists (such as Jean-Charles Lacretelle le Jeune, Joseph Fiévée, Alphonse Martainville, Isidore Langlois, and Louis-François Bertin). Other royalists such as Jean-Thomas-Élisabeth Richer de Sérizy adopted more uncompromising positions against the Republic.[49]

As president of the primary assembly of the Fontaine-de-Grenelle section, Quatremère declared that the capital's forty-eight primary assemblies should discuss the Law of Two Thirds as a single body, much like the defunct Commune. Copying earlier radical tactics by using the sections as a power base, he proposed that electors in the assemblies elect a national government because no legitimate government existed.[50] His speech outraged local republicans such as Alexandre Méchin, who complained that Quatremère placed himself 'at the head of an insurrection' by encouraging assemblies to violate the Republic's laws. For Méchin, Quatremère's advocacy of popular sovereignty was 'more Jacobinical than Chaumette or Robespierre', 'more anarchic than … the famous Constitution of 1793'.[51]

The Convention ordered sections that met daily to disband, but the primary assemblies of the Lepeletier and Théâtre Français sections instead planned an insurrection and other sections, including Fontaine-de-Grenelle, followed their lead.[52] On 24 September, Quatremère gave a heartfelt speech that differed drastically in tone from his jury reports and *Précis pour Miranda*. He urged citizens to take up arms against a regime that ruled through 'theft, brigandage, assassination and usurpation' and that perpetuated the 'anarchy' that allowed 'the multitude' to outlaw 'entire classes'.[53]

The Convention gathered troops in Paris, asked Jacobins to attend primary assemblies, and crushed a revolt in nearby Dreux, prompting many sections to convene on 4 October and mobilize national guard units. Quatremère asked Guerin, captain of a company of national guards in Fontaine-de-Grenelle section, to lead around 1,200 citizens willing to take up arms.[54] The police section of

---

[49] É. Barrault, 'Lacretelle, un écrivain face à la Révolution française (1766–1855)', *Annales historiques de la Révolution française*, no. 333 (2003), pp. 71–5; H. Zivy, *Le treize vendémiaire an IV* (Paris, 1898), p. 17.

[50] Archives de Paris, 6 AZ 1240.

[51] A.-E. Méchin, *De la souveraineté des assemblées primaires, ou lettre d'Al. Méchin, membre de l'assemblée primaire de la section de Fontaine de Grenelle au citoyen Quatremère* (n.p., n.d. [Paris, [11 Sept. 1795]), pp. 1–12; *Censeur des journaux*, no. 22, 18 Sept. 1795, pp. 2–3, and *Mercure de France*, vol. 18, no. 2, 2 Oct. 1795, pp. 33–7, summarized Méchin's tract.

[52] *Censeur des journaux*, no. 20, 16 Sept. 1795, pp. 1–3; M. Alpaugh, *Non-violence and the French Revolution: Political Demonstrations in Paris, 1787–1795* (Cambridge, 2014), pp. 197–203; Zivy, *Le treize vendémiaire*, pp. 23, 25, 30, 36, 42, 43, 46, 86.

[53] Bibliothèque de l'institut de la France, ms. 2555, dossier 1: Quatremère, *Discours du Citoyen Quatremère prononcé dans la séance du 2 vendémiaire, l'an quatrième de la République française, de l'Assemblée primaire et permanente de la section Fontaine de Grenelle* (Paris, n.d. [1796]), pp. 1–12.

[54] Archives de Paris, DQ10 617, dossier 1942; Zivy, *Le treize vendémiaire*, pp. 23, 25, 30, 36, 42, 43, 46, 86.

146 QUATREMÈRE DE QUINCY

the Committee of General Security reported declarations made by Quatremère and Mevolon. The commissioner Pierre Bénézech immediately wrote to the Committee of Public Safety to warn that the section was calling the roll and taking up arms.[55] The police section of the Committee of General Security also received additional reports about developments in Fontaine-de-Grenelle and other sections.[56] The following morning, the royalist central committee in the Théâtre Français section ordered around 25 000 insurgents from across Paris to converge on the Tuileries. Quatremère led volunteers from his section but they failed to advance beyond the Quai Voltaire and cross the Seine.[57] The insurrectionists failed despite their numerical advantage over the Convention's forces because they lacked military expertise, cannons, munitions, and support from the Paris Agency and 'pure' émigrés. Moreover, Barras defended the Convention with help from several military officers who were in Paris and willing to command soldiers to shoot citizens in defence of the Republic.[58]

Quatremère survived a day of violence that left several hundred dead, but he was forced to hide when a military tribunal found him guilty in absentia and condemned him to death: by inviting 'armed forces to gather, Quatremère and Saucede [secretary of the primary assembly] committed an act attacking the government, taking the character of revolt'.[59] Posters appeared around Paris with the verdict.[60]

Although after several months the new Directorial regime stopped pursuing the insurrection's organizers, Quatremère lived in fear, went out only in disguise, and hid until the following August. According to his first biographers, he initially returned to his own apartment via an unsealed entrance before living with an artist and a former national representative. Vaubertrand later recalled that Quatremère returned to him in the Madelonettes, and that his wife then fed and looked after Quatremère until he felt safe to leave six months later. It is therefore likely that Quatremère lived under the care of the Vaubertrands between February and early August 1796.[61] During this period in hiding, Quatremère used a

---

[55] AN, AF II 52, dossier 389, no. 13: 'Rapport de la section de police du Comité de Sûreté générale sur la déclaration des citoyens Quatremère et Mevolon, an IV, 12 vendémiaire [4 Oct. 1795]'.

[56] AN: AF II 52, dossier 390, no. 33: Bénézech to the Committee of Public Safety, 12 vendémiaire [4 Oct. 1795]; AF II 52, dossier 389, nos. 18–32, and dossier 390, nos. 18–32.

[57] Multiple reports show that the Convention monitored Quatremère's speeches and developments in his section; AN, AF II 52, dossier 389, nos. 40–5. These reports bear out his first biographers' claim that he was 'one of the chiefs of the insurrection' and 'most ardent' presidents of the primary assemblies;'Quatremère de Quincy', in Arnault ed., *Dictionnaire historique*, vol. 17, pp. 167–9; J.-D. Guigniaud, *Notice historique sur la vie et les travaux de M. Quatremère de Quincy* (Paris, 1866), p. 61.

[58] Lyons, *France under the Directory* (Cambridge, 1975), pp. 40–1; Popkin, *A New World Begins*, p. 445.

[59] Archives de Paris, DQ10 617, dossier 1942.

[60] *Courier de l'égalité*, no. 1148, 12 Oct. 1795, p. 144; Jouin, *Quatremère*, p. 30.

[61] Zivy, *Le treize vendémiaire*, pp. 99–100; Maury, 'Quatremère de Quincy', p. 610; Jouin, *Quatremère*, p. 31; Vaubertrand, *L'humanité pendant la terreur*, pp. 5, 27.

pseudonym ('Quintidi') and coded language in letters that he relayed using friends such Legrand ('L.G.', 'my ambassador'). He passed the time sculpting (in one letter he requested 'a little piece of gesso') and researching entries for the *Encyclopédie méthodique: architecture* on ancient Athens and modern Rome and Florence. His relationship with Miranda remained sufficiently cordial for him to request books and news even though Miranda had offered to help crush the Vendémiaire insurrection.[62] During this period, Miranda attracted the animus of the Directors who feared that he might disturb the war effort on the eastern front.[63]

Quatremère refrained from expressing any opinions between October 1795 and June 1796, but his writings over the subsequent months demonstrate his incisive grasp of Directorial political culture. We therefore need to summarize political developments at the start of the Directory before turning to his reactions.

The Constitution of 1795 was intended to allay the Thermidorians' fear that the ignorant populace would corrupt politics and support a tyrannical dictator. The Constitution therefore consolidated the social order, narrowed the franchise, and created a weak executive of five Directors who were elected by representatives in the Council of Five Hundred and the Council of Elders.[64] The legislative initially cooperated with the executive because the Law of Two Thirds ensured that the majority of representatives were former conventionnels. Since ex-conventionnels feared that they would be punished in the event of a restoration, the majority of representatives chose regicides as Directors—including their first pick, the anti-clerical former Girondin Louis Marie de La Révellière-Lépeaux. However, the tension between the Directors and moderate and royalist legislators betrayed the regime's underlying weakness. From the outset in October 1795, the Directory lacked legitimacy and republican elites agreed only that they wished to avoid revolution and restoration in equal measure. During its first year, the regime's reputation fell further as a result of economic hardship, financial scandal, the failure of two paper currencies, and banditry in the countryside.

In response to this crisis, the Directory exploited fear of 'anarchy' and 'royalism' to legitimize authoritarian centrism, and deployed the army to suppress bandits and support extraordinary measures against domestic enemies.[65] Yet the Directory's desire for a stable republic in a large democracy required not

---

[62] *Archivo del General Francisco Miranda*, vol. 13, pp. 142, 206, 211–12. Quatremère requested from Miranda: J. Stuart and N. Revett, *Antiquites of Athens* (London, 1762–94), 3 vols; P. Ferrerio and G. Falda, *Palazzi di Roma de' piu celebri architetti* (Rome, 1655–70), 2 vols; F. Ruggieri, *Studio d'architettura civile sopra gli ornamenti di porte e finestre colle misure, piante, modini, e profili, tratte da alcune fabbriche insigni di Firenze*, (Florence, 1722–8), 2 vols; F. Baldinucci, *Notizie de' professori del disegno da Cimabue* (Florence, 1681–1728), 6 vols.

[63] Robertson, *The Life of Miranda*, vol. 1, p. 157; Parra-Pérez, *Miranda*, p. 356; Cazotte, *Miranda*, p. 161; Mallet du Pan, Mallet du Pan, *Correspondance inédite*, vol. 1, p. 332.

[64] 'The Constitution of the Year III', in Stewart, ed., *A Documentary Survey of the French Revolution*, pp. 571–611; Ackroyd, *The French Debate*, pp. 11–54.

[65] H. Brown, *Ending the Revolution: Violence, Justice and Repression from the Terror to Napoleon* (Charlottesville, 2006), pp. 214–16.

148 QUATREMÈRE DE QUINCY

just repression but also enlightenment to educate the animalistic, superstitious populace and to expand and eventually reach *civilization*.[66] This previously ambiguous word now became a coherent and familiar concept thanks to Condorcet's posthumously published *Sketch for a Historical Picture of the Human Spirit*.[67] At the heart of the concept were three convictions: first, that art, science, and morality developed together; second, that humankind, once perfected, would live peacefully; and, third, that universal progress must defeat revealed religion to create a world in the image of enlightened France.[68]

Since the Directory's ambition required perfecting the arts and sciences to analyse, understand, and improve the populace, the regime wanted to gather information by experiments and exploratory voyages and by enriching the Republic's museums, libraries, archives, and scientific collections. The National Institute—decreed in October 1795 and formed in 1796—reflected the Directory's endeavour to 'enlighten the world' whilst serving 'the general utility and glory of the Republic' (Fig. 7.1). Pierre Daunou, a founding member, called the Institute an 'abridgment of the savant world, the representative body of the Republic of Letters' because it united one hundred and forty-four scientists, savants, writers, and artists.[69] The Institute included many former academicians, but the controversial Second Class of Moral and Political Sciences owed more to Condorcet than the academies. Its task to analyse sensations and ideas, ethics, social sciences, legislation, political economy, history and geography was unprecedented.[70] Until the early 1800s, the Second Class was dominated by the *idéologues* even if few members were self-proclaimed exponents of *idéologie*.[71] This 'science of ideas' contained two central planks: first, inspired by the writings of Étienne Bonnot de Condillac, *idéologie* deemed that the mind was malleable (hence improvable) and mechanistic (hence comprehensible and predictable) because the mind formed ideas by experiencing sensations; second, *idéologie* held dear the optimistic belief that the inductive

---

[66] See inter alia J.-L. Chappey, 'Raison et citoyenneté: les fondements culturels d'une distinction social et politique sous le Directoire', in R. Monnier, ed., *Citoyen et citoyenneté sous la révolution française* (Paris, 2006), pp. 279–88; and B. Gainot, 'La République comme association de citoyens solidaires: pour retrouver l'économie politique républicaine (1792–1799)', in J.-L. Chappey et al., eds, *Pour quoi faire la Révolution* (Marseille, 2012).

[67] Condorcet, *Esquisse d'un tableau historique des progrès de l'esprit humain* (Paris, year III [1795]). Sophie de Grouchy and Daunou edited the work, which was published in April 1795.

[68] D. Gilks, 'Civilization and Its Discontents: Quatremère de Quincy and Directorial Political Culture', *French Historical Studies*, vol. 45, no. 3 (2022), pp. 481–2.

[69] L. Aucoc, ed., *Lois, statuts et règlements concernant les anciennes Académies et l'Institut de 1635 à 1889* (Paris, 1889), pp. 3–4, 10, 14; Daunou cited in *Moniteur universel*, no. 203, 12 April 1796, p. 809. For an overview of the Institute and the election of its members, see M. Staum, *Minerva's Message: Stabilising the French Revolution* (Montreal, 1996), ch. 3.

[70] N. Claude, 'L'Institut des idéologues', *Mélanges de l'École française de Rome. Italie et Méditerranée*, vol. 108, no. 2 (1996), pp. 659–76.

[71] J.-L. Chappey, 'Révolution, régénération, civilisation. Enjeux culturels des dynamiques politiques', in Chappey et al., *Pour quoi faire la révolution*, p. 135. On the subtle yet important differences between *idéologues*, see M. Saad, *Cabanis. Comprendre l'homme pour changer le monde* (Paris, 2016).

Fig. 7.1 Abraham Girardet, *First Meeting of the National Institute, 15 Germinal Year Four of the Republic [4 April 1796]*. 1798. 29 × 37.7 cm. Engraved by Jean Duplessis-Bertaux. Musée Carnavalet. Inventory number G.29149.

method of the natural sciences could help decipher laws governing behaviour, and thus that the scientific study of humans could transform humanity in general. One prominent member of the Class, Constantin-François Volney, had already imagined several years earlier a vast programme of experimental rationalism: in the conclusion to his most famous writing, he described representatives of the world asking enlightened legislators to 'investigate the laws that nature...has implanted in our breasts' so that they could form 'an authentic and immutable code' that corrected 'the errors of religion'.[72]

At a practical level, the Directory's civilizing mission needed public instruction to promote civism and reason. The Directory channelled its limited resources for teaching into the Écoles Centrales (so that by summer 1797 these schools numbered around one hundred) and specialized schools of higher education.[73]

[72] C.-F. Volney, *Les ruines ou méditations sur les révolutions des empires* (Paris, 1791), pp. 320–30.
[73] J.-C. Buttier, 'L'école sous le Directoire: fonder moralement le régime républicain?', in L. Chavanette, ed., *Le Directoire: forger la République* (Paris, 2020), p. 199.

150 QUATREMÈRE DE QUINCY

However, the regime envisaged republicanizing adults through newspapers, festivals, artworks, music, and the revolutionary calendar.[74] Much to Quatremère's consternation, the regime also escalated the Republic's war against the Catholic Church: despite nominally supporting freedom of worship, the Directory outlawed refractory priests, processions, habits, inscriptions, bell-ringing, and religious foundations, sold places of worship to speculators, replaced Catholic school primers with republican textbooks, and sewed division over the status of the Pope.[75]

After six months of silence, in April 1796 Quatremère decided to attack the Directory in writing but to do so anonymously. Between June and October, he published several writings in the spirit of the right-wing of the Clichy club that met on the rue de Clichy. Moderate conventionnels founded the club after the fall of Robespierre, but the closure of the Jacobins undermined its rationale and membership declined until late 1795 when it developed ties with the right-wing press and attracted royalists and moderate republican legislators. During the first Directory, the club provided a forum for debating conservative policies and coordinating initiatives in the councils and press. Members included former and current deputies and journalists, some of whom wanted an entente with moderate republicans. However, an increasingly numerous and vocal body wanted to restore the Bourbons by election or force.[76] Quatremère and other clichyeans benefited from press freedom, but he wrote anonymously because a law passed in April threatened seditious writers with execution.[77]

The two writings by Quatremère that appeared in early summer targeted the Directory's origins, domestic policy, and abuse of the arts and sciences. The first was called *Glance at the Events of 13 Vendémiaire and Those That Followed*.[78] Quatremère denied writing this treatise after Jean-Baptiste Louvet accused him,

---

[74] J. Godechot, *La vie quotidienne en France sous le Directoire* (Paris, 1977), p. 175; M. Hermant, 'Monsieur dimanche face au citoyen décadi: les autorités révolutionnaires et la liberté de culte', in Chavanette, ed., *Le Directoire*, p. 187; M.-C. Chaudonneret, 'Les ministres de l'Intérieur et les arts sous le Directoire', *Livraisons de l'histoire de l'architecture*, no. 26 (2013), pp. 63–73.

[75] S. Desan, 'The French Revolution and Religion, 1795–1815' in S. Brown and T. Tackett, eds, *The Cambridge History of Christianity* (Cambridge, 2006), pp. 557–64; Kennedy, *A Cultural History of the French Revolution*, pp. 160, 361; D. Woronoff, *The Thermidorean Regime and the Directory, 1794–1799*, trans. J. Jackson (Cambridge, 1984), p. 119.

[76] On the Clichy club, see Challamel, *Les clubs contre-révolutionnaires*, pp. 483–5; W. Fryer, *Republic or Restoration in France? 1794–7. The Politics of French Royalism, with Particular Reference to the Activities of A. B. J. D'André* (Manchester, 1965), pp. 207–34; J. Popkin, 'Clichy, Club de', in J.-C. Martin, ed., *Dictionnaire de la Contre-Révolution* (Paris, 2011), p. 181; J. Popkin, *The Right-Wing Press in France, 1792–1800* (Chapel Hill, 1980), p. 85; J. Godechot, *Les institutions de la France sous la Révolution et l'Émpire* (Paris, 1998), p. 485; idem, *La Contre-Révolution. Doctrine et action, 1789–1804* (Paris, [1961] 1984), p. 247; Aulard, ed., *Paris pendant la reaction*, vol. 3, p. 91; Dumas, *Souvenirs*, vol. 3, pp. 87–9.

[77] L. Chavanette, 'La presse livre: une épine dans le pied du Directoire', in Chavanette, ed., *Le Directoire*, pp. 96–104.

[78] [Quatremère], *Coup d'œil sur la journée du 13 vendémiaire et ses suites* (Neuchâtel, 1796), pp. 1–31. References to Merlin de Douai as minister of police and minister of justice indicate that Quatremère wrote most of this treatise in April. It was printed in June.

but a close reading leaves little doubt that he penned it.[79] The treatise betrays first-hand knowledge of primary assemblies and the insurrection.[80] Its style is consistent with his known writings because it contains recherché citations of Latin and Italian sources besides erudite references to French and Roman history and Greek mythology.[81] Most tellingly, the treatise contained vocabulary and arguments that he reused in his *Letters on the Plan to Abduct Monuments of Art from Italy*. Just as the treatise contained several words (*dechirer, tarir, fléau*, and *funeste*) that reappeared in his *Letters*, it criticized the Directory's expansionist foreign policy along lines that he repeated in the *Letters*: the policy was, he said, as 'baneful to the victors as to the vanquished' and harmful to 'the arts and sciences' and 'republic of letters'.[82]

Quatremère wrote his *Glance at the Events of 13 Vendémiaire* to discredit the Directory in general. However, his more specific aim was to persuade ex-conventionnels in the councils that they could not rely upon the army, dishonest republican elites, and the threat of unleashing the popular movement. His message to these ex-conventionnels was that they should renounce war, abandon laws against émigrés and priests, and ally with newly elected legislators and the Parisians who had defended them during the Prairial uprising.[83]

He started the treatise by describing the Directory's illegal origins. The Convention, he claimed, mobilized the Jacobins and the army to repress electors who 'discussed their rights in legal assemblies' and protested, without any 'plan of attack or means of defence', against the Law of Two Thirds and violations of electoral procedure. 'Formidable batteries of cannons' cut down men and women until 'thousands of citizens were exterminated' and 'Paris was inundated with blood and littered with corpses'.[84] Throughout history, the kings of France had behaved magnanimously when they reclaimed Paris, he continued, but the vengeful Convention labelled all its opponents 'royalists, counter-revolutionaries, and Chouans', dissolved the primary assemblies and hunted down their presidents, and manipulated elections to fill the councils with ex-terrorists whose choice of Directors violated the Constitution.[85]

Quatremère then compared the Directory's record since November 1795 to the achievements of kings over the previous millennium. His opinion that the nation originated with Clovis's victory in 494 drew upon the aristocratic-Germanist thesis, widely accepted before the Revolution, that the nation originated with the Franks; he thus discarded the more recent republican commoner-Gaul thesis.[86] Over the centuries, he inisisted, France's kings sought

---

[79] J.-B. Louvet, *Sentinelle*, no. 420, 17 Aug. 1796, p. 683. At Quatremère's request, a conservative newspaper denied his authorship; *Nouvelles politiques*, no. 329, 18 Aug. 1796, pp. 1322–3.
[80] [Quatremère], *Coup d'œil*, pp. 6–7, 11–12.   [81] Ibid., pp. 3, 11–12, 21, 23.
[82] Ibid., pp. 19, 23, 26, 30.   [83] Ibid., pp. 29–31.   [84] Zivy, *Le treize vendémiaire*, pp. 31–3.
[85] [Quatremère], *Coup d'œil*, pp. 3–12.
[86] This historical debate is explored in detail in C. Nicolet, *La fabrique d'une nation: la France entre Rome et les Germains* (Paris, 2003), chs 3–4; and M. D'Auria, *The Shaping of French National Identity: Narrating the Nation's Past, 1715–1830* (Cambridge, 2020), ch. 6.

glory and happiness for the nation: they oversaw flourishing commerce, agriculture, and manufacturing; they created charities and houses of education; and they provided enlightened patronage for geniuses, founded academies to cultivate the arts and sciences, and erected monuments that 'will always be the eternal seal of the veritable glory of France'.[87] For Quatremère, the Directory had already squandered this material, spiritual, and intellectual collective inheritance: the Directory 'shook Europe to its foundations', incited other powers against France, depleted the treasury, encouraged atheism, and 'confused all ranks' by favouring new money over old.[88] He concluded by lambasting the Directory's most conspicuous abuse: its harm to the arts and sciences, despite its promise to reverse 'vandalism' and proscriptions against genius. The National Institute, he complained, embodied this abuse, not least because 'scum and ignominy' filled its ranks at the expense of illustrious figures whose achievements predated 1789, such as the poet and translator Jacques Delille, the editor and writer Suard, the devout Jean-François de La Harpe, and the political economist André Morellet.[89]

Quatremère here wilfully misrepresented the Institute by repeating Lakanal's boast that the regime had excluded aristocrats and royalists, when the Institute actually included figures whom Quatremère admired, such as the moralist, historian, and engraver Pierre-Charles Levesque.[90] Yet Quatremère resumed his polemic several weeks later in an article for the conservative *Courrier universel*.[91] Since France's greatest minds had been murdered, silenced, or exiled, he argued, the Institute was filled with political appointments and 'the principal destroyers of the divine Christian religion'. Just as public speeches by Jean-Baptiste Louvet, Marie-Joseph Chénier, and Joseph Lakanal interested no one, he claimed, members who advocated 'vandalism' during the year II now delivered 'blows against science and the arts through their false theories'.

Quatremère next extended his attack on the Institute to other schemes intended to revive the arts and sciences. All such innovations, he predicted, would fail because the Revolution had already destroyed education and religious inspiration. For instance, the Écoles Centrales would produce 'barbarians' because they taught 'atheism' whereas Old Regime colleges fostered learning and ethics. Similarly, the Directory's libraries and museums would merely encourage sterile analysis: collections of books and artworks, he complained, cause 'cold argumentation and

---

[87] [Quatremère], *Coup d'œil*, pp. 27, 23–4, 19, 23.   [88] Ibid., pp. 23, 26, 13–30.

[89] Ibid., pp. 19–20, 26. Quatremère's first library included an edition of Panckoucke's *Nouvelle grammaire raisonnée à l'usage d'une jeune personne* (Paris, year III [1794-5]), which included sections by La Harpe and Suard.

[90] J. Lakanal, *Rapport et projet de réglement de l'Institut national: présenté au nom de la commission d'examen* (Paris, [Feb.] 1796), pp. 1–14.

[91] [Quatremère], *Le véridique, ou Courrier universel*, 4 July 1796, pp. 1–2. This article expanded on a passage in the same author's *Coup d'œil*, pp. 19–20, and repeated themes found in his other writings. Note, for example, his praise for Charles Rollin, the Jansenist rector of the University of Paris who revived Greek studies at the end of the seventeenth century.

scholastic subtlety that leads us at great pace towards ruinous barbarism' whereas the 'great ideas' of 'ethics and religion' nourished France's greatest writers and artists. Alluding to the policy since 1794 of plundering foreign religious artworks and displaying them in the Louvre, he concluded that 'one piles up in vain the spoils of Europe in vast museums' because 'the sacred fire of genius is extinguished amongst the ruins of altars'.[92]

---

[92] [Quatremère], *Le véridique, ou Courrier universel*, 4 July 1796, pp. 1–2.

8

Justice to the Papacy, 1796

The previous chapter described several pieces, written anonymously in June and early July, in which Quatremère used violent language to attack the Directory's origins, domestic policy, and abuse of the arts. This chapter will show how, over the summer, he shifted his target slightly to take aim at the regime's foreign policy and seizure of cultural property from Italy. As the chapter will demonstrate, he also struck a different tone in the pseudo-epistolary *Letters on the Plan to Abduct the Monuments of Italy*, which used conciliatory language that, he hoped, would appeal to politicians, journalists, artists, and savants who supported the Republic but disliked the Directory.

The chapter reinterprets the *Letters* in the context of Quatremère's desire in the second half of 1796 to attack the Directory, and explaints why he described his work as an attempt to render 'justice to the papacy'.[1] Yet my interpretation goes against the grain of how scholars have approached the *Letters*. This writing made Quatremère known across erudite and artistic circles outside France during his lifetime, and, in recent decades, it has become his most reprinted and translated work. Despite the fame of the *Letters*, however, what Quatremère was *doing* remains unclear. Modern scholars are more concerned with the reception of the *Letters* and its place in wider histories than his reasons for writing or what his text meant when it first appeared. Some scholars use the *Letters* to articulate their own reflections about decontextualizing artworks, often treating this work and Quatremère's *Moral Considerations on the Destination of Artworks* (published in 1815) as a seamless whole.[2] Other scholars situate the *Letters* in the

---

[1] This short title (*Lettres sur le projet d'enlever les monumens de l'Italie*) appeared on the title page. The frontispiece provided a longer title: *Lettres sur le préjudice qu'occasionneraient aux arts et à la science le déplacement des monuments de l'art de l'Italie, le démembrement de ses écoles et la spoliation de ses collections, galeries, musées, etc., par A. Q* (Paris, an IV; 1796). I will henceforth refer to 'the *Letters*' and cite my English-language translation of the first Paris edition: Quatremère, *Letters on the Damage That Would Be Done to the Arts and to Science through the Displacement of the Monuments of Art from Italy, the Dismantling of Its Schools, and the Despoliation of Its Collections, Galleries, Museums, etc.*, in idem, *Letters to Miranda and Canova on the Abduction of Antiquities from Rome and Athens*, trans. C. Miller and D. Gilks (Los Angeles, 2012), pp. 92–123.
[2] B. Sherman, 'Quatremère/Benjamin/Marx: Art Museums, Aura, and Commodity Fetishism', in D. Sherman and I. Rogoff, eds, *Museum Culture: Histories Discourses, Spectacles* (Minneapolis, 1994), pp. 123–42; D. Maleuvre, *Museum Memories: History, Technology, Art* (Stanford, 1999), p. 15; A. McClellan, *The Art Museum from Boullée to Bilbao* (Los Angeles, 2008), p. 251; R. Labrusse, 'Muséophobies. Pour une histoire du musée du point de vue de ses contempteurs', *Romantisme*, vol. 173,

---

Quatremère de Quincy: Art and Politics during the French Revolution. David Gilks, Oxford University Press.
© David Gilks 2024. DOI: 10.1093/oso/9780198745563.003.0009

history of heritage and argue that Quatremère encouraged measures to protect Italy's historic and artistic patrimony.[3] Finally, some scholars situate the *Letters* in the history of cultural property seizures during the Revolutionary-Napoleonic Wars. According to Édouard Pommier, the leading exponent of this approach, Quatremère wrote the *Letters* between April and July as part of a real correspondence initiated by Miranda. The *Letters*, Pommier argued, demonstrated Quatremère's sensitivity for artworks' spiritual and physical surroundings and constituted a 'counter-revolutionary' response to the 'revolutionary' doctrine that the fruits of genius were 'the patrimony of liberty'.[4]

By contrast, my interpretation restores the context of political action to the *Letters*. The chapter first shows how the quarrel over plundering Italy brought to the fore underlying ideological divisions. After identifying the origins of these divisions, the chapter reconstructs the genesis of the *Letters*, showing how this work developed at length a short piece that he wrote and published anonymously in late June. The chapter then examines the work's structure, arguments, and sources and shows how Quatremère crafted, as his Francophone contemporaries recognized, a subtle polemic against the Directory.

By my reading, the *Letters* thus addressed deeper ideological fissures to attack the Republic subtly. Without a wider understanding of these fissures, Quatremère's intervention appears moderate, even apolitical. I argue that Quatremère used the word *civilization* to signal his acceptance of a republicanized concept whilst simultaneously accusing the Directory of pursuing a policy that would destroy the civilization that it claimed to protect. Consistent with the Clichy club's strategy before the 1797 elections, Quatremère wanted his work to fragment support for the Republic. His most famous writing from the revolutionary decade was therefore both a heartfelt defence of the papacy and Rome's heritage and a disingenuous

---

no. 3 (2016), pp. 68–78; E. Alloa, 'La mobilisation de l'aura. L'œuvre d'art à l'époque de sa déplaçabilité', in Quatremère, *Lettres à Miranda. Sur le déplacement des monuments de l'art de l'Italie (1796) de Quatremère de Quincy* (Paris, 2017), pp. 128–57; D. Rico Camps, 'El Patrimonio integral y universal de Quatremère de Quincy', in Quatremère, *Cartas a Miranda, con el anexo inventario de los robos hechos por los franceses en los países que han invadido sus ejércitos*, ed. D. Rico Camps and trans. I. Pintor Mazaeda (Murcia, 2007), pp. vii–xxiii.

[3] Pinelli, 'Storia dell'arte e cultura della tutela. Les lettres à Miranda di Quatremère de Quincy'; Poulot, 'The Cosmopolitanism of Masterpieces', pp. 62, 13–29; A. Emiliani, 'Introduzione', in Quatremère and Pio VII Chiaramonti, *Lo studio delle arti e il genio dell'Europa: Scritti di A.C. Quatremère de Quincy e di Pio VII Chiaramonti (1796-1802)* (Bologna, 1989), pp. 7–14; idem, *Leggi, bandi e provvedimenti per la tutela dei beni artistici e culturli negli antichi stati italiani* (Bologna, 1978), p. 17; J. Merryman, 'The Marquis de Somerueles: Vice-Admiralty Court of Halifax, Nova Scotia Stewart's Vice-Admiralty Reports 482 (1813)', *International Journal of Cultural Property*, vol. 5, no. 2 (1996), pp. 324–5; W. Sandholtz, *Prohibiting Plunder: How Norms Change* (Oxford, 2007), p. 56; and Griener, 'Fea and the Defence of the "Museum of Rome" (1783–1815)', pp. 102–4.

[4] Pommier: 'La Révolution et le destin des ouvrages de l'art de l'Italie', pp. 7–83; *L'art de la liberté*, esp. pp. 415–49; *Più antichi della luna, studi su J. J. Winckelmann e A. Ch. Quatremère de Quincy* (Bologna, 2000); 'Quatremère de Quincy et le patrimoine', pp. 459–80; 'Quatremère de Quincy et la destination des ouvrages de l'art', in R. Démoris, ed., *Les fins de la peinture* (Paris, 1990), pp. 31–51.

156 QUATREMÈRE DE QUINCY

political act that aped Condorcet's *Sketch* and commended authors approved by the *idéologues* whom he and other royalists despised.

Quatremère's attacks on the Directory need to be considered in light of earlier reactions to the seizure of artworks and antiquities. When the French Republic seized cultural property from the Low Countries and Rhineland in 1794, those who defended the policy distinguished this legitimate 'confiscation' by and for a free people from the pre-revolutionary dynastic 'abduction' of 'booty'. The dominant argument for seizing foreign cultural property reformulated recent justifications for preserving artefacts found within France that represented 'superstition' and royalty: since geniuses had worked towards liberty and enabled the Revolution to happen, their masterpieces should be preserved in the new home of liberty, irrespective of what subjects these artworks depicted and irrespective of where they were currently located—indeed, France's museum collections must transcend arbitrary dynastic frontiers, because gathering, classifying, and displaying artefacts advanced knowledge and inspired manufacturers.[5]

Some municipal administrators in occupied territories opposed French actions and justifications in 1794–5; they argued that artefacts belonging to communities rather than sovereigns should remain in situ.[6] However, writers and artists in Europe's cosmopolitan centres remained curiously silent.[7] In Paris, opponents of the policy merely questioned the wisdom of importing religious artwork that might encourage 'fanaticism' and that would certainly lose its original meaning once displaced. For example, one critic observed that French citizens saw a painting when they looked at Rubens' *Descent from the Cross* (1612–14) in Paris, whereas Flemish Catholics had encountered Christ when they prayed beneath this masterpiece in Antwerp cathedral.[8]

The invasion of Italy in 1796 eventually yielded many more opportunities to seize cultural property. In March, when Bonaparte became commander of the Army of Italy, the prospect of expropriating precious artworks and antiquities seemed unlikely because he was assigned a secondary role in a general offensive to force Austria to recognize France's extended eastern front. However, his victories against Piedmontese and Austrian forces enabled him to impose demands. For instance, the Piacenza armistice on 9 May required the Duke of

[5] D. Gilks, 'Attitudes to the Displacement of Cultural Property in the Wars of the French Revolution and Napoleon', *The Historical Journal*, vol. 56, no. 1 (2013), pp. 115–19.

[6] C. Piot, ed., *Rapport à M. le Ministre de l'Intérieur sur les tableaux enlevés à la Belgique en 1794 et restitués en 1815* (Brussels, 1883), pp. 5–6, 12–14, 168–70; and B. Savoy, '"Et comment tout cela sera-t-il conservé à Paris?": les réactions allemandes aux saisies d'œuvres d'art et de science opérées par la France autour de 1800', *Revue germanique internationale*, vol. 13 (2000), p. 108.

[7] Gilks, 'Attitudes to the Displacement of Cultural Property in the Wars of the French Revolution and Napoleon', pp. 129–30, 134–6.

[8] Y. Cantarel-Besson, ed., *La naissance du musée du Louvre: la politique muséologique sous la Révolution d'après les archives des musées nationaux* (Paris, 1981), vol. 1, p. 33; *Décade philosophique*, vol. 3, no. 20, 10 Nov. 1794, pp. 287–8.

Parma to surrender twenty paintings. Caught unprepared, the Directory dispatched a 'Commission for the research of the arts and sciences in Italy'.[9] Once Bonaparte advanced into Bologna—part of the papal legations—in mid-June, he soon demanded artefacts from papal collections in Rome. Experts from the National Institute listed obelisks in the city for the Republic to transfer to Paris, and an official newspaper boasted that 'French iron' had triumphed over 'British gold' in the race for antiquities. In the Bologna armistice of 23 June, the papacy duly agreed to surrender, alongside military fortresses and money, five hundred manuscripts and 'one hundred paintings, busts, vases or statues' from papal museums, libraries, and churches.[10] In these circumstances, the seizures and the papacy's future appeared inseparable. For some republicans, Bonaparte's advance was an opportunity to reshape Italy at the papacy's expense: since they wanted Catholicism to play no role in French public life and blamed Pius VI for provoking civil war, they embraced the idea that Bonaparte should, as the Directors requested, head south to 'totter the tiara of the alleged head of the universal church'. Catholics therefore feared that the French Republic intended to abolish the papacy even if, in practice, the Directors and Bonaparte recognized that public order in France required them to cajole the pope into legitimizing the Republic.[11]

Whereas earlier seizures had attracted relatively little opposition in France, in summer 1796 Bonaparte's demands in Italy provoked a quarrel in Paris that Quatremère exploited to attack the Directory. The quarrel escalated because events brought to the fore an underlying ideological fissure about the nature of civilization and its relationship to Christianity, the papacy, and the French Republic.

This fissure combined both long-term and more recent divisions, examined in previous chapters. The long-term division concerned the contrary attitudes towards Rome that Quatremère encountered on his travels during his youth (see Chapter 1). French visitors had long admired Rome, but their opinions became ambivalent during the eighteenth century. Critics contrasted Rome's historical grandeur to its modern decay, compared present-day Romans unfavourably to their ancient predecessors, and blamed the city's decline on papal incompetence or tyranny.[12] Critics often repeated various tropes, complaining that: the Catholic Church oppressed men of letters; native artists languished without patronage; Rome was

---

[9] M.-L. Blumer, 'La commission pour la recherche des objets de sciences et arts en Italie (1796–1797)', *La Révolution française*, vol. 87 (1934), p. 69; I. Richefort, 'La commission centrale des sciences et des arts en Italie (1796–1798)', in M. Favreau et al., eds, *De l'usage de l'art en politique* (Clermont-Ferrand, 2009), pp. 98–114.

[10] J. de Clercq, ed., *Recueil des traités de la France* (Paris, 1864), pp. 276–7; *CAFR*, vol. 16, no. 9549, pp. 420–1.

[11] A. Latreille, *L'église catholique et la Révolution française* (Paris, 1946), vol. 1, pp. 225–6; O. Chadwick, *The Popes and European Revolution* (Oxford, 1981), pp. 452–3.

[12] Montesquieu, *Considérations sur les causes de la grandeur des Romains*, ch. 18; Boyer d'Argens, *Lettres juives*: vol. 1, pp. 42–7, 81–6; vol. 2, p. 172; vol. 3, p. 77; P. Grossi, *Pierre-Louis Ginguené, historien de la littérature italienne* (Bern, 2006), pp. 141, 185; Gaspard Monge, letter dated 30 July 1796, Bibliothèque de l'Institut de France, ms 2191, paper 8C.

158 QUATREMÈRE DE QUINCY

pestilent; the papacy ensured that Romans depended on tourism and the court; and Christians destroyed, altered, neglected, or sold vestiges of 'pagan' Rome. In sum, for critical French writers, modern Romans were 'barbarians', not the legatees of antiquity.[13]

By contrast, some French antiquarians and long-term residents in Rome— including the young Quatremère—formed an alternative discourse that praised the papacy's custodianship and stressed the need to see antiquities in situ to appreciate their provenance and topographical context.[14] For instance, Jean-Jacques Barthélemy warned that research was futile without visiting Rome because the 'pile of statues, busts, inscriptions and bas-reliefs gathered in [the Capitoline] through the care of the last popes' meant that 'one will never surpass the Romans except in Rome'.[15] In a similarly positive vein, Jérôme Lalande's guidebook commended how cosmopolitan Rome combined 'erudition, languages, antiquities, monuments and medals'.[16] This positive discourse became more fulsome after 1775 as a result of enthusiasm for the new pontiff, Pius VI, and the Museo Pio-Clementino.[17]

The quarrel in 1796 rehearsed these contrary eighteenth-century views about papal Rome, but it also reflected the more recent division over the Republic presenting itself as the guardian of civilization (see Chapter 7). For republican elites, the Republic needed to distance itself from the terror by forming a narrative that repudiated the year II whilst reclaiming the Enlightenment and 1789.[18] In the year II, they claimed, an animalistic populace corrupted politics and dispersed 'the greatest men' whilst terrorists planned 'to annihilate the sciences and arts'.[19] 'Talent was never more atrociously treated than under Robespierre, Grégoire thus reminded his fellow representatives.[20] For republican elites, the Republic's

---

[13] Montesquieu, *Voyages*, vol. 1, p. 262; Boyer d'Argens, *Lettres juives*, vol. 1, pp. 169–74, 195–200; vol. 2, pp. 178–9; vol. 3, p. 123; F. de P. Latapie, *Ephémérides romaines*, 24 mars–24 octobre 1775, ed. G. Montègre (Paris, 2017), p. 335.

[14] Andrieux, *Les Français à Rome*, p. 131; Montègre, *La Rome des Français au temps des Lumières* pp. 108, 110–11, 118, 462; Cagiano, 'La Rome de Caylus'.

[15] Barthélemy, *Voyage en Italie*, pp. 29–30.

[16] J. Lalande, *Voyage d'un François en Italie, fait dans les années 1765 et 1766*, vol. 5 (Venice, 1769), pp. 263–5. Quatremère's first library included the 1786 edition of Lalande's work.

[17] Quatremère, 'Appienne (la voie)' and 'Belveder', in *EMA*, vol. 1, pp. 63–4, 263–4. On the wider context, see Collins, *Papacy and Politics*, ch. 4.

[18] B. Baczko, 'Le tournant culturel de l'an III', in R. Dupuy and M. Morabito, eds, *1795, pour une république sans révolution* (Rennes, 1996), pp. 17–37; Jones, '9 Thermidor: Cinderella among Revolutionary Journées', pp. 9–31; L. Chavanette, *Quatre-vingt-quinze—La terreur en procès* (Paris, 2017), pp. 119–53.

[19] J.-L. Chappey and J. Vincent, 'A Republican Ecology? Citizenship, Nature, and the French Revolution (1795–1799)', *Past and Present*, vol. 243, no. 1 (2019), p. 116; Daunou, quoted in *Moniteur universel*, no. 203, 12 April 1796, pp. 1–2; Antoine-François Fourcroy, quoted in L. de Launay, *Monge: Fondateur de l'Ecole Polytechnique* (Paris, 1933), p. 129.

[20] H. Grégoire, *Rapport sur les encouragements et récompenses à accorder aux savants, aux gens de lettres et aux artistes* (Paris, year III [1794]), p. 4.

immediate survival required restricting the franchise and eligibility for office, suppressing uprisings and Catholic influence, and eradicating 'barbarism', 'passion', and 'vandalism'.[21] Yet in the long term, preventing another year II and perfecting humanity required the 'reasonable elite', in other words 'the best educated and most interested in the maintenance of the laws', to study, understand, and improve the populace at home and abroad.[22] This civilizing process required applying reason rather than obeying the general will.[23] Since 'the happiness of the French people' was deemed 'inseperable from the perfection of the arts and sciences', the Directory was preoccupied with elite education, the National Institute, museums, and preserving evidence of the past.[24]

However, the Directory's civilizing mission was contested. Clandestine radicals opposed the domestic implications of the hierarchical Constitution of 1795.[25] Other republicans were sceptical about 'the Great Nation' subjecting foreign territories and vassal states to this mission.[26] French hegemony, they warned, would fuel resentment and undermine the cosmopolitan ideal of peaceful cooperation. Inspired by Condorcet's description of the 'Tenth Epoch', they favoured using French political and military power to foster international peace, equality, and mutual progress.[27]

Attitudes towards Rome and the Directory's recent attempt to refashion republican identity conditioned responses in Paris to Bonaparte's invasion of northern Italy and seizure of cultural property. For the executive Directors and their supporters, the civilizing mission necessitated gathering cultural property. Seizures, they argued, would civilize French citizens, 'repair...vandalism', and refute accusations that the French were 'barbarians' by proving that they valued artworks.[28] Other justifications combined tropes about Italy's inability to preserve Europe's heritage with boasts about how French science would restore neglected artworks for the Republic's museums to display before a large

---

[21] Serna, *La république des girouettes*, pp. 430, 417; H. Brown, *Ending the French Revolution: Violence, Justice, and Repression from the Terror to Napoleon* (Charlottesville, 2006), p. 43.

[22] C. Schröer, 'La République contestée: combats de politique symbolique', in Chavanette, ed., *Le Directoire*, pp. 144–50; Buttier, 'L'école sous le Directoire', in Chavanette, ed., *Le Directoire*, pp. 199, 209; A. Fourcroy, *Rapport et décret de la Convention nationale sur les Écoles de Santé de Paris, Montpellier et Strasbourg* (Paris, year III [1795]); F. Boissy d'Anglas, *Projet de constitution pour la République française, et discours préliminaire* (Paris, year III [1795]), p. 27.

[23] Sonenscher, *Sans-Culottes*, p. 36; P. Higgonnet, *Goodness beyond Virtue: Jacobins during the French Revolution* (Cambridge, MA, 1998), p. 65.

[24] *Décade philosophique*, vol. 7, no. 59, 1. Dec. 1795, p. 446; *Moniteur universel*, no. 203, 12 April 1796, pp. 1–2; H. Grégoire, *Second rapport sur le vandalisme* (Paris, year III [1794]), pp. 1–12.

[25] Serna, *Antonelle*, pp. 304–15.

[26] On the wider subject, see A. Jainchill, *Reimagining Politics after the Terror: The Republican Origins of French Liberalism* (Ithaca, 2008), ch. 4; Bélissa, *Repenser l'ordre européen*; and Kolla, *Sovereignty, International Law, and the French Revolution*, ch. 5.

[27] Miranda, *Opinion du Général Miranda*, pp. 13–19; Martin, 'Les enjeux diplomatiques dans le Magasin encyclopédique : du rejet des systèmes politiques à la redéfinition des rapports entre les nations (1795–1799)'.

[28] A. Debidour, ed., *Recueil des actes du Directoire exécutif: procès-verbaux, arrêtés, instructions, lettres et actes divers*, vol. 2 (Paris, 1911), pp. 333, 516; *Décade philosophique*, no. 76, 29 May 1796, p. 441.

160 QUATREMÈRE DE QUINCY

public.[29] The Commission selecting artefacts considered its work part of a larger process. As Gaspard Monge explained to his wife, his task as an expert sent to gather cultural property was a small contribution towards liberating Italians from the 'imprudent charlatan' Pius VI.[30]

Royalists such as Lacretelle and republicans such as Pierre-Louis Roederer countered this justificatory discourse. They initially opposed the Directory's strategy in general terms. For example, Lacretelle warned that Bonaparte's reckless command risked empowering generals, impoverishing Italians, and unleashing a larger 'war of extermination' whilst Roederer suggested that Parisians wanted peace rather than conquests.[31] From early June onwards, several publicists expressed specific fears for the arts if Bonaparte reached Rome. The monarchist Jean-Pierre Gallais suggested that abusing 'the right of fortunate brigands' would undermine peace by inciting retaliation. For Gallais, confiscating artwork was thus wrong because it might prove impolitic.[32]

Throughout spring, Quatremère remained silent on developments in Italy. He complained about France's 'broken' affairs and requested news about foreign affairs in his private letters, but it was only in late June, when he learned that Bonaparte had entered the papal legations, that he finally decided to stand against art seizures from Italy.[33] In response to this news, Quatremère wrote two anonymous pieces for the *Courrier universel* in the spirit of the Abbé de Boulogne's *Annales Catholiques*.[34] Whereas earlier criticism of plundering Italy suggested that the policy was impolitic, his argument that the seizures would harm the arts broadened and deepened opposition in ways that encouraged artists and scholars to share their opinions.[35] Importing masterpieces, he predicted, would not perfect France's unredeemable 'vandals', yet the resulting glut would disincentivize state commissions when artists already suffered from the loss of Church patronage, that 'most beautiful of paths...to genius'. He urged the Republic to preserve 'masterpieces

---

[29] *Moniteur universel*, no. 12, 3 Oct. 1796, pp. 45–6.

[30] Launay, *Monge*, pp. 143–4, 147, 155, 161.

[31] J.-C.-D. Lacretelle (le jeune), 'Réflexions sur le système d'administration à suivre dans les pays conquis', *Nouvelles politiques*, no. 265, 13 June 1796, p. 1058; Barrault, 'Lacretelle, un écrivain face à la Révolution française (1766–1855)', pp. 67–83; Roederer: *Journal de Paris*, no. 252, 31 May 1796, p. 1008, and no. 277, 25 June 1796, p. 1112.

[32] J.-P. Gallais, *Censeur des journaux*, no. 283, 5 June 1796, pp. 2–3.

[33] Quatremère's letters to Miranda transcribed in Dávila, ed., *Archivo del General Miranda*, vol. 13, pp. 150–2, 206–12.

[34] [Quatremère], *Véridique, ou Courrier universel*, 28 June 1796. The first of these pieces (a letter to the newspaper) sketched arguments that Quatremère developed in the *Letters*. Its language, style, and arguments also resembled his other writings. Consistent with his circumstances, it betrayed limited knowledge of current affairs.

[35] [Quatremère], *Véridique, ou Courrier universel*, 28 June 1796. In an argument that adapted Winckelmann's observation in *History of the Art of Antiquity* (pp. 324, 332–3) concerning ancient Roman plunder, Quatremère warned that Italian artists would lose models and patronage because nobles would sell their collections and cease to commission new work.

scattered over France' instead of despoiling Italy because 'sacrilegious attacks' in Paris threatened to consecrate religious paintings in the Louvre to 'the cherished demon of atheism'.[36] Gathering 'the spoils of Europe in vast museums', he concluded, was 'no less funereal than the very furor of vandalism' and could never replace the authentic culture rooted in religious ethics that the Revolution had destroyed.[37]

Contemporary readers did not fail to discern Quatremère's support for 'monarchy and superstition'.[38] They understood that he used these short pieces to celebrate Catholicism as the source of artistic inspiration, condemn the Revolution for irreligion, and dismiss the idea of perfectibility central to the concept of civilization. His partisan intervention nevertheless encouraged publicists to sustain the quarrel, not least because he asked republicans who were already doubtful about expansionist wars to explain whether plunder contradicted 'the rights of man that civilized nations have adopted'.[39] Once details of the Bologna armistice reached Paris in early July, writers associated with the faction of past frontiers were therefore primed to remonstrate against articles allowing French representatives to choose manuscripts, painting, and antiquities.

Lacretelle knew Quatremère from the Feuillant club and the Vendémiaire insurrection. His newspaper now warned against lusting after 'masterpieces...that Italy considers the most precious heritage from its ancestors'.[40] Such plundering, Lacretelle argued, would deprive Italy of revenue, force Italy into Austria's arms, and, by undermining war conventions, leave the French Republic exposed to retaliation.[41] Roederer also heeded Quatremère's appeal despite their political differences. Roederer possibly wanted to use art plunder to provoke public discussion, which he considered the means to establish public spirit and rational public opinion. More likely, however, he wrote about the subject because he feared that the Directory's seesaw politics and aggressive foreign policy risked destabilizing a republican settlement sooner secured through an alliance with moderate royalists.[42] (Roederer later recognized that the Clichy club threatened the Republic, but until that moment he allied with the likes of

---

[36] [Quatremère], *Véridique, ou Courrier universel*, 28 June 1796.

[37] [Quatremère], *Véridique, ou Courrier universel*, 4 July 1796, pp. 1–2.

[38] *Journal de patriotes de 89*, no. 231, 4 July 1796, p. 1293; *Rédacteur*, no. 203, 5 July 1796, p. 3.

[39] [Quatremère], *Véridique, ou Courrier universel*, 28 June 1796.

[40] J.-C.-D. Lacretelle (le jeune), 'Première lettre sur cette question: faut-il faire une révolution dans l'Italie?', *Nouvelles politiques*, no. 287, 5 July 1796, pp. 1147–8; idem, '*Nouvelles réflexions sur la guerre et la paix*', *Nouvelles politiques*, no. 289, 7 July 1796, p. 1555.

[41] *Journal de Paris*, no. 297, 15 July 1796, p. 1192.

[42] J.-L. Chappey, 'Pierre-Louis Roederer et la presse sous le Directoire et le Consulat: l'opinion publique et les enjeux d'une politique éditoriale', *Annales historiques de la Révolution française*, vol. 334, no. 4 (2003), pp. 6, 9; I. Rademacher, 'Élites et républicanisme: Pierre-Louis Rœderer, critique de la campagne d'Italie et brumairien', in J.-P. Barbe and R. Bernecker, eds, *Les intellectuels européens et la campagne d'Italie 1796-1798* (Münster, 1999), pp. 134–5. Roederer revisited the subject in 'De l'entrée de Bonaparte à Rome, des tableaux et statues d'Italie', *Journal d'économie publique*, vol. 3, no. 19, 28 Feb. 1797, pp. 39–45.

162   QUATREMÈRE DE QUINCY

Quatremère).[43] In his *Journal de Paris*, Roederer warned that displaced antiqui-
ties would lose much of their allure: the Apollo Belvedere was a god in Rome, he
observed, but in Paris the sculpture would become mere physical matter.[44]
Over the next weeks, Roederer also made the quarrel widely known by publishing
diverse short reflections, including a letter from the engraver Jean-Michel
Moreau that proposed asking the pope for casts rather than original antiquities.[45]
Another contributor repeated that undermining conventions exposed the
Republic to what it inflicted on others: henceforth, each change in fortune
would attach 'the arts ... to the chariot of victory'.[46]

The Directory's supporters and spokesmen, official newspapers, and senior
figures from the National Institute and Museum Commission responded immediately to these voices casting doubt on the wisdom and justice of seizing cultural
property from Italy. Some responses were vituperative, ad hominem attacks
that labelled opponents 'unpatriotic' and 'perennial antagonists of all government
measures'.[47] According to the *Censeur des journaux*, opponents filled newspapers
simply because the dispute had become a 'political affair and quarrel'.[48] Yet other
responses articulated in greater detail the nature of France's civilizing mission. As
the leading power, one contributor argued, France was duty-bound to protect the
corpus of 'statues that [modern Romans'] ancestors tore from subjugated Greece'.
Equally, France must punish Pius VI and perfect French museums, arts, and
manufacturing. As Joachim Lebreton insisted in his cogent response to critics,
other nations 'await their improvement from us'.[49]

Lebreton was an important intermediary between the Directory, artists, and
intellectuals as an editor of the *Décade philosophique*, head of the Committee of
Public Instruction's museum department, secretary of the Institute's Second
Class, and head of the Interior Ministry's office for the fine arts.[50] He argued
that seizing artwork was a regrettable necessity because Italy's decline meant
that the earlier exodus would accelerate and other powers would acquire what
the French Republic left behind. For Lebreton, the choice was therefore not
between Paris and Rome; instead, one could either disperse artefacts across capital

---

[43] Roederer, *Journal d'économie publique*, vol. 3, no. 20, 10 March 1797, p. 66; idem, *Journal de Paris*,
no. 196, 5 April 1797, pp. 791–2; J. Menichetti, 'Pierre-Louis Rœderer: la science sociale au Conseil
d'État', *Napoleonica. La Revue*, vol. 16, no. 1 (2013), pp. 17–18; Rademacher, 'Élites et républicanisme:
Pierre-Louis Roederer, critique de la campagne d'Italie et brumairien', p. 142.

[44] *Journal de Paris*, no. 289, 7 July 1796, pp. 1159–60.

[45] *Journal de Paris*, no. 291, 9 July 1796, p. 1168.

[46] *Journal de Paris*, no. 297, 15 July 1796, p. 1192. Quatremère incorporated both Moreau's
suggestion and this last argument into his seventh letter; *Letters*, pp. 119–20.

[47] G.B., *Miroir*, no. 75, 14 July 1796, p. 298.   [48] *Censeur de journaux*, no. 323, 16 July 1796, p. 1.

[49] *Rédacteur*, no. 211, 13 July 1796, pp. 3–4 and no. 217, 19 July 1796, p. 3; Lebreton, 'Réponse à
quelques objections contre le système d'importation en France de plusieurs chefs-d'œuvre des arts qui
possède l'Italie', *Décade philosophique*, no. 81, 18 July 1796, pp. 181–6.

[50] H. Jouin, *Joachim Lebreton, premier secrétaire perpétuel de l'Académie des Beaux-Arts* (Paris, 1892).
Lebreton taught rhetoric in a religious establishment before the Revolution; after 1789, he renonced his
vows and moved to Paris but remained an obscure figure until the Directory.

cities and English stately homes, or one could move the corpus of the finest pieces from Rome to Paris to preserve its integrity. Moreover, he added, by seizing antiquities, France would stimulate excavations to replenish Italy's collections, complete France's national museum, perfect France's school of art and inspire manufacturers. Lebreton's reasoning was also punitive. Pius VI, he reflected, 'ignited the civil war', 'rallied the coalition', and incited the populace that 'assassinated our diplomat, pillaged and devastated the Palais [Manchini], and pursued and insulted French citizens'. Since the pope and his subjects were 'no longer worthy trustees of Greek spoils', France must, as capital of the 'empire of the arts', preserve what 'the Romans seized from the Greeks'.[51]

Jean-Baptiste Pierre Lebrun also responded to opponents of the seizures. Lebrun's voice carried weight as a restorer, an authority on the Northern school of painting, and a member of the Museum Commission.[52] His letter to the *Journal de Paris* insisted that Italy would retain glory and fortune because large paintings and ancient monuments were immoveable. Responding to Roederer's fear that the Louvre would contain too many paintings, he explained that the museum would facilitate comparisons. Keen to use the dispute to further the Museum Commission's aims, however, Lebrun conceded the risk of arson, which, he argued, required paving the Louvre and sharing its collection with a second museum in southern France.[53]

Quatremère's *Letters* belongs to this stage of the quarrel in June–July when Rome was threatened.[54] Since Quatremère later recalled that he started writing when the papacy confronted 'the irreligious spirit' and 'revolt and rapine' resulting from the French advance, he likely planned the work in late June (when he wrote in the *Courrier universel* against the seizures) and wrote it in July from his hiding place under the care of the Vaubertrands.[55] He was unable to consult his library, but he followed the quarrel in newspapers.[56] An undated note, almost certainly written in July once Miranda returned to Paris, clarifies Quatremère's motive. Legrand told Miranda that 'our friend' was preoccupied 'with a small work that he would immediately like to publish anonymously'. This work showed that 'it would be

---

[51] Lebreton, 'Réponse à quelques objections contre le système d'importation en France de plusieurs chefs-d'œuvre des arts qui possède l'Italie', pp. 181–6; *Rédacteur*, no. 207, 19 July 1796, p. 3 printed an abridged version.

[52] D. Spieth, *Revolutionary Paris and the Market for Netherlandish Art* (Leiden, 2018), pp. 206–18; É. Pommier, 'Postface', in Lebrun, *Réflexions sur le Muséum national: 14 janvier 1793* (Paris, 1992); idem, *L'art de la liberté*, pp. 112–15, 197–200; G. Émile-Mâle, 'Jean-Baptiste-Pierre Lebrun (1748–1813). Son rôle dans l'histoire de la restauration des tableaux du Louvre', *Mémoires de la Fédération des sociétés historiques et archéologiques de Paris et de l'Île-de-France*, vol. 8 (1956), pp. 371–417.

[53] J.-B. Lebrun, *Journal de Paris*, no. 303, 21 July 1796, pp. 2014–5.

[54] The following account of the genesis of the *Letters* revises Pommier, 'La Révolution et le destin des ouvrages de l'art de l'Italie', pp. 8–18.

[55] Quatremère, *Canova*, pp. 74–5, 279; idem, *Lettres sur l'enlèvement des ouvrages de l'art antique à Athènes et à Rome* (Paris, 1836), p. xii.

[56] Quatremère, *Letters*, pp. 122–3, notes 30 and 40; Quatremère made mistakes as a result of his circumstances.

in the interests of the arts to insist that we do not export from Italy different masterpieces' and instead rendered 'the justice to the pontifical government that it merits for the zeal and care it has constantly demonstrated towards research into the arts and their conservation'. '[Our friend] would like to know promptly', Legrand concluded, 'what you think of [his work] and...know about our intentions regarding Italy. I heard the intention was to suppress the pope'. Besides seeking information and logistical support, Quatremère wanted reassurance that his work would 'not cause an inconvenience preventing it having the effect he desires'.[57]

Miranda surely encouraged Quatremère. He detested 'the conduct of the French in Italy & despoiling it of works of art', he later told his English hosts, but he probably assisted Quatremère because his former prison companion promised to discredit a foreign policy that he opposed for different reasons.[58] Changes between the 'small work' mentioned by Legrand and the published *Letters* imply that Miranda and other friends convinced Quatremère to forgo anonymity in practice and to use the last 'letter' and a follow-on petition to demand that the Directory consult expert opinion about seizing artworks.[59] At this stage, Quatremère also might have reworked his draft into one side of a pseudo-epistolary exchange (using Miranda as his imaginary anonymous interlocutor) and toned-down language that risked causing 'inconvenience' to help validate his work amongst readers ill-disposed to his political agenda.[60] Finally, to present himself as an impartial 'friend of the arts', Quatremère created the illusion that most of this exchange predated Bonaparte's victories and was therefore a prescient philosophical reflection rather than a reactive polemic.[61]

Quatremère probably made any such revisions around mid-July. During the second half of this month, he shared his reflections with several contacts before the *Letters* appeared in print in Paris. For instance, he sent a copy of his work in several instalments to Jean-Gabriel Peltier, a counter-revolutionary journalist and editor in London who was in the pay of the British government.[62] Between 23 July and 20 August, Peltier printed an incomplete, non-sequential version over several issues of *Paris pendant l'année 1796*, starting with the fourth letter.[63]

---

[57] Dávila, ed., *Archivo del General Miranda*, vol. 13, pp. 129, 153.

[58] J. Farington, *The Diary of Joseph Farington*, vol. 3 (New Haven, 1998), p. 1078.

[59] Several newspapers identified Quatremère as the author, including *Feuille de jour*, no. 106, 31 July 1796, p. 20.

[60] Quatremère, *Letters*, p. 94, quoted Miranda, *Opinion*, p. 13, in lieu of actual correspondence.

[61] In Quatremère's final letter, he identified an article in *Rédacteur* (no. 211, 13 July 1796) and claimed that he had finished writing whilst others started 'late in the day'. However, evidence cited above shows that he started writing later than he implied.

[62] H. Maspero-Clerc, *Un journaliste contre-révolutionnaire: Jean-Gabriel Peltier (1760–1825)* (Paris, 1973), p. 91.

[63] *Paris pendant l'année 1796*, no. 64, 23 July 1796, pp. 103–10; Peltier falsely claimed that he had received the entire collection of letters, which had 'appeared at the start of July'. However, in the issue dated 13 August (no. 68, p. 329), Peltier wrote that he printed Quatremère's letters in the order that he received them. He never printed the seventh letter.

Quatremère perhaps also shared his reflections with Angelo Petracchi and Serafino Casella, Roman representatives in Paris, and even gave them a printed copy of his new work because on 25 July their letter to the foreign minister eloquently summarized his arguments in the *Letters* without naming him.[64] His work was printed in its entirety in Paris sometime before 31 July, when the *Feuille de jour* mentioned it. The frontispiece left little doubt that he was the author: this work by 'A.Q.', it proclaimed, was available from 'QUATREMERE, Bookseller' (Fig. 8.1). The publisher Charles Crapelet printed two runs; each had seventy-four numbered pages, but the second run included an unnumbered page listing an error on page 41, and, unlike the first run, its title page spelled *Quatremère* with a grave accent. Quatremère later claimed that he sent Bonaparte a copy.[65]

The epistolary form of the *Letters* scarcely hides the fact that this tract followed a definite 'order of ideas', as Quatremère put it.[66] His central thesis was that 'displacing the monuments of Italy' and 'dismantling its schools and museums' would destroy 'civilization'.[67] To substantiate his warning, he imitated members of the Section of History in the Second Class who combined historical analysis and prophecy, thereby describing the story of Europe's past and imagining two possible futures that would result from present-day choices.[68]

Characteristic of how the *Letters* was simultaneously republican and conservative, Quatremère combined philosophical histories with Eusebius' thesis of continuity between ancient and modern Rome. To ensure his work appealed to republican readers, he eschewed theology, theocracy, or religious inspiration. He instead outlined a stadial, secular history that assumed humankind was improvable and that civilization was singular and general, a state and a process, 'the means instrumental to happiness and pleasure, to the advancement of instruction and reason, and finally to the improvement of mankind'. In keeping with Directorial political culture, *civilization* thus functioned in the *Letters* as a master word, justifying every end and purpose.[69] (This contrasted his *Courrier universel*

---

[64] *CAFR*, vol. 16, pp. 430–1.

[65] Quatremère, *Canova*, p. 280; idem, *Lettres sur l'enlèvement*, p. xiii. Not all extant copies from the second run still contain the errata page.

[66] Quatremère, *Letters*, p. 105. Contemporaries described the work as a *brochure* (implying that the pages were stitched together but not bound), and Quatremère later called it 'a tract [*un écrit*] in letter form' (*Canova*, p. 279).

[67] Quatremère, *Letters*, pp. 94–5, 105.

[68] A. Cook, '"The Great Society of the Human Species": Volney and the Global Politics of Revolutionary France', *Intellectual History Review*, vol. 23, no. 3 (2013), p. 322.

[69] Quatremère, *Letters*, pp. 94–5. Quatremère used the word *civilization* three times (pp. 94, 96, 117), but its conceptual centrality to the *Letters* is illustrated by his frequent use of cognate terms (such as *civilized Europe, perfection, lights, instruction, humanity*, and *commerce*) and opposite terms (such as *barbarians, barbary, night*, and *ignorance*).

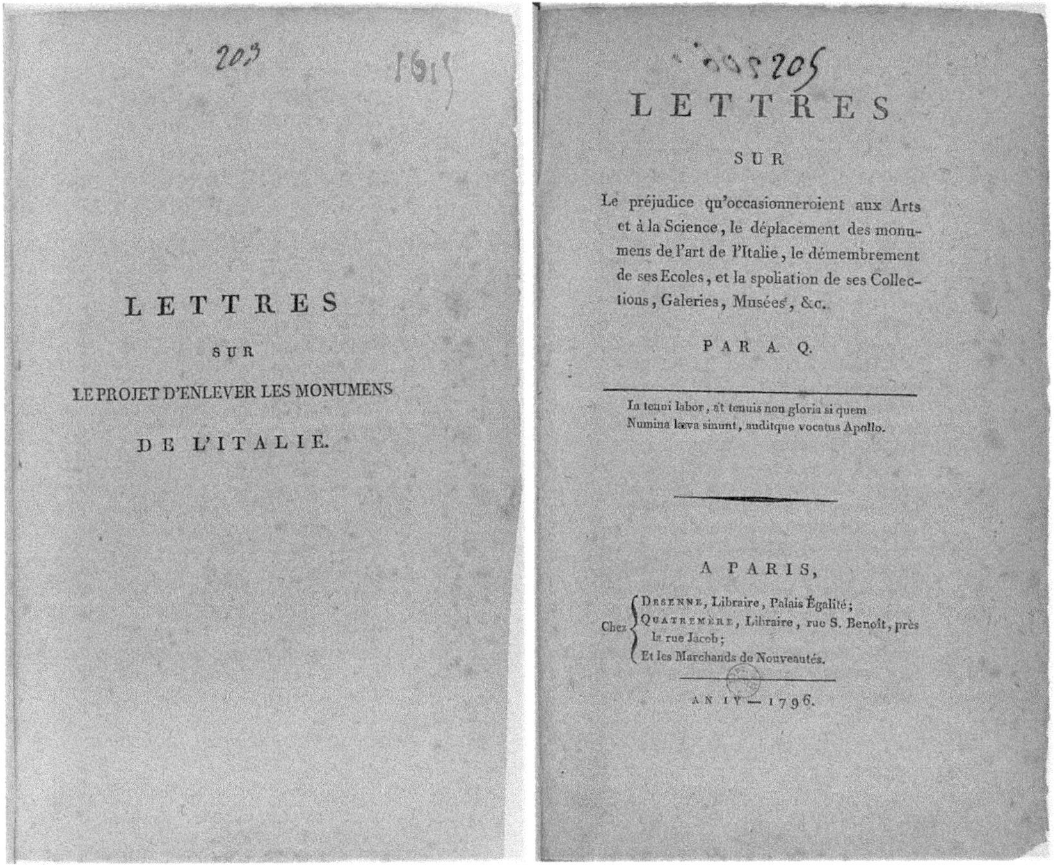

LETTRES

SUR

LE PROJET D'ENLEVER LES MONUMENS

DE L'ITALIE.

LETTRES

SUR

Le préjudice qu'occasionneroient aux Arts et à la Science, le déplacement des monumens de l'art de l'Italie, le démembrement de ses Ecoles, et la spoliation de ses Collections, Galeries, Musées, &c.

PAR A. Q.

In tenui labor, at tenuis non gloria si quem
Numina læva sinunt, audîtque vocatus Apollo.

A PARIS,

Chez { Desenne, Libraire, Palais-Egalité;
Quatremère, Libraire, rue S. Benoît, près la rue Jacob;
Et les Marchands de Nouveautés.

AN IV.—1796.

Fig. 8.1 Cover title (left) and frontispiece (right) of the first edition of Quatremère's *Letters on the Plan to Abduct the Monuments of Italy* (1796). BnF, Collection Deloynes.

writings in which he avoided the word and opposed the concept.)[70] However, Quatremère's history of the progress of civilization also subverted Directorial norms: against the discourse of Italian decline deployed to justify the seizures, he reworked the teleology joining ancient and modern Rome to depict the papacy as the custodian of civilization and the power that synthesized ancient genius with enlightened morals.

Quatremère's philosophical history of Europe consisted of three narratives, which together culminated in civilization. In order of importance for their consequences, these were narratives of science (scholarship and knowledge), art, and 'universal morality'.[71] According to his first narrative, science suffered during the Middle Ages and survived only thanks to ancient remains and monastic institutions in Italy. However, from the sixteenth century onwards, knowledge advanced through excavations, restorations, and museums. Unperturbed by inter-state rivalries, scholars in the 'general republic of the arts and sciences' pursued the truth. These scholars initially over relied on textual authorities, but the papacy's miraculous rediscovery of antiquities during the eighteenth century enabled the triumph of observation-based science.[72] For Quatremère, if Europe's powers respected the status quo then this new science would benefit everyone: hastened by the scholarly 'division of labour', a hitherto unknown 'light' would 'connect our knowledge with that of the past, revitalize...lost notions and bring ever new illumination to philosophy and the arts'. However, he warned that plundering Rome would undermine science and unleash 'ignorance and barbarity' once again.[73]

The second narrative concerned fine art and beauty. The Greeks perfected art, Quatremère insisted, but during the Middle Ages the 'lethargy of the mind and taste brought in its wake the neglect of all spirited and tasteful works'. Papal patronage alone ensured that taste survived, and helped Italy become Europe's 'seminary of the arts'. Raphael would have transformed the arts, Quatremère continued, but his legacy was ruined by Leo X's death and the sack of Rome,

---

[70] Elsewhere, with the notable exception of *Précis pour Miranda*, Quatremère he used the word *civilization* sparingly and differently to how he used it in the *Letters*. For instance, in the *Letters* he implied that the ancients never achieved civilization, but elsewhere he indicated that there were different types of civilization amongst the ancient Egyptians, Greeks, and modern Europeans—see *EMA*, vol. 1, pp. 109, 425, 501; vol. 2:1, pp. 172, 174, 238; and *Recueil de dissertations archéologiques* (Paris, 1835), p. 17.

[71] Quatremère, *Letters*, pp. 106, 108, 174–6. He implied in the *Letters* that science usually fertilized the arts, whilst the progress of the arts and sciences improved morality and politics. However, he suggested that this causal pattern was not universal; in early modern Italy, for instance, the nature of politics resulted in enlightened patronage for art, and the history of antiquity showed that wisdom and artistic genius did not always foster morality.

[72] Quatremère, *Letters*, pp. 94, 97, 101–2.

[73] Ibid., pp. 98–9, 101–3, 114, 117. Quatremère named Adam Smith as the source for his reference to the 'division of labour'. His first library included Jean-Antoine Roucher's 1790–1 translation of *The Wealth of Nations*. Roederer, Quatremère's ally in the quarrel, was Smith's most important interpreter in France; see R. Whatmore, 'Adam Smith's Role in the French Revolution', *Past and Present*, vol. 175, no. 1 (2002), p. 67.

168 QUATREMÈRE DE QUINCY

which dispersed his students and paintings.[74] Art's decline was exacerbated, Quatremère lamented, by the subsequent culture of collecting, because unmediated access to Old Master paintings hindered aspiring artists. Despite this pessimistic prognosis, he nevertheless concluded that art's future depended on the choices of European powers: the new science would foster 'a taste for the beautiful, simple, and true' whereas harming science and preventing students profiting from Rome would cause art to regress further.[75]

The third narrative described how 'universal morality' and instruction had finally replaced the right of conquest. According to Quatremère, the ancients' immorality meant that they never achieved civilization. The ancient Romans, he warned, were especially unworthy of imitation since they enslaved the vanquished, exterminated liberty, and left Europe a legacy of violent retribution that lasted until the recent 'happy revolution' in international relations and the rights of man.[76] In this enlightened age, Quatremère argued, plundering artwork had finally become unacceptable behaviour. Just as the spread of learning had diminished differences in Europe to the extent that no nation could call another 'barbaric', future learning promised to perfect humanity.[77] Yet, he warned, dismembering 'the museum of Rome' would undo this progress and replace peace with perpetual war.[78]

Quatremère's overall history from these three narratives took after several canonical writings by Montesquieu, Voltaire, and Condorcet. Following their example, his *Letters* attached moral values to periods, approached Europe as a community of nations, treated 'commerce' as the principal engine of progress, and described an enlightened age starting sometime between the treaties of Westphalia and Utrecht. As a pastiche of Condorcet's *Sketch*, in particular, the *Letters* bound all peoples, arts, and sciences into a shared trajectory of perfectibility.[79] Yet Quatremère also broke conspicuously with these philosophes: whereas they described the papacy as a tyrannical obstacle to humankind, he treated popes since Nicholas V as instigators of the revival of the arts and sciences. His idiosyncratic philosophical history thus adopted Condorcet's notion of civilization only to make Catholicism integral to it.

For Quatremère, this history of Europe culminated in a present-day dilemma: according to the cooperation problem running through the *Letters*, each power

---

[74] Quatremère, *Letters*, pp. 97, 110–13, 117, 119, 120.

[75] Ibid., pp. 97–9, 105–7, 109–10, 113–15, 119.   [76] Ibid., pp. 94–7, 116–17.

[77] Ibid., pp. 112, 119, 104–5, 96, 116, 94–5. Quatremère's argument about the status of cultural property during wartime copied Emmerich de Vattel, *Le droit des gens, ou principes de la loi naturelle, appliqués à la conduit et aux affaires des nations et des souverains*, vol. 3 (London, 1758), pp. 132–3. His first and second libraries contained this work; *Bibliothèque de M. Quatremère*, p. 137.

[78] Quatremère, *Letters*, pp. 99, 102, 111–12, 118, 104.

[79] Condorcet, 'The Sketch', in *Condorcet: Political Writings* (Cambridge, 2012), ed. S. Lukes and N. Urbitani, esp. 142–3. Quatremère's first library contained two editions of Condorcet's *Sketch*. In the *Letters*, he imitated Condorcet's idea of general perfectibility despite warning elsewhere that science stifled the arts. See, for example, his 'De la marche différente de l'esprit humain dans les sciences naturelles et dans les beaux-arts', *Recueil des lectures faites dans la séance publique annuelle de l'Institut royal* (Paris, 1834), pp. 35–43.

could either cooperate to sustain civilization or defect in the false hope of gaining short-term advantages.[80] His first letter outlined the broad consequences of cooperating and defecting, and the next five letters addressed the specific implications of each choice.

The second and third letters concerned the knowledge that scholars gained from antiquities. Quatremère argued in his second letter that cooperating required rediscovering and restoring neglected antiquities throughout former Roman colonies, on the one hand, and ensuring that tourist spending continued to finance excavation in Rome, on the other.[81] Plundering Rome, he warned, would break this virtuous cycle: just as Italians would not make insecure investments, any power that expropriated antiquities would not fund excavations with revenue gained from foreigners visiting its museum.[82] Quatremère's third letter explained that Rome was the ideal location for scholarship: Rome's antiquities, he argued, shed light on one another, and its museums facilitated firsthand observations that helped scholars elsewhere form general theories. 'Dismembering the museum of Rome', he concluded, would be a 'crime against public instruction' because 'to divide is to destroy'.[83] Quatremère therefore shared the encyclopedism of contemporaries such as Aubin-Louis Millin and Grégoire. However, unlike them, he insisted that Rome, rather than Paris, should host the materials of knowledge.

Quatremère's next three letters addressed artistic practice. His fourth and much of his fifth letters considered how dispersing antiquities would affect the plastic arts. Artists and connoisseurs learned to understand beauty, he argued, through studying masterpieces alongside their 'family' of inferior pieces. Living in Rome, he observed, enabled one to compare, classify, and judge artefacts under favourable light and within their natural landscape whilst imbibing a spiritual atmosphere conducive to beauty. But, he warned, defecting would destroy the understanding of beauty through undermining these opportunities.[84]

The end of Quatremère's fifth letter and his sixth letter concerned Italy's Renaissance and Baroque schools of painting. Europe's powers would benefit from an artistic golden age, he suggested, if they sustained science and contributed their Raphael paintings to Rome, where artists could study the master's oeuvre in one place. Above all, the powers must respect schools spread over the peninsula— these schools, he reasoned, formed unique natural and cultural environments in

---

[80] Quatremère did not use the terms *cooperate* and *defect*, but they draw attention to the game-theoric quality of the *Letters*. The cooperation problem he described featured numerous players, but, unlike the prisoner's dilemma, no repeat games and no benefits for defectors.

[81] Quatremère's point about rediscovering antiquities throughout former Roman colonies applied the reasoning laid out in Adam Smith, *An Inquiry into the Causes of the Wealth of Nations*, bk. 4 (London, 1776), 1.11: a 'country that has no mines of its own must...draw its gold and silver from foreign countries'.

[82] Quatremère, *Letters*, pp. 97–100. He repeated his argument from *Courrier universel*, 28 June 1796, but applied it to rediscovering antiquities rather than patronage for new artworks.

[83] Quatremère, *Letters*, pp. 100–4.   [84] Ibid., pp. 104–11.

170 QUATREMÈRE DE QUINCY

which students needed to immerse themselves and inspect both masterpieces and the imperfect and unfinished efforts that revealed Old Masters' techniques. If Quatremère agreed with Lebrun that students should contemplate a 'perfect assemblage' of 'paintings...arranged by order of school' and epoch, he tacitly criticized Lebrun's support for seizures by insisting that respecting the status quo would serve students' education better than filling the national museum in Paris with looted paintings.[85]

As the *Journal littéraire* recognized in its review, Quatremère's work spelled out a choice for Europe's powers: they could either be 'the true friend of the arts' or 'a modern-day Verres', taking after the example of the rapacious first-century BCE proconsul of Sicily condemned by Cicero.[86] Quatremère predicted that countries with 'sane politics' who loved the arts would cooperate to perfect scholarship, preserve peace, increase commerce, and create an artistic golden age. But ignorant or selfish powers would plunder Rome and discover that the resulting disaster hurt their own interests. Their artists and savants would find Rome depleted; perpetual war would impoverish their export markets; and eventually they would suffer the right of conquest that they had rekindled.[87]

Several books in Quatremère's library informed how he construed this cooperation problem. He borrowed from Montesquieu the idea that opposed parties must 'co-operate for the general good' and 'union of harmony'.[88] He also applied to Europe's shared heritage Emmerich de Vattel's principle of reciprocity, showing that mutual assistance was the basis for international happiness whilst nations endangered humankind through pursuing selfish interests.[89] However, Condorcet's *Sketch* was his most obvious source: like Condorcet, he depicted humankind standing between a cataclysm and greatness and reasoned that individuals and states, not fortune or divine will, shaped humanity's collective future.[90]

Quatremère feigned impartial detachment throughout most of the *Letters* so that it appeared moderate and reasonable. To make his work outwardly satisfy the norms of Directorial political culture, he therefore cast aside the counter-revolutionary language of his *Courrier universel* writings. He instead concealed his politics with classical erudition, mimicked his enemies' lexicon, cited approved modern writers (such as Buffon, Winckelmann, and Smith), and, as we have seen,

---

[85] Lebrun, *Réflexions sur le Muséum national* (n.p, n.d, [Paris, 1793]), pp. 5–6; Quatremère, *Letters*, pp. 111–15.

[86] *Journal littéraire*, no. 7, 1 Sept. 1796, p. 210.

[87] Quatremère, *Letters*, pp. 102–3, 94, 111–13, 109, 95, 118–20, 98. These arguments followed Vattel, *Le droit des gens*, vol. 1, pp. 438–40.

[88] Montesquieu, *Considérations sur les causes de la grandeur des Romains*, ch. 9. Quatremère's first library included the 1748 Paris edition besides the 1769 London edition of Montesquieu's complete writings.

[89] Vattel, *Le droit des gens*, vol. 1, p. 11.

[90] Quatremère, *Letters*, pp. 7, 95; Condorcet, 'Sketch', pp. 94–5, 98–9.

selectively imitated Condorcet, bête noire of royalist intellectuals.[91] He even played to anti-clerical readers by mocking relics and praising the Holbachian materialist Charles-François Dupuis.[92] Just as disingenuously, he also condemned slavery, which the following year he and other clichyeans in the Council of Five Hundred tried to reimpose in the colonies.[93]

Alongside this strategy of dissimulation, Quatremère crafted a veiled polemic aginst the Directory's civilizing mission. In large part, he attacked the regime implicitly through eulogizing the pope at precisely the moment when republicans blamed the papacy for the Revolution's misfortunes and for destabilizing Europe, spreading superstition, impoverishing Italy, and failing to protect Europe's heritage. Against their hostile opinion, he insisted that the papacy, not the French Republic, should be entrusted with protecting civilization. Outrageously, given the circumstances, Quatremère even suggested that France should resume paying annates to support Pius VI's 'learned conquests' and enrich the capital of the true 'republic'.[94] After all, the papacy had ensured 'the unbroken cultivation of the arts', created 'sumptuous museums', hosted scholars and artists from all nations, and acted as the spiritual *civitas maxima* whose neutrality placed Rome outside the right of conquest. For all that was opportunistic in the *Letters*, Quatremère repeated throughout his life his belief in the inviolability of papal property and Catholicism's power to inspire art and learning.[95]

Alongside this general defense of the papacy, his *Letters* also defended the papacy's specific right to retain antiquities. Given widespread disbelief in teleologies that cast the papacy as the successor of pagan emperors, Quatremère prudently identified other continuities in Roman history and devised other justifications for respecting papal ownership. Since 'nature' had placed these antiquities in the 'museum of Rome', he insisted, only here could students draw objects surrounded by unmovable monuments and geographical, social, and spiritual conditions that had taken root over centuries.[96] In sum, even if antiquities

---

[91] For royalist criticism of Condorcet, see Murray, *The Right-Wing Press*, pp. 215–16; J. de Maistre, *Considerations on France*, ed. and trans. R. Lebrun (Cambridge, 2006), p. 29; L. de Bonald, 'Observations sur un ouvrage postume de M. Condorcet', in *Théorie du pouvoir politique et religieux dans la société civile, démontrée par le raisonnement et par l'histoire*, vol. 2 (Paris, 1796), pp. 482–520.

[92] Quatremère called Dupuis a man of 'vaster intellect' with 'profound theories'; *Letters*, pp. 103, 112. However, Dupuis's *Origine de tous les cultes, ou la réligion universelle* (Paris, year III [1795]) outraged nonconstitutional Catholics. *Annales catholiques*, vol. 2, no. 25, 1796, pp. 542–64, condemned this work as the most audacious rallying cry to incredulity written during the century. Quatremère's unpublished obituary of Dupuis criticized his systemic thinking and conviction that he could explain everything through the zodiac. Dupuis, he lamented, 'flattered himself to have found in the sky the key to all the errors of the earth' and 'to all mysteries of history'; Quatremère, 'Notice historique sur M. Charles-François Dupuis' [1809], Bibliothèque de l'Institut de France, ms. 2555, no. 27.

[93] Quatremère, *Letters*, p. 96; Quatremère, *Rapport fait par Quatremère au nom d'une commission spéciale sur la responsabilité des ministres et celle des agents du Directoire dans les colonies* (Paris, year V [1797]).

[94] Quatremère, *Letters*, pp. 97–8, 101–2, 108, 119.

[95] See e.g. Quatremère, 'Rome', in *EMA*, vol. 3, p. 300; and Quatremère, *Dictionnaire historique d'architecture*, vol. 2 (Paris, 1832), p. 217. Quatremère's praise for the papacy resembled what he previously wrote about Biscari; *EMA*, vol. 1, pp. 556–7.

[96] Quatremère, *Letters*, pp. 101, 105–7.

originated from ancient Greece and elsewhere, they had become part of Rome by dint of their extended stay and usefulness. For Quatremère, then, it was futile to create a universal museum elsewhere at the expense of this '*mappa mundi* in relief'.[97] Contrary to a common misconception in recent scholarship, Quatremère did not argue that these antiquities belonged to their so-called original context. Indeed, antiquities in Rome were invaluable, in his eyes, because their recontextualization in the city transformed them from idols of pagan worship into objects of beauty and knowledge.

For Quatremère, then, the papacy's past and present record, on the one hand, and the utility and beauty of antiquities in Rome, on the other, justified why antiquities should remain in the city. Beyond these reasons, he also insisted that the papacy had a twofold legal claim to this property. He drew the first claim from the idea of *jus commune*: Rome, he asserted, safeguarded what served public instruction and therefore belonged to the community.[98] He borrowed the second claim from political economists. To disarm republicans who favoured expropriating the expropriator, he argued that Rome's antiquities were a mined resource that required labour and investment to wrest them from the earth. Implicitly, this meant that modern Rome's claim was legitimate, even if ancient Rome had possessed Greek sculptures through the right of the strongest or *faustrecht*, which, according to the 1790 Committee on Feudal Rights, was an illegitimate means of acquiring property.[99]

Quatremère attacked the Directory indirectly by praising and defending the papacy in all these respects, but he also attacked the regime itself for imperilling the civilization that it claimed to advance and for exporting a revolution that had overturned 'every cause of social harmony'.[100] In the first six letters, he contrasted tacitly the advance of art, science, and morality during the Old Regime to the harm caused under the Republic. For instance, he implied that the Crown had nourished geniuses (such as Buffon), whereas the Republic murdered savants (such as Jean-Sylvian Bailly and Jean-Paul Rabault de Saint-Étienne). In the same vein, he reminded readers how the Crown had restored Gallo-Roman monuments that the Republic then abandoned. Finally, to warn against the Republic hoarding displaced artefacts, the *Letters* juxtaposed the example of the useful Museum of Natural History (founded under Louis XIII) with arbitrary Baroque collecting.[101]

---

[97] Ibid., p. 108.

[98] Ibid., pp. 94–5, 98, 112, 119. Quatremère expressed contrary views about the extent of this community: on one occasion, he claimed that the 'common inheritance' of 'the arts and sciences belong to all of Europe', but elsewhere he called antiquities 'the most national … of … properties' (pp. 94, 98).

[99] Ibid., pp. 98, 112. On the Committee on Feudal Rights and the wider context of the debate over property, see R. Blaufarb, *The Great Demarcation: The French Revolution and the Invention of Modern Property* (Oxford, 2016), esp. 48–81.

[100] Quatremère, *Letters*, p. 103.

[101] Ibid., pp. 100–1, 114–15, 118–20. Quatremère drew upon the familiar distinction between useful and vain collections; see Poulot, *Musée, nation, patrimoine*, pp. 83, 280.

His seventh letter dispelled any lingering ambiguity, naming the French Republic explicitly for the first time in the text.[102] Treating masterpieces in monetary terms, he mused in this final letter, was an abomination of his times that raised a pertinent if perverse question: what 'would [they] fetch if... put up for sale' by France, and 'used as securities, so that bank notes can be issued on the surety of antique statues?' Edmund Burke had judged selling Church land to secure bank notes an 'outrage upon credit, property, and liberty'.[103] Following Burke's example, Quatremère warned that papal cultural property might serve an equally futile end. For both thinkers, property rights belonged not only to individuals but also to corporate bodies and institutions. Stripping those rights was tyrannical and harmful.[104]

The immediate reception of the *Letters* demonstrates how Quatremère's contemporaries understood his polemic. Unsurprisingly, conservative Parisian newspapers praised his 'politically and morally just' work and identified its underlying argument that papal Rome was the cultural fortress that protected masterpieces against the 'barbarism' spread by the *idéologues*.[105] In the same vein, the *Annales catholiques* repeated Quatremère's defense of Pius VI (that 'protector of the arts, benefactor of humanity..., respected by... Europe') and his regret that 'one abducts... the resources of [the pope] and the wealth of his people'.[106] Francophone royalists abroad understood the *Letters* equally well. For example, Mallet du Pan betrayed his incisive reading when he lamented that Italy, after drawing Europe from 'barbarism', had fallen 'prey to a troop of *philosophy-banditti* and sacrilegious spoilers' who violated Rome's 'national property', 'fruit of the genius, sacrifices, and labours of a country'. Similarly, Louis XVI's former navy minister recognized how Quatremère punctured the Directory's claim to be 'the restorer of the arts and sciences' and showed the tragic consequences of its spoliation of sacred property, originally commissioned and excavated through the 'constant zeal of... the popes'.[107] In London, Peltier praised Quatremère's 'delicious letters', 'so full of taste, talent, and wisdom'.[108]

Royalists thus understood and admired Quatremère's work. Readers who favoured preserving the Republic had a more complex response, but eventually

---

[102] Quatremère, *Letters*, pp. 116, 118, 120.

[103] E. Burke, *Reflections on the Revolution in France*, ed. J. Pocock (Indianapolis, 1987), p. 107.

[104] Quatremère, *Letters*, p. 117; J. Pocock, 'The Political Economy of Burke's Analysis of the French Revolution', *The Historical Journal*, vol. 25, no. 2 (1982), pp. 331–49.

[105] *Nouvelles politiques*, no. 325, 12 Aug. 1796, p. 1299; *Feuille de jour*, no. 106, 31 July 1796, p. 20; *Journal littéraire*, no. 7, 1 Sept. 1796, p. 210.

[106] *Annales catholiques*, vol. 3, no. 26, 1797, p. 17.

[107] J. Mallet du Pan, 'A Summary of the Tributes Exacted, and Other Robberies Committed, by the French Republic', *The British mercury; or, Historical and critical views of the events of the present times*, vol. 2, no. 10, 15 Jan. 1799, p. 88; A.-F. Bertrand de Moleville, *Histoire de la Révolution de France*, vol. 4 (Paris, 1803), pp. 254–8. Lally-Tollendal also grasped that Quatremère spoke out against those who wished to destroy the papacy, but he seemingly fell for Quatremère's conceit by calling him 'a republican'; T.-G. de Lally-Tollendal, *Défense des émigrés français: adressée au peuple français* (London, 1797), p. 330.

[108] *Paris pendant l'année 1796*, no. 72, 3 Sept. 1796, pp. 506, 600.

174 QUATREMÈRE DE QUINCY

they also grasped what Quatremère was doing. The initial reaction of the executive Directors, their spokesmen and official newspapers, and influential readers who were critical of the regime but loyal to the Republic was to ignore Quatremère. For example, Millin refrained from mentioning the *Letters* in the *Magasin encyclopédique*, even though his journal reported on the experts sent to Italy to gather cultural property. Millin's silence reflected his ambivalence towards the seizures. On the one hand, he opposed expansionist wars, shared many of Quatremère's assumptions, and later opposed the spoliation of enlightened private collectors such as Cardinal Borgia. On the other hand, he wanted to enrich Paris with a judicious selection of artefacts, arguing that measured seizures would stimulate education and publicize treasures otherwise 'buried' in religious sanctuaries or princely cabinets.[109]

Whilst Millin remained silent, the Directors were compelled to react in mid-August because many distinguished artists and savants voiced support for Quatremère in ways that threatened to undermine the regime's civilizing claims. Quatremère solicited support through an artists' petition, which he alluded to at the end of the *Letters*. Legrand and an inner circle of signatories perhaps drafted the petition and gathered signatures in early August when Quatremère was preoccupied with other affairs, but Quatremère inspired it and surely persuaded many artists to sign.[110] The petition proclaimed that fear of 'ignorant friends', 'love of the arts [and] the desire to preserve their masterpieces for the admiration of all peoples' motivated its authors. Whilst alluding to the *Letters*, the petition was worded impartially, eschewing further comment on the seizures ('We shall allow ourselves no reflections on this subject already submitted to public opinion by savant discussions') and simply requesting that a commission report on 'whether it is advantageous for France and... artists in general to displace from Rome the monuments of antiquity and the masterpieces of painting and sculpture composing the galleries and museums of that capital of the arts'. Besides David, the forty-seven petitioners included the painters Vien, Girodet, Robert, and Clérisseau, the sculptors Pajou, Julien, and Boizot, the architects Legrand and Molinos and the engraver (and future Director of the

---

[109] Martin, 'Les enjeux diplomatiques'; *Magasin encyclopédique*, vol. 1 (1796), p. 407; A.-L. Millin, 'Lettres de Millin', in *Aubin-Louis Millin et l'Allemagne: le Magasin encyclopédique—les lettres à Karl August Böttiger*, eds G. Espagne and B. Savoy (Hildesheim, 2005), pp. 312, 345–6, 361, 366.

[110] Quatremère proposed asking artists their opinion in *Letters*, pp. 114, 117–18. An editorial note in the second edition denied his authorship of the petition; Quatremère, *Lettres sur le projet d'enlever les monumens de l'Italie* (Rome, 1815), p. 95. According to Barras, *Mémoires*, vol. 2, pp. 396–7, the royalists deployed Quatremère to trick David: 'Unable to resist against such a mind..., [David] yielded to make peace with his fellow professionals.... A great meal sealed the reconciliation and the imbecile David dishonoured himself with his signature.' The purported dinner is consistent with the layout of signatures on the manuscript; AN, F17 1279, dossier 1 ('Pétition d'artistes au Directoire exécutif'), verso 1. However, David's response to the triumphal entry of art into Paris, reported in É. Delécluze, *Louis David: son école et son temps* (Paris, 1855), p. 209, suggests that his scepticism was genuine.

Musée Napoléon) Denon.[111] Many signatories were friends and acquaintances who Quatremère knew from Coustou's studio, his Italian voyages, the Panthéon, or his administrative work since 1789 for art juries, museums, and public instruction.

One perceptive contemporary observed that political differences between the artists—who included former terrorists and ardent republicans—made them an unlikely group. Embarrassingly for the Directors, these artists were amongst the most famous in Paris and their diverse politics made Quatremère's petition appear authoritative and impartial. Quatremère's masterstroke lay in exploiting a shared grievance amongst them. If few supported his desire to discredit the Republic and defend the papacy, most shared his appreciation of the importance of Rome in young artists' formation. As a group, they approached the petition less as a principled stand against the displacement of art and more as an opportunity to reassert their credentials and regain status.[112]

After signing the petition, Legrand and several other petitioners presented a letter to La Révellière, the acting president and Director most closely associated with public instruction and the Commission sent to Italy, in his Petit-Luxembourg office: 'Citizen President, A deputation of artists, tasked with meeting the executive Directory, asks to be admitted to a private audience to present a petition concerning the progress of the plastic arts that they practice.'[113] More provocatively, this deputation also appealed to public opinion by printing the petition in Roederer's *Journal de Paris*. This adversarial gesture linked the petition to earlier opposition so that other newspapers assumed that the petitioners were 'against the displacement of masterpieces, even if they do not express their opinion'.[114] Facing a backlash, some petitioners felt obliged to clarify their positions.[115] When legislators wondered why artists had allied with 'enemies of our glory', journalists suggested that foreign powers had bribed them.[116] Patriots demanded the deportation of these 'cowardly and anti-French' artists whilst the Commission in Italy complained that 'our artists...find nothing of beauty...that is not in Italy'.[117] The artists' ostensible support for Quatremère's agenda also threatened to divide the Directors. Bruised by the petition, La Révellière scotched ambitions to take

---

[111] D. Gilks, 'Art and Politics during the "First" Directory: Artists' Petitions and the Quarrel over the Confiscation of Works of Art from Italy in 1796', *French History*, vol. 26, no. 1, pp. 64–6, 75–7.

[112] Ibid., pp. 64–6. Over half the petitioners had been academicians. Most had spent more than two years studying in Italy and benefited from patronage that the Revolution had ruined. On how Quatremère knew most signatories, see Gilks, 'Art and Politics during the "First" Directory', p. 58 n. 63.

[113] AN, F 17 1279, dossier 1 ('Paris ce 28 thermidor l'an 4 de la République. Des artistes français au Directoire Exécutif').

[114] *Journal de Paris*, no. 330, 17 Aug. 1796, p. 1323.

[115] *Nouvelles politiques*, no. 329, 18 Aug. 1796, p. 1323; Gilks, 'Art and Politics during the "First" Directory', p. 67.

[116] A. Thibaudeau, *Mémoires sur la Convention et le Directoire*, vol. 2 (Paris, 1824), p. 134.

[117] AN, F17 1279, dossier 5.

176   QUATREMÈRE DE QUINCY

Trajan's column whilst Barras was angered by David's hypocrisy and Carnot's suggestion that the Republic return a Corregio painting to the Duke of Parma.[118]

Although the petition was merely an anodyne request for a commission, its publication in an adversarial journal combined with the petitioners' status thus threatened to legitimize Quatremère's earlier interventions and broaden opposition to the victories in Italy that provided the state with a lifeline. La Révellière and his allies therefore turned on Quatremère by trying to discredit the *Letters* without naming the work or its author. They dismissed the idea that most petitioners supported Quatremère and implied that David had misunderstood the *Letters*.[119] They also publicized the reactionary implications of Quatremère's interventions. For instance, Charles-Joseph Trouvé, general secretary of the Directory, warned that heeding the petition's demand would benefit the counter-revolution: if the Directors returned confiscated art, Trouvé mused, then they would next send Italy what 'we already possess'—an obvious reference to Quatremère's plea to return Raphael's paintings. Such concessions, Trouvé speculated in jest, would inspire critics to demand the return of 'weapons, money and towns ... and that, most importantly, the republican government be destroyed'.[120] A counter-petition, probably also penned by Trouvé, provided another means to discredit Quatremère.[121] Drawing from earlier critiques of papal Rome, the petition argued that the city's masterpieces, and the visitors that they attracted, trapped ordinary Romans in poverty by discouraging investment in manufacturing and agriculture. Seizing this 'servile and precarious resource' was therefore a duty because sustaining the status quo 'would entrench the worthlessness and pride of that indolent and superstitious city and ensure that it is forever dependent on a corrupt and corrupting government'.[122] Contemporaries recognized that the petition took aim at 'Quatremère's short book'.[123] Its thirty-seven signatories included Lenoir, the painters Jean-Baptiste Regnault and François Gérard, and the sculptor Chaudet, but as a whole the counter-petitioners were relatively younger and less distinguished that the signatories of Quatremère's petition.[124]

This state-backed criticism paved the way for others to name and ridicule Quatremère's *Letters* as 'seventy-four pages of nonsense', 'pretexts, assumptions and sophistry' that betrayed his 'tender interest for the enemies of France'.[125] Despite his efforts to make the *Letters* appear part of the 'centre', the regime

---

[118] Gilks, 'Art and Politics during the "First" Directory', p. 68.

[119] Barras, *Mémoires*, vol. 2, pp. 396–7; *Décade philosophique*, no. 85, 17 Aug. 1796, pp. 431–2 and no. 87, 16 Sept. 1796, p. 564.

[120] C.-J. Trouvé, *Moniteur universel*, no. 335, 22 Aug. 1796, p. 1.

[121] [C.-J. Trouvé], 'Pétition présentée par les artistes au Directoire exécutif', *Moniteur universel*, no. 12, 3 Oct. 1796, pp. 45–6; citing my translation printed in Quatremère, *Letters*, pp. 171–3.

[122] Ibid., p. 46. On the source of this argument, see F. Venturi, *Italy and the Enlightenment: Studies in a Cosmopolitan Century*, trans. S. Corsi (New York, 1972), p. 239.

[123] [Trouvé], 'Pétition présentée par les artistes au Directoire exécutif', pp. 45–6.

[124] Gilks, 'Art and Politics during the "First" Directory', pp. 71–3.

[125] Quatremère-Disjonval, *Lettre du citoyen Quatremère Disjonval*, pp. 45–9; Monge quoted in N. Dhombres, 'Gaspard Monge, membre de l'institut et commissaire des sciences et des arts en

JUSTICE TO THE PAPACY, 1796   177

and its supporters thus identified his ploy and took action to make it appear extreme.

Given that Quatremère's Francophone contemporaries across the political spectrum discerned his polemic, why is the *Letters* now so misunderstood? Part of the explanation lies in how foreign readers during the late 1790s and early 1800s interpreted the *Letters* through the prism of their own concerns. In Germany, for instance, the work was read as a philosophical reflection on displacing artwork from organic habitats.[126] Readers in Italy, by contrast, considered the work an exhortation for export restrictions and a reformulation of the venerable Roman Catholic vision of classical culture.[127] Such responses conditioned modern scholars' rediscovery of the *Letters*.

However, the greater part of the explanation lies with Quatremère. During the Consulate and the Empire, Quatremère wanted the *Letters* forgotten because his lip service to perfecting humankind and implicit criticism of General Bonaparte belonged to a bygone moment.[128] In 1815, he allowed a second edition when its new function as a manifesto for returning artefacts from Paris to Rome obscured his original motives.[129] The third edition of 1836 caused even greater obfuscation. Changes and corrections erased traces of his original circumstances, and the octogenarian Quatremère—or his publisher—embellished the foreword with falsities. The most consequential fiction concerned the name and origins of his work: although earlier editions neglected to mention Miranda, this foreword claimed that the deceased general had proposed the original

---

Italie: regards sur une correspondance (juin 1796–octobre 1797)', in Barbe and Bernecker, eds, *Les intellectuels européens*, pp. 122–3; F. Pommereul, *Campagne du Général Buonaparte en Italie, pendant les années IVe et Ve de la République française* (Paris, 1797), p. 367.

[126] Johann Wilhelm Archenholz introduced the *Letters* to German readers with his translation. However, Archenholz excluded the explicitly polemical seventh letter, thereby reinforcing the tendency to ignore Quatremère's circumstances: 'Ueber den nachtheiligen Einfluss der Versetzung der Monumente aus Italien auf Kunste und Wissenschaften', *Minerva*, Oct. 1796, pp. 87–120, and Nov. 1796, 271–307. *Allgemeiner litterarischer*, no. 5, Dec. 1796, p. 577, reviewed the *Letters*.

[127] C. Fea, *Discorso intorno alle belle arti in Roma recitato nell'adunanza degli arcadi* (Rome, 1797), p. xv; idem, *Relazione di un viaggio ad Ostia* (Rome, 1802), p. 80; B. Chiaramonti, *Chirografo della Santità di Nostro signore Papa Pio VII. in data del primo ottobre 1802, sulle antichità, e belle arti in Roma, e nello Stato Ecclesiastico* (Rome, 1802), pp. 6–14; Quatremère, *Canova*, p. 196. On the context of this reception, see F. Boyer, *Autour de Canova et de Napoléon* (Paris, 1937), p. 229; B. Steindl, 'Leopoldo Cicognaras *Storia della Scultura* und die Lettres à Miranda von Quatremère de Quincy', in *Pratum Romanum: Richard Krautheimer zum 100. Geburtstag*, ed. R. Colella (Wiesbaden, 1997), p. 326; and Griener, 'Fea and the Defence of the Museum of Rome', pp. 102–5, 109, which shows that Carlo Fea printed unauthorized facsimiles of the *Letters* after 1803.

[128] F. Jacobi, *Briefwechsel zwischen Goethe und Friedrich Jacobi*, ed. M. Jacobi (Leipzig, 1846), p. 230. Jacobi wrote to Goethe in 1803 explaining how the *Letters* was 'completely out of print, and, as is self-evident, must not be reissued' (p. 230).

[129] Quatremère, *Lettres sur le projet d'enlever les monumens de l'Italie* (Rome, 1815). An article in *Ami de la religion et du roi journal ecclésiastique, politique et littéraire*, no. 105, Nov. 1815, saw the *Letters* as a restitution manifesto.

'epistolary commerce'.[130] In the context of the July monarchy, making this hero of Latin American independence integral to the work surely helped make it appear less retrograde. The *Letters on the Plan to Abduct the Monuments of Italy* henceforth became the 'Letters to Miranda'.

[130] Quatremère, *Lettres sur l'enlèvement des ouvrages de l'art antique à Athènes et à Rome écrites les unes au célèbre Canova, les autres au général Miranda* (Paris, 1836), pp. v, xii, xvi.

9

The Mask of Constitutionalism, 1796–9

Shortly after publishing the *Letters*, Quatremère left his hiding place under the care of the Vaubertrands.[1] He hoped to profit from the judiciary's recent leniency towards leaders of the uprising even though his involvement led newspapers to call him 'Quatremère de Quincy of 13 Vendémiaire'.[2] He was detained briefly in La Force prison until the Criminal Tribunal's Jury of Accusation tried him for conspiring against the Republic.[3] Representing himself, his peculiar closing speech made no mention of his role in the uprising. He argued that he had no motive to provoke violence and sow political discord because he understood that power gained through arming the populace was only ever temporary. He reminded the jury that he was a man of integrity, elected repeatedly to defend 'justice, order, and morality'. As in the *Letters*, he used his speech to appeal to different factions. On the one hand, he paid lip-service to the Directory for ensuring 'liberty's triumph abroad to efface all traces of anarchy inside France'. On the other, he appealed to royalists by describing his imaginary conversation with 'martyrs of liberty' and attacking 'power acquired through the bloody means of anarchy' that enslaved politicians to their minions.[4]

On 9 August, the jury decided in Quatremère's favour and cast doubt on whether there had even been 'a conspiracy to arm citizens against the legitimate authority'. Conservative newspapers claimed that spectators applauded the verdict, but republicans argued that he and other insurrectionists had been 'whitewashed by the tribunals'.[5] The *Décade philosophique* asked why they had been tried for

---

[1] Vaubertrand, *L'humanité pendant la terreur*, p. 27.

[2] *Gazette d'Amsterdam*, no. 12, 9 Feb. 1796; *Feuille du jour*, no. 108, 2 Aug. 1796, p. 2, and no. 112, 6 Aug. 1796, p. 1; R. Beaulaincourt-Marles, *Boniface-Louis-André de Castellane, 1758–1837* (Paris, 1901), p. 79.

[3] J. Godechot, *Les institutions de la France sous la Révolution et l'Empire* (Paris, 1985), p. 479, explains that such a jury included a representative of the Directory, officials chosen by the Department's electoral assembly, and four judges chosen by the civil tribunal.

[4] Quatremère, *Discours prononcé par le citoyen Quatremère-Quincy au tribunal criminel du département de la Seine, le 22 thermidor, an quatrième de la République* (Paris, n.d. [1796]), pp. 1–8. Quatremère's friend Le Clère printed his speech, which Peltier reprinted in *Paris pendant l'année 1796*, vol. 8, no. 70, 27 Aug. 1796, pp. 507–10.

[5] Guigniaut, *Notice historique*, p. 61; *Feuille de jour*, no. 116, 10 Aug. 1796, p. 1; Dhombres, 'Gaspard Monge, membre de l'Institut et commissaire des sciences et des arts en Italie: Regards sur une correspondance (juin 1796–octobre 1797)', pp. 122–3; Anon., *Dictionnaire des Jacobins vivans, dans lequel on verra les hauts faits de ces messieurs* (Hambourg, 1799), pp. 146–7; J.-B. Louvet, *Sentinelle*, no. 420, 17 Aug. 1796, p. 683, and no. 429, 26 Aug. 1796, p. 719.

Quatremère de Quincy: Art and Politics during the French Revolution. David Gilks, Oxford University Press.
© David Gilks 2024. DOI: 10.1093/oso/9780198745563.003.0010

conspiracy rather than revolt, and complained that they had been spared only because they failed comprehensively.[6]

After his acquittal, Quatremère was embroiled in two disputes over his father's inheritance. The first stemmed from the fact that Jean Tondu de Muiroger had given the state 40 000 francs that he owed Quatremère's late father.[7] The distinguished lawyer Nicolas-François Bellart argued on Quatremère's behalf that only profit on capital, not actual capital, could be sequestered from individuals condemned in absentia, and that the law and common practice amongst 'civilized peoples' dictated that inherited assets be set aside until claimed. The court recognized that Quatremère had been wronged, but the dispute continued over the next decade.[8] The second dispute was with his brother, who returned to Paris in July 1796 and accused Antoine Quatremère of paying Stadhouder William V to prolong his sentence after he was detained in 1787 as a prisoner of war. The legislative committee divided the estate between the quarrelsome siblings, meaning that Antoine Quatremère received just 267 722 livres—a modest sum given the family's fortune before the Revolution.[9]

Despite these frustrations, Quatremère perhaps enjoyed his freedom after hiding for almost a year. He paid 1,000 livres a year to rent a five-room, first-floor apartment at 209 rue Saint Domingue, section Fontaine-de-Grenelle.[10] He remained part of Miranda's circle of artists, art dealers, and publishers despite finding Miranda 'obstinate and blind to [his own] interest' when he refused to accept his proposal for settling a financial dispute with John Hurford Stone.[11] Since Quatremère loathed the Directory's efforts to republicanize culture, he perhaps found solace in the cultural reaction in Paris at a time when the word *patriot* became an insult.[12]

During the year after his acquittal, Quatremère expressed contrary attitudes towards museums. In October 1796, he penned an anonymous letter to the *Journal littéraire* that criticized museums created during the Revolution.[13]

---

[6] *Décade philosophique*, no. 83, 7 Aug. 1796, p. 316, and no. 84, 17 Aug. 1796, p. 384.

[7] Archives de Paris, DQ10 617, dossier 1942.

[8] G. Roche and F. Lebon, eds., *Recueil général des arrêts du Conseil d'état: comprenant les arrêtés, décrets, arrêts et ordonnances rendus en matière contentieuse, depuis l'an 8 jusqu'à 1839*, vol. 1 (Paris, 1839), p. 27; Bibliothèque de l'Institut, dossier d, paper 45: N.-F. Bellart, *Précis du Conseil de Préfecture pour le cit. Quatremère de Quincy contre le cit. Tondu de Muiroger* (n.p, n.d. [Paris, 1796]), pp. 1–7.

[9] Quatremère-Disjonval, *Lettre du Citoyen Quatremère Disjonval*, pp. 42, 1–12; Lemay, ed., *Dictionnaire des législateurs*, vol. 2, p. 621.

[10] Archives de Paris, DQ10 617, dossier 1942; BHVP, MS-NA-121, fol. 77.

[11] *Archivo del General Miranda*, vol. 14, pp. 166–7, 186, 189, 193–4, 201. Stone was an English printer who welcomed the Revolution in 1789, but his behaviour in Paris aroused suspicion; M. Stern, 'The English Press in Paris and Its Successors, 1793–1852', *Papers of the Bibliographical Society of America*, vol. 74, no. 4 (1980), pp. 307–59.

[12] J. Godechot, *La vie quotidienne en France sous le Directoire* (Paris, 1977), pp. 113, 140, 160, 166; Aulard, ed., *Paris pendant la réaction thermidorienne et sous le Directoire*, vol. 3, pp. 144, 171.

[13] Anon. [Quatremère], 'Lettre à l'auteur du Journal littéraire', *Journal littéraire*, vol. 1, no. 11, 16 Oct. 1796, pp. 361–7.

THE MASK OF CONSTITUTIONALISM, 1796–9   181

The letter repeated arguments and a citation from his earlier writings against plundering Italy and used examples that he recycled later.[14] Responding to the recent petition in favour of plundering Italy, he argued that only a 'barbarian' could imagine that depriving Rome would civilize France given the appalling state of French museums and artistic heritage. The plight of Versailles illustrated this sad state of affairs, he continued: citing Richer de Sérizy approvingly, he reported the palace's degradation and the transformation of heroic figures in its garden into inanimate stone statues. (If many visitors to Versailles shared this regret, Quatremère conveniently ignored the creation several months earlier of the Special Museum of the French School in Versailles.)[15]

For Quatremère, the state of Paris museums created since 1789 further undermined the case for plundering Rome. He urged readers to witness for themselves the Museum of Antiquities and French Monuments:

> Go to the Museum of the Petits-Augustins: you will see an old church, an old cloister and a garden filled with paintings and statues stacked as if in a fair or market. You will see columns whose capitals lean against and tear large paintings. You will see a Cardinal Richelieu, François I, Louis XII, and Christ situated between a mutilated Bacchus and hermaphrodite.[16]

Quatremère had previously wanted to purge superfluous artefacts from the Petits-Augustins, but his animus towards Lenoir hardened during the Directory when Lenoir acquired fragments from the royal tombs at Saint-Denis and won official support to transform the repository into this museum with a collection of around two hundred marble sculptures, three hundred and fifty columns and fragments, and numerous paintings.[17]

Quatremère also poured scorn on the National Museum of the Arts. His critique came at a time when the museum was blighted by political interference, delayed renovations, and accusations against its restorers. Moreover, during this period, the public could see little art in the Louvre. The Grande Galerie was closed and the Salon was yet to open. The recent exhibition of highlights from the French, Italian, and Flemish Schools had shown just 161 paintings, far fewer than the 538 paintings displayed when the museum opened in August 1793. However, Quatremère ignored these obvious targets and instead attacked what the museum displayed.[18]

---

[14] For instance, the letter's references to Le Brun, Le Sueur, and Rubens reappeared in Quatemère's *Considérations morales*, pp. 110–13, and *Recueil de notices historiques*, pp. 14–15.

[15] C. Jones, *Versailles* (London, 2018), p. 134.

[16] Anon. [Quatremère], 'Lettre à l'auteur du Journal littéraire', p. 362. These artefacts match those described in A. Lenoir, *Notice historique des monuments des arts réunis au dépot national des monumens* (Paris, year IV [1795]), pp. 11, 13–14, 18, 21–2, 24–5.

[17] Ibid.; Poulot, *Musée, nation, patrimoine*, pp. 288, 291, 295, 318.

[18] *Décade philosophique*, no. 28, 29 January 1795, pp. 211–12; D. Spieth, *Revolutionary Paris and the Market for Netherlandish Art* (Leiden, 2017), p. 81; Cantarel-Besson, ed., *La naissance du Musée du Louvre*, vol. 2, pp. 56–7, 67.

Contrary to the curators' claim that the exhibition enabled visitors to compare masterpieces and discover less-famous paintings, he complained that the uneven light and superabundance of artworks left him too exhausted to see 'anything but frames, canvases and colours'.

Quatremère then took to task the National Museum for devaluing seventeenth-century religious paintings previously displayed in locations that shrouded them in 'a little magic and much illusion'. The diminished aura of these paintings, he argued, showed that one should 'leave...each piece at the place for which it was originally destined and for which the artist often made it' and resist the 'fit of rage...to turn everything upside down'.[19] He recalled enjoying Poussin's *Winter* (1660–4) in the Luxembourg palace during his youth, but now he searched in vain in the Louvre for 'this miracle of painting'. Rubens's *Elevation of the Cross* (1610) and *Descent from the Cross* (1612–14) were 'sublime' in the cathedral of Our Lady in Antwerp, but in the Louvre 'ignoramuses mock them' and artists 'no longer recognize them'.[20] Paintings in the recent exhibition also suffered from their displacement.[21] Charles Le Brun's *Penitent Magdalen* (1656–7) 'spoke to all hearts' as part of the decorative ensemble in the chapel of the Magdalen in the Carmelite church. The fictitious legend that Le Brun depicted Louis XIV's mistress, Louise de La Vallière, added another layer of meaning, he argued, because spectators saw the painting inside the convent where she lived after retiring from court. Alas, Quatremère lamented, such sensory stimuli and sentimental associations were lost in the Salon Carré, where visitors examined Le Brun's painting 'with the eyes of a severe critic'.[22] Worse still was the plight of Eustache Le Sueur's life of Saint Bruno cycle (1645–8), the twenty-two paintings removed from the walls of the cloister of the Chartreuse de Vauvert and transferred to canvas. He claimed that, in his youth, an artist fell into a reverie inside the cloister and confused real monks with Le Sueur's representations, but the recent exhibition prevented such 'soft emotions and charming errors' and displayed just two paintings from the series.[23] Although Quatremère correctly implied that Le Sueur's paintings were highly regarded before the Revolution, the ideological nature of his critique led him to ignore well-publicized

---

[19] Anon. [Quatremère], 'Lettre à l'auteur du Journal littéraire', pp. 363–4.

[20] Ibid., pp. 362–3. These paintings by Rubens were displayed in the Louvre in 1794–5 and Poussin's *Winter* was displayed in the Luxembourg museum during Quatremère's youth; *Catalogue des tableaux du cabinet du roi au Luxembourg. Nouvelle édition* (Paris, 1774), p. 9.

[21] *Notice des tableaux des trois écoles choisis dans la collection du Muséum des arts* (Paris, 1796), pp. 41–2, 45–6.

[22] Anon. [Quatremère], 'Lettre à l'auteur du Journal littéraire', p. 363; A. McClellan, 'La mort de Charles Lebrun dans les galeries de la Révolution', in J. Guillerme, ed., *Les collections: fables et programmes* (Paris, 1993), pp. 344–6. Quatremère repeated concerns about Le Brun's painting raised in the exhibition catalogue; *Notice des tableaux des trois écoles choisis dans la collection du Muséum des arts* (Paris, 1796), pp. 41–2.

[23] Anon. [Quatremère], 'Lettre à l'auteur du Journal littéraire', pp. 363–4.

Fig. 9.1 Engraved by François Chauveau (c. 1660) after the original painting by Eustache Le Sueur, *The body of Saint Bruno is laid out in state and surrounded by mourning Carthusian monks*. Etching with engraving. 33.5 × 22.2 cm. Wellcome Collection. Reference 44180i. Public Domain Mark. This print was made after one of the twenty-two paintings depicting the life of Saint Bruno, which Le Sueur painted for the Petit Cloître des Chatreux de Paris (1645–48).

complaints in the late 1780s when the Crown bought and restored the cycle. At that time, one critic complained that Le Sueur's work had been 'disfigured by a sacrilegious hand'.[24]

Quatremère was therefore critical of the Museum of French Monuments and the National Museum, but his comments about these institutions hardly prove that he despised museums per se. Indeed, several months later, he offered practical advice for supplementing and reorganizing museums. In March 1797, Dufourny asked him to recommend an ancient statue of Apollo that the Central Museum of the Arts (the new name for the Louvre museum) could acquire as a pendant for the Apollo Belvedere.[25] Around the same time, Quatremère helped create the Special Museum of the French School in Versailles. The interior minister, Pierre Bénézech, decided that the former palace should display works by French masters, which, he hoped, would create space in the Louvre for sculptures from Italy and placate local demands in Versailles for a second national museum.[26] Quatremère joined an eight-man committee that assisted the Central Museum examine thousands of objects. He attended most meetings between April and September 1797 to discuss how to light the museum in Versailles and divide series such as Joseph Vernet's seaports of France and Le Sueur's life of Saint Bruno.[27]

Quatremère became more directly involved in politics again after his acquittal in August 1796. His writings in June and July 1796 had rehearsed clichyean criticism of the Directory, but from August onwards he was an active member of the Clichy club that met in the Tivoli gardens and the residences of Jean-Louis Gibert des Molières and Louis-François Bertin. As before, the club attracted both royalists and moderate republican legislators.[28]

Club members disagreed about how to respond to recent setbacks. Some hoped that an alliance with moderate republicans might lead to a constitutional monarchy under Louis Philippe d'Orléans, but others shared Mallet de Pan's view that they should pursue a Bourbon restoration whilst avoiding talk of punishing regicides and returning *bien nationaux*. In early 1797, however, members rallied behind Louis XVIII's new strategy for a gradual, legal restoration by gaining

---

[24] *Journal de Paris*, no. 4, 4 Jan. 1787, p. 14. The purchase is documented in AN, O1 1913 76, folios 256–71. The cycle's admirers included J.-B. de La Curne de Sainte Palaye, *Lettre à M. de B. [Bachaumont] sur le bon gout dans les arts et dans les lettres* (Paris, 1751), pp. 6–10, and H. Walpole, 'Letter to John Chute' [1771], in *Private Correspondance of Horace Walpole, Earl of Orford*, vol. 3 (London, 1820), p. 379.

[25] AN, F17 1279, dossier 4, document 3: letter from Dufourny to Lebreton, 5 March 1797.

[26] T. Gaehtgens, 'Le Musée historique de Versailles', P. Nora, ed., *Lieux des mémoires*, vol. 2 (Paris, 1986), pp. 144–5; Y. Cantarel-Besson, ed., *Musée du Louvre, janvier 1797–juin 1798: procès-verbaux du conseil d'administration du 'Musée central des arts'* (Paris, 1992), pp. 43, 48, 71.

[27] Cantarel-Besson, ed., *Musée du Louvre, janvier 1797–juin 1798*, pp. 18, 45, 47, 71–2. The Special Museum opened in 1801, but during the Empire its collection was dispersed and it closed in 1810.

[28] Popkin, 'Clichy, Club de', p. 181; Popkin, *The Right-Wing Press*, p. 85; Godechot, *Les institutions*, p. 485; idem, *La contre-révolution. Doctrine et action 1789–1804* (Paris, 1984), p. 247; Aulard, ed., *Paris pendant la réaction thermidorienne et sous le Directoire*, vol. 3, p. 91; Dumas, *Souvenirs*, vol. 3, p. 88.

royalist majorities in the councils, changing the Constitution, and replacing the executive Directors with the monarch.[29]

Quatremère's loyalty to Louis XVIII meant that he supported this strategy and donned 'the mask of constitutionalism' to hide his absolutist convictions.[30] In late February 1797, he joined royalist efforts to capitalize on the Directory's unpopularity in wealthy urban areas by penning an essay that, at first glance, appeared to dispute candidate lists in the forthcoming legislative elections.[31] The revolutionaries had previously feared that lists of self-nominating candidates would encourage factionalism and result in the election of vainglorious politicians. However, in February 1797 the Directory gambled that lists might help republican candidates in the spring elections.[32]

Quatremère composed his essay rapidly in response, but he pretended that it was the fruit of disinterested contemplation. He claimed, for instance, that the version appearing in 1797 was the 'Second Edition, reviewed and corrected' even though no 'first' edition existed. Far from advancing a philosophical argument, his essay reflected the strategy of Louis XVIII and the Clichy club. On the one hand, he exploited the backlash against candidate lists to appeal to republicans such as Roederer, who feared that introducing lists risked returning radical legislators whereas unimpeded elections without lists would allow public opinion to reach a consensus.[33] His essay therefore attacked the Directory for restoring the 'reign of crime' through this 'foreign' innovation and other 'experimental politics'.[34] On the other hand, he devoted most of the essay, ironically, to declaring his candidature in all but deed and sketching a clichyean election manifesto. He thus advised voters to reject terrorists and sophists and choose experienced candidates who would end the war, defend 'order and justice', and restore France's religion, commerce, and colonies.[35] He concluded with a thinly veiled autobiography: the ideal candidate studied the ancients, profited from his honest wealth to live a life of impartial reflection, and had first-hand political experience.[36]

The experiment with lists ultimately backfired for the Directory in the 1797 elections because the clergy and conservative newspapers directed voters towards

---

[29] P. Mansel, *Louis XVIII* (Stroud, 1999), pp. 133, 116.

[30] Quatremère in Mallet du Pan, *Mémoires et correspondance*, vol. 2, p. 414; Mansel, *Louis XVIII*, pp. 110–11, 93, 118.

[31] Quatremère, *La véritable liste des candidats, précédée d'observations sur la nature de l'institution des candidats, et son application au gouvernement représentatif* (Paris, 1797). *Feuille du jour*, no. 313, 5 March 1797, p. 3, mentioned this essay.

[32] M. Crook, 'Le candidat imaginaire, ou l'offre et le choix dans les élections de la Révolution française', *Annales historiques de la Révolution française*, vol. 321, no. 3 (2000), pp. 93–8; P. Rosanvallon, *The Demands of Liberty: Civil Society in France since the Revolution*, trans. A. Goldhammer (Cambridge, MA, 2007), ch. 2; B. Gainot, 'Le contentieux électoral sous le Directoire. Monisme et pluralisme dans la culture politique de la France révolutionnaire', *Revue historique*, vol. 2, no. 642 (2007), p. 329; Edelstein, *The French Revolution*, p. 322.

[33] Quatremère, *La véritable liste*, pp. 51, 64. Roederer praised Quatremère's essay in *Journal d'économie publique*, vol. 3, no. 20, 10 March 1797, p. 66.

[34] Quatremère, *La véritable liste*, pp. 4–7, 20–7.   [35] Ibid., pp. 27–57.   [36] Ibid., pp. 57–67.

186   QUATREMÈRE DE QUINCY

their preferred candidates.[37] For example, Joseph-François Michaud's *Feuille du jour* advised Parisians to elect Quatremère, La Harpe, Lacretelle, Richer de Sérizy, Claude-François Chauveau-Lagarde, and Antoine Balthazar Joachim d'Andre.[38] The royalists consequently won half the seats for renewal and became the majority in the Council of Five Hundred. Quatremère was the first-choice candidate in Fontaine-de-Grenelle section and one of four new legislators elected by the Seine Department. Royalists abroad read the news with delight. In Brno, the Marquis de Bombelles hoped that the results would lead to 'the only government... suitable for France'. From Berne, Mallet du Pan wrote that he was 'well acquainted with Quatremère de Quincy, a man full of courage, imagination, talent and inflexible principle'. 'Parisians never decided better', Mallet du Pan added; by choosing 'men of property, upright and moderate men', they vindicated the decision 'to rebuild the monarchy stone by stone, even, if necessary, by means of the Constitution itself, and without running the danger of setting off revolutionary violence'.[39]

Quatremère returned to the Salle du Manège on 20 May 1797 as one of the most experienced legislators on the right. He found several allies in the Council of Five Hundred: Joseph Bernardi and Pierre Royer-Collard shared his belief that Catholicism was the proper foundation for popular morality; and he considered General Amédée Willot 'brave, frank, active, [and] clever'. However, he mistrusted General Jean-Charles Pichegru (perhaps because his brother had served as Pichegru's adjunct in the Netherlands) and found no obvious clichyean leader who could coordinate royalist efforts to overturn legislation.[40]

This vacuum of leadership meant that Quatremère was, for several months over the summer, amongst the most active clichyeans in the Council. He used his membership of the Committee of Public Instruction to advance the club's agenda and mitigate the harm that he believed the Revolution had caused education.[41] For example, he opposed selling rectories housing primary school teachers. The long-serving deputy Louis-Alexandre Jard-Panvillier argued that selling rectories would

---

[37] J. Suratteau, 'Les élections de l'an V aux conseils du Directoire', *Annales historiques de la Révolution française*, vol. 30 (1958), pp. 21–63; C. Lucas, 'The First Directory and the Rule of Law', *French Historical Studies*, vol. 10, no. 2 (1977), p. 254; Crook, 'Le candidat imaginaire, ou l'offre et le choix dans les élections de la Révolution française', pp. 99–105; H. Mitchell, *The Underground War against Revolutionary France. The Missions of William Wickham 1794–1800* (Oxford, 1965), pp. 149–50, 154, 156.

[38] *Feuille du jour*, no. 343, 5 April 1797, p. 3.

[39] Bombelles, *Journal*, vol. 5, p. 180; Mallet du Pan, *Mémoires et correspondance*, vol. 2, pp. 307–9.

[40] A. Philippe, *Royer-Collard, sa vie publique, sa vie privée, sa famille* (Paris, 1857), p. 43; Quatremère, [Review of Bernardi, *De l'origine et des progrès de la législation française*] *Journal des savans*, Dec. 1817, p. 750; A.-C. Thibaudeau, *Mémoires sur la Convention et le Directoire* (Paris, 1824), vol. 2, pp. 177–8; Quatremère in Mallet du Pan, *Mémoires et correspondance*, vol. 2, p. 416; Viénot de Vaublanc, *Mémoires de M. le comte de Vaublanc*, p. 331; Mitchell, *The Underground War*, p. 159.

[41] Quatremère, *Motion d'ordre faite par Quatremère, au nom de la commission de l'instruction publique, sur le projet présenté par la commission de l'aliénation des presbytères. Séance du 11 thermidor, an V* [29 July 1797] (Paris, year V [1797], p. 2.

THE MASK OF CONSTITUTIONALISM, 1796–9   187

prevent the Catholic Church reacquiring these buildings, which, in any case, faced ruin because teachers could not afford to maintain them.[42] However, Quatremère countered that selling rectories would exacerbate the damage to education that had been caused by contradictory laws and utopian ambitions since 1789. Successive Committees of Public Instruction, he lamented, had denied priests their traditional pedagogical role without replacing them with salaried teachers. As for maintaining the rectories, he argued that the best method of conservation required respectful and continuous use.[43] His report convinced the Council of Five Hundred to suspend selling rectories until public instruction had been reorganized.[44]

Quatremère also tried to protect education by consolidating scholarships for Paris colleges after the number of scholarship students fell from around 325 in 1793 to sixty in 1795. He proposed that his alma-mater, the Collège Égalité (formerly Louis-le-Grand), should control scholarships currently scattered across colleges. Despite the 'revolutionary thunderstorms', he argued, this 'solitary asylum of the sacred fire of science, love of study, and the precious traditions of ancient disciplines of learning that the Greeks and Romans handed us' had thrived under Jean-François Champagne's leadership.[45] If Quatremère's suggestion was ignored at the time, his general idea was realized the following year with the creation of the Prytanée.[46]

Quatremère exploited his position in the Council of Five Hundreds to make politicized interventions concerning visual culture. In June, he proposed creating a commission to survey the consistency and legality of inscriptions on monuments—a measure intended to expunge traces of the year II.[47] In July, he joined a committee tasked with examining plans to sell the Palais de l'Égalité (formerly the Palais-Royal) and its gardens to rid Paris of a hotspot for counter-revolutionary activity. Ignoring the site's recent political use, he convinced the other members that the Palais should not be sold because Victor Louis's design beautified Paris and was part of France's architectural heritage.[48]

---

[42] *Collection générale des lois et des actes du corps législatif et du Directoire exécutif* (Paris, 1797), pp. 159–61; L. Merle, 'Louis-Alexandre Jard-Panvillier', *La revue du Bas-Poitou et des provinces de l'Ouest*, vols 5–6 (1969), p. 343; L.-A. Jard-Panvillier, *Rapport fait au nom d'une commission spéciale sur l'aliénation des presbytères, 8 nivôse, an V* (Paris, year V [1797]), pp. 3, 4, 6–7.

[43] Quatremère, *Motion d'ordre*, pp. 2–4, 12–14.

[44] *La clef du cabinet des souverains*, no. 192, 30 July 1797, p. 1716, and no. 193, 31 July 1797, p. 1722; P.-S.-F. Cardonnel, *Opinion du citoyen Cardonnel, député du Tarn, sur l'aliénation des presbytères proposée par Jard-Panvillier, au nom de la commission dont il est le rapporteur* (Paris, year V [1797]), pp. 1–14.

[45] Quatremère, *Corps législative. Conseil des Cinq Cents. Rapport fait par Quatremère au nom de la commission d'instruction publique sur le mode et l'organisation des bien affectes aux bourses des ci-devant collèges de Paris, séance du 9 fructidor an V* [15 August 1797] (Paris, year V [1797]), pp. 1–14.

[46] For the background, see Palmer, ed., *The School of the French Revolution*, pp. 32–3, 113–83; idem, *The Improvement of Humanity*, p. 177; idem, 'Le Prytanée français et les écoles de Paris (1798–1802)', *Annales historiques de la Révolution française*, no. 243 (1981), pp. 123–52.

[47] *Journal des débats et lois du corps législatif*, no. 24, 7 June 1797, p. 339.

[48] Schneider, *Quatremère*, p. 32.

188 QUATREMÈRE DE QUINCY

Quatremère's politics even came to the fore when he tried to persuade other legislators to exempt painters and sculptors from paying tax. Quatremère was asked to report on artists' behalf after Louis-Sébastien Mercier's eccentric efforts failed to convince the Council of Five Hundred.[49] Quatremère's underlying argument that the 'arts of genius' differed from the mechanical arts and from the commercial activities of art dealers rearticulated the hierarchical ethos of the Academy of Painting and Sculpture.[50] He reasoned that it was absurd for painters and sculptors to pay tax whilst exempting composers, poets, and architects because all artists studied nature for glory, not financial profit. Painters and sculptors differed merely in their choice of instruments and the 'organs that they address to reach the soul'. In any case, he concluded, taxing artists was both impossible because their productivity and the value of their art fluctuated, and un-enforceable because artists could declare themselves 'amateurs'.[51]

However, Quatremère failed to convince the Council. One legislator countered that taxing artists was preferable to taxing agriculture and poorer citizens. Others insisted that the state should tax all profits and that Parisian artists should not live at the nation's expense.[52] Quatremère's response betrayed his frustration and his politics: taxing artists would raise just 2,000 écus yet dishonour a profession that 'had lost everything to the revolution'. His opponents on the issue, he complained, used 'language that does not belong to a country that is ... illustrious thanks to arts, but rather to the times when vandalism exercised its ravages'. Despite his efforts, however, the majority of legislators opposed deliberating on his amendment.[53]

Alongside his work on behalf of artists and the Committee of Public Instruction, in summer 1797 Quatremère joined clichyean attempts to confront the Directory when the royalist press exploited division between the Executive Directors, lobbied for peace, and denigrated Bonaparte's victories. Like other royalist legislators, he opposed restrictions on refractory priests and émigrés, criticized arbitrary deportations, and defended a purported émigré who had worked with the Austrian occupiers in Valenciennes in 1793.[54] Similarly, he tried to remove local impediments to royalist electoral gains by demanding the

---

[49] *Journal des débats et des décrets*, vol. 83, no. 420, pp. 427–30 and vol. 83, no. 421, pp. 433–40.

[50] P. Michel, *Le Commerce du tableau à Paris: dans la seconde moitié du XVIIIe siècle* (Paris, 2007), p. 101.

[51] Quatremère, *Rapport fait par Quatremère, au nom d'une commission spéciale, sur l'exemption du droit de patente en faveur des peintres, sculpteurs, graveurs & architectes: séance du 13 messidor, an V* (Paris, Year V [1797]), pp. 1–14.

[52] *La clef du cabinet des souverains*, no. 192, 30 July 1797, p. 1714; BnF, 8-YA3-27 (54, 1623), MSS 418–20 (J.-C. Deloynes, 'Rapport de quatremere de quinci sur les patentes des artistes. 10 thermidor an 5. 28 juillet 1797').

[53] Ibid., MSS 419–20.

[54] *Journal des débats et lois du Corps législatif*, no. 31, 10 June 1797, p. 463; T.-J.-N. Vasse-Saint-Ouen, *Rapport fait par Vasse, au nom d'une commission, composée des représentants du peuple Dissandes-Moullevade, Quatremer et Vasse, chargée d'examiner la pétition de J.-J. Desmarets, ancien directeur des subsistances militaires à Valenciennes, mis hors la loi et inscrit comme émigré à l'époque de l'invasion par les Autrichiens. Séance du 5 fructidor an V* (Paris, Year V [1797]), pp. 1–8.

THE MASK OF CONSTITUTIONALISM, 1796–9   189

replacement of personnel in the central offices responsible for urban policing and subsistence so that they reflected the Councils' political composition.[55] He also joined Vaublanc and Pastoret's campaign to ban political clubs and remove the threat from Constitutional circles, which royalists considered 'temples of Jacobinism' and republican legislators deemed sources of free expression to 'nourish the sacred fire of patriots'.[56]

Quatremère's allegiance to the Clichy club led him to adopt some inconsistent positions in the Council. For example, despite previously condemning slavery, in June–July during debates on colonial affairs he supported restoring white-settler interests in Saint-Domingue by reimposing military force. Similarly, despite his earlier opposition to denunciation, he supported legislation to enable the Council to denounce ministers, generals, and colonial agents.[57]

If Quatremère wore the 'mask of constitutionalism' in the Council, his contemporaries nevertheless saw in him an 'agitator' who wanted to overthrow the Directory. He supplied Mallet du Pan with intelligence, met François Barthélemy (the Director sympathetic to the royalist cause), criticized moderate clichyans such as Mathieu Dumas and his 'sect of constitutionalists', and conspired with 'absolutist' clichyans several times a week at the Place Vendôme.[58] His reputation lends plausibility to Barras's story that he and Pierre Lenormand told General Hoche in late July that they needed 'to act immediately' because they had already lost allies and time 'making small attacks on the Directory'.[59] Quatremère, Barras suggested, wanted to evaluate Hoche's willingness to lead a coup, but this ploy backfired. Over the next weeks, the Directors removed conservative ministers, eased pressure on radicals, and solicited military support. By contrast, the royalists only mobilized around fifteen hundred men despite their strength in the Councils.[60] Dumas later regretted

[55] Quatremère, *Corps legislatif. Conseil des Cinq-cents. Opinion de Quatremère sur le renouvellement des bureaux centraux. Seance du 19 messidor an V* [7 July 1797] (Paris, year V [1797]), pp. 1–7. *La clef du cabinet des souverains*, no. 171, 9 July 1797, pp. 1542–3, summarized the debate.

[56] Quatremère, *Opinion de Quatremère, sur le second projet relatif aux réunions politiques* (Paris, n.d. [1797]), pp. 4, 6, 8, 10–11. The British Library's *Bibliothèque historique de la Révolution, Conseil des Cinq Cents, Rapports etc.*, no. 358, contains speeches from the debate. On the context, see C. Peyrard, 'Les débats sur le droit d'Association et de réunion sous le Directoire', *Annales historiques de la Révolution française*, vol. 3, no. 297 (1994), pp. 463–78.

[57] Quatremère, *Rapport fait par Quatremère au nom d'une commission spéciale sur la responsabilité des ministres et celle des agents du Directoire dans les colonies Séance du 30 messidor, an 5* [18 July 1797] (Paris, year V [1797]), pp. 6, 18, 31; Quatremère, *Suite aux considérations sur les arts du dessin*, p. 16. On the context, see B. Gainot, 'The constitutionalization of general freedom under the Directory', in M. Dorigny, ed., *The Abolitions of Slavery: From L. F. Sonthonax to Victor Schoelcher, 1793, 1794, 1848* (New York, 2003), pp. 183–6.

[58] Thibaudeau, *Mémoires sur la Convention et le Directoire*, vol. 1, p. 189; A. Nettement, *Histoire du coup d'état du 18 fructidor an IV* (Paris, 1851), pp. 17–18; Quatremère in Mallet du Pan, *Mémoires et correspondance*, vol. 2, pp. 412–6. Quatremère's reference to previous letters ('You wish, Monsieur, that I should continue writing to you') suggests that they had corresponded over a lengthy period.

[59] Barras, *Mémoires*, vol. 2, pp. 489–90.

[60] J. Godechot, 'The Internal History of France during the Wars, 1793–1814', in C. Crawley, ed., *The New Cambridge Modern History*, vol. 9 (Cambridge, 1995), p. 290; Mansel, *Louis XVIII*, p. 127; D. Sutherland, *The French Revolution and Empire: the Quest for a Civic Order* (Oxford, 2002), p. 286.

190 QUATREMÈRE DE QUINCY

his failure to contain the Clichy club's 'royalist party' whose poorly concealed plots provided the pretext for the Fructidor coup.[61]

Quatremère was amongst the most experienced royalists removed from office on 3–4 September 1797 as a result of the coup—he was one of just thirteen legislators expelled who had served as national representatives *before* the Directory. He was expelled because of his politics rather than papers found on d'Antraigues, which made no mention of him.[62] Royalists in Hamburg claimed that Quatremère-Disjonval demanded his brother's arrest, but there is no evidence for this.[63] The triumvir of Directors—Barras, La Révellière, and Rewbell—instigated the coup because it feared royalist electoral gains. However, the triumvir presented the coup as a public-safety measure against the 'royalist conspiracy' that Bonaparte uncovered when he caught d'Antraigues and found evidence of Pichegru's treason and Wickham's contact with legislators.[64] During the coup, General Augereau's soldiers surrounded the Councils and the triumvir closed royalist newspapers, arrested fifty-three legislators and their fellow Directors Carnot and Barthélemy, and annulled many election results.[65] Although bloodless, the coup crushed the greatest royalist threat to the Republic's survival since 1793 and marked the start of a new phase of the Directory characterized by the regime's disregard for the law.[66]

The Directory ordered Quatremère to leave Paris immediately and France within a fortnight, but he had fled elsewhere by the time that the police raided his apartment and seized his papers.[67] Contrary to what Quatremère's biographers have claimed, he did not leave France right away. If the cold winter prevented him from travelling to London, after February 1798 the French occupation of Rome deterred him from returning to Italy. For over a year, he therefore lay low in Paris, rented out his properties, and moved from place to place, perhaps assisted by Royer-Collard, Miranda, and the foreign minister,

---

[61] Dumas, *Souvenirs*, vol. 3, pp. 88–9; Mitchell, *The Underground War*, pp. 225–6; E. Jovy, *De Royer-Collard à Racine. Quelques recherches sur une partie de la descendance de Racine, à propos d'une lettre inédite de Royer-Collard* (Paris, 1917), p. 13; F. de Rovéréa, *Mémoires de F. de Rovéréa*, vol. 2 (Berne, 1848), p. 56; F. de Barthélemy, *Mémoires historiques et diplomatiques* (NP, 1799), p. 71.

[62] AN, AF III 44, dossier 158.

[63] *Le 18 fructidor, ou anniversaire des fêtes directoriales* (Hamburg, 1798), p. 18; and anon., *Dictionnaire des Jacobins vivans, dans lequel on verra les hauts faits de ces messieurs* (Hambourg, 1799), pp. 146–7.

[64] G. Caudrillier, *La trahison de Pichegru et les intrigues royalistes dans l'est avant fructidor* (Paris, 1908), pp. 354–86.

[65] I.-É. Larue, *Histoire du dix-huit fructidor: la déportation des députés à la Guyane, leur évasion et leur retour en France*, vol. 2 (Paris, 1895), pp. 251–92; A. Meynier, *Les coups d'état du Directoire*, vol. 1 (Paris, 1927), pp. 5–20.

[66] Lucas, 'The First Directory and the Rule of Law', pp. 231–60.

[67] *Moniteur universel*, vol. 28, no. 354, 10 Sept. 1797, pp. 809–10; AN, T1662, no. 11 ('Quatremère de quincy, deporte', report 3706); Archives de Paris: DQ10 422, dossier 3202; DQ10 1396, dossier 1037; DQ10 51, file 28, no. 5937.

THE MASK OF CONSTITUTIONALISM, 1796–9   191

Talleyrand.[68] During this time, he joined the plot to encourage popular uprisings, undermine the Directory, and form a provisional government until Louis XVIII returned.[69]

Whilst Quatremère kept out of sight in Paris, the Directory renounced the national debt, executed around a hundred and sixty royalists, purged local authorities that had tolerated counter-revolutionary violence, and adopted harsher measures against Catholics. He was in the city in July 1798 during the triumphal entry of monuments of art and science from Rome and Venice whose expropriation he had warned against.[70] In November, however, he decided to leave for Frankfurt, perhaps because he feared that his property would be sequestered or that he would be caught if he remained. Talleyrand obtained on his behalf a passport issued by the Kingdom of Sardinia to 'Monsieur Alessandro Quartini, Piedmontese painter and dealer of paintings, prints and other curiosities', but the hasty nature of his departure prevented him from finding anyone to look after his collection of artworks and books.[71] He complained to Mallet du Pan that he was expelled 'with the utmost rudeness' before he could plan how to serve 'the good cause' with 'the very few friends [he] then possessed'.[72] Before setting out on his journey, he did not know 'a word of German', he confessed, and his only contact in Frankfurt was the son of Miranda's friend Barrois.[73]

Quatremère slipped out of Paris on 27 November, carrying antique medals to help him pass for Quartini and sell along the way. His subterfuge was so successful that the Directory, assuming he remained in France, wanted him taken to the

[68] Quatremère was not banished to Guiana for doubting Madame de Staël's sex, as quipped in G. Canning, 'New Morality', *The Anti-Jacobin; or, Weekly Examiner*, no. 36, 9 July 1798, p. 285. Quatremère's previous biographers claim that he left France in 1797; see, for example, Schneider, *Quatremère*, p. 12. For evidence of properties he rented out, see Bibliothèque de l'Institut, MS 2555, dossier 4, paper 52. Quatremère's letter to Miranda in 1798 (in which he explained 'you can see … that I am no longer where you left me') suggests that he hid with Miranda's assistance, or at least somewhere known to him, until Miranda left Paris in December 1797; AN: F7 6285 (police generale), no. 5819, dossier titled 'Correspondence du C. Quatremère avec Miranda pour les annes 1798 et 1799', paper 14. Royer-Collard recalled meeting Quatremère most days in Passy, where they 'conspired together'; H. Jouin, *David d'Angers, sa vie, son oeuvre, ses écrits et ses contemporains*, vol. 1 (Paris, 1878), p. 164.

[69] Godechot, *Contre-révolution*, pp. 145, 149; Mitchell, *The Underground War*, pp. 225–6; Jovy, *De Royer-Collard à Racine*, p. 13; Rovéréa, *Mémoires*, vol. 2, p. 56.

[70] P. Mainardi, 'Assuring the Empire of the Future: The 1798 Fête de la Liberté', *Art Journal*, vol. 48, no. 2 (1989), pp. 155–63.

[71] AN, F7 6285, no. 5819, paper 14. Quatremère told Adolphe Leclère in 1828 that Talleyrand was 'the most loyal man in friendship I have known' and added that the foreign minister warned him to escape, gave him a false passport, and lent him 10 000 gold francs; Guigniaud, *Notice historique*, p. 32. During the early Revolution, Quatremère worked with Talleyrand on several committees; AP, vol. 34, p. 498; M. Guillaume, ed., *Procès-verbaux du Comité d'Instruction publique de l'Assemblée législative* (Paris, 1889), p. xviii; R. Stamp, 'Educational Thought and Educational Practice during the Years of the French Revolution', *History of Education Quarterly*, vol. 6, no. 3 (1966), pp. 34–5. During the Restoration, Talleyrand often hosted Quatremère, whom he called him a man of 'intelligence, probity, and knowledge'; *Extraits des memoires du prince de Talleyrand*, vol. 2, p. 323; and G. Lacour-Gayet, *Talleyrand* (Paris, 1990), p. 1215.

[72] Quatremère in Mallet du Pan, *Mémoires et correspondance*, vol. 2, p. 416.

[73] AN, F7 6285, no. 5819, paper 14.

192 QUATREMÈRE DE QUINCY

Île d'Oléron. Even in 1799, the United States ambassador in London believed that he was still in Paris.[74] The daily Paris-Dresden stagecoach that he perhaps caught took a week to cover six hundred kilometres through eastern France and the annexed left bank of the Rhine before reaching the medieval walled city of Frankfurt. However, he found no reason to remain and soon complained that Frankfurt lacked the libraries that he needed for his history of the Revolution. Convinced that the Directory's spies were omnipresent, he spoke only Italian to preserve his disguise and avoided the Francophone community of Huguenots and merchants.[75]

The following week Quatremère travelled to Hamburg. He led what he described as 'a discreet and constrained life', away from his compatriots, Francophone theatres, newspapers, and cafés. 'Germany displeases me greatly', he complained. His letters expressed boredom ('I cannot see what I should do here, where I know no one and I have no perspective on things') and loneliness ('I have no other company, amusement or occupation than my heating stove'). His only help, he wrote, came from 'a young man employed by a banker, who can do me a few favours but is only available intermittently'. The weather worsened his plight; he described the 'deluge of snow' and 'cold worthy of Lapland' that froze the Elbe and prevented him from travelling and receiving news and letters. 'To hell with the ice and port and city of Hamburg and its inhabitants for building a commercial city on a river than can remain frozen for three months!', he lamented. In early January 1799, he described his hunger, penury, and broken thumb and concluded that 'nothing approaches the isolation in which I find myself.... I am a dead man'.[76]

It was in this state of despair that Quatremère agreed to meet Dumas in Eutin, Holstein. Dumas recalled that Quatremère was welcomed as 'one of the French writers most distinguished by his taste for the arts and profound knowledge' because his 'celebrated letters on the removal of monuments and artworks from Italy had already made him famous in Germany and commended him to all friends of literature and the fine arts'.[77] Such hospitality meant that Quatremère was 'infinitely better here in this small and inconspicuous town', as he put it.[78] Although he initially only planned to spend several days here, he decided to remain as Friedrich Stolberg's guest. However, his letters describe the tension when he surprised his hosts by criticizing Dumas and Friedrich Heinrich Jacobi's

---

[74] National Archives, London, HO 42/46/125, ff. 273–4.

[75] AN, F7 6285, no. 5819, papers 14–15.

[76] AN, F7 6285, no. 5819, paper 14–16. Other émigrés also complained about the weather. For example, see Balliol College Archives & Manuscripts: Mallet Family Papers, Letter from Portalis to Mallet du Pan, 27 Jan. 1799. This section draws upon F. Baldensperger, *Le mouvement des idées dans l'émigration française (1789–1815)*, vol. 1 (Paris, 1924), p. 140; M. Lindemann, *Patriots and Paupers: Hamburg, 1712–1830* (Oxford, 1990), pp. 48–52; N. Boyle, *Goethe: The Poet of the Age* (Oxford, 1991), p. 43.

[77] Dumas, *Souvenirs*, vol. 3, p. 161.   [78] *Archivo del General Miranda*, vol. 6, p. 341.

constitutionalism. Angered by the 'stupid infatuation' with the Revolution, he praised Mallet du Pan for attacking German 'apes' who considered 1789 the 'immaculate conception of human reason'.[79] If he no longer feared spies, he believed that the Directory's influence meant that eight in ten newspapers in northern Germany 'write at [its] discretion'.[80]

Quatremère still hoped to reach England, which he described in a letter to Miranda as 'the nation that is truly great that is not the great nation'. 'There is a god for travellers', he mused, and the sea voyage from Harburg to Great Yarmouth could hardly be worse than covering by land 'five hundred leagues in Germany'.[81] Miranda obtained entry papers for him through Wickham and Rufus King, but he sent them to Hamburg and they only reached Eutin several months later. After finally receiving the papers, Quatremère postponed his voyage until May because of heavy rain and a lack of travel companions. However, his voyage was then foiled by unusual spring weather and his papers ceased to be valid. Around this time, Miranda discovered that his secretary was a royalist spy and his support for Quatremère waned, hence their correspondence stopped abruptly in April 1799. Quatremère asked Mallet du Pan for help reaching London, but their efforts never materialized.[82]

Quatremère found his year in Holstein instructive despite his desire to leave for England. An extract from one of his letters provides an insight into his milieu in this atypical corner of Germany: 'several... respectable members of the true republic... of the arts and sciences', he told Miranda, had introduced him to new 'types of knowledge'.[83] Other sources suggest that this 'republic' was hosted by Christian Stolberg in Tremsbüttel, Friedrich Stolberg in Eutin, and Friedrich Reventlow in Emkendorf. These pious scholars invited émigrés such as d'Angiviller, Dumas, and Portalis to meet savants and men of letters such as the poets Johann Heinrich Voss and Friedrich Gottlieb Klopstock, the Danish mathematician and cartographer Karsten Niebuhr and the philosopher Jacobi.[84] This environment tended to reinforce what most émigrés already thought rather than convert them to the latest currents in Germany philosophy. Just as Portalis dismissed Fichte and Kant as 'sophists' who wrote abstract philosophy for other philosophers, Quatremère ignored Kant and other German writers on aesthetics. 'Germany', Quatremère complained, 'is cankered far deeper than might be

---

[79] Ibid., p. 356. [80] Quatremère in Mallet du Pan, *Mémoires et correspondance*, vol. 2, p. 418.
[81] *Archivo del General Miranda*, vol. 6, pp. 341–2, 356.
[82] National Archives, London: HO 42/46/125, folios 273–4 (Rufus King letter dated 21 Jan. 1799); *Archivo del General Miranda*, vol. 6 pp. 355–7; Quatremère in Mallet du Pan, *Mémoires et correspon-dance*, vol. 2, p. 421. Significantly, Miranda made no contact with Quatremère in November 1800 when he visited Paris. However, Quatremère later sent him a copy of *De l'architecture égyptienne* (Paris, 1803)—*Archivo del General Miranda*, vol. 16, pp. 281–2.
[83] *Archivo del General Miranda*, vol. 6, p. 356.
[84] Dumas, *Souvenirs*, vol. 3, pp. 158–69; Balliol College Archives & Manuscripts, Mallet Family Papers, Letters from Portalis to Mallet du Pan, 2 June and 24 June 1797; J. Silvestre de Sacy, *Le comte d'Angiviller: dernier directeur général des bâtiments du roi* (Paris, 1953), ch. 18.

194 QUATREMÈRE DE QUINCY

supposed; and scholastic philosophy is more certainly noxious than even the worldly and frivolous philosophy of France'.[85]

Quatremère spent most time in Eutin amongst 'several...famous literary figures...who have come in search of a port against tempests'. He formed close ties with three of these men.[86] The first was his host, Friedrich Stolberg, who was president of the Lübeck episcopal court. He described Stolberg as a man 'after my own heart', 'virtuous and religious', a 'genius', and an 'anti-revolutionary' Francophile.[87] Stolberg's earlier reflections on Italy, Pius VI, and the connection between the ancient and Christian worlds had in some respects foreshadowed his own *Letters*, but Stolberg was more critical of Rome's museums in ways that might have shaped his future writings.[88] For example, Stolberg regretted the displacement of ancient sarcophagi from their 'proper place' in Rome to fill museums 'in which the number of objects destroys the effect of each'.[89] Stolberg also introduced Quatremère to Christian Heyne's scholarship on the ancient Greeks' use of ivory, mosaic, and ebony, which Quatremère cited critically in his writings on ancient polychromatic monumental sculptures.[90]

The second figure, Charles Vanderbourg, tutored Stolberg's children.[91] Vanderbourg perhaps inspired Quatremère to learn German. (Quatremère learned the language sufficiently well to develop a taste for Christoph Wieland's novels, read German scholarship on antiquity, and start translating Heinrich Meyer reflections on landscape history.)[92] Vanderboug also introduced his

---

[85] Quatremère in Mallet du Pan, *Mémoires et correspondance*, vol. 2, p. 416–17; Guigniaud, *Notice historique*, p. 48. Revealingly, Quatremère never cited Kant's *Critique of the Power of Judgement* (1790) and never used the word *ésthétique*. He used Kant simply as a strawman in a single note to *Essai sur la nature, le but et les moyens de l'imitation dans les beaux-arts* (Paris, 1823), p. vi, n. 1; and his second library only contained one of Kant's writings, namely Peyer-Imhoff's 1796 French translation of *Observations on the Feeling of the Beautiful and Sublime* (1764)—*Bibliothèque*, p. 46. Quatremère's exposure to and interest in Kantian philosophy and German aesthetics is greatly exaggerated by Schneider, *L'ésthetique classique*, pp. 83–92, and J. Rubin, 'The Politics of Quatremère to Quincy's Romantic Classicism', in G. Levitine, ed., *Culture and Revolution: Cultural Ramifications of the French Revolution* (College Park, MD, 1989), p. 230; idem, 'Allegory versus Narrative in Quatremère de Quincy', *Journal of Aesthetics and Art Criticism*, vol. 44, no. 4 (1986), pp. 383–4, 389.

[86] Quatremère in Mallet du Pan, *Mémoires et correspondance de Mallet du Pan*, vol. 2, pp. 411–12. Quatremère's letters imply that he saw few people outside Eutin—an impression supported by Portalis, who wrote in May 1799 that he was yet to see Quatremère in Germany.

[87] Quatremère in Mallet du Pan, *Mémoires et correspondance de Mallet du Pan*, vol. 2, pp. 412–13.

[88] F. Stolberg, *Travels through Germany, Switzerland, Italy, and Sicily* [1794], trans. T. Holcroft, vol. 1 (London, 1796), pp. 360, 386, 432. Stolberg remains a relatively obscure figure in recent scholarship despite meriting a place in A.-L.-G. de Staël, *De l'Allemagme*, vol. 2 [1813] (Paris, 1980), pp. 258–60. See, however, E. Joshua, *Friedrich Leopold Graf Zu Stolberg and the German Romantics* (Bern, 2005), ch. 4.

[89] Stolberg, *Travels*, p. 432.

[90] Quatremère later wrote a sympathetic biography of Heyne in Michaud, ed., *Biographie universelle ancienne et moderne*, vol. 19 (Paris, 1857), pp. 404–11. Revealingly, Quatremère's *Le jupiter olympien, ou, l'art de la sculpture antique, considéré sous un nouveau point de vue* (Paris, 1815) contained more references to Heyne than to Winckelmann or Caylus.

[91] R. Mortier, 'Un "germanisant" sous l'Empire et la Restauration. Charles Vanderbourg (1765–1827)', *Revue belge de philologie et d'histoire*, vol. 29, no. 4 (1951), pp. 1003–27.

[92] Quatremère, '[Review of] Cratès et Hipparquie, roman de Wieland, suivi des Pythagoriciennes, par le même; traduit par M. de Vanderbourg, 1818', *Journal des savants* (Sept. 1818), p. 535; idem, *Essai sur la nature, le but et les moyens de l'imitation*, p. 329. Quatremère's *Le jupiter olympien* cited German

companion to some simple if useful terminology glossed from his understanding of German philosophy, such as the distinction between 'materialism' and 'idealism'. Quatremère arrived when Vanderbourg was translating Lessing's *Laocoön: An Essay on the Limits of Painting and Poetry* (1766). Responding to Winckelmann's belief that signs were images that depended on nature, Lessing argued that signs were like words, whose meaning relied on convention.[93] However, Vanderbourg and Quatremère reinterpreted Lessing's work as the first step towards a fuller 'comparative anatomy of the arts', such as Quatremère provided in his later reflections on the nature, the ends, and the means of the imitative arts.[94] For Quatremère, Lessing thus provided a theoretical justification for insisting that artists work within the rules of their art because he had demonstrated that the 'system of similitude between painting and poetry' hinged on misinterpretations of Horace's *ut pictora poesis*. Artists, Quatremère demanded, must respect the 'inalienable patrimony' that nature assigned each art: artists who stole from other arts failed to recognize that the mind could appreciate just one art at a time, and that the purpose of art was not verisimilitude but 'imitation' (i.e. the creation of a representation that resembled, yet remained distinct from, the subject).[95]

The affable bisexual widower Jacobi was the third figure in Quatremère's Eutin circle. Like Quatremère, Jacobi came from a merchant family, had first-hand experience of politics, abhorred *ex nihilo* abstractions, and was a prolific author whose most famous writings were contributions to quarrels.[96] Jacobi was known for his philosophical tracts on Spinoza and Hume, but his most recent work, *On Divine Things and Their Revelation*, remained unpublished until 1811.[97]

---

scholarship by Meiners, Spengler, Boettiger, Uffenbach, and Volkel besides Heyne (pp. 274, 281–2, 286, 305, 412). Quatremère explained in an unpublished manuscript (Bibliothèque de l'Institut de France, 2555, dossier 2, paper 20) that he started translating Meyer's chapter in Goethe's *Winckelmann und sein Jahrhundert* (Tübingen, 1805) but decided to develop instead his own ideas on the subject. The result was his 'Essai historique sur l'art du paysage à Rome', *Archives littéraires de l'Europe*, vol. 10 (1807), p. 376.

[93] G. Lessing, *Laocoön: An Essay on the Limits of Painting and Poetry* [1766], ed. J. Bernstein (Cambridge, 2002), pp. 25–130; E. Gombrich, 'The Diversity of the Arts: The Place of the Laocoon in the Life and Work of G. E. Lessing (1729–1781)', in idem, *Tributes: Interpreters of our Cultural Tradition* (Oxford, 1984), pp. 30–50.

[94] C. Vanderbourg, 'Avertissment du traducteur', *Du Laocoon, ou des limites respectives de la poésie et de la peinture: traduit de l'allemand de G.E. Lessing* (Paris, 1802), pp. i–x; Quatremère, 'Littérature—Beaux-arts', *Moniteur universel*, no. 252, 1 June 1803, p. 1142.

[95] Quatremère, *Essai sur la nature, le but et les moyens de l'imitation*, pp. 19, 45–52. Quatremère made the same arguments in in several articles that appeared in *Archives littéraires de l'Europe*, a journal that Vanderbourg cofounded: 'Notice sur Canova, sur sa réputation, ses ouvrages et sa statue du Pugilateur', vol. 3 (1804), pp. 3–6; idem, 'Sur le passage de Pline: *Graeca res est nihil velare*', vol. 9 (1806), pp. 53–4. Vanderbourg summarized Quatremère's *Essai* in *Moniteur universel*, no. 12, 12 Jan. 1824, pp. 45–8, and no. 33, 2 Feb. 1824, p. 130.

[96] G. di Giovanni, 'The Unfinished Philosophy of Friedrich Heinrich Jacobi', in F. Jacobi, *The Main Philosophical Writings and the Novel Allwill*, trans. and ed. G. di Giovanni (Montreal, 1994), pp. 3–12, 18–19.

[97] De Staël, *De l'Allemagne*, vol. 2, pp. 205–12; Mortier, 'Un "germanisant" sous l'Empire et la Restauration, Charles Vanderbourg, 1765–1827', p. 1024; Baldensperger, *L'émigration française*, vol. 2, p. 168; Dumas, *Souvenirs*, vol. 3, pp. 138, 160–1.

196 QUATREMÈRE DE QUINCY

Quatremère described Jacobi with uncharacteristic fondness in a letter to Mallet du Pan in 1799: 'Amongst true philosophers you may rank Jacobi, whose opinions and character I value and love increasingly highly.... In the main, his opinions are excellent.'[98] Quatremère's admiration for Jacobi was both long-lasting and reciprocated: he later collected Jacobi's philosophical and literary writings whilst Jacobi recommended him to Goethe, visited him in Paris, and made him an honorary member of the Academy of Munich.

Quatremère imbibed Jacobi's central philosophical message. For Jacobi, the assumption that everything must have a reason, cause, or ground resulted in atheism, moral fatalism, and nihilism. Jacobi argued that any demonstration was founded on principles that were founded on additional principles and so forth, until one reached a first principle grounded in belief, which required a 'moral somersault' to internalize. He complained that philosophers abused reason and transformed 'life into stone' by searching for a 'scientific system' of ethics or 'religion within the limits of reason', and urged philosophers to accept that God was an extension of our dependency on belief to understand our bodies and the surrounding world. In practical terms, politics should therefore remove obstacles to spiritual expression because religion was the only means to rescue humanity from modern abstractions and the obsession with money and material utility, and to restore moral values, such as community and justice.[99]

Jacobi's philosophy shaped how Quatremère later framed his critique of the *idéologues* and materialist theories of the fine arts. During the early 1800s, Quatremère's first target was an interpretation of beauty that subverted the Platonic ideal in art. Incensed by Émeric-David's thesis that ancient Greek artists created beautiful art because they were surrounded by beautiful nude figures, Quatremère countered that Greek artists discovered the ideal in nature and represented the human species, rather than individual specimen, through a creative process nourished by religion.[100] Moreover, the example of Greece had ramifications for contemporary art: since Greek nudity was an

---

[98] Quatremère in Mallet du Pan, *Mémoires et correspondance de Mallet du Pan*, vol. 2, pp. 412–13; Guigniaud, *Notice historique*, pp. 79–80, n. 64; Bibliothèque de l'Institut, 2555, dossier 1, paper 2; É. Décultot, 'Le cosmopolitisme en question. Goethe face aux saisies françaises d'œuvres d'art sous la Révolution et sous l'Empire', *Revue germanique internationale*, vol. 12 (1999), p. 165; *Bibliothèque de M. Quatremère*, pp. 2–4, 30–1.

[99] F. Beiser, *The Fate of Reason: German Philosophy from Kant to Fichte* (Cambridge, MA, 1987), p. 89; T. Pinkard, *Hegel: A Biography* (Cambridge, 2001), pp. 124–5; idem, *German Philosophy 1760–1860: The Legacy of Idealism* (Cambridge, 2002), pp. 85, 91–4, 96, 124–5.

[100] T.-B. Émeric-David, *Recherches sur l'art statuaire, considéré chez les anciens et chez les modernes, ou Mémoire sur cette question proposée par l'Institut national de France: Quelles ont été les causes de la perfection de la sculpture antique et quels seroient les moyens d'y atteindre?* (Paris, 1805); Quatremère, 'Sur l'idéal dans les arts du dessin', *Archives littéraires de l'Europe*, vol. 6 (1805), pp. 385–404, and vol. 7, pp. 3–37, 289–337. On the tradition that Quatremère defended, the classic work is E. Panofsky, *Idea: A Concept in Art Theory*, trans. J. Peake (Columbia, SC, 1968). Émeric-David's perplexed response (Bibliothèque de l'Arsenal, MS 5906, fol. 104) underlines that Quatremère targeted the essay less for its content than how it embodied a trend that he feared.

artistic device rather than a habit, he argued that contemporary sculptors such as Canova should use the idealized nude form.[101]

Quatremère's second target was the materialist eye. Although he had previously attacked how the Revolution resulted in a uniquely pernicious way of looking at art, his friendship with Jacobi led him to sharpen his critique. Over the next decades, he articulated an alternative theory of seeing. He argued that the mind's innate faculties enabled individuals to perceive art, and that these faculties were stimulated by various contexts surrounding artworks. Since 'half beauty's power resides...in the faculties' of the beholder, our perception of art was subjective. He therefore rejected the theory that treated the mind as a passive vessel that received sense impressions and gazed at artworks as physical objects devoid of spiritual associations. Fearing that the abuse of reason harmed the act of looking at art, he condemned 'that cold, arrogant spirit of calculation and analysis' that destroys 'all moral principle in man and his works [and] reduces everything to an organized mechanism'. Echoing Jacobi, he warned that this 'spirit' would leave 'the universe without God, man without a soul, society without morals, the joys of life without perspective, our desires without illusion, the arts without passions, and the products of art without effect'.[102]

For Quatremère, the materialist eye went hand in hand with the 'mania for collections' spawned by revolutionary upheaval. The belief that sensations resulted from mechanical principles led to the dangerous conclusion that 'art should always, in all situations, produce similar effects' and that, as a result, artworks could be displaced and sold at whim. Although Quatremère defended museums displaying antiquities whose objective beauty could survive displacement, in the early 1800s he thus railed against 'repositories' overflowing with 'dead' matter seized from churches. Such repositories contained the 'physical substance' of Christian artworks without the 'train of ideas and illusions' that made them powerful in their former environments. Displaying 'pious objects' in the Museum of French Monuments, he complained, treated 'a religious language that is still vigorous like those signs of a dead or forgotten language'. According to both Quatremère and Jacobi, objects exist independently of our experience of them but we need faith for these objects to reveal themselves to us.[103] Quatremère's practical response to the mania in question was to return or repurpose religious artworks and tomb monuments.[104]

---

[101] Quatremère, 'Sur la diversité du génie et des moyens des différents arts', *Archives litteraires de l'Europe*, vol. 4 (1804), pp. 70–5; idem, 'Sur les médailles', *Magasin encyclopédique*, vol. 5 (1807), p. 440.

[102] Ibid. pp. 42–3, 46, 58, 65, 81.

[103] Quatremère, *Considérations morales*, pp. 55, 58, 65–7, 85; Quatremère, *Rapport fait au Conseil général du département de la Seine sur l'instruction publique et autres sujets* (Paris, year VIII [1800]), pp. 31, 33, 40; Schneider, '*Un ennemi du musée des monuments français*', pp. 358–9.

[104] *Carteggio*, pp. 182–5; AN, F2 (I) 123, pp. 6–7 (Quatremère, 'Rapport fait au conseil municipal de la ville de Paris, par un de ses membrés sur les concessions de terrains dans les cimetières', Paris, 29 germinal 13).

Quatremère regretted another legacy of this mania and the materialist eye: namely, that living artists aspired to display their work in museums and they therefore created technically accomplished yet useless artwork that only connoisseurs and other artists admired. In response, during the first decades of the nineteenth century, he encouraged artists to create artwork for socially useful purposes and places, such as public squares and churches.[105]

Quatremère and other émigrés were pessimistic in mid-1799 about developments in France and Europe.[106] 'Events have already steeled me for the unhappy certitude that soon there will no longer be a corner of Europe where one can demand asylum', he complained to Miranda: 'I swear...that this year will see general catastrophe.... Never has France appeared stronger and Germany so feeble.'[107] However, over the next months the Directorial Republic suffered military defeats in Italy against Russian forces and political upheaval at home. Sieyès and his allies used the Prairial coup to change the Directors and then plotted to strengthen the executive. They struck in November when the Councils were at odds, Napoleon Bonaparte was back from Egypt, and the Republic's armies had averted military disaster. Under the pretext of a Jacobin plot, the Directors resigned and forced the Councils to form a Provisional Government whilst Lucien Bonaparte, as president of the Council of Five Hundred, relocated deputies to Saint-Cloud, where his brother commanded troops. On 9 November, sceptical deputies resisted against Napoleon Bonaparte until Lucien rallied soldiers; a subjugated quorum then adjourned the legislative and handed power to an executive Consulate consisting of Napoleon Bonaparte, Sieyès, and Roger Ducos.[108]

Quatremère seized the opportunity to return to France after the Brumaire coup. He travelled with Portalis and Dumas via Osnabrück and reached Paris in mid-February. He rented a property in Chaillot because, although the Consulate allowed émigrés to return, he was obliged to live outside the capital and report to the police.[109] 'At my eventual return to Paris', he wrote to Canova, 'I found myself without a house, without furniture, and obliged to argue with everyone'. The regime had seized his library, which he struggled to retrieve.[110]

---

[105] Quatremère, *Canova*, pp. 266–71; *Carteggio*, pp. 169–71; AN, O3 1390 (Quatremère letter to Chabrol, 13 Jan. 1822).

[106] Balliol College Archives & Manuscripts: Mallet Family Papers: Portalis letters to Mallet du Pan, 2 June and 24 June 1798.

[107] Quatremère, Letter to Miranda in *Archivo del General Miranda*, vol. 6, pp. 342, 356.

[108] P. Dwyer, *Napoleon: The Path to Power* (New Haven, 2007), pp. 480–504.

[109] *Journal de Francfort*, no. 52, 21 Feb. 1800, p. 3; *Bulletin des lois de la République française*, no. 340, law 3507, pp. 14–6; J.-E. Portalis, *De l'usage et de l'abus de l'esprit philosophique durant le XVIIIe siècle* (Paris, 1820), p. 32; Dumas, *Souvenirs*, vol. 3, pp. 169, 172.

[110] *Carteggio*, pp. 19, 113. Quatremère's struggle to reclaim his library is documented in: AN, F17 1042; Bibliothèque de l'Institut, MSS 2555, papers 61–5.

THE MASK OF CONSTITUTIONALISM, 1796–9   199

He also petitioned in vain for the rent owed from one of his properties, number 140 rue Saint Honoré, that had been sequestered after Fructidor.[111] Although aggrieved by these misfortunes, he perhaps found some consolation in Pierre-Narcisse Guèrin's *The Return of Marcus Sextus* (1799), displayed in Jean-Baptiste Decretôt's Place des Victoires gallery. This celebrated painting, he later noted, 'appeared to be an allusion to the return of those that one called the émigrés'.[112]

[111] Archives de Paris: DQ10 51, file 28, no. 5937; DQ10 422, dossier 3202; DQ10 1396, dossier 1037.

[112] J. Bottineau, 'De Bélisaire à Marcus Sextus: genèse et histoire d'un tableau de Pierre Guérin (1774–1833)', *Révue du Louvre et des Musées de France*, vol. 3 (1993), p. 50; Quatremère, *Recueil de notices historiques*, pp. 418–19.

Conclusion: Art, Crown, and Altar

This book has restored the context of political action to Quatremère's biography and demonstrated that his Catholic faith shaped how he navigated the tempestuous revolutionary decade. That religion guided him should hardly suprise us. He was raised in a devout household; his closest acquaintances (such as Canova, Friedrich Stolberg, Jacobi, and Royer-Collard) were also pious; and he considered the Church the fountainhead of artistic patronage and inspiration. Although his family was Jansenist, his Italian voyages led him to an ultramontanism that buttressed his ideal republic of letters. For him, the papacy had ensured 'the unbroken cultivation of the arts', hosted scholars and artists from all nations, and acted as Europe's spiritual *civitas maxima*. Defending Pius VI against the Directory in 1796, he praised the papacy's historic contribution to art and knowledge and argued for its right to retain antiquities in the encyclopaedic museum that was Rome. Quatremère was thus part of a wider cosmopolitan counter-revolution.[1] His preferred Europe was a federation in which knowledge circulated freely irrespective of frontiers; he feared that the Revolution would lead to a retrograde universal empire or an extended conflict between nation states that would extinguish art and knowledge.

The book has also demonstrated Quatremère's commitment to the Crown and substantiated contemporary verdicts that he was 'devoted to [Louis XVI]' and 'served the counter-revolution with distinction'. His convictions remained strikingly consistent in an age of turncoats: he joined royalist clubs; he was allied to conservative politicians such as Viénot de Vaublanc; he defended Feuillant causes and voted consistently with right-wing national representatives in the Legislative Assembly; he co-organized an armed insurrection against the Republic in 1795; he tried to undermine the Directory with his writings in 1796; he was among the clichyeans in the Council of Five Hundred in 1797 who publicly supported constitutional means to advance royalist interests whilst plotting to overthrow the regime by illegal means.

I showed how Quatremère was a significant politician, but my book also made the case that he was a counter-revolutionary theorist and publicist. By his reckoning, the revolutionaries unleashed atheism and materialism, murdered

---

[1] Matthijs Lok identifies and explains the significance of this cosmopolitan counter-revolution in *Europe against Revolution: Conservatism, Enlightenment, and the Making of the Past* (Oxford, 2023).

Quatremère de Quincy: Art and Politics during the French Revolution. David Gilks, Oxford University Press. © David Gilks 2024. DOI: 10.1093/oso/9780198745563.003.0011

savants, committed vandalism, and neglected historic monuments, thereby squandering the material, spiritual, and intellectual inheritance that kings since Clovis had nurtured and protected for France. His alternative to revolutionary nihilism was a conservative philosophy grounded in antiquarian scholarship: 'only the history of peoples, monuments, and the arts of antiquity', he explained in December 1794, 'can expand the philosopher's horizon and transform into a complete theory the fleeting observations that the brevity of human life otherwise condemns us to make'.[2]

Why, given such evidence of Quatremère's committment to Crown and altar, do modern scholars confuse or overlook his politics? The answer lies in an argument central to the book: namely, that his commitment coexisted with his talent as a resourceful political actor capable of deploying the language of his opponents to feign support for their causes. Just as he was accused of hiding beneath a 'cloak of democracy and liberty', he confessed that he had worn 'the mask of constitutionalism'. Examples from across the book illustrate his talent for simulation. He supported the 'liberty of theatres' in 1789–90, but later adopted contrary positions on free speech and the free market for the arts. In 1791, he bemoaned the 'despotism' of the Academy of Painting and Sculpture, yet, behind such condemnatory language, he wanted to save this institution from abolition. Despite his absolutist convictions, as a national representative in 1791–2 and 1797 he embraced royalist strategies to work within constitutional arrangements that he disputed in private. On some occasions, he feigned support for causes far removed from his convictions. For example, his desire in 1793–4 to show that the Panthéon was synonymous with the Revolution's victory over Catholicism meant that he designed a colossal sculpture group representing the Republic and helped pantheonize Lepeletier. His *Letters* was also at least partly disingenuous. In this celebrated pseudo-epistolary tract, he mobilized the secular concept of civilization dear to republican elites, even though his underlying aim was to pen papist and clichyean propaganda. Appropriately, the *Letters* first appeared in 1796 in a counter-revolutionary London periodical subsidized by the British government.

Many modern scholars err by interpreting Quatremère's diverse pronouncements as if he lived in unchanging times, thereby paying insufficient attention to the specific historical and biographical contexts that conditioned and occasioned these interventions. The detailed portrait in the preceding chapters provides the means to reinterpret his most famous writings during the revolutionary decade, but my book has implications that extend beyond the confines of Quatremère scholarship. By shedding light on the contradictory, even hypocritical, character of revolutionary politics, the book confronts the convenient assumption that individual actors embodied fixed ideologies. My book also demonstrates the case for a particular

---

[2] [Quatremère], *Précis pour Miranda*, p. 5.

approach to writing the history of political thought during the Revolution. Instead of identifying and scrutinizing a canon of substantial texts by celebrated theorists, this approach treats the political thought of the period as fluid and episodic, and therefore draws upon a wide and fragmentary source base that includes newspaper articles, pamphlets, essays, official reports, and speeches. The discourses articulated in such sources were created by numerous authors and editors, sometimes collaboratively and anonymously; since they were often disingenuous, contradictory, and tactical, they defy conventional anthologizing.

One claim made throughout the book is that Quatremère's politics, reflections on the arts, and uses of the arts were intertwined. These connections can be summarized in conclusion. The most significant finding was that Quatremère thought about art first and politics second, meaning that his pre-revolutionary writings on the arts constituted the foundation for his post-1789 politics. His account of the genesis of the Doric order, his theory of 'character' (intended as a civic-minded, neo-sumptuary law for Paris architecture), his desire to preserve and adapt historic masterpieces of architecture and sculpture, and his defence of academic principles led logically towards his political philosophy, which favoured gradual social and political evolution over experimentation, innovation, and invention. The Revolution did not change Quatremère's theories of art and architecture, but its events compelled him to apply, adapt, and sharpen his earlier reflections. For instance, the Revolution led him to turn his sights on the spirit of calculation and materialism that would leave 'the universe without God, man without a soul, society without morals, the joys of life without perspective, our desires without illusion, the arts without passions, and the products of art without effect'.[3] During the Revolution, Quatremère also tried to use artistic media to serve political ends. For example, he proposed redesigning the Manège to ensure order and reduce popular participation. In the same vein, he envisaged using the former church of Sainte-Geneviève and the Festival of the Law to display artistic media that made the case for constitutional monarchy. Similarly, many of his writings served a political agenda that is not immediately apparent to modern readers. For instance, several of his short writings in 1796 might be read as apolitical reflections on the arts, but, on closer inspection, he wrote them to rally monarchists against the Directory or appeal to republican artists and writers critical of the regime.

The present work has reinterpreted Quatremère's writings during the first half of his life and focused on those that he produced during the Revolution. It has said little about his life after 1800, but casting an eye over the second half of his life—as a postscript of sorts—sheds light on his deeds during the Revolution. On the one hand, looking at his later life confirms the depth of his political and religious

---

[3] Quatremère, *Considérations morales*, pp. 107–8.

CONCLUSION   203

convictions; on the other hand, it draws attention to how the revolutionary decade was a unique period when politics preoccupied him.

Quatremère returned to France after the Brumaire coup, but he set aside his royalist politics and did not plot against the Consulate. Since the restoration of the Bourbons appeared unlikely, he hoped for peace and invested his energies trying to influence state patronage of the arts and urban improvements in Paris. He rekindled his friendship with David and tried to ingratiate himself with Napoleon Bonaparte. His condemnation of 'vain abstractions' resulting from 'a religion without God' chimed with Napoleon's desire to placate Catholics and to expunge the influence of the *idéologues*.[4] Enjoying the support of Prefect Nicolas Frochot, his appointment to the General Council of the Seine Department enabled him to propose repairing public monuments, creating cemeteries, and erecting, on the site of the Grand Châtelet, a triumphal arch honouring the First Consul.[5] During discussions about the Concordat, he exploited his position to campaign against the Museum of French Monuments and force Lenoir to relinquish tomb sculptures to families and churches. He thus urged Jean-Antoine Chaptal, the interior minister, to regulate the 'mania' that had seen 'collectors of monuments solicit spoliations and advocate demolitions to swell their collections'.[6] A case in point was Lenoir's support for demolishing the Paris church of Saint-Nicolas-du-Chardonnet, which Quatremère and seventy other artists, writers, and scientists petitioned to save.[7]

Quatremère's obsequiousness, and his belated publication of old research, facilitated his election to the Institute's Class of History and Ancient Literature in February 1804.[8] He continued to praise Napoleon publicly during the Empire. For example, several years after attending the coronation, he penned a sycophantic article thanking the Emperor for gathering 'treasures of genius from all centuries'. He also encouraged Canova to flatter Napoleon to win funding to

---

[4] Quatremère, 'De M. de Paw, et de son opinion sur la beauté des femmes de la Grèce', *Archives littéraires de l'Europe*, vol. 4 (1804), p. 430; Quatremère's report on festivals, cited in Schneider, *Quatremère*, p. 60; A. Canova, *Scritti*, vol. 1, eds. H. Honour and P. Mariuz (Salerno, 2007), p. 376.

[5] Schneider, *Quatremère*, p. 63; Quatremère, *Rapport fait au conseil général, le 15 thermidor an 8 [3 Aug. 1800], sur l'instruction publique, le rétablissement des bourses, le scandale des inhumations actuelles, l'érection des cimetières, la restitution des tombeaux, mausolées, etc.* (Paris, n.d.); idem, *Rapport fait au Conseil général du département de la Seine... par le C. Quatremère-Quincy, au nom de la commission de ce conseil, chargée de présenter le mode et les moyens d'exécution du monument voté en l'honneur du premier consul Bonaparte. Séance du 8 frimaire an X* (Paris, n.d.); A. Aulard, ed., *Paris sous le Consulat. Recueil de documents pour l'histoire de l'esprit public à Paris*, vol. 2 (Paris, 1903), pp. 389, 683–84; Quatremère, 'Sur le procédé antique de l'encaustique', Bibliothèque de l'Institut, 2555, dossier 2, no. 3; Quatremère and Molinos, 'Examen par Quatremère de Quincy et Molinos des sculptures de la fontaine de Grenelle' (6 Dec. 1803), BHVP, CGM 33, fol. 156.

[6] Poulot, *Musée, nation, patrimoine*, p. 271; L.-P. Deseine, *Opinion sur les musées, où se trouvent retenus tous les objets d'arts qui sont la propriété des temples consacrés à la religion catholique* (Paris, year XI [1803]); J.-C. Beugnot, 'Lettre au ministre, 3 fructidor an IX', in *Moniteur universel*, no. 158, 7 June 1819, p. 738.

[7] AN, F13 910 (petition dated 8 May 1800).   [8] Schneider, *Quatremère*, p. 162.

excavate antiquities for the Accademia di San Luca.[9] Yet Quatremère's doubts about Napoleon grew. In a letter in 1803, he feared that the resumption of war 'will...be deadly for the arts', and during the Empire he played a more limited role than before in Paris improvements. He instead preoccupied himself finishing his masterpiece on ancient Greek polychromic sculptures, writing philosophical reflections on the fine arts, and promoting Canova's reputation in Paris.[10] Unable to comment on politics directly, during the Empire's zenith he reverted to his earlier strategy of writing about the arts as a subtle means to criticize the regime. His 1806 lectures on the 'Moral considerations on the destination of artworks' thus lamented how Denon, as Director general of museums, commissioned and displayed artworks, and how Lenoir's Museum of French Monuments accumulated disembodied religious sculptures.[11] Once Napoleonic rule unravelled, he resumed the sort of royalist plotting that he had practised during the Revolution. In 1814, he thus complained that he was exhausted after spending two years preparing the fall of 'Attila' or 'Ahriman' (the Zoroastrian spirit of destruction). During the Hundred Days in 1815, he wisely declined offers of official roles.[12]

Quatremère exercised restraint expressing his political and religious convictions throughout most of the Revolutionary-Napoleonic era, but during the Restoration he could finally speak his mind. He refused to help ex-conventionnels such as David and Daunou.[13] His loyalty to the Bourbons meant that he was showered with honours and gifted influential positions as royal censor and general intendant of the arts and public monuments. He was appointed to the Royal Council of Public Instruction, Honorary Museum Council, and Office for Improvements in the General Council of the Seine.[14] He now deployed his rhetorical talents in the service of Louis XVIII to justify restricting press freedom: 'liberty must be limited', he reasoned, to avoid unleashing grievances after the 'miracle' of the Restoration 'saved us from tyranny, usurpation, enemy invasion, and civil war'.[15] However, he sided with the ultra-royalist faction rather than the liberal monarchists whom the king initially favoured. He returned to national

---

[9] *Le couronnement de Napoléon Premier, Empereur des français* (Paris, 1806), p. 429. Quatremère, 'Sur les vases céramographiques appelés jusqu'à présent vases étrusques', *Moniteur universel*, no. 287, 14 Oct. 1807, pp. 1110–11; idem, *Canova*, p. 193.

[10] F. Haskell, 'More about Sommariva', *The Burlington Magazine*, vol. 114, no. 835 (1972), p. 691.

[11] Lebreton wrote a sympathetic summary of Quatremère's lectures in his 'Notice des travaux de la classe des beaux-arts de l'Institut national', *Magasin encyclopédique*, vol. 6 (1806), pp. 163–8.

[12] *Carteggio*, p. 36; [Quatremère], *L'ultimatum du parti révolutionnaire* (n.p., n.d. [1815]); Schneider, *Quatremère*, p. 273.

[13] G. Bourgin, 'Quelques textes sur Daunou, garde des archives', *Bibliothèque de l'École des chartes*, vol. 102 (1941), pp. 322–3; Schneider, *Quatremère*, p. 400.

[14] Schneider, *Quatremère*, p. 16; Bibliothèque de l'Institut, 2555, dossier 4, no. 81 ('Extrait de l'ordonnance du Roi qui nomme un intendant géneral des arts et des monuments publiques et détermine les attributions de cet intendant').

[15] Quatremère, *Considérations pratiques et de circonstance sur la liberté de la presse* (Paris, 1814), p. 21.

politics for the last time as a representative of the Seine Department in the Chamber of Deputies in 1820–2 when the king moved closer to the ultras after the Duc de Berry's assassination. In the Palais Bourbon, Quatremère sided with the ministry of Joseph de Villèle and looked to the Comte de Artois, future Charles X, for leadership.[16] His library included writings by ultra-royalist ministers, such as Bonald and Denis-Antoine-Luc de Frayssinous.[17]

During the Restoration, Quatremère became synonymous with the Academy of Fine Arts. As its permanent secretary, he exercised considerable power over the arts for twenty-three years. Ironically, however, he only obtained the position because Dufourny declined it despite winning most votes in 1816.[18] Quatremère's academic eulogies established the dominant narrative about art history in France, warned young artists against 'innovations', celebrated the Bourbons, and chastised the Revolution as 'a sort of lacuna, a deserted and sterile space for the history of the arts, as for artists'.[19] Consistent with the ultra-royalist programme to strengthen the Church's influence and benefit from the religious revival, as permanent secretary he used Crown patronage to redecorate places of worship. If his general idea was inspired by his pre-Revolution experience of churches in Paris and Rome, his programme began in earnest with the proposal to repurpose artworks 'hidden' inside the Museum of French Monuments so that they could decorate chapels in the church of Saint-Sulpice. Over the following years: he encouraged and commended Christian artworks by Canova, Prud'hon, Abel de Pujol, and Dominique Ingres; argued that, to decorate churches, the Crown should commission immoveable frescos, murals, and enamel paintings; and remained silent when the return of the Panthéon to the Church meant removing much of his decorative programme.[20] He helped redecorate the church of Saint-Germain-des-Prés by returning tombs and, during the restoration overseen by his ally Hippolyte Godde, designing the pulpit.[21] Quatremère's dogma about the purpose of art became the Crown's unofficial doctrine under Charles X. The prefect of the Seine Department, Gaspard de Chabrol, thus proclaimed:

---

[16] P. Duvergier de Hauranne, *Histoire du gouvernement parlementaire en France*, vol. 6 (Paris, 1864), pp. 63–4; Jouin, *David d'Angers*, vol. 1, p. 164.

[17] *Bibliothèque de M. Quatremère*, pp. 11, 15, 135, 137.

[18] J.-M. Leniaud, ed., *Procès-verbaux de l'Académie des beaux-arts*, vol. 2 (Paris, 2002), p. ii, viii; Fontaine, *Journal*, vol. 1, p. 517.

[19] Quatremère, *De l'invention et de l'innovation dans les ouvrages des beaux-arts* (Paris, 1828); idem, 'Notice historique sur la vie et les ouvrages de Van-Spaendonck', in *Institut royal de France. Séance publique de l'Académie royale des beaux-arts* (Paris, 1822), p. 8. Quatremère's eulogies were published in *Recueil de notices historiques lues dans les séances publiques de l'Académie royale des beaux-arts a l'Institut* (Paris, 1834) and *Suite du recueil de notices historiques* (Paris, 1837).

[20] *Carteggio*, pp. 182–5; Schneider, *Quatremère*, p. 125; Quatremère, *Discours prononcé par Quatremère de Quincy aux funérailles de Pierre-Paul Prud'hon* (Paris, 1823); M.-C. Chaudonneret, *L'état et les artistes: de la Restauration à la monarchie de Juillet, 1815–1833* (Paris, 1999), pp. 172, 244.

[21] See the overview and copies of documents: École nationale des Chartes, 'Restauration de l'église Saint-Germain-des-Prés', http://elec.enc.sorbonne.fr/saintgermaindespres/.

206 QUATREMÈRE DE QUINCY

'Works of art are made for Churches; it is their first and their noblest destination, and, at the outset, religious edifices were the cradle of the arts.'[22]

During the Restoration, Quatremère also played his part in the history of museums. As historians of collecting have rightly noted, his attitude towards museums was far more ambivalent than his twentieth-century reputation as a 'museophobe' implies.[23] Before the Revolution, he admired museums and private collections in Italy and subscribed to the conventional enlightened opinion that some cabinets reflected the vanity of their owners whilst well-organized collections enabled artists, scholars, and amateurs to study previously scattered artefacts. However, as this book has documented, during the Revolution he expressed conflicted views. On the one hand, he supported using the Louvre as a museum, urged the nation to purchase private collections, helped create the museum in Versailles, and defended papal museums. On the other hand, he warned against assembling discordant objects and encouraging artists to create useless artworks intended for museums, and he condemned the 'mania' for collecting that arose from and encouraged destruction, plunder, and displacement. For him, Lenoir embodied this mania because he disfigured artefacts and arranged them as illustrative markers of political eras rather than respecting their material authenticity and trying to understand their styles. During the Restoration, political circumstances meant that Quatremère once again approached museums positively, although he remained sufficiently sceptical to suggest that societies that collected art rarely produced great art.[24] In 1814–15, he struggled to reconcile his support for the Royal Museum with the alliance's restitution demands, which he publicly ignored yet, depending on the claimant, privately criticized or supported.[25] Faced with the return of so many masterpieces, his longer-term solution to was reorganize the Museum into distinct collections for Old Masters and recent French artists, and encourage the Crown to purchase a Raphael painting and Greek antiquities.[26] However, no museum nationalist, he was delighted to visit the British Museum and study the Parthenon sculptures,

---

[22] Schneider, *Quatremère*, p. 74.

[23] Pomian, *Le musée, une histoire mondiale*, vol. 2, p. 154; Poulot, 'The Cosmopolitanism of Masterpieces'.

[24] Quatremère, 'Extrait d'un ensemble de recherches historiques et philosophiques sur la cause principale du développement et de la perfection des beaux-arts chez toutes les nations', in *Recueil des discours prononces dans la séance publique annuelle de l'Institut royal de France, le lundi 24 avril 1826* (Paris, 1826), pp. 30–45.

[25] K. Eustace, *Canova. Ideal Heads* (Oxford, 1997), p. 28; C. Pietrangeli, 'Un ambasciatore d'eccezione: Canova a Parigi', in G. Pavanello, ed., *Canova* (Milan, 2003), pp. 15–22; E. Stengel, *Private und amtliche Beziehungen der Bruder Grimm zu Hessen*, vol. 2 (Marburg, 1886), p. 83.

[26] AN: O3 1389, 16 Nov. 1815; O3 1311, no. 880; F21 571, part III; Schneider, *Quatremère*, p. 354; J.-M. Leniaud, 'Joachim Le Breton et Antoine Quatremère de Quincy, secrétaires perpétuels de l'Académie des Beaux-Arts: deux conceptions divergentes du musée', in M.-T. Caracciolo and G. Toscano, eds, *Jean-Baptiste Wicar et son temps 1762–1834* (Villeneuve d'Ascq, 2007), pp. 79–91; Quatremère, *Sur la statue antique de Vénus découverte dans l'île de Milo* (Paris, 1821); idem, *Lettrés écrits de Londres à Rome, et addressées à M. Canova, sur les marbres d'Elgin, ou les sculptures du temple de Minerve à Athènes* (Rome, 1818), pp. 5–6, 160.

which, he wrote, Lord Elgin had saved from Ottoman 'barbarism'.[27] Besides defending large museums in capital cities, he also supported site-specific museums, such as the project to reuse the Gallo-Roman Thermes de Julien in Paris as a museum of antiquities, and private provincial collections, such as those created by Esprit Calvet and the 'patriot antiquarian' Claude-Madeleine Grivaud de la Vincelle. The Crown must encourage private collectors, he argued, because they were knowledgeable and wanted the public to enjoy their treasures, even if, he conceded, some collectors were motivated by 'sterile mania' or 'ostentation'.[28]

Quatremère was a diminished force during his last decades. Student revolts against the Academy of the Fine Arts and spats with Horace Vernet and Henri Labrouste in the late 1820s sapped his authority.[29] Bedridden for several months after the July Revolution in 1830, when he finally resumed his duties as permanent secretary his role was increasingly administrative and ceremonial until he retired at the end of the decade.[30] He published numerous books during the second half of his life, but most were based on older research or were revised editions or collections of earlier writings, sometimes lavishly printed and illustrated. During the July monarchy, he alienated former allies such as Ingres and the younger generation derided him as an anachronistic, hollow imitation of Louis XIV's academicians. This generation misunderstood or ignored altogether his exploits during the Revolution of 1789—exploits that the present book has finally explained in their proper context for the first time.

---

[27] *Carteggio*, pp. 214–16.

[28] AN, F13 910, file 'Thermes de Julien, rue de la Harpe'; Schneider, *Quatremère*, pp. 86–9; Quatremère, [Review of Grivaud de la Vincelle, *Recueil de monumens antiques*], *Journal des savants*, Oct. 1817, p. 598. The private collectors of nineteenth-century France have found a worthy historian, who has artfully described the public implications of their efforts; see Tom Stammers, *The Purchase of the Past: Collecting Culture in Post-Revolutionary Paris c. 1790–1890* (Cambridge, 2020).

[29] M. Bressani, 'The Paestum Controversy', in C. Belier et al., eds, *Henri Labrouste: Structure Brought to Light* (New York, 2012), pp. 89–93; S. Bann, 'Quarrels between Painting and Sculpture in Post-revolutionary France', Canadian Centre for Architecture Mellon Lectures, 17 April 2003, pp. 1–13: https://www.cca.qc.ca/cca.media/files/1484/1385/Mellon04-SB.pdf

[30] Leniaud, ed., *Procès-verbaux de l'Académie des beaux-arts*, vol. 5 (Paris, 2004), p. 67; and vol. 6 (Paris, 2003), p. 313.

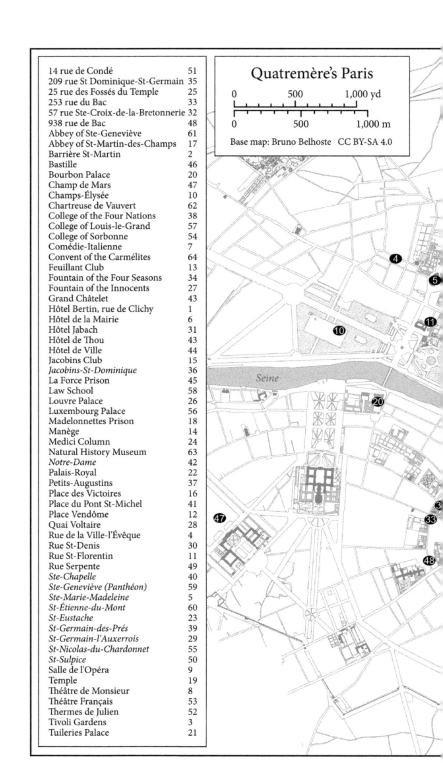

14 rue de Condé	51
209 rue St Dominique-St-Germain	35
25 rue des Fossés du Temple	25
253 rue du Bac	33
57 rue Ste-Croix-de-la-Bretonnerie	32
938 rue de Bac	48
Abbey of Ste-Geneviève	61
Abbey of St-Martin-des-Champs	17
Barrière St-Martin	2
Bastille	46
Bourbon Palace	20
Champ de Mars	47
Champs-Élysée	10
Chartreuse de Vauvert	62
College of the Four Nations	38
College of Louis-le-Grand	57
College of Sorbonne	54
Comédie-Italienne	7
Convent of the Carmélites	64
Feuillant Club	13
Fountain of the Four Seasons	34
Fountain of the Innocents	27
Grand Châtelet	43
Hôtel Bertin, rue de Clichy	1
Hôtel de la Mairie	6
Hôtel Jabach	31
Hôtel de Thou	43
Hôtel de Ville	44
Jacobins Club	15
Jacobins-St-Dominique	36
La Force Prison	45
Law School	58
Louvre Palace	26
Luxembourg Palace	56
Madelonnettes Prison	18
Manège	14
Medici Column	24
Natural History Museum	63
Notre-Dame	42
Palais-Royal	22
Petits-Augustins	37
Place des Victoires	16
Place du Pont St-Michel	41
Place Vendôme	12
Quai Voltaire	28
Rue de la Ville-l'Évêque	4
Rue St-Denis	30
Rue St-Florentin	11
Rue Serpente	49
Ste-Chapelle	40
Ste-Geneviève (Panthéon)	59
Ste-Marie-Madeleine	5
St-Étienne-du-Mont	60
St-Eustache	23
St-Germain-des-Prés	39
St-Germain-l'Auxerrois	29
St-Nicolas-du-Chardonnet	55
St-Sulpice	50
Salle de l'Opéra	9
Temple	19
Théâtre de Monsieur	8
Théâtre Français	53
Thermes de Julien	52
Tivoli Gardens	3
Tuileries Palace	21

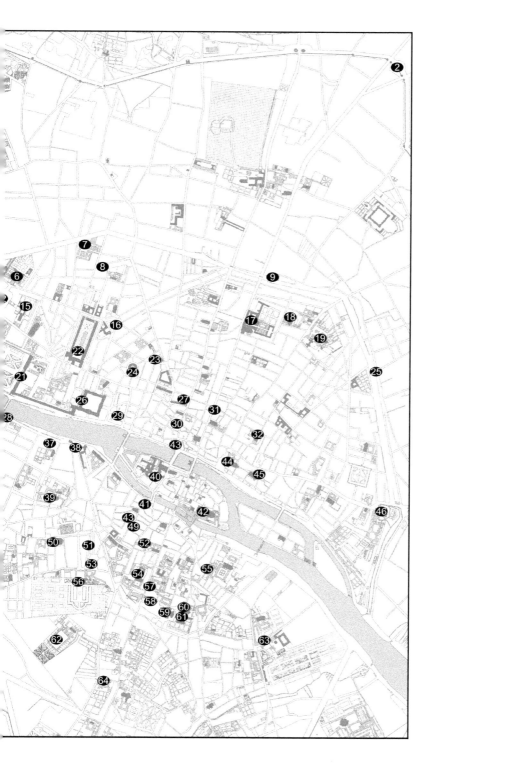

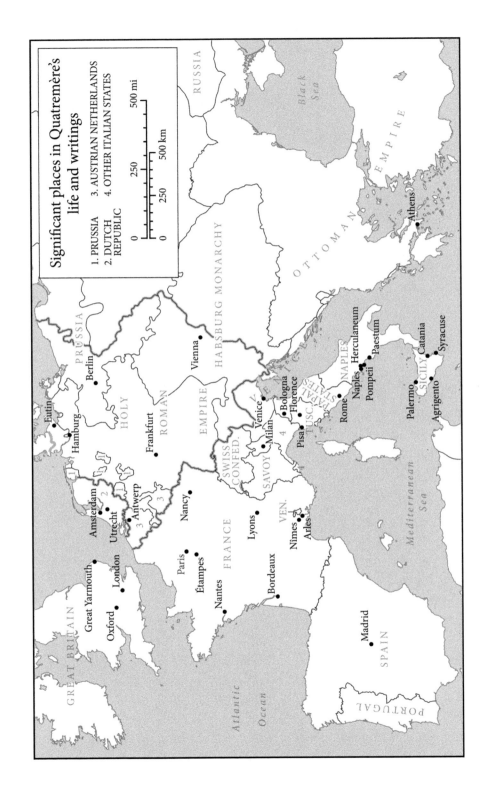

Bibliography

MANUSCRIPTS

London
National Archives
HO 42/46/125

Los Angeles
Getty Institute Research Library
Ms 850209

Oxford
Balliol College Archives & Manuscripts
Mallet Family Papers

Paris
Archives de l'Institute
D74, Prix Caylus 1785
E305

Archives de Paris
6 AZ 1240
D10 U13
DQ10 51
DQ10 617
DQ10 422
DQ10 1396
DQ 1447

Archives nationales
284AP/9
ADVIII
AF III 44
C76, no. 749
CP NIII Seine 213
CP NIII Seine 882
DIII 384
F2 (I) 123
F7A 1307A
F7 4884 79
F7 6285
F7 7645

212 BIBLIOGRAPHY

F13 212
F13 325
F13 333
F13 335
F13 910
F13 1136
F13 1137
F13 1138
F13 1925
F13 1935
F13 1938
F17 1025A
F17 1042
F17 1057
F17 1065
F17 1084
F17 1088
F17 1195
F17 1281
F17 1279
F17 1280
F17 1307A
F17 1310
F17 2780 2
F21 0048
H2 1959
H748 231
H1023 17
K1009
O1 1073
O1 1147
O1 1702
O1 1913 76
O1 1920
O3 1389
T 1662
W 313

Archives nationales—Minutier central des notaires
ET II 624
ET II 516
ET II 767
ET II 1061
MC II 770
MC II 767
MC ET II 624

Bibliothèque de l'Arsenal
Ms 6498, vol. 12

Bibliothèque de l'Institute
Ms 2555: Papiers d'A.-C. Quatremère de Quincy, Secrétaire perpétuel de l'Académie des beaux-arts

Bibliothèque historique de la ville de Paris
814, ff. 430–8
1212, f. 15
Cp 3435, ff. 124–9
NA-121, f. 77
NA-191, ff. 161, 492
MA-NA-191

Bibliothèque nationale
'Rapport de Mr. Quatremère sur la pétition des artistes du 19 8bre [octobre] der. 14 9bre [novembre] 1791'. Transcribed by Jean-Charles Deloynes.
'Extrait de la séance du juri des arts au sujet du concours' [2 Jan. 1795], p. 272.
'Jury des Arts. Prix décernés aux esquisses de peintures présentées au concours ouvert par la Convention Nationale et soumises au jugement du jury des arts, en vertu de la loi du 9 frimaire de l'an troisième' [1795].
'Jury des arts. Prix décernés aux esquisses de sculpture, présentées aux divers concours ouverts par la Convention Nationale et soumises au jugement du jury des arts, en vertu de la loi du 9 frimaire de l'an troisième' [1795].
'Jury des Arts. Prix décernés aux projets d'architecture, présentés aux divers concours ouverts par la Convention Nationale et soumis au jugement du Jury des Arts, en vertu de la loi du 9 frimaire de l'an troisième' [1795].

PRINTED SOURCES

Primary sources
Edited volumes
Anon., ed., *Collection générale des décrets rendus par l'Assemblée Nationale, avec la mention des sanctions et acceptations données par le Roi*, vol. 25 (Paris, 1792).
Anon., ed., *Collection générale des lois, proclamations, arrêtés et autres actes du Directoire exécutif* (Paris, 1797).
Baczko, Bronislaw, ed., *Une éducation pour la démocratie: textes et projets de l'époque révolutionnaire* (Paris, 1982).
Berger, Robert, ed., *Public Access to Art in Paris: A Documentary History from the Middle Ages to 1800* (University Park, PA, 1999).
Blanc, Olivier, ed., *Last Letters: Prisons and Prisoners of the French Revolution, 1793–1794*, trans. Alan Sheridan (New York, 1987).
Bonnaire, Marcel, ed., *Procès-verbaux de l'Académie des beaux-arts*, 3 vols (Paris, 1937–43).
Cantarel-Besson, Yveline, ed., *La naissance du Musée du Louvre: la politique muséologique sous la Révolution daprès les archives des musées nationaux*, 2 vols (Paris, 1981).
——ed., *Musée du Louvre, janvier 1797-juin 1798 : procès-verbaux du conseil d'administration du 'Musée central des arts'* (Paris, 1992).
Charavay, Étienne, ed., *Assemblée électorale de Paris, 26 août 1791–12 août 1792 : procès-verbaux de l'élection des députés à l'assemblée législative* (Paris, 1894).

214 BIBLIOGRAPHY

Clercq, Jules de, ed., *Recueil des traités de la France, publié sous les auspices du ministère des affaires étrangères* (Paris, 1864).

David, Jules, ed., *Le peintre Louis David, 1748–1825 : souvenirs & documents inédits* (Paris, 1880).

Davila, Vincete, ed., *Archivo del General Francisco Miranda*, 23 vols (Caracas, 1929–50).

Debidour, Antonin, ed., *Recueil des actes du Directoire exécutif : procès-verbaux, arrêtés, instructions, lettres et actes divers*, 4 vols (Paris, 1911).

Furcy-Raynaud, Marc, ed., *Procès-verbaux des assemblées du jury élu par les artistes exposant au Salon de 1791 pour la distribution des prix d'encouragement, publié d'après le manuscrit original* (Paris, 1906).

Guillaume, James, ed., *Procès-verbaux du Comité d'instruction publique de l'Assemblée législative* (Paris, 1889).

——, *Procès-verbaux du Comité d'instruction publique de la Convention nationale*, 7 vols (Paris, 1891–1907).

Hippeau, Celestin, ed., *L'instruction publique en France pendant la Révolution*, 2 vols (Paris, 1881–3).

Lacroix, Sigismond, ed., *Actes de la Commune pendant la Révolution*, 1st series, 7 vols (Paris, 1894–9) and 2nd series, 7 vols (Paris, 1900–9).

Lallement, Guillaume, ed., *Choix de rapports, opinions, et discours prononcés à la tribune nationale depuis 1789 jusqu'à ce jour : recueillis dans un ordre chronologique*, 15 vols (Paris, 1818–21).

Lapauze, Henri, ed., *Procès-verbaux de la Commune générale des arts, de peinture, sculpture, architecture et gravure (18 juillet 1793—tridi de la 1ère décade du 2ème mois de l'an II) et de la Société populaire et républicaine des arts (3 nivôse an II–28 floréal an III)* (Paris, 1903).

Lemonnier, Henri, ed., *Procès-verbaux de l'Académie royale d'architecture, 1671–1793*, 9 vols (Paris, 1911–29).

Lichtenstein, Jacqueline, and Michel, Christian, eds, *Conférences de l'Académie royale de peinture et de sculpture*, 6 vols (Paris, 2006–15).

Mavidal, Jérôme, and Laurent, Emile, eds, *Archives parlementaires de 1787 à 1860: recueil complet des débats législatifs et politiques des chambres françaises*, 82 vols, first series (Paris, 1862–1912).

Montaiglon, Anatole de, and Guiffrey, Jules, eds, *Correspondance des directeurs de l'Académie de France à Rome, avec les surintendants des Bâtiments*, 18 vols (Paris, 1887–1912).

Pinelli, Antonio, and Emiliani, Andrea, eds, *Lo studio delle arti e il genio dell'Europa. Scritti di A.C. Quatremère de Quincy – Pio VII Chiaramonti (1796–1802)* (Bologna, 1989).

Pavanello, Giuseppe, ed., *Il carteggio Canova-Quatremère de Quincy, 1785–1822* (Ponzano, 2005).

Roche, Germain, and Lebon, Félix, eds, *Recueil général des arrêts du Conseil d'état: comprenant les arrêtés, décrets, arrêts et ordonnances rendus en matière contentieuse, depuis l'an 8 jusqu'à 1839*, vol. 1 (Paris, 1839).

Stewart, John, ed., *A Documentary Survey of the French Revolution* (New York, 1951).

Tuetey, Alexandre, ed., *Répertoire général des sources manuscrites de l'histoire de Paris pendant la Révolution française*, 11 vols (Paris, 1892).

——, *Procès-verbaux de la Commission des monuments (1790–1794)*, vol. 1 (Paris, 1902).

Periodicals

Allgemeiner litterarischer Anzeiger oder Annalen der gesammten Litteratur für die geschwinde Bekanntmachung verschiedener Nachrichten aus dem Gebiete der Gelehrsamkeit und Kunst. Leipzig, 1796.

Ami de la religion et du roi journal ecclésiastique, politique et littéraire. Paris, 1815.

Annales catholiques; ou suite des Annales religieuses, politiques et littéraires. Paris, 1796–7.

BIBLIOGRAPHY 215

Bulletin des lois de la République française. Paris, 1799–1800.
Censeur des journaux. Paris, 1795–7.
Chronique de Paris. Paris, 1790–1.
Clef du cabinet des souverains, nouveau journal du soir et du matin, historique, politique, économique, moral et littéraire. Paris, 1797.
Courrier des LXXXIII départements. Paris, 1792.
Courrier de l'égalité. Paris, 1795.
Décade philosophique, littéraire et politique. Paris, 1794–6.
Esprit des Journaux, françois et etrangers. Par une société de gens-de-lettres. Paris, 1786.
Feuille du jour. Paris, 1796.
Gazette d'Amsterdam. Amsterdam, 1796.
Journal de Francfort. Frankfurt, 1800.
Journal de la municipalité et du département de Paris. Paris, 1791.
Journal de Paris. Paris, 1782–96.
Journal des débats. Paris, 1792–7.
Journal des patriotes de 89. Paris, 1796.
Journal des savants, Paris, 1791 and 1817–8.
Journal littéraire. Paris, 1796.
Mercure de France. Paris, 1765 and 1795.
Miroir. Paris, 1796.
Moniteur universel. Paris, 1791–8.
Nouvelles politiques, nationales et étrangères. Paris, 1796.
Paris pendant l'année 1796. London, 1796.
Quotidienne, ou Feuille du jour. Paris, 1797.
Rédacteur. Paris, 1796.
Révolutions de Paris. Paris, 1792.
Thermomètre du jour. Paris, 1792.
Véridique, ou Courrier universel. Paris, 1796.

Original publications
Amaury-Duval, Eugène, *L'atelier d'Ingres. Souvenirs* (Paris, 1878).
Anon., *Catalogue des tableaux du cabinet du roi au Luxembourg. Nouvelle édition* (Paris, 1774).
Anon., *Etrennes à la vérité, ou Almanach des aristocrates pour la présente année, seconde de la liberté, 1790* (Paris, n.d. [1790]).
Anon., *Vœu des artistes* (Paris, 1789).
Anon., *Ouvrages de peinture, sculpture et architecture, gravures, dessins, modèles, etc., exposés au Louvre par ordre de l'assemblée nationale au mois de septembre 1791, l'an III de la liberté* (Paris, 1791).
Anon., ['M. le Cte'], *Lettre anonyme contre le graveur Miger, au sujet de sa Lettre à J. Vien* (n.d., n.p. [Paris, 1791]).
Anon., *Détails de la cérémonie arête par le directoire du département de Paris pour la fête décrète par l'assemblée nationale* (Paris, 1792).
Anon., *Convention nationale. Rapport et décret sur la fête de la Réunion républicaine du 10 août 1793* (Paris, 1793).
Anon., *Notice des tableaux des trois écoles choisis dans la collection du Muséum des arts: rassemblés au Sallon d'exposition pendant les travaux de la Gallérie* (Paris, 1795).
Anon., 'Observations sur l'article concernant les tableaux d'Italie, insère dans le Journal de Paris, du 19 messidor', *Rédacteur*, no. 211, 13 July 1796, pp. 3–4.

216 BIBLIOGRAPHY

Anon., *Dictionnaire de l'Académie française*, 5th edn (Paris, 1798).

Anon., *Le 18 fructidor, ou anniversaire des fêtes directoriales* (Hamburg, 1798).

Anon., *Dictionnaire des Jacobins vivans, dans lequel on verra les hauts faits de ces messieurs* (Hamburg, 1799).

Anon., *Le Couronnement de Napoléon Premier, Empereur des français* (Paris, 1806).

Anon., 'Sketches of Parisian Society, Politics and Literature, Paris, October 18, 1826', in *The New Monthly Magazine and Literary Journal*, vol. 17 (Paris, 1826), pp. 422–3.

Artaud de Montor, Alexis-François, *Histoire du Pape Pie VII*, vol. 1 (Paris, 1837).

d'Aviler, Augustin-Charles, *Dictionnaire d'architecture*, 2 vols (Paris, 1693).

Bachaumont, Louis Petit de, et al., *Mémoires secrets pour servir à l'histoire de la République des Lettres en France depuis 1762 jusqu'à nos jours*, vol. 11 (London, 1779).

Baillot, Pierre, *Récit de la mort de Guillaume Simonneau, maire d'Étampes, lu le 22 mars 1792 dans la société patriotique de Dijon* (Dijon, 1792).

Ballet, Augustin-François, *Eloge de M. Augustin-François Ballet, prêtre du diocèse de Paris* (Paris, 1808).

Barras, Paul, *Mémoires de Barras, membre du Directoire*, ed. George Duruy, 3 vols (Paris, 1895).

Barthélemy, François, *Mémoires historiques et diplomatiques de Barthélemy, depuis le 14 julliet jusqu'au 30 prairial an VII* (Paris, 1799).

Barthélemy, Jean-Jacques, *Voyage en Italie de M. l'Abbé Barthélemy* (Paris, 1802).

Barthélemy-Saint-Hilaire, Jules, *M. Victor Cousin, sa vie et sa correspondance*, 3 vols (Paris, 1895).

Belgrano, Jacopo, *Dell'architettura egiziana* (Parma, 1786).

Bellart, Nicolas, *Précis du Conseil de Préfecture pour le cit. Quatremère de Quincy contre le cit. Tondu de Muiroger* (Paris, 1796).

Bertrand de Moleville, Antoine-François de, *Histoire de la Révolution de France*, 14 vols (Paris, 1801–3).

Beugnot, Jean-Charles, *Opinion de Jean-Charles Beugnot* (Paris, 1792).

Blanc, Charles, *Grammaire des arts du dessin* (Paris, [1880] 2000).

Bombelles, Marc-Marie, *Journal*, vol. 5 (Geneva, 2002).

de Bonald, Louis, 'Observations sur un ouvrage postume de M. Condorcet', in *Théorie du pouvoir politique et religieux dans la société civile, démontrée par le raisonnement et par l'histoire*, vol. 2 (Paris, 1796), pp. 482–520.

Boyer d'Argens, Jean-Baptiste, *Lettres juives, ou correspondance philosophique, historique, et critique, entre un Juif voyageur à Paris & ses correspondans en divers endroits*, 6 vols (The Hague, 1738).

Brosses, Charles de, *Le président de Brosses en Italie: lettres familières écrites d'Italie en 1739 et 1740*, vol. 2 (Paris, 1869).

Burke, Edmund, *Reflections on the Revolution in France*, ed. John Pocock (Indianapolis, 1987).

Canning, George, 'New Morality', *The Anti-Jacobin; or, Weekly Examiner*, no. 36, 9 July 1798.

Canova, Antonio, *Scritti*, eds Hugh Honour and Paolo Mariuz, vol. 1 (Salerno, 2007).

Cardonnel, Pierre, *Opinion du citoyen Cardonnel, député du Tarn, sur l'aliénation des presbytères proposée par Jard-Panvillier, au nom de la commission dont il est le rapporteur* (Paris, 1797).

Caylus, Anne-Claude, *Histoire et mémoires de l'Académie des inscriptions et belles letters*, vol. 23 (Paris, 1756).

BIBLIOGRAPHY 217

Champagneaux, Luc-Antoine, 'Notice de l'éditeur, sur quelques circonstances de sa détention dans les années 1793 et 1794, pour servir de supplément aux Notices historiques de J. M. Ph. Roland', in idem, ed., *Œuvres de J. M. Ph. Roland, femme de l'ex-ministre d'intérieur*, vol. 2 (Paris, year VIII [1800]).

Chenier, Marie-Joseph, *Adresse de M. J. de Chénier, auteur de la Tragédie de Charles IX, aux soixante districts de Paris* [1790] (Paris, 1795).

Clérisseau, Charles-Louis, *Antiquités de France. Tome premier – monuments de Nismes* (Paris, 1778).

Chiaramonti, Barnaba, *Chirografo della Santità di Nostro signore Papa Pio VII. in data del primo ottobre 1802, sulle antichità, e belle arti in Roma, e nello Stato Ecclesiastico* (Rome, 1802).

Coissin, Philippe-Edmund, *Tableau des prisons de Paris, sous le règne de Robespierre* (Paris, 1795).

Condorcet, Nicolas de Caritat, *Rapport sur l'instruction publique présenté à l'Assemblée législative les 20 et 21 avril 1792* (Paris, 1792).

——, *Fragments sur la liberté de la presse* (Paris, 1776), reprinted in François Arago, ed., *Oeuvres de Condorcet*, vol. 2 (Paris, 1847).

——, *Esquisse d'un tableau historique des progrès de l'esprit humain. Ouvrage posthume de Condorcet* (Paris, an III [1795]), translated as 'The Sketch', in Steven Nukes and Nadia Urbinati, eds, *Political Writings* (Cambridge, 2012).

Courtois, Edme-Bonaventure, *Rapport fait au nom de la commission chargée de l'examen des papiers trouvés chez Robespierre et ses complices* (Paris, year III).

La Curne de Sainte Palaye, Jean-Baptiste de, *Lettre à M. de B. (Bachaumont) sur le bon goût dans les arts et dans les lettres* (Paris, 1751).

David, Jacques-Louis, *Discours du citoyen David, député du Département de Paris; sur la nécessité de supprimer les Académies* (Paris, 1793).

——, *Rapport fait à la Convention nationale par David, Imprimé par ordre de la Convention nationale* (Paris, 1793).

Delécluze, Étienne, *Louis David: son école et son temps* (Paris, 1855).

Deseine, Louis-Pierre, *Réfutation d'un projet de statuts et règlements, pour l'Académie centrale de peinture, sculpture, gravure et architecture, présenté à l'Assemblée nationale, par la majorité des Membres de l'académie royale de peinture et sculpture en assemblée délibérante* (Paris, 1791).

——, *Considérations sur les académies, et particulièrement sur celles de peinture, sculpture et architecture, présentées à l'Assemblée nationale par M. Deseine* (Paris, 1791).

——, *Réponse au 'Mémoire sur l'Académie royale de peinture et sculpture, par plusieurs membres de cette Académie'* (Paris, 1791).

——, *Notices historiques sur les anciennes académies royales* (Paris, 1814).

Desmoulins, Camille, *Révolutions de France et de Brabant*, no. 85 (July 1791).

Dumas, Mathieu, *Souvenirs du lieutenant-général Comte Mathieu Dumas de 1770 à 1836. Publiés par son fils*, 3 vols (Paris, 1839).

——, *Memoirs of His Own Time: Including the Revolution, the Empire, and the Restoration*, 2 vols (London, 1839).

Dupaty, Charles, *Lettres sur l'Italie en 1785* (Paris, 1790).

Dupuis, Charles-François, *Origine de tous les cultes, ou réligion universelle*, 12 vols (Paris, 1795).

Emeric-David, Toussaint-Bernard, *Recherches sur l'art statuaire, considéré chez les anciens et chez les modernes, ou Mémoire sur cette question proposée par l'Institut national de France:*

218 BIBLIOGRAPHY

quelles ont été les causes de la perfection de la sculpture antique et quels seroient les moyens d'y atteindre. Ouvrage couronné par l'Institut national, le 15 vendémiaire an IX (Paris, 1805).

Eynard, Étienne, and Tardieu, Pierre-Alexandre, *Considérations sur l'état actuel des arts sur les concours de peinture, sculpture, architecture et gravure, et sur le mode de jugement* (n.p., n.d. [Paris, 1794]).

Farington, Joseph, *The Diary of Joseph Farington*, vol. 3 (New Haven, 1998).

Fea, Carlo, *Discorso intorno alle belle arti in Roma recitato nell'adunanza degli arcadi* (Rome, 1797).

——, *Relazione di un viaggio ad Ostia* (Rome, 1802).

Fleury, Joseph-Abraham, *Mémoires de Fleury de la Comédie française*, vol. 2 (Paris, 1844).

Fontaine, Pierre François Léonard, *Journal: 1799–1853*, 2 vols (Paris, 1987).

Fourcroy, Antoine-François, *Rapport et projet de décret sur l'enseignement libre des sciences et des arts 19 frimaire an II* (Paris, 1793).

——, *Rapport et décret de la Convention nationale sur les écoles de santé de Paris, Montpellier et Strasbourg* (Paris, 1795).

Fournel, Alexandre, ed., *Catalogue d'objets d'arts: antiquités égyptiennes, grecques et romaines, vases grecs, terres cuites, figurines en bronze, sculptures en marbre, dont deux bustes de Canova, médailles, miniatures, dessins et belles estampes anciennes et modernes, composant le cabinet de feu M. Quatremère de Quincy* (Paris, 1850).

——, *Bibliothèque de M. Quatremère de Quincy, la vente 27 mai–6 juin 1850* (Paris, 1850).

Français, Antoine, *Opinion de M. Français, député de Loire inférieure* (Paris, 1792).

Garnerey, Jean-François, et al., *Mémoire et plan relatifs à l'organisation d'une Ecole nationale des beaux-arts qui ont le dessin pour base; par une société d'artistes* (Paris, 1791).

Gaucher, Charles-Etienne, *Lettre à M. Quatremère de Quincy, sur la gravure* (n.p., n.d. [Paris, 1791]).

Goethe, Johann, *Italian Voyage, 1786–1788*, trans. William Auden and Elizabeth Mayer (London, 1962).

Gregoire, Henri, *Discours prononcé dans l'église cathédrale de Blois en présence des corps administratifs, tribunaux, garde nationale et troupes de ligne, pour Jacques Guillaume Simonneau, maire d'Etampes, assassiné le 3 mars 1792 pour avoir défendu la loi, par M., évêque du département de Loir-et-Cher* (Rennes, 1792).

——, *Rapport sur les encouragements, récompenses et pensions à accorder aux savants, aux gens de lettres et aux artistes* (Paris, 1794).

——, *Second rapport sur le vandalisme: séance du 8 Brumaire, l'an III* (Paris, 1794).

Gresset, Jean-Baptiste, *Épître à M. de Tournehem, directeur et ordonnateur général des bâtimens, jardins, arts et manufactures de Sa Majesté, sur la colonne de l'hostel de Soissons* (Paris, 1752).

Jacobi, Friedrich, *Briefwechsel zwischen Goethe und Friedrich Jacobi*, ed. Max Jacobi (Leipzig, 1846).

Jal, Auguste, *Esquisses, croquis, pochades, ou tout ce qu'on voudra sur le Salon de 1827* (Paris, 1828).

Jard-Panvillier, Louis Alexandre, *Rapport fait au nom d'une commission spéciale sur l'aliénation des presbytères, 8 nivôse, an V* (Paris, 1797).

Hankins, Thomas, and Silverman, Robert, *Instruments and the Imagination* (Princeton, 1999).

Hegel, Georg, *Hegel's Aesthetics. Lectures on Fine Art* [1823–30], trans. Thomas Knox (Oxford, 1998).

Héron, François, *Représentation d'un citoyen à la nation* (Paris, 1791).

BIBLIOGRAPHY   219

Houdon, Jean-Antoine, *Réflexions sur les concours en général et sur celui de la statue de J.-J. Rousseau en particulier* (Paris, 1791).

Hoüel, Jean, *Voyage pittoresque des isles de Sicile* (Paris, 1782).

Huet-Froberville, Jean-Baptiste, *Opinion de M. Huet-Froberville, . . . sur le rapport du Comité d'instruction publique et sur la pétition des artistes concernant la nomination des juges pour les prix d'encouragement accordés aux arts par l'Assemblée nationale constituante* (Paris, 1791).

Jaucourt, Louis de, 'Rome', in Denis Diderot and Jean-Le Rond d'Alembert, eds, *Encyclopédie, ou dictionnaire raisonné des sciences, des arts et des métiers*, vol. 14 (Neuchâtel, 1765).

Laffon, André-Daniel, Rapport fait à l'Assemblée nationale, sur l'achèvement du Panthéon français au nom du comité de l'ordonnance des finances, le 24 décembre 1791 (Paris, 1791).

La Harpe, Jean-François, *Du fanatisme dans la langue révolutionnaire, ou De la persécution suscitée par les barbares du dix-huitième siècle, contre la religion chrétienne et ses ministres* (Paris, 1797).

Labat, Pierre-Daniel, *Vie de Demoiselle Anne-Charlotte Bourjot: épouse de M. Quatremère l'aîné* (Paris, 1791).

Lacretelle, Charles, 'Réflexions sur le système d'administration à suivre dans les pays conquis', *Nouvelles politiques*, no. 265, 13 June 1796.

——, *Histoire de la révolution française*, 3 vols (Paris, 1825).

Lacroix, Antoine, 'Eloge historique de Soufflot [1785]', in *L'œuvre de Soufflot à Lyon: études et documents* (Lyon, 1982).

Laffon de Ladebat, André-Daniel, *Rapport fait . . . sur l'achèvement du Pantheon francais au nom du comité de l'ordinance des finances, le 24 decembre 1791* (Paris, 1791).

Lakanal, Joseph, *Rapport et projet de réglement de l'Institut national: présenté au nom de la commission d'examen* (Paris, 1796).

Lalande, Joseph-Jérome de, *Voyage en Italie*, 9 vols (Paris, 1786).

Latapie, François de Paule, *Ephémérides romaines, 24 mars–24 octobre 1775*, ed. Gilles Montègre (Paris, 2017).

Le Roy, Julien-David, *The Ruins of the Most Beautiful Monuments of Greece* [1770], ed. Robin Middleton and trans. David Britt (Los Angeles, 2004).

Lebreton, Joachim, *Notice historique sur la vie et les ouvrages de Pierre Julien* (Paris, 1805).

——, *Notice historique sur la vie et les ouvrages de M. Moitte* (Paris, 1812).

——, 'Réponse a quelques objections contre le système d'importation en France de plusieurs chefs-d'œuvre des arts que possède de l'Italie', *Décade Philosophique*, no. 81, 18 July 1796, pp. 181–6.

——, Lebreton, Joachim, 'Notice des travaux de la Classe des beaux-arts de l'Institut national', *Magasin encyclopédique*, vol. 6 (1806), pp. 155–75.

Lebrun, Jean Baptiste, et al., *Essai sur les moyens d'encourager la peinture, la sculpture, l'architecture et la gravure* (Paris, 1794).

Lebrun, Jean Baptiste, *Réflexions sur le Muséum national* (n.p, n.d, [Paris, 1793]).

Lenoir, Alexandre, *Notice succinte des objets de sculpture et architecture réunis au dépôt provisoire national, rue des Petits-Augustins, par Alexandre Lenoir, garde dudit depot* (Paris, 1793).

——, *Notice historique des monumens des arts réunis au dépôt national des monumens* (Paris, 1795).

Lessing, Gotthold Ephraim, *Laocoön: An Essay on the Limits of Painting and Poetry* [1766], ed. Jay Bernstein (Cambridge, 2002).

220 BIBLIOGRAPHY

Louis, Victor, 'Lettre sur les monumens des arts en Italie', *Nouvelles politiques*, no. 351, 7 Sept. 1796, pp. 1403–4.

de Maistre, Joseph, *Considerations on France*, ed. and trans. Richard Lebrun (Cambridge, 2006).

Mallet du Pan, Jacques, *Correspondance inédite de Mallet du Pan avec la cour de Vienne (1794–1798)* (Paris, 1884).

——, *Mémoires et correspondance de Mallet du Pan pour servir à l'histoire de la Révolution française*, ed. Pierre-André Sayous, 2 vols (Paris, 1851).

——, *Memoirs and Correspondence of Mallet du Pan, Illustrative of the History of the French Revolution*, ed. Pierre-André Sayous, 2 vols (London, 1852).

——, 'A Summary of the Tributes Exacted, and other Robberies Committed, by the French Republic, among Foreign Nations, since the Year 1794', *The British mercury; or, Historical and critical views of the events of the present times*, vol. 2, no. 10, 15 Jan. 1799.

Martainville, Alphonse-Louis, *Merdiana, ou Manuel des chieurs, suite de l'almanach des gourmands* (Paris,1803).

Mechin, Alexandre, *De la souveraineté des assemblées primaires, ou lettre d'Al. Méchin, membre de l'assemblée primaire de la section de Fontaine de Grenelle au citoyen Quatremère* (Paris, 1795).

Mercier, Louis-Sebastien, *Le tableau de Paris*, vol. 7 (Amsterdam, 1783).

——, *Paris delineated*, vol. 1 (London, 1802).

Meyer, Frederic, *Fragments sur Paris*, 2 vols, trans. Charles-François Dumouriez (Paris, 1798).

Miger, Simon-Charles, *Lettre à M. Vien, chevalier de l'ordre du Roi, premier peintre et directeur de l'Académie royale de peinture* (Paris, 1789).

Millin, Aublin-Louis, *Aubin-Louis Millin et l'Allemagne: le Magasin encyclopédique—les lettres à Karl August Böttiger*, ed. Geneviève Espagne and Bénédicte Savoy (Hildesheim, 2005).

Miranda, Francisco, *Opinion du général Miranda sur la situation actuelle de la France, et sur les remèdes convenables à ses maux* (Paris, 1795).

Montesquieu, Charles-Louis Secondat, *Voyages de Montesquieu*, vol. 1 (Paris, 1894).

——, *Considérations sur les causes de la grandeur des Romains et de leur décadence* (Paris, 1748).

Mopinot de la Chapotte, Antoine-Rigobert, *Proposition d'un monument à élever dans la capitale de la France* (Paris, 1790).

Panckoucke, Charles, 'Avis . . . aux souscripteurs' [14 May 1787], in Amédée-Louis-Michel Lepeletier, *Encyclopédie méthodique. Histoire naturelle*, vol. 3 (Paris, 1787).

Paroy, Jean-Philippe, *Opinions religieuses, royalistes et politiques de M. Antoine Quatremère de Quincy* (Paris, 1810).

——, *Précis historique de l'origine de l'Académie royale de peinture, sculpture et gravure* (Paris, 1816).

——, *Mémoires du comte de Paroy: souvenirs d'un défenseur de la famille royale pendant la Révolution* (Paris, 1895).

Perry, Sampson, *The Argus; Or, General Observer: A Political Miscellany* (London, 1796).

Pingré, Alexandre-Gui, *Mémoire sur la colonne de la halle aux bleds et sur le cadran cylindrique que l'on construit au haut de cette colonne* (Paris, 1764).

Piranesi, Givovanni-Battista, *Différentes vues de quelques restes de trois grands edifices qui subsistent encore dans le milieu de l'ancienne ville de Pesto autrement Posidonia qui est située dans la Lucanie* (Rome, 1778).

——, 'Divers Manners of Ornamenting Chimneys [1769]', in John Wilton-Ely, ed., *Givoanni Battista Piranesi: The Polemical Works* (Farnborough, 1972).

——, *Observations on the Letter of Monsieur Mariette: With Opinions on Architecture* [1765], trans. Caroline Beamish and David Britt (Los Angeles, 2002).

Pitra, Louis-Guillaume, 'Lettre de M. Pitra, électeur de 1789', in Maurice Tourneux, ed., *Correspondance littéraire, philosophique et critique*, vol. 17 (Paris, 1882).

Poisson de La Chabeaussière, Auguste-Étienne-Xavier, *Catéchisme français, ou Principes de philosophie, de morale et de politique républicaine, à l'usage des écoles primaires* (Paris, year IV [1795]).

Pommereul, François-René, *Campagne du général Buonaparte en Italie: pendant les années IVe et Ve de la République française* (Paris, 1797).

Portalis, Jean-Étienne, *De l'usage et de l'abus de l'esprit philosophique durant le XVIIIe siècle* (Paris, 1820).

Portiez, Louis-François-René, *Rapport fait au nom du Comité d'instruction publique, sur les concours de sculpture, peinture et architecture, ouverts par les décrets de la Convention nationale* (Paris, 1795).

Prudhomme, Louis-Marie, *Histoire générale et impartiale des erreurs, des fautes et des crimes commis* (Paris, 1797).

Puthod de la Maisonrouge, François-Marie, *Les monuments ou le pèlerinage historique* (Paris, 1790–1).

Quatremère, Marc-Étienne, *Motion de M. Quatremère* (Paris, 1789).

——, *Pétition à l'Assemblée nationale, relative au transport de Voltaire* (Paris, 1791).

Quatremère de Quincy, Antoine-Chrysostôme, 'ARTS. Aux auteur du Journal. Paris 31 January 1787', *Journal de Paris*, no. 42, 11 Feb. 1787, pp. 181–3.

——, *Encyclopédie méthodique, ou Par ordre de matières; Par une société de gens de lettres, de savans et d'artistes . . . Architecture*, 3 vols (Paris, 1788–1825).

——, 'De la nature des opéras bouffons italiens et de l'union de la comédie et de la musique dans ces poëmes', *Mercure de France*, no. 12, March 1789, pp. 124–48.

——, 'Tableau, bas-reliefs, statues et pierres gravées de la Galerie de Florence et du Palais Pitti', *Mercure de France*, no. 38, 19 Sept. 1789, pp. 62–8.

——, *Discours prononcé a l'Assemblée des représentants de la commune, le vendredi 2 Avril 1790, sur la liberté des theatres, et le rapport des commissaires* (Paris, 1790).

——, *Considérations sur les arts du dessin en France, suivies d'un plan d'académie, ou d'école publique, et d'un système d'encouragements* (Paris, 1791).

——, *Suite aux Considérations sur les arts du dessin en France; ou réflexions critiques sur le projet de statuts et règlements de la majorité de l'Académie de peinture et sculpture* (Paris, 1791).

——, *Seconde suite aux Considérations sur les arts du dessin, ou projet de règlement pour l'école publique des arts du dessin; et de l'emplacement convenable a l'Institut national des sciences, lettres & arts* (Paris, 1791).

——, *Réflexions nouvelles sur la gravure, par M. Quatremère de Quincy* (Paris, 1791).

——, *Rapport et projet de decret présentés a l'Assemblée Nationale, par M. Quatremère, au nom du Comité de l'instruction publique, le 14 novembre 1791, sur les réclamations des artistes qui ont exposé au Salon du Louvre* (Paris, 1791).

——, *Rapport sur l'édifice dit de Sainte-Geneviève, fait au Directoire du département de Paris, par M. Quatremère-Quincy* (Paris, 1791). [Abridged reprint as *Extrait du premier rapport présenté au Directoire dans le mois de mai 1791, sur les mesures propres à transformer l'églises dite de Sainte-Geneviève, au Panthéon français* (Paris, 1792).]

222   BIBLIOGRAPHY

——, 'Rapport et projet de décret relatif au payement des appointements dus aux professeurs de l'école publique de chant et de déclamation' [5 Feb. 1792], in James Guillaume, ed., *Procès-verbaux du Comité d'Instruction publique de l'Assemblée legislative* (Paris, 1889), pp. 107–9.

——, *Projet de décret présenté à l'Assemblée nationale, au nom du Comité d'instruction publique, relatif au paiement des appointements dus aux professeurs de l'École publique de chant et de déclamation* (Paris, n.d.).

——, 'Rapport et projet de decret sur la petition de monsieur de Rossel fait au nom de Comité d'instruction publique' [25 Avril 1792], in James Guillaume, ed., *Procèsverbaux du Comité d'Instruction publique de l'Assemblée legislative* (Paris, 1889), pp. 173–6.

——, 'Rapport et projet de décret sur les honneurs à accorder à la mémoire de Jacques-Guillaume Simonneau, maire d'Etampes. Par M. Quatremère' [9 May 1792], James Guillaume, ed., *Procès-verbaux du Comité d'Instruction publique de l'Assemblée legislative* (Paris, 1889), pp. 284–6.

—— *Décret sur les honneurs a rendre a la mémoire de Jacques-Guillaume Simonneau, maire d'Etampes, précédé du rapport fait au nom du Comite d'instruction publique* (Paris, 1792).

——, *Opinion ... sur les dénonciations faites contre M. Duport, ci-devant ministre de la justice. Prononcée le 2 juin 1792.* (Paris, n.d. [1792]).

——, *Opinion de M. Quatremère, député du département de Paris, qui n'a pu être prononcé dans la séance du 13 juillet, sur la suspension de MM. Pétion et Manuel, maire et procureur de la commune de Paris* (Paris, n.d. [1792]),

——, *Opinion ... sur les dénonciations dirigées contre M. Lafayette* (Paris, 1792).

——, *Rapport approuvé par le comité d'instruction publique de l'assemblée législative, sur les réclamations des directeurs de théatre, & la proprieté des auteurs dramatiques* (Paris, 1792).

——, *Rapport fait au Directoire du département de Paris, le 13 novembre 1792, l'an Ier de la République ... sur l'état actuel du Panthéon français, sur les changements qui s'y sont opérés, sur les travaux qui restent à entreprendre, ainsi que sur l'ordre administratif établi pour leur direction et la comptabilité* (Paris, n.d. [1792]).

——, *Rapport fait au Directoire du département de Paris: sur les travaux entrepris, continués ou achevés au Panthéon français depuis le compte-rendu le 17 novembre 1792 & sur l'état actuel du monument, le deuxième jour du second mois de l'an 2 de la République française, une & indivisible; imprimé par ordre du Directoire* (Paris, n.d. [1793]).

——, [Published anonymously] *Précis pour Miranda* (n.p, n.d. [Paris, 1794]).

——, *Jury des arts. Prix décernés aux esquisses de peintures présentées au concours ouvert par la Convention Nationale et soumises au jugement du Jury des Arts, en vertu de la loi du 9 frimaire de l'an troisième* (Paris, n.d. [1795]).

——, *Discours du Citoyen Quatremère Prononcé dans la Séance du 2 vendémaire, l'an quatrième de la république française, de l'Assemblie primaire et permanente de la section Fontaine de Grenelle* (Paris, n.d. [1795]), Bibliothèque de l'Institut de France, Ms 2555, dossier 1.

——, [Published anonymously], *Coup d'œil sur la journée du 13 vendémiaire et ses suites* (Neuchâtel, 1796).

——, [Published anomymously], 'Variétés. Sur les arts', *Véridique, ou Courrier universel*, 28 June 1796, pp. 2–3.

——, [Published anonymously], *Véridique, ou Courrier universel*, 4 July 1796, pp. 1–2.

——, [Published under 'A.Q.',] *Lettres sur le préjudice qu'occasionneraient aux Arts & à la Science le Déplacement des Monuments de l'Art de l'Italie* (Paris, 1796). [Partially printed by Jean-Gabriel Peltier in *Paris pendant l'année 1796* between 23 July and 20 August

BIBLIOGRAPHY   223

1796. Reprinted with changes as *Lettres sur le préjudice qu'occasionneroient aux arts et à la science le déplacement des monumens de l'art de l'Italie, le démembrement de ses écoles et la spoliation de ses collections, galeries, musées,...par M. Quatremère de Quincy. Nouvelle édition faite sur celle de Paris de 1796* (Rome, 1815). Translated into German by Johann Wilhelm Archenholz as 'Ueber den nachtheiligen Einfluss der Versetzung der Monumente aus Italien auf Kunste und Wissenschaften', *Minerva*, Oct. 1796 and Nov. 1796. Translated into English by David Gilks in Quatremère, *Letters to Miranda and Canova on the Abduction of Antiquities from Rome and Athens* (Los Angeles, 2012), pp. 92–123.]

——, *Discours prononcé, par le citoyen Quatremère-Quincy, au tribunal criminel du département de la Seine, le 22 thermidor, an quatrième de la République* [9 Aug. 1796] (Paris, n.d. [1796]).

——, [Published anonymously], 'Lettre à l'auteur du Journal Littéraire', *Journal littéraire*, vol. 1, no. 11, 16 Oct. 1796, pp. 361–7.

——, *La véritable liste des candidats: précédée d'observations sur la nature de l'institution des candidats et son application au gouvernement représentatif* (Paris, 1797).

——, *Rapport fait par Quatremère, au nom d'une commission spéciale, sur l'exemption du droit de patente en faveur des peintres, sculpteurs, graveurs et architectes, séance du 13 messidor, an V. Corps législatif. Conseil de Cinq-Cents* (Paris, 1797).

——, *Corps législatif. Conseil des Cinq-cents. Opinion de Quatremère sur le renouvellement des bureaux centraux. Séance du 19 messidor an V* (Paris, 1797).

——, *Corps législatif. Conseil des Cinq-cents. Rapport fait par Quatremère, au nom d'une commission spéciale, sur la responsabilité des ministres et celle des agens du Directoire dans les colonies. Séance du 30 messidor an V* (Paris, 1797).

——, *Opinion de Quatremère sur les second projet relatif aux réunions politiques* (Paris, 1797): British Library, London, Bibliothèque historique de la Révolution, Conseil des Cinq Cents, Rapports etc., vol. 358, tract 9.

——, 'Rapport de quatremere de quinci sur les patentes des artistes. 10 thermidor an 5': BnF, transcribed by J.-C. Deloynes.

——, *Corps législatif. Conseil des Cinq-cents. Motion d'ordre fait par Quatremère au nom de la commission d'instruction publique, sur le projet présenté par la commission de l'aliénation des presbytères. Séance du 11 thermidor an V* (Paris, 1797).

——, *Corps législatif. Conseil des Cinq-cents. Rapport fait par Dehaussy-Robécourt, au nom d'une commission composée des représentans du peuple Noaille, Quatremère de Quincy et Dehaussy-Robécourt, sur les opérations des assemblées primaires de la commune de Valenciennes. Séance du 15 messidor an V* (Paris, 1797).

——, *Rapport fait par Quatremère au Nom de la Commission d'instruction publique sur le mode d'organisation des biens affectés aux bourses des ci-devant Collèges de Paris—Séance du 9 Fructidor an V* (Paris, 1797), in AN, AD XXIA 360.

——, [Several letters to Miranda, 1795–6]', in *Archivo del General Miranda*, vol. 6 (Caracas, 1930), pp. 341–2, 356.

——, [Several unpublished letters to Miranda, 1798–9], AN, F7 6285.

——, [Letter to Mallet du Pan, 18 Aug. 1799] in Pierre-André Sayous, ed., *Mémoires et correspondance de Mallet du Pan*, vol. 2 (Paris, 1851), pp. 412–13.

——, *Rapport fait au Conseil général du Département de la Seine, le 15 thermidor an 8, sur l'instruction publique, le rétablissement des bourses, le scandale des inhumations actuelles, l'érection des cimetières, la restitution des tombeaux, mausolées, etc.* (Paris, 1800).

——, 'Littérature-Beaux-arts' [review of Lessing, *Laocoon*], *Moniteur universel*, no. 252, 1 June 1803, p. 1142.

224 BIBLIOGRAPHY

——, *De l'architecture égyptienne considérée dans son origine, ses principes et son gôut, et compare sous les memes rapports à l'architecture grecque. Dissertation qui a remporté, en 1785, le prix proposé par l'Académie des Inscriptions et Belles-Lettres* (Paris, 1803).

——, 'Dissertations sur la diversité du génie et des moyens poétiques des différens arts', *Archives littéraires de l'Europe*, vol. 4 (1804), pp. 46–75.

——, 'Rapport fait au conseil municipal de Paris … sur les concessions de terrains dans les cimetières' [19 April 1805], in AN, F2 (I) 123, pp. 6–7.

——, 'Sur le Démos de Parrhasius', *Archives littéraires de l'Europe*, vol. 4 (1805), pp. 258–82.

——, 'Sur la restitution du temple de Jupiter Olympien à Agrigente. Extraite d'un Mémoire destiné à être lu dans la séance publique de la troisiemè class de l'Institut national, le Ier vendredi de germinal 1805', *Archives littéraires de l'Europe*, vol. 6 (1805), pp. 72–87.

——, 'Sur l'idéal dans les arts du dessin', *Archives littéraires de l'Europe*, vol. 6 (1805), pp. 385–404; vol. 7, pp. 3–37, 289–337.

——, 'Deuxième partie: les palais', in Jacques-Guillaume Legrand and Charles-Paul Landon, eds, *Description de Paris, et de ses édifices*, vol. 1 (Paris, 1806), pp. 1–93.

——, 'Réflexions critiques sur les mausolées en général, et en particulier sur celui exécuté par M. Canova, et placé depuis peu dans l'église de Saint-Augustin, à Vienne', *Archives littéraires de l'Europe*, vol. 9 (1806), pp. 266–92.

——, 'Essai historique sur l'art du paysage à Rome', *Archives littéraires de l'Europe*, vol. 10 (1807), pp. 193–208, 376–91.

——, 'Sur les vases céramographiques appelés jusqu'à présent vases étrusques', *Moniteur universel*, no. 287, 14 Oct. 1807, pp. 1110–11.

——, *Institut de France. Funérailles de M. Moitte, le 3 mai 1810* (Paris, 1810).

——, *Quelques considérations pratiques et de circonstances sur la constitution et la liberté de la presse* (Paris, 1814).

——, *Le Jupiter olympien, ou l'Art de la sculpture antique considéré sous un nouveau point de vue, ouvrage qui comprend un essai sur le goût de la sculpture polychrome, l'analyse explicative de la toreutique et l'histoire de la statuaire en or et en ivoire, chez les Grecs et les Romains* (Paris, 1814).

——, *Considérations morales sur la destination des ouvrages de l'art* (Paris, 1815).

——, [Published anonymously], *L'Ultimatum du parti révolutionnaire* (n.p., 1815).

——, 'Un discours sur les monumens d'art dues à la Restauration', *Recueil des discours prononcés dans la séance publique annuelle de l'Institut royal de France, le mercredi 24 avril 1816* (Paris, 1816), pp. 43–50.

——, '[Review of] Bernardi, *De l'origine et des progrès de la législation française, ou Histoire du Droit public et privé de la France, depuis la fondation de la monarchie jusques et compris la revolution', Journal des savants*, Dec. 1817, pp. 748–51.

——, [Review of Grivaud de la Vincelle, *Recueil de monumens antiques*], *Journal des savants*, Oct. 1817.

——, *Lettrés écrits de Londres à Rome, et addressées à M. Canova, sur les marbres d'Elgin, ou les sculptures du temple de Minerve à Athènes* (Rome, 1818).

——, 'Traité théorique et pratique de l'art de bâtir, par J. Rondelet', *Journal des savants*, June 1818, pp. 365–8.

——, 'Extrait du Discours de M. Quatremère de Quincy, aux funérailles de M. Dufourny', *Journal des savants*, Oct. 1818, p. 629.

——, *Éloge historique de M. Van Spaendonck: séance publique de l'Académie royale des beaux-arts du 5 octobre 1822* (Paris, 1822).

——, *Essai sur la nature, le but et les moyens de l'imitation dans les beaux-arts* (Paris, 1823).

——, 'Extrait d'un ensemble de recherches historiques et philosophiques sur la cause principale du développement et de la perfection des beaux-arts chez toutes les nations', in *Recueil des discours prononces dans la séance publique annuelle de l'Institut royal de France, le lundi 24 avril 1826* (Paris, 1826), pp. 30–45.

——, 'Une lettre de Quatremère de Quincy [to Lemonnier, April 1828]', *Archives de l'Art français, nouvelle série*, vol. 1 (1907), pp. 189–92.

——, *Histoire de la vie et des ouvrages de Raphaël* (Paris, 1824; expanded 2nd edn, 1833).

——, *Dictionnaire historique d'architecture comprenant dans son plan les notions historiques, descriptives, archéologiques...de cet art*, 2 vols (Paris, 1832).

——, 'De la marche différente de l'esprit humain dans les sciences naturelles et dans les beaux-arts', *Recueil des lectures faites dans la seance publique annuelle de L'Institut royal r France, du vendredi 2 mai 1834* (Paris, 1834), pp. 35–43.

——, *Canova et ses ouvrages, ou Mémoires historiques sur la vie et les travaux de ce célèbre artiste* (Paris, 1834).

——, *Recueil de notices historiques, lues dans les séances publiques de l'Académie royal des beaux-arts à l'Institut* (Paris, 1834).

——, *Histoire de la vie et des ouvrages de Michel-Ange Bonarroti* (Paris, 1835).

——, *Lettres sur l'enlèvement des ouvrages de l'art antique à Athènes et à Rome, écrites les unes au célèbre Canova, les autres au général Miranda,...nouvelle édition* (Paris, 1836).

——, *Essai sur l'idéal dans ses applications pratiques aux œuvres de l'imitation propre des arts du dessin* (Paris, 1837).

——, *Suite du recueil des notices historiques lues dans les séances publiques de l'Académie royale des beaux-arts à l'Institut* (Paris, 1837).

Quatremère-Disjonval, *Lettre du citoyen Quatremère-Disjonval, adjudant-général batave, au c[itoy]en Cochon, ministre de la Police générale de la République française* (n.p, n.d. [1796]).

Reb..., 'Essai sur les tombeaux des grands hommes dans les sciences, les lettres et les arts', *Mercure de France*, Jan. 1765, pp. 17–20.

Renou, Antoine, *Esprit des statuts et réglemens de l'Académie royale de peinture et de sculpture, pour servir de réponse aux détracteurs de son régime* (Paris, 1790).

——, *Réfutation de la 'Seconde suite aux considérations sur les arts de dessin' par M. Quatremère de Quincy* (Paris, 1791).

Renou, Antoine, et al., *Précis motivé par les officiers de l'Académie royale de peinture & sculpture, & plusieurs Académiciens qui s'y sont joints, pour servir de réfutation à un projet de statuts d'académie centrale, par quelques académiciens* (Paris, 1791).

——, *A Messieurs du Comité de constitution par les officiers de l'Académie royale de peinture et de sculpture en apportant leur nouveau plan de statuts* (Paris, 1791).

Restout, Jean-Bernard, *Discours prononcé dans l'Académie royale de peinture et sculpture, le samedi 19 décembre 1789* (Paris, 1790).

Robin, Jean-Baptiste, 'Plan pour la formation d'une société des arts du dessin à Paris', *Extrait du tribut de la société nationale des neuf soeurs. 14 avril 1791* (n.p. [Paris], n.d. [1791]), pp. 1–16.

Roederer, Pierre-Louis, 'Mélangés. Des Tableaux d'Italie', *Journal de Paris*, no. 289 7 July 96, pp. 1159–60.

——, *Journal d'économie publique, de morale et de politique*, vol. 2, no. 20, 10 March 1797, p. 66.

——, 'De l'entrée de Bonaparte à Rome, des tableaux et statues d'Italie', *Journal d'économie publique*, vol. 19, 28 Feb. 1797, pp. 39–45.

——, *Journal de Paris*, 5 April 1797, pp. 791–2.

——, 'Des candidates proposés', *Oeuvres du comte P.-L. Roederer*, vol. 6 (Paris, 1853).

226 BIBLIOGRAPHY

Roland le Virloy, Charles-François, *Dictionnaire d'architecture* (Paris, 1770–1).

Rossel de Cercy, Auguste-Louis, *Mémoire pour M. de Rossel* (Paris, 1792).

Rousseau, Jean-Jacques, *The Discourses and Other Early Political Writings*, ed. and trans. Victor Gourevitch (Cambridge, 1997).

Roverea, Ferdinand de, *Mémoires de Ferdinand de Rovéréa* (Berne, 1848).

Saint-Non, Jean-Claude-Richard de, *Voyage pittoresque: ou, Description des royaumes de Naples et de Sicile* (Paris, 1781).

Saint-Victor, Jacques-Benjamin de, *Tableau historique et pittoresque de Paris* (Paris, 1808).

Sainte-Beuve, Charles-Augustin, *Nouveaux lundis*, vol. 2 (Paris, 1883).

Section des Marchés, *Pétition de la section des Marchés…à la Convention nationale, le 21 ventôse 3e année républicaine, tendante principalement à rétablir honorablement la mémoire du citoyen Quatremère, marchand de draps, rue Denis, assassiné au tribunal révolutionnaire* (Paris, n.d. [1795]).

Semper, Gottfried, *Vier Elemente der Baukunst* (Brunswick, 1851).

Smith, Adam, *An Inquiry into the Causes of the Wealth of Nations* (London, 1776).

Soufflot, Jacques-Germain, *Plan général de l'église de Sainte-Geneviève, de la place & de la rüe au devant, suivant le dernier projet présenté au Roy par Mr le Marquis de Marigny, approuvé par Sa Majesté le 2 mars 1757, inventé et dessiné par J. G. Soufflot* (Paris, 1757).

Staël, Germaine de, *Corinne, or Italy*, trans. Sylvia Raphael (Oxford, 2008).

——, *De l'Allemagne* [1813], 2 vols (Paris, 1993).

Stendhal, *Paris-Londres: Chroniques*, ed. R. Dénier (Paris, 1997).

——, *Correspondance générale*, ed. Victor del Litto, vol. 3 (Paris, 1968).

Stolberg, Friedrich, *Travels through Germany, Switzerland, Italy, and Sicily* [1794], 4 vols, trans. Thomas Holcroft (London, 1796).

Talleyrand-Perigord, Charles-Maurice, *Rapport sur l'instruction publique, fait au nom du Comité de Constitution à l'Assemblée nationale, les 10, 11 et 19 septembre 1791* (Paris, 1791).

——, *Extraits des mémoires du prince de Talleyrand-Périgord* (Paris, 1838).

Thibaudeau, Antoine-Claire, *Mémoires sur la Convention: et le Directoire*, vols 1–2 (Paris, 1824).

Todeschi, Claudio, *Opere di monsignore Claudio Todeschi* (Rome, 1779).

Trouvé, Charles-Joseph, *Moniteur universel*, no. 335, 22 Aug. 1796, p. 1.

——, [Attributed to this author] 'Pétition présentée par les artistes au Directoire exécutif', *Moniteur universel*, no. 12, 3 Oct. 1796, pp. 45–6.

Vanderbourg, Charles, 'Avertissement du Traducteur', in Gotthold Lessing, *Du Laocoon, ou des limites respectives de la poésie et de la peinture: traduit de l'allemand de G. E. Lessing* (Paris, 1802).

Vasse, Thomas, *Rapport fait par Vasse, au nom d'une commission, composée des représentants du peuple Dissandes-Moullevade, Quatremer et Vasse, chargée d'examiner la pétition de J.-J. Desmarets, ancien directeur des subsistances militaires à Valenciennes, mis hors la loi et inscrit comme émigre à l'époque de l'invasion par les Autrichiens. Séance du 5 fructidor an V* (Paris, year V [1797]).

Vattel, Emmerlich de, *Droit des gens, ou principes de la loi naturelle* (London, 1758).

Vaubertrand, François, *L'humanité pendant la terreur, récit en vers, avec des notes historiques* (Paris, 1861).

Vaublanc, Vincent-Marie Viénot de, *Mémoires sur la Révolution de France et recherches sur les causes qui ont amené la Révolution de 1789 et celles qui l'ont suivie*, 4 vols (Paris, 1833).

——, *Mémoires de M. le comte de Vaublanc* (Paris, 1857).

Vaudoyer, Antoine, *Idées d'un citoyen françois sur le lieu destiné à la sépulture des hommes illustres de France* (Paris, 1791).

Verniquet, Edme, *Atlas du plan général de la ville de Paris* (Paris, 1795).

Villette, Charles, *Lettres choisies de Charles Villette: sur les principaux évènemens de la Révolution* (Paris, 1792).

Viollet-le-Duc, Eugène Emmanuel, *Dictionnaire raisonné de l'architecture française*, vol. 6 (Paris, 1863).

Volney, Constantin-François de, *Les ruines ou méditation sur les révolutions des empires* (Paris, 1791).

Voltaire, François-Marie, *Letters Concerning the English Nation* [1734] (Oxford, 2009).

Walpole, Horace, 'Letter to John Chute' [1771], in *Private Correspondence of Horace Walpole, Earl of Orford*, vol. 3 (London, 1820).

Winckelmann, Johann Joachim, *Reflections on the Imitation of Greek Works in Painting and Sculpture* [1755], trans. Henri Fuseli (London, 1765).

——, *History of the Art of Antiquity* [1764], trans. H. Mallgrave (Los Angeles, 2006).

Secondary sources

Adkins, Gregory, 'The Renaissance of Peiresc: Aubin-Louis Millin and the Post-revolutionary Republic of Letters', *Isis*, vol. 99 (2008), pp. 675–700.

Agulhon, Maurice, *Marianne into Battle: Republican Imagery and Symbolism in France, 1789–1880*, trans Janet Lloyd (Cambridge, 1981).

Alloa, Emmanuel, 'La mobilisation de l'aura', in Quatremère, *Lettres à Miranda. Sur le déplacement des monuments de l'art de l'Italie (1796) de Quatremère de Quincy* (Paris, 2017).

Alpaugh, Michael, *Non-violence and the French Revolution: Political Demonstrations in Paris* (Cambridge, 2014).

Andrieux, Maurice, *Les français à Rome* (Paris, 1968).

Anon., 'Fragments d'histoire de la protection littéraire: la lutte entre les auteurs dramatiques et les directeurs de théâtre sous l'Assemble législative française (1791–1792)', *Le droit d'auteur: organe officiel du Bureau de l'union internationale pour la protection des œuvres littéraires et artistiques*, no. 10, 15 Oct. 1890, pp. 105–10.

Argan, Giulio, 'On the Typology of Architecture', *Architectural Design*, vol. 33 (1963).

Arnault, Antoine-Vincent, et al., 'Quatremère', in 'Quatremère de Quincy (Antoine-Chrysosthôme)', *Dictionnaire historique et raisonné de tous les hommes depuis la Révolution française*, vol. 17 (Paris, 1827), pp. 167–9.

Aulard, François-Alphonse, ed., *La société des Jacobins: recueil de documents pour l'histoire du club des Jacobins de Paris*, vol. 3 (Paris, 1892).

——, *Paris pendant la réaction thermidorienne et sous le Directoire*, vol. 2 (Paris, 1898).

——, *Les orateurs de la Législative et de la Convention: l'éloquence parlementaire pendant la Révolution française*, vol. 1 (Paris, 1885).

Auricchio, Laura, *Adélaïde Labille-Guiard: Artist in the Age of Revolution* (Los Angeles, 2009).

Avin, Louis, 'Quelques mots touchant l'application du droit de conquête aux monuments de l'art', *Bulletins de l'Académie royale des sciences, des lettres et des beaux-arts de Belgique*, vol. 41 (1872), pp. 263–91.

Baczko, Bruno, *Ending the Terror: The French Revolution after Robespierre*, trans. Michael Petheram (Cambridge, 1994).

——, 'Le tournant culturel de l'an III', in Roger Dupuy and Marcel Morabito, eds, *Pour une république sans révolution* (Rennes, 1996), pp. 17–37.

228 BIBLIOGRAPHY

Baldensperger, Ferdinand, *Le mouvement des idées dans l'émigration française (1789–1815)*, 2 vols (Paris, 1924).

Balsamo, Isabelle, et al., eds, *La Manufacture du Dijonval et la draperie sedanaise, 1650–1850* (Châlons-sur-Marne, 1984).

Bann, Stephen, 'Quarrels between Painting and Sculpture in Post-revolutionary France', CCA Mellon Lectures (17 April 2003): https://www.cca.qc.ca/cca.media/files/1484/1385/Mellon04-SB.pdf.

Barasch, Mosche, *Theories of Art: From Plato to Winckelmann*, 2 vols (New York, 1985–90).

Baridon, Laurent, 'Le Dictionnaire d'architecture de Quatremère de Quincy: codifier le néoclassicisme', in Claude Blanckaert and Michel Porret, eds, *L'Encyclopédie méthodique (1782–1832). Des Lumières au positivisme* (Geneva, 2006), pp. 691–718.

Barrault, Éric, 'Lacretelle, un écrivain face à la Révolution française (1766–1855)', *Annales historiques de la Révolution française*, vol. 333, no. 1 (2003), pp. 67–83.

Barrière, François, 'M. Quatremère de Quincy', *Revue de Paris*, vol. 5, May 1850, p. 286.

Barroero, Liliana, 'I primi anni della scuola del Nudo in Campidoglio', in Donatella Biagi Maino, ed., *Benedetto XIV e le arti del disegno* (Rome, 1998), pp. 367–76.

Barthelemy-Saint-Hilaire, Jules, 'Notice sur Étienne Quatremère', *Journal des savants* (Nov. 1857), pp. 708–23.

Beaulaincourt-Marles, Sophie, *Boniface-Louis-André de Castellane, 1758–1837* (Paris, 1901).

Becq, Anne, *La genèse de l'esthétique française moderne: de la raison classique à l'imagination créatrice, 1680–1814* (Pisa, 1984).

Beiser, Frederick, *The Fate of Reason: German Philosophy from Kant to Fichte* (Cambridge, MA, 1987).

Belayé, Simone, 'Les enrichissements de la Bibliothèque nationale', in Alfred Fierro, ed., *Patrimoine parisien 1789–1799: destructions, créations, mutations* (Paris, 1989), pp. 48–63.

Belhoste, Jean-François, et al., *La Manufacture du Dijonval et la draperie sedanaise, 1650–1850* (Charleville-Mézières, 1984).

Belhoste, Bruno, *Paris Savant: Capital of Science in the Age of the Enlightenment*, trans. Susan Emanuel (Oxford, 2018).

Belissa, Marc, *Repenser l'ordre Européen (1795–1802). De la société des rois aux droits des nations* (Paris, 2006).

Bell, David, *The Cult of the Nation in France: Inventing Nationalism, 1680–1800* (Cambridge, MA, 2003).

Benhamou, Reed, *Public and Private Art Education in France: 1648–1793* (Oxford, 1993).

——, *Regulating the Académie: Art, Rules and Power in 'Ancien Régime' France* (Oxford, 2009).

Benisovich, Michel, 'Le Général Francisco de Miranda et ses amis Parisiens (1792–1798)', *Gazette des beaux-arts*, vol. 59, no. 6 (1962), pp. 345–52.

Benoit, François, *L'Art français sous la Révolution et l'Empire* (Paris, 1897).

Benzaken, Jean-Charles, 'Hercule dans la Revolution Francaise (1789–1799) ou les "Nouveaux travaux d'Hercule"', in Michel Vovelle, ed., *Les images de la Revolution Française* (Paris, 1989), pp. 203–14.

Bergdoll, Barry, *European Architecture 1750–1890* (Oxford, 2000).

——, ed., *Le Panthéon symbole des révolutions. De l'église de la nation au temple des grands hommes* (Paris, 1989).

Berger, Guy, et al., *Paris, lieux de pouvoir et de citoyenneté* (Paris, 2006).

Bertoncini Sabatini, Paolo, 'Da Agrigento verso Atene: il viaggio alla sorgente del genio ellenico di Quatremère de Quincy', in Alessandro Carlino, ed., *La Sicilia e il Grand Tour: la riscoperta di Akragas. 1700–1800* (Palermo, 2011), pp. 51–71.

Bertrand, Gilles, *Le grand tour revisité: pour une archéologie du tourisme: le voyage des Français en Italie (milieu XVIIIe siècle—début XIXe siècle)* (Rome, 2008).

Biard, Michel, *La liberté ou la mort. Mourir en député, 1792–1795* (Paris, 2015).

Bignamini, Ilaria, and Wilton, Andrew, *Grand Tour: The Lure of Italy in the Eighteenth Century* (London, 1996).

Biver, Marie-Louise, *Le Panthéon à lépoque révolutionnaire* (Paris, 1982).

——, *Fêtes révolutionnaires à Paris* (Paris, 1979).

Blanning, Timothy, 'The Role of Religion in European Counter-Revolution 1789–1815', in Derek Beales and Geoffrey Best, eds, *History, Society and the Churches: Essays in Honour of Owen Chadwick* (Cambridge, 1985), pp. 195–214.

——, *The Pursuit of Glory: Europe 1648–1815* (London, 2008).

——, *Reform and Revolution in Mainz 1743–1803* (Cambridge, 1974).

——, *The French Revolution in Germany: Occupation and Resistance in the Rhineland, 1792–1802* (Oxford, 1983).

Blanckaert, Claude, and Porret, Michel, eds, *L'Encyclopédie méthodique (1782–1832) des Lumières au positivisme* (Geneva, 2006).

Blaufarb, Rafe, *The Great Demarcation: The French Revolution and the Invention of Modern Property* (Oxford, 2016).

Blumer, Marie-Louise, 'La Commission pour la recherché des objets de sciences et arts en Italie (1796–1797)', *La Révolution française*, vol. 87, no. 1 (1934), pp. 62–88, 124–50, 222–59.

Bonnet, Jean-Claude, *Naissance du panthéon: essai sur le culte des grandes homes* (Paris, 1998).

——, 'La mort de Simonneau', in Jean Nicolas, ed., *Mouvements populaires et conscience sociale* (Paris, 1987), pp. 671–6.

——, ed., *La Carmagnole des muses. L'homme de lettres et l'artiste dans la Révolution* (Paris, 1988).

Bordes, Philippe, *Le Serment du Jeu de Paume de Jacques-Louis David. Le peintre, son milieu et son temps de 1789 à 1792* (Paris, 1983).

——, *Jacques-Louis David: Empire to Exile* (New Haven, 2005).

——, 'Le Musée Napoleon', in Jean-Claude Bonnet, ed., *L'Empire des Muses. Napoléon, les Arts et les Lettres* (Paris, 2004).

Bordes, Philippe, and Michel, Régis, eds, *Aux armes et aux arts! Les arts de la Révolution 1789–99* (Paris, 1988).

Boschot, Adolphe, 'Le centenaire d'un esthéticien, Quatremère de Quincy', in *Institut de France, Publications Diverses de l'année 1940* (Paris, 1940), pp. 17–40.

Bottineau, Josette, 'De Bélisaire à Marcus Sextus: génese et histoire d'un tableau de Pierre Guérin (1774–1833)', *Révue du Louvre*, vol. 43, no. 3 (1993), pp. 41–53.

Bourgin, Georges, 'Quelques textes sur Daunou, garde des archives', *Bibliothèque de l'École des chartes*, vol. 102 (1941), pp. 318–28.

Bourne, Henry, 'Improvising a Government in Paris in July, 1789', *American Historical Review*, vol. 10, no. 2 (1905), pp. 280–308.

Bowron, Edgars, 'Academic Life Drawing in Rome, 1750–1790', in Richard Campbell, ed., *Visions of Antiquity: Neoclassical Figure Drawings* (Los Angeles, 1993).

Boyer, Ferdinand, 'L'organisation des conquêtes artistiques de la Convention en Belgique', *Revue belge de philologie et d'histoire*, vol. 49, no 2 (1971), pp. 490–500.

230 BIBLIOGRAPHY

——, *Autour de Canova et de Napoléon* (Paris, 1937).

Boyle, Nicholas, *Goethe: The Poet of the Age* (Oxford, 1991).

Brassart, Patrick, *Paroles de la Révolution. Les Assemblées parlmentaires, 1789–1794* (Paris, 1988).

Bresc-Bautier, Geneviève, et al., *Un musée révolutionnaire. Le musée des monuments français d'Alexandre Lenoir* (Paris, 2016).

Bressani, Martin, 'The Paestum Controversy', in Corinne Belier et al., eds, *Henri Labrouste: Structure Brought to Light* (New York, 2012).

Brette, Armand, *Histoires des édifices où ont siégé les assemblées parlementaires de la Révolution française*, vol. 1 (Paris, 1902).

Briggs, Robin, *Early Modern France* (Oxford, 1998).

Brockliss, Laurence, *Calvet's Webb: Enlightenment and the Republic of Letters in Eighteenth-Century France* (Oxford, 2002).

Brown, Howard, *Ending the French Revolution: Violence, Justice and Repression from the Terror to Napoleon* (Charlottesville, 2006).

Buchez, Philippe, *Histoire de l'assemblée constituante*, vol. 5 (Paris, 1846).

——, *Histoire parlementaire de la révolution française*, vol. 3 (Paris, 1846).

Burke, Peter, *The Fabrication of Louis XIV* (New Haven, 1994).

Buttier, Jean-Charles, 'L'école sous le Directoire: fonder moralement le régime républicain?', in Loris Chavanette, ed., *Le Directoire. Forger la République (1795–99)* (Paris, 2020).

——, 'Les trois vies du Catéchisme républicain, philosophique et moral de La Chabeaussière', *Annales historiques de la Révolution française*, no. 364 (2011), pp. 163–92.

Byrnes, Joseph, *Priests of the French Revolution: Saints and Renegades in a New Political Era* (Philadelphia, 2014).

Carlson, Marvin, *Theatre: A Very Short Introduction* (Oxford, 2014).

Cassanelli, Roberto, 'Ancient and Modern Rome: Places and Memory', in Roberto Cassanelli et al., eds, *Ruins of Ancient Rome: The Drawings of French Architects Who Won the Prix de Rome* (Los Angeles, 2002).

Caubisens-Lasfargues, Colette, 'Le Salon de Peinture pendant la Révolution', *Annales historique de la Révolution française*, vol. 33, no. 164 (1961), pp. 193–214.

Caudrillier, Gustaaf, *La trahison de Pichegru et les intrigues royalistes dans l'est avant fructidor* (Paris, 1908).

Cazotte, Jacques, *Miranda, 1750–1816. Histoire d'un séducteur* (Paris, 2000).

Ceserani, Giovanna, 'Antiquarian Transformations in Eighteenth-Century Europe', in Alain Schnapp, ed., *World Antiquarianism: Comparative Perspectives* (Los Angeles, 2013).

——, *Italy's Lost Greece: Magna Graecia and the Making of Modern Archaeology* (Oxford, 2012).

——, 'The Charm of the Siren: The Place of Sicily in Historiography', in Christopher Smith and John Serrati, eds, *Ancient Sicily from Aeneas to Cicero* (Edinburgh, 2000).

Chadwick, Owen, *The Popes and European Revolution* (Oxford, 1981).

Challemel, Augustin, *Les clubs contre-révolutionaires* (Paris, 1895).

Chappey, Jean-Luc, 'Pierre-Louis Rœderer et la presse sous le Directoire et le Consulat: l'opinion publique et les enjeux d'une politique éditoriale', *Annales historiques de la Révolution française*, no. 334 (2003), pp. 1–21.

——, 'Raison et citoyennete: les fondements culturels d'une distinction sociale et politique sous le Directoire', in Raymonde Monnier, ed., *Citoyen et citoyenneté sous la Révolution française* (Paris, 2006), pp. 279–88.

——, 'The New Elites. Questions about Political, Social and Cultural Reconstruction after the Terror', in David Andress, ed., *The Oxford Handbook of the French Revolution* (Oxford, 2015), pp. 556–72.

——, 'Du peuple enfant au peuple malheureux: Questions sur les mutations des dominations sociales et politiques entre la république thermidorienne et l'Empire', *La Révolution française: cahiers de l'Institut d'histoire de la Révolution française*, no. 9 (2015), pp. 67–91.

——, 'Révolution, régénération, civilisation. Enjeux culturels des dynamiques politiques', in Jean-Luc Chappey et al., eds, *Pour quoi faire la révolution* (Marseille, 2012).

Chappey, Jean-Luc, and Vincent, Julien, 'A Republican Ecology? Citizenship, Nature, and the French Revolution (1795–1799)', *Past and Present*, vol. 243, no. 1 (2019), pp. 109–40.

Charavay, Étienne, *Assemblée électorale de Paris, 18 Novembre 1790 15 Juin 1791* (Paris, 1894).

Chaudonneret, Marie-Claude, 'Les ministres de l'Intérieur et les arts sous le Directoire', *Livraisons de l'histoire de l'architecture*, no. 26 (2013), pp. 63–73.

——, *L'État et les artistes: de la Restauration a la monarchie de Juillet* (Paris, 1999).

Chavanette, Loris, *Quatre-vingt-quinze: la terreur en procès* (Paris, 2017).

——, 'La presse livre: une épine dans le pied du Directoire', in Loris Chavanette, ed., *Le Directoire. Forger la République (1795–1799)* (Paris, 2020), pp. 96–104.

Chevallier, Pierre, and Rabreau, Daniel, *Le Panthéon* (Paris, 1977).

Clarke, Joseph, *Commemorating the Dead in Revolutionary France: Revolution and Remembrance 1789–1799* (Cambridge, 2009).

Clay, Lauren, 'Patronage, Profits, and Public Theatres: Rethinking Cultural Unification in Ancien Régime France', *Journal of Modern History*, vol. 79, no. 4 (2007), pp. 729–71.

——, *Stragestruck: The Business of Theatre in Eighteenth-Century France and Its Colonies* (Ithaca, 2013).

Cobb, Richard, *The Police and the People* (Oxford, 1993).

Collins, Jeffrey, *Papacy and Politics in Eighteenth-Century Rome: Pius VI and the Arts* (Cambridge, 2004).

——, 'Museo Pio-Clementino, Vatican City: Ideology and Aesthetics in the Age of the Grand Tour', in Carole Paul, ed., *The First Modern Museum of Art: The Birth of an Institution in 18th- and Early-19th-Century Europe* (Los Angeles, 2012), pp. 113–44.

Connelly, Jeffrey, 'Forerunner of the Louvre', *Apollo*, vol. 45 (1972), pp. 382–9.

——, 'The Grand Gallery of the Louvre and the Museum Project: Architectural Problems', *Journal of the Society of Architectural Historians*, vol. 31, no. 2 (1972), pp. 120–32.

Cook, Alexander, '"The Great Society of the Human Species": Volney and the Global Politics of Revolutionary France', *Intellectual History Review*, vol. 23, no. 3 (2013), pp. 309–28.

Cormack, William, *Revolution and Political Conflict in the French Navy 1789–1794* (Cambridge, 1995).

Coupin, Pierre-Alexandre, 'Notice nécrologique sur Jacques-Louis David', *Revue encyclopédique*, no. 34 (April 1827), pp. 34–58.

Crook, Malcolm, *Elections in the French Revolution: An Apprenticeship in Democracy, 1789–1799* (Cambridge, 1996).

——, 'The New Regime: Political Institutions and Democratic Practices', in David Andress, ed., *The Oxford Handbook of the French Revolution* (Oxford, 2015), pp. 218–35.

——, 'Le candidat imaginaire, ou l'offre et le choix dans les élections de la Révolution française', *Annales historiques de la Révolution française*, no. 321 (2000), pp. 91–110.

Crow, Thomas, *Painters and Public Life in Eighteenth-Century Paris* (New Haven, 1985).

Darlow, Mark, *Staging the French Revolution: Cultural Politics and the Paris Opera, 1789* (Cambridge, 2012).

Darnton, Robert, *The Business of the Enlightenment: A Publishing History of the Encyclopédie, 1775–1800* (Cambridge, MA, 1979).

232 BIBLIOGRAPHY

D'Auria, Matthew, *The Shaping of French National Identity: Narrating the Nation's Past, 1715–1830* (Cambridge, 2020).

David d'Angers, Pierre-Jean, 'Notes rétrospectives', *L'almanach du people pour 1851* (Paris, 1851).

Davidson, Ian, *Voltaire: A Life* (London, 2012).

Décultot, Elisabeth, 'Le cosmopolitisme en question. Goethe face aux saisies françaises d'œuvres d'art sous la Révolution et l'Empire', *Revue germanique internationale*, no. 12 (1999), pp. 165–75.

Deming, Mark, *La Halle au blé de Paris, 1762–1813* (Paris, 1984).

——, 'Le Panthéon révolutionnaire', in Barry Bergdoll, ed., *Le Panthéon symbole des révolutions. De l'église de la nation au temple des grands hommes* (Paris, 1989).

Dendena, Francesco, 'A New Look at Feuillantism: The Triumvirate and the Movement for War in 1791', *French History*, vol. 26, no. 1 (2012), pp. 6–33.

——, *I nostri maledetti scranni!: il movimento fogliante tra la fuga di Varennes e la caduta della monarchia (1791–1792)* (Milan, 2013).

——, 'L'expérience révolutionnaire dans les mémoires des leaders feuillants. Le récit de soi comme interprétation de l'histoire de la Révolution', in Olivier Ferret and Anne-Marie Mercier-Faivre, eds, *Biographie & politique. Vie publique, vie privée, de l'Ancien Régime à la Restauration* (Lyon, 2014), pp. 183–98.

——, 'La haine des honnêtes gens. Stratégies éditoriales de la presse feuillante et construction des identités collectives', *Annales historiques de la Révolution française*, vol. 384, no. 2 (2016), pp. 83–108.

Desan, Suzanne, 'The French Revolution and Religion, 1795–1815', in Steward Brown and Timothy Tackett, eds, *The Cambridge History of Christianity* (Cambridge, 2006), pp. 557–64.

Dhombres, Nicole, 'Gaspard Monge, membre de l'institut et commissaire des sciences et des arts en Italie. Regards sur une correspondance (juin 1796–octobre 1797), in Jean-Paul Barbe and Roland Bernecker, eds, *Les intellectuels européens face à la campagne d'Italie (1796–1798)* (Münster, 1999).

Dorigny, Marcel, 'La mort de Simonneau: un révélateur des conflits politiques au printemps de 1792', in Comité du bicentenaire de la révolution en Essonne, ed., *L'Essonne, l'Ancien Régime et la Révolution* (Saint-Georges-de-Luzençon, 1991), pp. 155–61.

Dowd, David, *Pageant-Master of the Republic: Jacques-Louis David and the French Revolution* (Lincoln, NE, 1948).

Dowley, Francis, 'D'Angivillier's Grands Hommes and the Significant Moment', *Art bulletin*, vol. 39, no. 4 (1957), pp. 259–77.

Doyle, William, *Oxford History of the French Revolution* (Oxford, 2003).

Draper, James, and Scherf, Guilhem, *Augustin Pajou. Royal Sculptor 1730–1809* (New York, 1997).

Dubin, Nina, *Features and Ruins: Eighteenth-Century Paris and the Art of Hubert Robert* (Los Angeles, 2013).

Dupuy, Marie-Anne, ed., *Dominique-Vivant Denon: L'oeil de Napoléon* (Paris, 1999).

Dupuy, Pascal, ed., *La Fête de la Fédération* (Rouen, 2012).

Durnerin, Augustin, *Tableau généalogique de la famille Quatremère* (Paris, 1896).

Duvergier de Hauranne, Prosper, *Histoire du gouvernement parlementaire* (Paris, 1864).

Dwyer, Philip, *Napoleon: The Path to Power* (New Haven, 2007).

École nationale des Chartes, 'Restauration de l'église Saint-Germain-des-Prés', http://elec.enc.sorbonne.fr/saintgermaindespres/.

Edelstein, Melvin, *The French Revolution and the Birth of Electoral Democracy* (Ashgate, 2014).

Émile-Mâle, Gilberte, 'Jean-Baptiste-Pierre Lebrun (1748–1813). Son rôle dans l'histoire de la restauration des tableaux du Louvre', *Mémoires de la fédération des sociétés historiques et archéologiques de Paris et de l'Île-de-France*, vol. 8 (1956), pp. 371–417.

Emiliani, Andrea, 'Introduzione', in Antonio Pinelli and Andrea Emiliani, eds, *Lo studio delle arti e il genio dell'Europa. Scritti di A.C. Quatremère de Quincy – Pio VII Chiaramonti (1796–1802)* (Bologna, 1989).

——, *Leggi, bandi e provvedimenti per la tutela dei beni artistici e culturli negli antichi stati italiani* (Bologna, 1978).

Émond, Gustave, *Histoire du collège de Louis-le-Grand, ancien collège des jésuites à Paris* (Paris, 1845).

Etlin, Richard, *Symbolic Space: French Enlightenment Architecture* (Chicago, 1994).

Eustace, Katherine, *Canova: Ideal Heads* (Oxford, 1997).

Farinati, Valeria, 'Storia e fortune di un dizionario. Quatremère de Quincy in Italia', in Valeria Farinati and Georges Teyssot, eds, *Dizionario storico de architettura* (Venice, 1985).

Faroult, Guillaume, ed., *Hubert Robert (1733–1808): un peintre visionnaire* (Paris, 2016).

Fayolle, Caroline, and Buttier, Jean-Charles, eds, *Pédagogies, utopies et révolutions (1789–1848)*, special edition of La Révolution française: Cahiers de l'Institut d'histoire de la Révolution française, no. 4 (2013).

Feuga, Paul, *Luc-Antoine Champagneux ou le destin d'un Rolandin fidèle* (Lyon, 1991).

Fittipaldi, Arturo, 'Museums, Safeguarding and Artistic Heritage in Naples in the Eighteenth Century: Some Reflections', *Journal of the History of Collections*, vol. 19, no. 11 (2007), pp. 191–202.

Fitzsimmons, Michael, 'Sovereignty and Constitutional Power', in David Andress, ed., *The Oxford Handbook of the French Revolution* (Oxford, 2015).

Foucart, Bruno, *Le renouveau de la peinture religieuse en France Paris* (Paris, 1987).

Fraser, Elisabeth, *Mediterranean Encounters: Artists between Europe and the Ottoman Empire, 1774–1839* (Philadelphia, 2017).

Freund, Amy, *Portraiture and Politics in Revolutionary France* (Philadelphia, 2014).

Fryer, Walter, *Republic or Restoration in France? 1794–7. The Politics of French Royalism, with Particular Reference to the Activities of A. B. J. D'André* (Manchester, 1965).

Fumaroli, Marc, 'Le comte de Caylus et l'académie des inscriptions', *Comptes rendus des séances de l'Académie des inscriptions et belles-lettres*, vol. 139, no. 1 (1995), pp. 225–50.

Gaehtgens, Thomas, 'Le Musée historique de Versailles', in Pierre Nora, ed., *Lieux des mémoires*, vol. 2 (Paris, 1986), pp. 143–68.

——, 'Du Parnasse au Panthéon: la représentation des *hommes illustres* et des *grands hommes* dans la France du XVIIIe siècle', in Thomas Gaehtgens and Gregor Wedekind, eds, *Le culte des grands hommes 1750–1850* (Paris, 2010), pp. 135–71.

Gaehtgens, Thomas, and Lugand, Jacques, *Joseph-Marie Vien: peintre du roi (1716–1809)* (Paris, 1988).

Gainot, Bernard, 'Le contentieux électoral sous le Directoire. Monisme et pluralisme dans la culture politique de la France révolutionnaire', *Revue historique*, vol. 2, no. 642 (2007), pp. 325–53.

——, 'The Constitutionalization of General Freedom under the Directory', in Marcel Dorigny, ed., *The Abolitions of Slavery: From L. F. Sonthonax to Victor Schoelcher, 1793, 1794, 1848* (New York, 2003), pp. 180–96.

——, 'La République comme association de citoyens solidaires: pour retrouver l'économie politique républicaine (1792–1799)', in Jean-Luc Chappey et al., eds, *Pour quoi faire la Révolution* (Marseille, 2012), pp. 87–118.

234 BIBLIOGRAPHY

Garrioch, David, *The Formation of the Parisian Bourgeoisie, 1690–1830* (Cambridge, MA, 1996).

——, *The Making of Revolutionary Paris* (Los Angeles, 2002).

Gélis, Jacques, 'Émeute de marché et pouvoir local: le cas Simonneau, 1792', in Comité du bicentenaire de la révolution en Essonne, ed., *L'Essonne, l'Ancien Régime et la Révolution* (Saint-Georges-de-Luzençon, 1991), pp. 145–54.

Gendron, François, *La jeunesse dorée: épisodes de la révolution française* (Montreal, 1979).

Genty, Maurice, 'Les élections municipales à Paris sous le Directoire', *Annales historiques de la Révolution française*, no. 319 (2000), pp. 47–70.

Geoffroy-Schwinden, Rebecca, *From Servant to Savant. Musical Privilege, Property, and the French Revolution* (Oxford, 2022).

Gerbino, Anthony, 'Architectural Theory in the Service of the Crown: The Foundation of the Académie royale d'architecture', in Mark Swenarton et al., eds, *The Politics of Making* (Abington, 2007), pp. 95–104.

Gilks, David, 'The Fountain of the Innocents and its Place in the Paris Cityscape, 1549–1788', *Urban History*, vol. 45, no. 1 (2018), pp. 45–73.

——, 'Attitudes to the Displacement of Cultural Property in the Wars of the French Revolution and Napoleon', *Historical Journal*, vol. 56, no. 1 (2013), pp. 113–43.

——, 'Civilization and Its Discontents: Quatremère de Quincy and Directorial Political Culture', *French Historical Studies*, vol. 45, no. 3 (2022), pp. 481–510.

——, 'Art and Politics during the "First" Directory: Artists' Petitions and the Quarrel over the Confiscation of Works of Art from Italy in 1796', *French History*, vol. 26, no. 1 (2012), pp. 53–78.

Gillispie, Coulston, *Science and Polity: The Revolutionary and Napoleonic Years* (Princeton, 2004).

Ginsberg, Jane, 'A Tale of Two Copyrights: Literary Property in Revolutionary France and America', *Tulane Law Review*, vol. 64, no. 5 (1990), pp. 991–1031.

Giovanni, George di, 'The Unfinished Philosophy of Friedrich Heinrich Jacobi', in Friedrich Jacobi, *The Main Philosophical Writings and the Novel Allwill*, trans. and ed. George di Giovanni (Montreal, 1994), pp. 1–170.

Glénard, Guillaume, *L'exécutif et la constitution de 1791* (Rennes, 2009).

Gob, Andre, *Des musées au-dessus de tout soupçon* (Paris, 2007).

Godechot, Jacques, 'Fragments des Mémoires de Charles-Alexis Alexandre sur les Journées Révolutionnaires de 1791 et 1792', *Annales historiques de la Révolution française*, no. 126 (1952), pp. 113–251.

——, 'La presse sous la Révolution française et l'Empire', in Claude Bellanger et al., eds, *Histoire générale de la presse française* (Paris, 1969), vol. 1, pp. 403–568.

——, *La grande nation: l'expansion révolutionnaire de la France dans le monde de 1789 à 1799* (Paris, [1956] 1983).

——, *La vie quotidienne en France sous le Directoire* (Paris, 1977).

——, *Les institutions de la France sous la Révolution et l'Empire* (Paris, 1985).

——, *La contre-révolution, doctrine et action, 1789–1804* (Paris, [1961] 1984).

——, 'The Internal History of France during the Wars, 1793–1814', in Charles Crawley, ed., *The New Cambridge Modern History*, Vol. 9: *War and Peace in an Age of Upheaval, 1793–1830* (Cambridge, 1995), pp. 275–306.

Gombrich, Ernst, 'The Diversity of the Arts: The Place of the Laocoon in the Life and Work of G. E. Lessing (1729–1781)', in Ernst Gombrich, *Tributes: Interpreters of Our Cultural Tradition* (Oxford, 1984), pp. 30–50.

Goodman, Jessica, ed., *Commemorating Mirabeau: Mirabeau aux Champs-Elysées and Other Texts* (Cambridge, 2017).

Grammacini, Gisela, 'Moitte, Quatremère de Quincy, l'architecture et la sculpture historique au Panthéon', in *L'art et les révolutions, XXXVIIe congrès international d'histoire de l'art* (Strasbourg, 1992), pp. 157–77.

——, *Jean-Guillaume Moitte (1746–1810): Leben und Werk* (Berlin, 1993).

Grandjean, Gilles, and Scherf, Guilhem, eds, *Pierre Julien 1731–1804* (Paris, 2004).

Greenhalgh, Michael, 'Quatremère de Quincy as a Popular Archaeologist', *Gazette des beaux-arts*, vol. 71, no. 1 (1968), pp. 249–56.

Grell, Chantal, *Le dix-huitième siècle et l'antiquité en France 1680–1789*, 2 vols (Oxford, 1995).

Griener, Pascal, 'De Dupuis à Quatremère de Quincy. Les enjeux du paradigme hiéroglyphique dans la théorie de l'art à la fin du XVIIIème siècle', in Jackie Pigeaud and Jean-Paul Barbe, eds, *La redécouverte de la Grèce et de l'Egypte au XVIIIe siècle et au début du XIXe siècle* (Nantes, 1997), pp. 131–42.

——, 'Carlo Fea and the Defence of the Museum of Rome, 1783–1815', *Georges-Bloch-Jahrbuch des Kunstgeschichtlichen Seminars der Universität Zürich*, vol. 7 (2000), pp. 96–109.

Grossi, Paolo, *Pierre-Louis Ginguené, historien de la littérature italienne* (Bern, 2006).

Groult, Martine, 'De la science à l'esthétique. L'architecture dans l'*Encyclopédie* de Diderot et d'Alembert et la *Méthodique* de Quatremère de Quincy', *Dix-huitième siècle*, no. 31 (1999), pp. 525–40.

Guffey, Elizabeth, *Drawing an Elusive Line: The Art of Pierre-Paul Prud'hon* (Newark, 2001).

Guichard, Charlotte, *Les amateurs d'art à Paris au XVIIIe siècle* (Paris, 2008).

——, 'Arts libéraux et arts libres à Paris au XVIIIe siècle: peintres et sculpteurs entre corporation et Académie royale', *Revue d'histoire moderne et contemporaine*, no. 49 (2002/3), pp. 54–68.

Guiffrey, Jules, *Liste des pensionnaires de l'Académie de France à Rome: donnant les noms de tous les artistes récompensés dans les concours du Prix de Rome de 1663 à 1907* (Paris, 1908).

Guigniaut, Joseph-Daniel, *Notice historique sur la vie et les travaux de M. Quatremère de Quincy* (Paris, 1864).

Guilhaumou, Jacques, 'Nous/vous/tous: la fête de l'union du 10 aout 1793', *Mots. Les langages du politique*, no. 10 (1985), pp. 91–108.

Hardman, John, *The Life of Louis XVI* (New Haven, 2016).

——, *Marie-Antoinette: The Making of a French Queen* (New Haven, 2019).

——, *Barnave: the Revolutionary who Lost his Head for Marie Antoinette* (New Haven, 2023).

Hargrove, June, *Les statues de Paris. La représentation des grands hommes dans les rues et sur les places de Paris* (Paris, 1989).

Hargrove, June, ed., *The French Academy: Classicism and its Antagonists* (Newark, 1990).

Harloe, Katherine, *Winckelmann and the Invention of Antiquity: History and Aesthetics in the Age of Altertumswissenschaft* (Oxford, 2013).

Haskell, Francis, *History and Its Images: Art and the Interpretation of the Past* (New Haven, 1993).

——, 'More about Sommariva', *Burlington Magazine*, vol. 114, no. 835 (1972), pp. 691–5.

Haskell, Francis, and Penny, Nicholas, *Taste and the Antique: The Lure of Classical Sculpture, 1500–1900* (New Haven, 1981).

236 BIBLIOGRAPHY

Hayworth, Jordan, *Revolutionary France's War of Conquest in the Rhineland* (Cambridge, 2019).

Hermant, Maxime, 'Monsieur dimanche face au citoyen décadi: les autorités révolutionnaires et la liberté de culte', in Loris Chavanette, ed., *Le Directoire. Forger la République (1795–1799)* (Paris, 2020), pp. 179–96.

Hesse, Carla, 'Enlightenment Epistemology and the Laws of Authorship in Revolutionary France, 1777–1793', *Representations*, no. 30 (1990), pp. 109–37.

Heurtin, Jean-Philippe, *L'Espace public parlementaire: essai sur les raisons du législateur* (Rennes, 1999).

Higonnet, Patrice, *Paris: Capital of the World*, trans. Artur Goldhammer (Cambridge, MA, 2002).

——, *Goodness beyond Virtue: Jacobins during the French Revolution* (Cambridge, MA, 1998).

Hoefer, Jean, ed., 'Quatremère', *Nouvelle biographie générale*, vol. 41 (Paris, 1862), pp. 286–7.

Honour, Hugh, 'Canova's Studio Practice—I: The Early Years', *Burlington Magazine*, vol. 114, no. 828 (1972), pp. 146–59.

Horn, Jeff, *Alexandre Rousselin and the French Revolution* (Oxford, 2020).

Hunt, David, 'The People and Pierre Dolivier: Popular Uprisings in the Seine-et-Oise Department (1791–1792)', *French Historical Studies*, vol. 11, no. 2 (1979), pp. 184–214.

Hunt, Lynn, *Politics, Culture and Class in the French Revolution* (Los Angeles, 1984).

——, 'Hercules and the Radical Image in the French Revolution', *Representations*, no. 2 (1983), pp. 95–117.

Jainchill, Adam, *Reimagining Politics after the Terror: The Republican Origins of French Liberalism* (Ithaca, 2008).

Jong, Sigrid de, *Rediscovering Architecture: Paestum in Eighteenth-Century Architectural Experience and Theory* (New Haven, 2015).

Jones, Colin, *The Great Nation: France from Louis XV to Napoleon* (London, 2003).

——, 'The Overthrow of Maximilien Robespierre and the "Indifference" of the People', *American Historical Review*, vol. 119, no. 3 (2014), pp. 689–713.

——, '9 Thermidor: Cinderella among Revolutionary *Journées*', *French Historical Studies*, vol. 38, no. 1 (2015), pp. 9–31.

——, *Versailles* (London, 2018).

Joshua, Eleoma, *Friedrich Leopold Graf Zu Stolberg and the German Romantics* (Bern, 2005).

Jouffre, Valérie, and Andia, Béatrice, et al., eds, *Fêtes et Révolutions* (Paris, 1989).

Jouin, Henri, *David d'Angers: sa vie, son oeuvre, ses écrits et ses contemporains*, 2 vols (Paris, 1878).

——, *Antoine-Chrysostôme Quatremère de Quincy. Deuxième secrétaire perpétuel de l'Académie des beaux-arts* (Paris, 1892).

——, *Antoine Renou premier secrétaire perpétuel de l'École nationale des beaux-arts (1793–1806)* (Paris, 1905).

Jourdan, Annie, *Les monuments de la Révolution 1770–1804. Une histoire de représentation* (Paris, 1997).

——, 'Les concours de l'an II. En quête d'un art républicain', in Martine Lapied and Christine Peyrard, eds, *La révolution française au carrefour des recherches* (Aix-en-Provence, 2003), pp. 263–78.

Jovy, Ernest, *De Royer-Collard à Racine. Quelques recherches sur une partie de la descendance de Racine, à propos d'une lettre inédite de Royer-Collard* (Paris, 1917).

Julia, Dominique, 'Instruction publique/éducation nationale', in Albert Soboul, ed., *Dictionnaire historique de la Révolution française* (Paris, 1989), pp. 575–81.

Kaplan, Steven, *La fin des corporations* (Paris, 2001).

Kennedy, Emmet, *A Cultural History of the French Revolution* (New Haven, 1989).

Kohle, Hubertus, 'The road from Rome to Paris: The Birth of a Modern Neoclassicism', in Dorothy Johnson, ed., *Jacques-Louis David: New Perspectives* (Newark, 2006), pp. 71–80.

Kolla, Edward, *Sovereignty, International Law, and the French Revolution* (Cambridge, 2017).

Körner, Hans, and Piel, Friedrich, '"A mon ami A. Quatremère de Quincy". Ein unbekanntes Werk Jacques-Louis David, aus dem Jahre 1779', *Pantheon*, vol. 43 (1985), pp. 89–96.

Kubben, Raymond, *Regeneration and Hegemony: Franco-Batavian Relations in the Revolutionary Era, 1795–1803* (Leiden, 2011).

Labrusse, Rémi, 'Muséophobies. Pour une histoire du musée du point de vue de ses contempteurs', *Romantisme*, vol. 3, no. 173 (2016), pp. 68–78.

Lacour-Gayet, Georges, *Talleyrand* [1947] (Paris, 1990).

Lajer-Burcharth, Ewa, *Necklines: The Art of Jacques-Louis David after the Terror* (New Haven, 1999).

Lang, Suzanne, 'The Early Publications of the Temples at Paestum', *Journal of the Warburg and Courtauld Institutes*, vol. 13, no. 1 (1950), pp. 48–64.

Lapied, Martine, and Peyrard, Christine, eds, *La Révolution française au carrefour des recherches* (Aix-en-Provence, 2003).

Latreille, André, *L'Église catholique et la Révolution française*, 2 vols (Paris, 1946–50).

Launay, Louis de, *Monge: fondateur de l'École Polytechnique* (Paris, 1933).

Laurent, Jeanne, *A propos de l'École des beaux-arts* (Paris, 1987).

Lavin, Sylvia, *Quatremère de Quincy and the Invention of a Modern Language of Architecture* (Cambridge, MA, 1992).

——, 'In the Names of History: Quatremère de Quincy and the Literature of Egyptian Architecture', *Journal of Architectural Education*, vol. 44, no. 3 (1991), pp. 131–7.

Le Bihan, Alain, *Francs-maçons parisiens du Grand Orient de France (fin du XIIIe)* (Paris, 1966).

Leben, Ulrich, 'New Light on the École Royale Gratuite de Dessin: The Years 1766–1815', *Studies in the Decorative Arts*, vol. 1, no. 1 (1993), pp. 99–118.

Lebensztejn, Jean-Claude, *De l'imitation dans les beaux-arts* [1982] (Paris, 1996).

Leith, James, *Space and Revolution: Projects for Monuments, Squares, and Public Buildings in France 1789–1799* (Montreal, 1991).

Lemay, Edna, 'Les législateurs de la France révolutionnaire (1791–1792)', *Annales historiques de la Révolution française*, vol. 347 (2007), pp. 3–28.

——, ed., *Dictionnaire des Législateurs (1791–1792)*, 2 vols (Paris, 2007).

Lemonnier, Henri, 'Cinquante années de l'Académie royale d'architecture (1671–1726)', *Journal des savants* (Oct. 1915), pp. 445–60.

——, 'Introduction', *Procès-verbaux de l'Académie royale d'architecture, 1671–1793* (Paris, 1926), vol. 1.

Leniaud, Jean-Michel, 'Joachim Le Breton et Antoine Quatremère de Quincy, secrétaires perpétuels de l'Académie des beaux-arts: deux conceptions divergentes du musée', in Maria-Teresa Caracciolo and Gennaro Toscano, eds, *Jean-Baptiste Wicar et son temps 1762–1834* (Villeneuve d'Ascq, 2007), pp. 79–91.

Leoni, Marina, *Quatremère de Quincy e il primo tomo (1788–1790) del Dizionario di architettura dell'Encyclopédie Méthodique*. Unpublished doctoral thesis, Politecnico di Torino (2012).

238   BIBLIOGRAPHY

——, 'Art, morale et politique. Les écrits de Quatremère de Quincy sur le théâtre, à l'aube de la Révolution française', in Corinne Doria, ed., *La morale de l'homme politique* (Paris, 2015), pp. 17–34.

Leroy-Jay Lemaistre, Isabelle, 'De Sainte-Geneviève au Panthéon, les différents programmes de sculpture, à la lumière des récentes découvertes', in Barry Bergdoll, ed., *Le Panthéon symbole des révolutions. De l' église de la nation au temple des grands hommes* (Montreal, 1989).

Lilti, Antoine, *Figures publiques: l'invention de la célébrité* (Paris, 2014).

Lindemann, Mary, *Patriots and Paupers: Hamburg, 1712–1830* (Oxford, 1990).

Loisselle, Kenneth, *Brotherly Love: Freemasonry and Male Friendship in Enlightenment France* (Ithaca, 2014).

Lok, Matthijs, *Europe against Revolution: Conservatism, Enlightenment, and the Making of the Past* (Oxford, 2023).

Lucas, Colin, 'The First Directory and the Rule of Law', *French Historical Studies*, vol. 10, no. 2 (1977), pp. 231–60.

Luke, Yvonne, 'The Politics of Participation: Quatremère de Quincy and the Theory and Practice of "*Concours publiques*" in Revolutionary France 1791–1795', *Oxford Art Journal*, vol. 10, no. 1 (1987), pp. 15–43.

——, 'Quatremère de Quincy', in Jane Turner, eds, *The Grove Dictionary of Art*, vol. 25 (Oxford, 1996), pp. 798–9.

Lunel, Ernest, *Le théâtre and la Révolution* (Paris, 1910).

Lüsebrink, Hans-Jürgen, and Reichardt, Rolf, *The Bastille: A History of a Symbol of Despotism and Freedom* (Chapel Hill, 1997).

Lyon-Caen, Nicholas, 'Territoire paroissial et investissement nobiliaire. Marc-Étienne Quatremère et les limites de Saint-Germain-l'Auxerrois', *Hypothèses 2005. Travaux de l'école doctorale d'histoire*, vol. 1 (Paris, 2006), pp. 79–88.

——, *La Boite à Perrette. Le jansénisme parisien au XVIIIe siècle* (Paris, 2010).

——, 'Les jansénistes, le commerce, et l'argent au dix-huitième siècle', in Francesco Armannachi, ed., *Religion and Religious Institutions in the European Economy, 1000–1800* (Florence, 2012), pp. 585–94.

Lyons, Martyn, 'The 9 Thermidor: Motives and Effects', *European Studies Review*, vol. 5, no. 2 (1975), pp. 123–46.

——, *France under the Directory* (Cambridge, 1975).

Mainardi, Patricia, 'Assuring the Empire of the Future: The 1798 Fête de la Liberté', *Art Journal*, vol. 48, no. 2 (1989), pp. 155–63.

Maleuvre, Didier, *Museum Memories: History, Technology, Art* (Stanford, 1999).

Malpero-Clerc, Hélène, *Un journaliste contre-révolutionnaire: Jean Gabriel Peltier (1760–1825)* (Paris, 1973).

Mansel, Philip, *Louis XVIII* (London, 1981).

Marc, Bayard, et al, eds, L'Académie de France à Rome au XVIIIe siècle. Le palais Mancini: un foyer artistique dans l'Europe des Lumières (1725-1792) (Rennes, 2016).

Margerison, Kenneth, 'P.-L. Rœderer: Political Thought and Practice during the French Revolution', *Transactions of the American Philosophical Society*, vol. 73, no. 1 (1983), pp. 77–84.

Maricourt, André, *Prisonniers et prisons de Paris pendant la terreur* (Paris, 1924).

Martin, Virginie, 'Les enjeux diplomatiques dans le Magasin encyclopédique (1795–1799): du rejet des systèmes politiques à la redéfinition des rapports entre les nations (1795-1799)', *La Révolution française: cahiers de l'Institut d'histoire de la Révolution française*, no. 2 (2012).

Maslam, Susan, *Revolutionary Acts: Theater, Democracy, and the French Revolution* (Baltimore, 2005).

Maspero-Clerc, Hélène, *Un journaliste contre-révolutionnaire: Jean-Gabriel Peltier (1760–1825)* (Paris, 1973).

Maury, Alfred, 'Quatremère de Quincy', in Louis Michaud, ed., *Biographie universelle ancienne et moderne, nouvelle édition*, vol. 34 (Paris, n.d. [post-1853]), pp. 608–14.

Mazeau, Guillaume, 'La Révolution, les fêtes et leurs images: spectacles publics et représentation politique (Paris, 1789–1799)', *Images Re-vues*, no. 6 (2018).

Mazzei, Otello, *L'ideologia del Restauro Archittonico da Quatremère a Brandi* (Milan, 1984).

McClellan, Andrew, 'Mobilité et fortunes critique. La mort de Charles Lebrun dans les galeries de la Révolution', in Jacques Guillerme, ed., *Les collections: fables et programmes* (Paris, 1993), pp. 341–9.

——, *Inventing the Louvre: Art, Politics, and the Origins of the Modern Museum in Eighteenth-Century Paris* (Los Angeles, [1994] 1999).

——, *The Art Museum from Boullée to Bilbao* (Los Angeles, 2008).

——, 'D'Angiviller's "Great Men" of France and the Politics of the Parlements', *Art History*, vol. 13 (1990), pp. 174–91.

McClellan, Michael, 'The Italian Menace: Opera Bouffa in Revolutionary France', *Eighteenth-Century Music*, vol. 1, no. 2 (2004), pp. 249–63.

McMachon, Denis, *Enemies of the Enlightenment: The French Counter-Enlightenment and the Making of Modernity* (Oxford, 2001).

McManners, John, *Death and the Enlightenment: Changing Attitudes to Death among Christians and Unbelievers in Eighteenth-Century France* (Oxford, 1981).

McPhee, Peter, *Robespierre: A Revolutionary Life* (New Haven, 2012).

——, *Liberty or Death: The French Revolution* (New Haven, 2016).

Menichetti, Johan, 'Pierre-Louis Rœderer: la science sociale au Conseil d'État', *Napoleonica. La Revue*, vol. 16, no. 1 (2013), pp. 17–48.

Merle, Louis, 'Louis-Alexandre Jard-Panvillier. Le coup d'Etat du 18 brumaire et la constitution de l'an VIII', *La revue du Bas-Poitou et des provinces de l'ouest*, nos. 5–6 (1969), pp. 343–67.

Merriman, John, 'The Marquis de Somerueles: Vice-Admiralty Court of Halifax, Nova Scotia Stewart's Vice-Admiralty Reports 482 (1813)', *International Journal of Cultural Property*, vol. 5, no. 2 (1996), pp. 319–29.

Messina, Maria, 'L'arte di Canova nella critica di Quatremère de Quincy', *Quaderni sul Neoclassico*, vols 1–2 (1973), pp. 119–51.

Meynier, Albert, *Les coups d'état du Directoire*, 2 vols. (Paris, 1927).

Michel, Christian, *Charles-Nicholas Cochin et l'art des lumières* (Rome, 1993).

——, *The Académie Royale de Peinture et de Sculpture: The Birth of the French School, 1648–1793*, trans. Chris Miller (Los Angeles, 2018).

——, *L'Académie royale de peinture et de sculpture (1648–1793). La naissance de l'Ecole Française* (Geneva, 2012).

Michel, Patrick, *Le Commerce du tableau à Paris: dans la seconde moitié du XVIIIe siècle* (Paris, 2007).

Michel, Régis, 'L'art des Salons', in Philippe Bordes and Régis Michel, eds, *Aux armes et aux arts! Les arts de la Révolution 1789–99* (Paris, 1988), pp. 26–39.

——, ed., *David contre David: actes du colloque organisé au musée du Louvre par le service culturel du 6 au 10 décembre 1989*, 2 vols (Paris, 1993).

Middleton, Robin, and Baudouin-Matuszek, Marie-Noelle, *Jean Rondelet: The Architect as Technician* (New Haven, 2007).

240 BIBLIOGRAPHY

Mitchell, Christopher, *The French Legislative Assembly of 1791* (Leiden, 1988).

Mitchell, Harvey, *The Underground War against Revolutionary France: The Missions of William Wickham, 1794–1800* (Oxford, 1965).

Montègre, Gilles, *La Rome des Français au temps des Lumières: capitale de l'antique et carrefour de l'Europe, 1769–1791* (Rome, 2011).

——, 'François de Paule Latapie, un savant voyageur français au cœur de la Rome des Lumières', *Mélanges de l'École française de Rome. Italie et Méditerranée*, vol. 117, no. 1 (2005), pp. 371–422.

Mortier, Roland, 'Un "germanisant" sous l'Empire et la Restauration, Charles Vanderbourg, 1765–1827', *La revue belge de philologie et d'histoire*, vol. 29, no. 4 (1951), pp. 1003–27.

——, *Les 'Archives Littéraires de l'Europe' (1804–1808) et le cosmopolitisme littéraire sous le premier Empire* (Brussels, 1957).

Murray, William, *The Right-Wing Press in the French Revolution, 1789–1792* (Woodbridge, 1986).

Mustoxydes, Theodosios, *Histoire de l'esthétique française, 1700–1900* (Paris, 1920).

Naginski, Erika, *Sculpture and Enlightenment* (Los Angeles, 2009).

Nettement, Alfred, *Histoire du coup d'état du 18 fructidor* (Paris, 1851).

Nicolet, Claude, *La fabrique d'une nation: la France entre Rome et les Germains* (Paris, 2003).

Norci-Cagiano, Letizia, 'La Rome de Caylus et "l'idea del bello"', in Nicholas Cronk and Kris Peeters, eds, *Le comte de Caylus: les arts et les lettres* (Leiden, 2004), pp. 111–24.

Nowinski, Judith, *Baron Dominique Vivant Denon (1747–1825): Hedonist and Scholar* (Cranbury, 1970).

Ozouf, Mona, *La fête révolutionnaire, 1789–1799* (Paris, 1977).

——, 'Le Panthéon. L'École normale des morts', in Pierre Nora, ed., *Les lieux de Mémoire*, vol. 1 (Paris, 1984), pp. 129–66.

——, 'De-Christianization', in François Furet and Mona Ozouf, eds, *A Critical Dictionary of the French Revolution*, trans. A. Goldhammer (Cambridge, MA, 1989), pp. 21–32.

——, L'École de la France: essais sur la Révolution, l'utopie et l'enseignement (Paris, 1984).

Palmer, Robert, *The Improvement of Humanity Education and the French Revolution* (Princeton, 1985).

——, ed., *The School of the French Revolution: A Documentary History of the College of Louis-le-Grand and Its Director, Jean-Francois Champagne 1762–1824* (Princeton, 1975).

——, 'Le Prytanée français et les écoles de Paris (1798–1802)', *Annales historiques de la Révolution française*, no. 243 (1981), pp. 123–52.

Panofsky, Erwin, *Idea: A Concept in Art Theory*, trans. Joseph Peake (Columbia, SC, 1968).

Parra-Pérez, Caracciolo, *Miranda et la Révolution française* (Paris, 1926).

Pascal, André, *Pierre Julien sculpteur (1731–1804). Sa vie et son œuvre* (Paris, 1904).

Pasquali, Susanna, 'From the Pantheon of Artists to the Pantheon of Illustrious Men: Raphael's Tomb and Its Legacy', in Richard Wrigley and Matthew Craske, eds, *Pantheons: Transformations of a Monumental Idea* (Aldershot, 2004), pp. 35–56.

——, 'Neoclassical Remodelling and Reconception', in Tod Marder and Mark Jones, eds, *The Pantheon: From Antiquity to the Present* (Cambridge, 2015), pp. 330–53.

Pearson, Roger, *Voltaire Almighty. A Life in Pursuit of Freedom* (London, 2005).

Pellegrin, Nicole, 'Les femmes et le don patriotique: les offrandes d'artistes de septembre 1789', in Marie-France Brive, ed., *Les Femmes et la Révolution française*, vol. 2 (Toulouse, 1990), pp. 361–80.

Petridou, Vassiliki, 'A.C. Quatremère de Quincy et son mémoire sur l'architecture égyptienne', in Chantal Grell, ed., *L'Egypte imaginaire de la Renaissance à Champollion* (Paris, 2001), pp. 173–86.

Pevsner, Nikolaus, *Academies of Art, Past and Present* (Cambridge, 1940).

Peyrard, Christine, 'Les débats sur le droit d'association et de réunion sous le Directoire', *Annales historiques de la Révolution française*, no. 297 (1994), pp. 463–78.

Philippe, Adrien, *Royer-Collard, sa vie publique, sa vie privée, sa famille* (Paris, 1857).

Pietrangeli, Carlo, 'Un ambasciatore d'eccezione: Canova a Parigi', in Giuseppe Pavanello, ed., Canova (Milan, 2003), pp. 15–22.

Pinelli, Antonio, 'Storia dell'arte e cultura della tutela. Les Lettres à Miranda di Quatremère de Quincy', *Ricerche di storia dell' arte*, vol. 8 (1975–6), pp. 43–62.

Pingaud, Léonce, *Choiseul-Gouffier: la France en Orient sous Louis XVI* (Paris, 1887).

Pinkard, Terry, *Hegel: A Biography* (Cambridge, 2001).

——, *German Philosophy 1760–1860: The Legacy of Idealism* (Cambridge, 2002).

Piot, Charles, ed., *Rapport à M. le Ministre de l'Intérieur sur les tableaux enlevés à la Belgique en 1794 et restitués en 1815* (Brussels, 1883).

Plongeron, Bernard, *L'abbé Grégoire et la république des savants* (Paris, 2001).

Pocock, John, *Barbarism and Religion*, 6 vols (Cambridge, 1999–2015).

——, 'The Political Economy of Burke's Analysis of the French Revolution', *Historical Journal*, vol. 25, no. 2 (1982), pp. 331–49.

Pomian, Kristian, 'Leçons italiennes: les musées vus par les voyageurs français au xviiie siècle', in Édouard Pommier, ed., *Les musées en Europe à la veille de l'ouverture du Louvre* (Paris, 1995), pp. 337–61.

——, *Le musée, une histoire mondiale. T. 2: L'Ancrage européen, 1789–1850* (Paris, 2021).

Pommier, Édouard, *L'art de la liberté. Doctrines et débats de la Révolution française* (Paris, 1991).

——, 'La Révolution et le destin des ouvrages de l'art de l'Italie', in Quatremère, *Lettres à Miranda*, ed. Édouard Pommier (Paris, 1989), pp. 7–83.

——, 'Une intervention de Quatremère de Quincy', in Michel Fleury and Guy-Michel Leproux, eds, *Le cimetière des Saints Innocents* (Paris, 1990), pp. 144–58.

——, 'Quatremère de Quincy et la destination des ouvrages de l'art', in René Démoris, ed., *Les fins de la peinture* (Paris, 1990), pp. 31–51.

——, 'Postface', in Jean-Baptiste Pierre Lebrun, *Réflexions sur le Muséum national: 14 janvier 1793* (Paris, 1992).

——, *Più antichi della luna, studi su J. J. Winckelmann e A. Ch. Quatremère de Quincy* (Bologna, 2000).

——, 'Quatremère de Quincy et le patrimoine', in Giuseppe Pavanello, ed., *Antonio Canova e il suo ambiente artistico fra Venezia, Roma e Parigi* (Venice, 2000), pp. 459–80.

——, *Winckelmann, inventeur de l'histoire de l'art* (Paris, 2003).

Poniatowski, Michel, *Talleyrand: les années occultées 1789–1792* (Paris, 1995).

Popkin, Jeremy, *The Right-Wing Press in France, 1792–1800* (Chapel Hill, 1980).

——, 'Clichy, Club de', in Jean-Clément Martin, ed., *Dictionnaire de la contre-Révolution* (Paris, 2011).

——, *A New World Begins: The History of the French Revolution* (New York, 2020).

Portalis, Roger, and Draibel, Henri, *Charles-Etienne Gaucher, graveur. Notice et catalogue* (Paris, 1879).

Portet, Élisabeth, 'Les collections du Panthéon. Étude, inventaire et perspectives scientifiques', *In situ. Revue des patrimonies*, no. 29 (2016).

242 BIBLIOGRAPHY

Potofosky, Allan, *Constructing Paris in the Age of Revolution* (Basingstoke, 2009).

Poulet, Anne, et al., *Jean-Antoine Houdon: Sculptor of the Enlightenment* (Chicago, 2005).

Poulot, Dominique, 'The Cosmopolitanism of Masterpieces', in Quatremère, *Letters to Miranda and Canova on the Abduction of Antiquities from Rome and Athens* (Los Angeles, 2012), pp. 1–91.

——, *Musée, nation, patrimoine, 1789–1815* (Paris, 1997).

——, *Surveiller et s'instruire: la Révolution française et l'intelligence de l'héritage historique* (Oxford, 1996).

——, 'Alexandre Lenoir et les musées de monuments français', in Pierre Nora, ed., *Les lieux de mémoire. La nation*, vol. 2 (Paris, 1986), pp. 497–531.

——, 'Pantheonisations in Eighteenth-Century France: Temple, Museum, Pyramid', in Richard Wrigley and Matthew Craske, eds, *Pantheons: Transformations of a Monumental Idea* (Aldershot, 2004), ch. 6.

Pouradier, Maud, 'Le débat sur *la liberté* des *théâtres*: le répertoire en question', in Martial Poirson, ed., *Le théâtre sous la Révolution: politique du répertoire (1789–1799)* (Paris, 2008), ch. 1.

Profio, Alessandro Di, *La Révolution des Bouffons: l'opera italien au théâtre de Monsieur 1789–1792* (Paris, 2003).

Quatremère, Étienne, 'Notice historique sur la vie de M. Quatremère de Quincy', *Journal des savants* (1853), pp. 657–69.

Racine, Karen, *Francisco de Miranda: A Translatantic Life in the Age of Revolution* (Wilmington, DE, 2003).

Rademacher, Ingrid, 'Élites et républicanisme: Pierre-Louis Rœderer, critique de la campagne d'Italie et brumairien', in Jean-Paul Barbe and Roland Bernecker, eds, *Les intellectuels européens et la campagne d'Italie. 1796–1798* (Munster, 1999), pp. 129–60.

——, 'La science sociale républicaine de Pierre-Louis Roederer', *Revue française d'histoire des idées politiques*, no. 13 (2001), pp. 25–55.

Rapport, Michael, 'Belgium under French Occupation: Between Collaboration and Resistance, July 1794 to October 1795', *French History*, vol. 16, no. 1 (2002), pp. 53–82.

Rasmussen, Jasper, 'Continuity and Destruction: Quatremère de Quincy and History', in Uwe Fleckner et al., eds, *Der Sturm der Bilder* (Berlin, 2011), pp. 77–100.

Ravel, Jacques, *The Contested Parterre: Public Theater and French Political Culture, 1680–1791* (Ithaca, 1999).

Reichardt, Rolf, 'The Heroic Deeds of the New Hercules', in Ian Germani and Robin Swales, eds, *Symbols, Myths and Images of the French Revolution* (Regina, 1998), pp. 37–45.

Reichardt, Rolf, and Kohle, Hubertus, *Visualizing the French Revolution: Politics and the Pictorial Arts in Late Eighteenth-Century France* (London, 2008).

Renouvier, Jules, *Histoire de l'art pendant la Révolution 1789–1804* (Paris, [1863] 1996).

Richefort, Isabelle, 'La commission centrale des sciences et des arts en Italie (1796–1798)', in Marc Favreau et al., eds, *De l'usage de l'art en politique* (Clermont-Ferrand, 2009), pp. 98–115.

Rico Camps, Daniel, 'El patrimonio integral y universal de Quatremère de Quincy', in Daniel Rico Camps, ed., *Cartas a Miranda, con el anexo inventario de los robos hechos por los franceses en los países que han invadido sus ejércitos*, trans. Ilduara Pintor Mazaeda (Murcia, 2007), pp. vii–xxiii.

Ridley, Ronald, *The Pope's Archaeologist: The Life and Times of Carlo Fea* (Rome, 2000).

——, *Magick City: Travellers to Rome from the Middle Ages to 1900*, vol. 2 (London, 2020).

Robertson, William, *Life of Miranda*, 2 vols (Chapel Hill, 1929).

Robinet, Jean-François, *Condorcet: sa vie, son œuvre, 1743–1794* (Geneva, 1968).

Robiquet, Paul, *Le personnel municipal de Paris pendant la Révolution, période constitutionnelle* (Paris, 1890).

Roche, Daniel, *France in the Enlightenment*, trans. Arthur Goldhammer (Cambridge, MA, 1993).

Role, Claude, 'Roucher, Gossec, Simonneau ou le triomphe de la loi', *Études Heraultes*, no. 35 (2005), pp. 121–3.

Rosanvallon, Pierre, *The Demands of Liberty: Civil Society in France since the Revolution*, trans. Arthur Goldhammer (Cambridge, MA, 2007).

Rossi, Aldo, *L'architettura della città* (Padua, 1966).

Rowlands, Thomas, 'Quatremère de Quincy: The Formative Years 1785–1795', Unpublished doctoral thesis, Northwestern University (1987).

Rubin, James, 'The Politics of Quatremère to Quincy's Romantic Classicism', in George Levitine, ed., *Culture and Revolution: Cultural Ramifications of the French Revolution* (College Park, MD, 1989), pp. 230–44.

——, 'Allegory versus Narrative in Quatremère de Quincy', *Journal of Aesthetics and Art Criticism*, vol. 44, no. 4 (1986), pp. 383–92.

Saad, Mariana, *Cabanis. Comprendre l'homme pour changer le monde* (Paris, 2016).

Saint-Hilaire, Barthélemy, *Notice sur M. Étienne Quatremère* (Paris, 1858).

Saint-Victor, Jacques, *Tableau historique et pittoresque de Paris* (Paris, 1808).

Saisselin, René, 'Quatremère de Quincy and the Internal Contradictions of Bourgeois Aesthetics', *Marxist Perspectives*, vol. 3 (1980), pp. 100–15.

Sandholtz, Wayne, *Prohibiting Plunder: How Norms Change* (Oxford, 2007),

Sanson, Rosemonde, *Les 14 juillet, fête et conscience nationale, 1789–1975* (Paris, 1976).

Sanyal, Sukla, 'The 1792 Food Riot at Etampes and the French Revolution', *Studies in History*, vol. 18, no. 1 (2002), pp. 23–50.

Sargentson, Caroline, *Merchants and Luxury Markets: The Marchands Merciers of Eighteenth-Century Paris* (London, 1996).

Savoy, Benedicte, '"Et comment tout cela sera-t-il conserve à Paris?": les réactions allemandes aux saisies d'œuvres d'art et de science opérées par la France autour de 1800', *Revue germanique internationale*, no. 13 (2000), pp. 107–30.

——, *Patrimoine annexé. Les biens culturels saisis par la France en Allemagne autour de 1800*, 2 vols (Paris, 2003).

Scherf, Guilhem, 'Pierre Julien, "Le Vrai statuaire"', in Gilles Grandjean and Guilhem Scherf, eds, *Pierre Julien 1731–1804: Sculpteur du Roi* (Paris, 2004).

Schnapper, Antoine, *David témoin de son temps* (Paris, 1980).

Schnapper, Antoine, and Sérullaz, Arlette, et al., *Jacques-Louis David, 1748–1825* (Paris, 1989).

Schneider, René, 'Quatremère de Quincy et l'art de la médaille (1806–1830)', *Gazette numismatique française*, 12th year (1908), pp. 363–86.

——, 'Un ennemi du musée des monuments français', *Gazette des beaux-arts*, vol. 1, no. 2 (1909), pp. 353–70.

——, *Quatremère de Quincy et ses interventions dans les arts* (Paris, 1910).

——, *L'esthétique classique chez Quatremère de Quincy (1805–1823)* (Paris, 1910).

Schroer, Christina, 'La République contestée: combats de politique symbolique', in Loris Chavanette, ed., *Le Directoire: forger la République (1795–1799)* (Paris, 2020), pp. 144–50.

Scott, Katie, *Becoming Property: Art, Theory and Law in Early Modern France* (New Haven, 2019).

Sepinwall, Alyssa, *The Abbé Grégoire and the French Revolution: The Making of Modern Universalism* (Los Angeles, 2005).

Serna, Pierre, *Antonelle, aristocrate révolutionnaire (1747–1817)* (Paris, 1997).

244 BIBLIOGRAPHY

——, *La république des girouettes, 1789–1815 et au-delà: une anomalie politique; la France de l'extrême centre* (Paris, 2005).

Serra, Joselita, ed., *Paestum and the Doric Revival, 1750–1830* (Florence, 1986).

Shapiro, Barry, *Traumatic Politics: The Deputies and the King in the Early French Revolution* (Philadelphia, 2009).

Sherman, Daniel, 'Quatremère/Benjamin/Marx: Art Museums, Aura, and Commodity Fetishism', in Daniel Sherman and Irit Rogoff, eds, *Museum Culture: Histories Discourses, Spectacles* (Minneapolis, 1994), pp. 123–43.

Silvestre de Sacy, Jacques, *Le comte d'Angiviller, dernier directeur général des bâtiments du roi* (Paris, 1953).

Sire, Marie-Anne, *La France du Patrimoine. Les choix de la mémoire* (Paris, 2005).

Sluhovsky, Moshe, *Patroness of Paris: Rituals of Devotion in Early Modern France* (Leiden, 1998).

Smentek, Kristel, *Mariette and the Science of the Connoisseur in Eighteenth-Century Europe* (Cambridge, MA, 2014).

Soboul, Albert, and Monnier, Raymonde, *Répertoire du personnel sectionnaire parisien en l'an II* (Paris, 1985).

Sonenscher, Michael, *Sans-culottes: An Eighteenth-Century Emblem in the French Revolution* (Princeton, 2008).

Souchal, François, 'Le monument funéraire du Dauphin, fils de Louis XV, a la cathédrale de Sens', in Bernard Barbiche and Yves-Marie Bercé, eds, *Études sur l'ancienne France offertes en hommage à Michel Antoine* (Paris, 2003), pp. 369–87.

——, *Le vandalisme de la Révolution* (Paris, 1993).

Spary, Emma, *Utopia's Garden: French Natural History from the Old Regime to the Revolution* (Chicago, 2000).

Spieth, Darius, *Revolutionary Paris and the Market for Netherlandish Art* (Leiden, 2017).

Stammers, Tom, *The Purchase of the Past. Collecting Culture in Post-Revolutionary Paris c. 1790–1890* (Cambridge, 2020).

Stamp, Robert, 'Educational Thought and Educational Practice during the Years of the French Revolution', *History of Education Quarterly*, vol. 6, no. 3 (1966), pp. 35–49.

Stara, Alexandra, *The Museum of French Monuments 1795–1816: 'Killing Art to Make History'* (Farnham, 2013).

Staum, Martin, *Minerva's Message: Stabilizing the French Revolution* (Montreal, 1996).

Stein, Perrin, ed., *Jacques Louis David: Radical Draftsman* (New York, 2022).

Steindl, Barbara, 'Leopoldo Cicognaras *Storia della Scultura* und die *Lettres a Miranda* von Quatremère de Quincy', in Renate Colella et al., eds, *Pratum Romanum: Richard Krautheimer zum 100. Geburtstag* (Wiesbaden, 1997), pp. 325–39.

Stengel, Edmund, *Private und amtliche Beziehungen der Bruder Grimm zu Hessen*, vol. 2 (Marbourg, 1886).

Stern, Madeleine, 'The English Press in Paris and Its Successors, 1793–1852', *The Papers of the Bibliographical Society of America*, vol. 74, no. 4 (1980), pp. 307–59.

Suratteau, Jean-René, 'Les élections de l'an V aux conseils du Directoire', *Annales historiques de la Révolution française*, vol. 30, no. 154 (1958), pp. 21–63.

Sutherland, Donald, *The French Revolution and Empire: The Quest for a Civic Order* (Malden, MA, 2003).

Sweet, Rosemary, *Cities and the Grand Tour: The British in Italy, c. 1690–1820* (Cambridge, 2012).

Szambien, Werner, *Le musée de l'architecture. Le musée d'architecture (1776–1836): projet inachevé* (Paris, 1984).

——, [Review of 1989 edition] 'Quatremère de Quincy: Lettres à Miranda sur le déplacement des monuments de l'art de l'Italie (1796)', *Revue de l'art*, no. 87 (1990), p. 88.

——, *Les projets de l'an II, concours d'architecture de la période révolutionnaire* (Paris, 1986).

Tackett, Timothy, *When the King Took Flight* (Cambridge, MA, 2003).

——, *The Coming of the Terror in the French Revolution* (Cambridge, MA, 2015).

——, *The Glory and the Sorrow. A Parisian and His World in the Age of the French Revolution* (Oxford, 2022).

——, 'Les députés de l'Assemblée législative, 1791–1792', in Christine Le Bozec and Éric Wauters, eds, *Pour la Révolution française: recueil d'études en hommage à Claude Mazauric* (Rouen, 1998), pp. 139–44.

Taws, Richard, *The Politics of the Provisional: Art and Ephemera in Revolutionary France* (University Park, PA, 2013).

Tourneaux, Maurice, 'Notice préliminaire: Journal intime de l'abbé Mulot, bibliothécaire et grand-prieur de l'abbaye de Saint-Victor (1777–1782)', *Mémoires de la Société de l'histoire de Paris et de l'Ile-de-France*, vol. 29 (1902), pp. 19–36.

Trinchero, Christina, 'Regards sur l'Italie entre XVIIIe et XIXe siècles: le Magasin encyclopédique de Millin', *Annales historiques de la Révolution française*, no. 351 (2008), pp. 59–75.

Tucoo-Chala, Suzanne, *Tucoo-Chala, Charles-Joseph Panckoucke et la librarie francaise 1736–1798* (Paris, 1977).

Turnovsky, Geoffrey, *The Literary Market: Authorship and Modernity in the Old Regime* (Philadelphia, 2010).

Van de Sandt, Udolpho, 'Institutions et concours', in Régis Michel and Phillipe Bordes, eds, *Aux Armes et aux Arts! Les Arts de la Révolution, 1789–1799* (Paris, 1989).

Vardi, Liana, *The Physiocrats and the World of the Enlightenment* (Cambridge, 2012).

Venturi, Franco, *Italy and the Enlightenment: Studies in a Cosmopolitan Century*, trans. Susan Corsi (New York, 1972).

Vidler, Anthony, *The Writing on the Walls: Architectural Theory in the Late Enlightenment* (Princeton, 1987).

——, 'The Idea of Type: The Transformation of the Academic Ideal, 1750–1830', *Oppositions*, no. 8 (1977), pp. 95–115.

Vitet, Louis, *L'Académie royale de peinture et de sculpture: étude historique* (Paris, 1861).

Vovelle, Michel, *L'irrésistible ascension de Joseph Sec, bourgeois d'Aix* (Paris, 1975).

——, *The Fall of the French Monarchy, 1787–1792*, trans. Susan Burke (Cambridge, 1984).

——, 'Agricol Viala ou le héros malheureux', *Annales historiques de la Révolution française*, vol. 52, no. 241 (1980), pp. 345–64.

Wahnich, Sophie, 'Un avocat sensible dans l'émotion de l'événement: le curé Dolivier face au meurtre du maire d'Etampes, printemps 1792', *Nuevo Mundos* (2006), http://journals.openedition.org/nuevomundo/1984.

Wallon, Henri, 'Centenaire de l'élection de Quatremère de Quincy à l'Institut, classe d'histoire et de littérature ancienne', *Comptes rendus des séances de l'Académie des inscriptions et belles-lettres*, vol. 47, no. 6 (1804), pp. 538–80.

Walton, Charles, *Policing Public Opinion in the French Revolution: The Culture of Calumny and the Problem of Free Speech* (Oxford, 2009).

Wardropper, Ian, and Rowlands, Thomas, 'Antonio Canova and Quatremère de Quincy: The Gift of Friendship', *Art Institute of Chicago Museum Studies*, vol. 15, no. 1 (1989), pp. 38–46.

Watkin, David, *Sir John Soane. Enlightenment Thought and the Royal Academy Lectures* (Cambridge, 1996).

Watt, Alexander, 'Notes from Paris', *Apollo*, vol. 27, no. 157 (1938).

246   BIBLIOGRAPHY

Will, Frederick, 'Two Critics of the Elgin Marbles: William Hazlitt and Quatremère de Quincy', *Journal of Aesthetics and Art Criticism*, vol. 14, no. 4 (1956), pp. 462–74.

Williams, Hannah, 'Saint Geneviève's Miracles: Art and Religion in Eighteenth-Century Paris', *French History*, vol. 30, no. 3 (2016), pp. 322–53.

Wittkower, Rudolf, 'Piranesi and Eighteenth-Century Egyptomania', in idem, *Studies in the Italian Baroque* (London, 1975), pp. 258–73.

Wittmann, Richard, *Architecture, Print Culture, and the Public Sphere in Eighteenth-Century France* (London, 2007).

Worley, Michael, 'The Image of Ganymede in France, 1730–1820: The Survival of a Homoerotic Myth', *Art Bulletin*, vol. 76, no. 4 (1994), pp. 630–43.

——, *Pierre Julien: Sculptor to Queen Marie-Antoinette* (New York, 2003).

Woronoff, Denis, Woronoff, *The Thermidorean Regime and the Directory, 1794–1799*, trans. Julian Jackson (Cambridge, 1984).

Wrigley, Richard, 'Transformations of a Revolutionary Emblem: The Liberty Cap in the French Revolution', *French History*, vol. 11, no. 2 (1997), pp. 131–69.

Younés, Samir, 'Part I', in *The True, The Fictive, and The Real. The Historical Dictionary of Architecture of Quatremère de Quincy*, ed. and trans. Samir Younés (London, 1999), pp. 9–58.

Zivy, Henri, *Le treize vendémiaire an IV* (Paris, 1898).

Index

For the benefit of digital users, indexed terms that span two pages (e.g., 52–53) may, on occasion, appear on only one of those pages.

Abel de Pujol, Alexandre-Denis (1785–1861: painter) 205–6
academies
    Academy of Architecture 34, 54, 56, 58–9, 62–3
    Academy of Fine Arts 1–2, 205–7
    Academy of Inscriptions and Belles-Lettres 2, 16, 30–1, 34
    Academy of Painting and Sculpture 7, 17–18, 54–6, 58–9, 61, 64–7, 94, 188, 201
    Academy of Saint-Luke 55
Alberti, Leon Battista (1404–72: architect) 38
antiquarianism 21–36, 158, 200–1
archaeological excavations and rediscoveries 24–5, 37, 46–7, 162–3, 167, 169
art education 17–18, 21–2, 55–6, 58–9, 61, 63–4, 67
d'Angiviller, Charles-Claude Flahaut de la Billarderie (1730–1809: Director of Royal Buildings) 56–7, 61–4, 66–7, 140, 193–4
Auger, Louis (active 1790s: sculptor) 127–8

Baccarit, Louis-Antoine (active 1790s: sculptor) 128
Bachaumont, Louis Petit de (1690–1771: writer) 42–3, 182–4
Bailly, Jean-Sylvain (1736–93: astronomer and politician) 49–51, 114–15, 125–6, 172
Barère de Vieuzac, Bertrand (1755–1841: politician) 66–7
Barnave, Antoine (1761–93: politician) 90–1, 114–15, 125–6
Barras, Paul (1755–1829: politician and Director) 137–8, 145–7, 174–6, 189–90
Barrois, Louis-François (1748–c.1835: printer) 141–2, 191
Barthélemy, François (1747–1830: politician and diplomat) 142–3, 189–90
Barthélemy, Jean-Jacques (1716–95: antiquarian) 158
Beaumarchais, Pierre-Augustin Caron de (1732–99: playwright) 50–1, 99

Beauharnais, Alexandre de (1760–94: army officer and politician) 68, 94
Bellart, Nicolas-François (1761–1826: magistrate) 180
Bénézech, Pierre (1749–1802: politician) 145–6, 184
Bertin, Louis-François (1766–1841: author and newspaper owner) 144–5, 184
Bertrand de Molleville, Antoine-François (1744–1818: navy minister) 101, 173
Biscari, Ignazio Paternò-Castello (1719–86: antiquarian) 27–8, 140–1, 171
Blondel, François (1618–86: architect) 34, 39–42
Boissy d'Anglas, François-Antoine de (1756–1826: author and politician) 142–4, 158–9
Boichot, Guillaume (1735–1814: sculptor) 121–2, 127, 130
Boizot, Louis-Simon (1743–1809: sculptor) 174–5
Bologna armistice 156–7
Bonald, Louis de (1754–1840: philosopher and politician) 13–14, 170–1, 205–6
Bonaparte, Napoleon (1769–1821: Corsican nobleman) 142–3, 156–7, 159–61, 165, 177–8, 188–90, 198, 203–4
Bonenfant, Claude-Louis (active 1793–4: commissioner for section Fontaine-de-Grenelle) 125, 135
Boulogne, Étienne-Antoine (1747–1825: cleric and editor) 160–1
Bourdaloue, Louis, (1632–1704: Jesuit preacher) 13
Boujot family (Antoine Quatremère's maternal family) 15
Brissot de Warville, Jacques-Pierre (1754–93: politician) 70–1, 91–2, 102–3, 136–7
Brottier, Gabriel (1723–89: librarian and historian) 35–6
Brumaire coup 198–9
Buffon, Georges-Louis-Leclerc (1707–88: naturalist) 170–2
Burke, Edmund (1729–97: statesman and philosopher) 13–14, 173

248 INDEX

Calvet, Esprit (1728–1810: physician and
collector) 206–7
Canova, Antonio (1757–1822: sculptor) 3–4,
12–13, 29–31, 45–6, 54, 196–200, 203–6
Cassas, Louis-François (1756–1827: artist) 97
Caylus, Anne-Claude-Philippe de Tubières
(1692–1765: antiquarian) 30–1, 34
Cellerier, Jacques (1742–1814: architect) 49–50,
84–6
Catholicism 9, 20, 39, 156–8, 161, 168, 171, 186,
191, 201, 204–5
censorship 20, 37, 45, 50–1, 53, 65–6, 98–9,
204–5
Cicero (106BC–43BC: Roman philosopher and
consul) 170
Clichy club 5–6, 8–9, 150, 154–6, 161–2, 170–1,
184–90, 200–1
Champagne, Jean-François (1751–1813: scholar
and educator) 187
Champagneux, Luc-Antoine (1744–1807: lawyer
and journalist) 135–6
Champ de Mars. *See* Field of the Federation
Chateaubriand, François-René (1768–1848:
author and politician) 13
Chénier, Andre (1762–94: poet and
journalist) 102, 106, 124
Chénier, Marie-Joseph (1764–1811: dramatist
and politician) 50–1, 152
Clérisseau, Charles-Louis (1721–1820: architect
and draughtsman) 28–9, 174–5
Condillac, Étienne Bonnot de (1714–80:
philosopher) 13–14, 148–9
Coustou le Jeune, Guillaume (1716–77:
sculptor) 17–18, 81, 87, 119–20, 174–5
Couthon, Georges (1755–94: lawyer and
politician) 92–3
Chabrol, Gilbert-Joseph-Gaspard (1773–1843:
administrator and prefect of Paris) 198,
205–6
Chaisneau, Charles (1749–1817: author, poet,
and entomologist) 84, 122–3
Chaptal, Jean-Antoine (1756–1832: scientist and
minister of the interior) 203
Charles X (1757–1836; comte d'Artois; king of
France 1824–30) 204–6
Chaudet, Antoine-Denis (1763–1810:
sculptor) 122, 128, 176
churches
Notre-Dame cathedral, Paris 49–50, 87
Saint-Denis 75–6, 83–4
Sainte-Geneviève abbey, Paris 79–80
Sainte-Geneviève, Paris. *See* Panthéon
Saint-Germain-des-Prés, Paris 205–6
Saint-Germain l'Auxerrois, Paris 12–13, 15–16

Saint-Étienne-du-Mont, Paris 79–80, 119
Saint-Eustache, Paris 75–6
Sainte-Marie-Madeleine, Paris 75
Saint-Nicolas-du-Chardonnet, Paris 203
Saint-Sulpice, Paris 205–6
Santissima Trinità dei Monti, Rome 23
Santa Croce, Florence 73–4
Santa Maria dei Fiori, Florence 19
Sistine chapel, Rome 21
Westminster Abbey, London 83–4
civilization, theory of 141–2, 147–8, 155–9, 161,
165–9, 171–2, 201
College of Louis-le-Grand 16–17, 64, 187
Commission of Monuments 95–7
Committee of Public Instruction 64, 68,
77–8, 93–101, 106–7, 118, 140–1, 162–3,
186–7
Commune of the Arts 59, 63, 67–8, 104, 123–4
Condorcet, Nicolas de (1743–94: mathematician
and philosopher) 13–14, 68, 70–1, 93–4,
99, 147–8, 155–6, 158–9, 168, 170–1
Courrier universel 152, 160–1, 163–7, 170–1
Crapelet, Charles (1762–1809: printer) 165

Danton, Georges (1759–94: politician) 114–15,
125, 133
David, Jacques-Louis (1748–1825: painter and
politician) 3–4, 8–9, 23, 25–6, 29–30, 56–7,
65–71, 82–3, 106–7, 125–7, 130–1, 138–42,
174–6, 203–5
Daunou, Pierre-Claude-François (1761–1840:
idéologue, politician, and historian) 148–9,
158–9, 204–5
Décade philosophique, littéraire et politique 156,
162–3, 179–80
Dejoux, Claude (1732–1816: sculptor) 17–18,
120, 126, 129, 141
Del Rosso, Giuseppe (1760–1831:
architect) 30–1, 35–6
Denon, Dominique-Vivant (1747–1825:
diplomat, author, and artist) 30–1, 35–6,
174–5, 203–4
Deseine, Louis-Pierre (1749–1822:
sculptor) 29–30, 62–3
Désilles, André (1767–90: army officer killed in
the Nancy mutiny) 106–7, 110
Desjardins, Martin (1640–94: sculptor) 57
Desmoulins, Camille (1760–94: journalist and
politician) 16–17, 84–6
Directory, political culture of the 147–55, 162,
170–3, 184–5
Drouais, Jean-Germain (1763–88: painter) 56
Dufourny, Léon (1754–1818: architect) 28–9,
139–41, 184, 205–6

INDEX 249

Dumas, Mathieu (1753–1837: army officer and politician) 90–1, 103, 113–15, 189–90, 192–4, 198–9
Duport, Adrien (1759–98: lawyer and politician) 91, 114–15
Duport du Tertre, Marguerite-Louis-François (1774–93: minister of justice) 16–17, 90–1, 104
Dupuis, Charles-François (1742–1809: author) 13–14, 64, 170–1

Egypt. See Quatremère de Quincy, Egyptian art and architecture
Elgin marbles 206–7
Eméric-David, Toussaint-Bernard (1755–1839: art historian) 196–7
émigrés 54, 90–1, 97, 101–4, 114–15, 125, 138, 145–6, 151, 188–9, 193–4, 198–9
Eusebius (d. 339: historian of early Christianity) 165–7

Feuillant club 89–94, 101–7, 111–12, 116, 119, 123, 144–5, 161–2, 200–1
festivals in Paris:
    Festival of the Federation (1790) 48–9, 54
    Festival of the Law (1792) 105–11, 122, 202
    Festival of Liberty (1792: celebrating the Châteauvieux regiment) 102, 106
    Festival of Liberty (1798: celebrating the arrival of artefacts from Italy) 191
Field of the Federation 75–6, 90–1, 106, 110
Florence 19, 38–9, 57, 73–4, 146–7
Fortin, Augustin-Félix (1763–1832) 122
Fountain of the Innocents 40–4
Franklin, Benjamin (1706–90: statesman and scientist) 75–6
Frayssinous, Denis-Luc de (1765–1841: prelate and orator) 13, 204–5
free market 53, 59–60, 201
Frochot, Nicolas (1761–1828: prefect of the Seine Department) 203
Fructidor coup 190

Gallais, Jean-Pierre (1756–1820: journalist) 160
Genius, visual representations of 120–1, 128
Gérard, Denis-Stanislas (d. 1830s: companion of Antoine Quatremère) 12
Girardin, Louis-Stanislas (1762–1827: army officer and politician) 90–1
Girodet, Anne-Louis (1767–1824: painter) 174–5
Girondins 102–3, 125, 131, 135–6, 142–3, 147
Ginguené, Pierre-Louis (1748–1816: author) 157–8

Godde, Hippolyte (1781–1869: architect) 205–6
Goethe, Johann Wolfgang von (1749–1832: author) 25–6, 177–8, 195–6
Gossec, François-Joseph (1734–1829: composer) 107, 110
Gouges, Olympe de (1748–93: author) 107
Goujon, Jean (c.1510–c.1565: sculptor) 40–4
Greece. See Quatremère de Quincy, Greek art and architecture
Grégoire, Henri (1750–1831: priest and politician) 57–8, 105–6, 142, 158–9, 169
Grivaud de la Vincelle, Claude-Madeleine (1762–1819: antiquarian) 206–7
Guérin, Pierre-Narcisse (1774–1833: painter) 198–9
Guibert, Joseph (active 1792–4: ornamental sculptor) 124, 128–9
Guillaumot, Charles-Axel (1730–1807: architect) 58–9

Hegel, Georg (1770–1831: philosopher) 1
Hercules, visual representations of 87, 120–1, 127–8, 131
Heyne, Christian Gottlob (1729–1812: classical scholar) 194
Hoche, Louis (1768–97: army officer) 189–90
Houdon, Jean-Antoine (1741–1823: sculptor) 59, 119–20, 122–3
Huet de Froberville, Claude-Jean-Baptiste (1752–1838: politician) 94–5

Idéologues 13–14, 148–9, 155–6, 173, 196–7, 203
Ingres, Jean-Auguste-Dominique (1780–1867: painter) 205–7

Jacobin club 90–3, 102, 105, 111–12, 138, 145–6, 150–1, 184
Jacobi, Friedrich Heinrich (1743–1819: philosopher) 177–8, 193–7, 200
Jal, Auguste (1795–1873: author) 1
Jard-Painvillier, Louis-Alexandre (1757–1822: politician) 186–7
Journal de Paris 40–2, 102, 105–6, 161–3, 175–6
Julien, Pierre (1731–1804: sculptor) 17–18, 58–9, 139, 174–5
July Monarchy 177–8, 207

Kant, Immanuel (1724–1804: philosopher) 193–4
Kersaint, Armand-Guy-Simon de Coetnempren (1742–93: naval officer and politician) 97–8

250 INDEX

Labrouste, Henri (1801–75) 207
Lacretelle (le jeune), Jean-Charles-Dominique de
(1766–1855: historian and
journalist) 144–5, 160–2, 185–6
Lacretelle, Pierre-Louis de (1751–1824:
lawyer) 64
Lafayette, Gilbert du Motier de (1757–1834:
army officer and politician) 49–50,
112–14
La Fontaine, Jean de (1621–95: author) 12
La Harpe, Jean-François de (1739–1803:
author) 151–2, 185–6
Lakanal, Joseph (1762–1845: educator and
politician) 100, 152
Lalande, Jérôme (1732–1807: astronomer and
author) 21, 158
Lameth, Alexandre (1760–1829: soldier and
politician) 91, 114–15
La Révellière-Lépeaux, Louis-Marie de
(1753–1824: politician and Director) 147,
175–6, 190
La Rochefoucauld, Louis-Alexandre de (1743–92:
naturalist and politician) 75–6
La Rochefoucauld-Liancourt,
François-Alexandre-Frédéric de
(1747–1827: politician and president of the
Paris Department) 76–8, 84, 86
Lavin, Sylvia (theorist and historian of
architecture) 4–5, 46
Lebreton, Joachim (1760–1819: professor and
administrator) 162–3, 203–6
Le Brun, Charles (1619–90: painter and Director
of the Academy of Painting and
Sculpture) 182–4
Lebrun, Jean-Baptiste-Pierre (1748–1813: painter
and art dealer) 163, 169–70
Le Chapelier, Isaac René Guy (1754–94: jurist
and politician) 53–4, 99–100, 114–15, 123
Leclère, Adolphe Jean-Baptiste (1800–61: actor
and Antoine Quatremère's adopted
son) 12, 125, 191–2
Ledoux, Charles-Nicolas (1736–1806:
architect) 33–4, 81–2
Lefevre (head of accounts for the
Pantheon) 116–18
Legrand, Jacques-Guillaume (1753–1807:
architect) 28–9, 69–70, 110, 141–3, 146–7,
163–4, 174–6
Lenoir, Alexandre (1761–1839: archaeologist and
curator) 96–7, 176, 181, 203, 206–7
Lepeletier de Saint-Fargeau, Louis-Michel
(1760–93: politician) 128–9, 201
Lessing, Gotthold Ephraim (1729–81) 194–5
Le Sueur, Eustache (1617–1655: painter) 182–4

Lesueur, Jacques-Philippe (1757–1830:
sculptor) 122, 130–1
liberty of theatres, debate about the 7, 51, 201
Lorta, Jean-François (1752–1837:
sculptor) 122, 128
Louis, Victor (1731–1800: architect) 187
Louis XVI (1754–93; king of France 1774–92) 7,
28, 48–50, 58, 60, 65–7, 83–6, 89–92,
97–8, 102–3, 108–9, 111–15, 121–2, 125,
190–1, 200
Louis XVII (1785–95; king of France, claimant,
1793–95) 144–5
Louis XVIII (1755–1824: comte de Provence;
king of France 1815–1824;) 144–5, 185,
190–1, 204–5
Louvet, Jean-Baptiste (1760–97: author and
journalist) 150–2
Lucas de Montigny, Jean-Robert-Nicolas
(1747–1810: sculptor) 122, 128
Luckner, Nicolas (1722–94: army
officer) 112–13
Luxembourg palace and gardens 12–13, 17,
175–6, 182–4

Maistre, Joseph de (1753–1821:
philosopher) 13–14
Malesherbes, Guillaume-Chrétien de
Lamoignon de (1721–94: statesman and
minister) 37, 68
Mallet du Pan, Jacques (1749–1800:
journalist) 9, 45, 89, 136–7, 173, 185–6,
189–93, 195–6, 200
Marie-Antoinette (1755–93: queen of France
1774–92) 7, 17–18, 44, 46–7, 69–70, 91,
104, 112
Méchin, Alexandre (1772–1849: administrator
and elector in primary assembly of the
Fontaine-de-Grenelle section) 145
Mercier, Louis-Sébastien (1740–1814: author
and politician) 42–3, 188
Michaud, Joseph-François (1767–1839: historian
and publicist) 185–6
Millin, Aubin-Louis de Grandmaison (1759–1818:
antiquary and naturalist) 169, 173–5
Mirabeau, Honoré-Gabriel Riqueti (1749–91:
author and politician) 8, 75–6, 84–6, 122–3
Miranda, Francisco de Miranda (1756–1816:
army officer and Venezuelan
revolutionary) 9, 136–7, 141–7, 154–5,
163–4, 177–8, 180, 190–1, 193–4, 198
Molinos, Jacques (1743–1831: architect) 28–9,
143, 146–5, 203
Moitte, Jean-Guillaume (1746–1810:
sculptor) 17–18, 119–22, 128, 130, 140

INDEX 251

Monge, Gaspard (1746–1818: mathematician) 68, 157–60, 176–7
Montagnards 125, 130–1, 133, 137–8
Montesquieu, Charles-Louis de Secondat (1689–1755: magistrate and political philosopher) 20, 168, 170
moral hazard 53
Moreau, Jean-Michel (1741–1814: draughtsman and engraver) 161–2
Mulot, François-Valentin (1749–1804: constitutional priest and politician) 124
museums and collections
  British Museum, London 206–7
  Charles collection of scientific instruments, Paris 96
  Calvet collection, Avignon 206–7
  Grivaud de la Vincelle collection 206–7
  Louvre, Paris 63–6, 96–7, 152–3, 160–3, 181–4
  Museum of French Monuments, Paris 3–4, 96–7, 181, 184, 197, 203–6
  Museum of Natural History, Paris 172
  Museo Ercolanese, Portici 24
  Museo Pio-Clementino, Rome 21–3, 158
  Orleans collection, Paris 17
  Palazzo Biscari, Catania 27–8
  Palazzo degli Studi, Naples 23–4
  Palazzo Pitti, Florence 57
  Special Museum of the French School, Versailles 180–1
  Townley collection of antiquities, London 45
  Uffizi Gallery, Florence 57

National Institute 68, 148–9, 151–2, 156–9, 162, 165

Paestum 24–6, 32–4
Palloy, Pierre-François (1755–1835: building contractor) 107–9
Panthéon, Paris 8, 43–4, 68, 70–88, 116–34, 202
pantheonizations 84–6, 105–6, 122–3, 128–9
Paris Opera (Royal Academy of Music) 44, 50, 53
paradox of plenty 34–5
Pétion de Villeneuve, Jérôme (1756–94: politician and mayor of Paris) 111–12
Pajou, Augustin (1730–1809: sculptor) 69–70, 119–20, 141, 174–5
Panckoucke, Charles-Joseph (1736–98: publisher) 36–7, 40, 45, 50–1, 100
papacy 7–9, 20–1, 149–50, 154–67, 171, 173
Paroy, Jean-Philippe-Gui (1750–1824: painter) 10, 67–8, 72

Pastoret, Claude-Emmanuel Joseph Pierre (1755–1840: writer and politician) 71, 75–6, 86, 90–1, 114–15, 124, 144–5
patronage of the arts 18, 22, 35, 47, 55–6, 58–62, 68, 71, 98–9, 122, 141–2, 151–2, 157–8, 160–1, 200
Peltier, Jean-Gabriel (1760–1825: journalist) 9, 164–5, 173, 179
Phrygian cap 87, 119, 131
Pichegru, Jean-Charles (1761–1804: army officer) 142–3, 186, 190
Piranesi, Giambattista (1720–78: artist) 21–2, 34, 37
Pius VI, Giovanni Angelo Braschi (1717–99: pope 1775–99) 21, 154–60, 162–3, 171, 173, 194, 200
Pommier, Édouard (1925–2018: art historian) 4–5, 42–3, 163–4
Poncet, Pierre (masonry contractor at Panthéon) 86, 123, 128–9
Portalis, Jean-Étienne-Marie (1746–1807: jurist and politician) 142–3, 193–4, 198–9
Prudhomme, Louis-Marie (1752–1830: journalist) 76, 90–1
Prud'hon, Pierre-Paul (1758–1823: painter) 31, 205–6

Quatremère, Marc-Étienne (1751–94: textile merchant) 15–16, 49, 84–6, 125–6, 138–9
Quatremère, Étienne-Marc (1782–1857: orientalist) 15–16
Quatremère de Quincy, Antoine-Chrysostôme (1755–1849: author and politician)
  allegory, use of 81–2, 87, 111
  appearance and personality 10–14, 89
  apprenticeship as a sculptor 17–18
  artworks created by him 12, 21–2, 131, 135–6, 205–6
  authenticity in art, reflections on 27, 43–4, 206–7
  beauty, theory of 37–8, 46, 167, 169, 171–2, 196–7
  cemeteries, reflections on 19, 27–8, 39, 76–7, 203
  Chamber of Deputies, national representative in 1820–2 in the 204–5
  character, architectural theory of 39–42, 87
  collection of books and artworks 12–14, 28, 125, 170, 191–2, 204–5
  Committee of Public Instruction for Paris, membership of the 64, 68–70
  Committee of Public Instruction in the Legislative Assembly, membership of the 93–101

252 INDEX

Quatremère de Quincy, Antoine-Chrysostôme (1755–1849: author and politician) (*cont.*)
conservation of monuments 27, 46–7, 72, 163–4, 186–7, 203
Considerations on the Arts of Drawing in France (1791) 59–62
Council of Five Hundred, representative in the 170–1, 185–90
education 16–17
destruction of Paris heritage, reflections on the 7, 38–9, 42–3, 72, 206–7
Doric order, reflections on the 10, 23, 25–6, 30–5, 38, 202
Egyptian art and architecture 1, 30–1, 34–8
Encyclopédie méthodique: Architecture 36–40, 77, 146–7
England, his travels in and reflections on 45–6, 92–3, 114–15, 190–1, 193–4, 206–7
Enlightenment, his positive vision of the 13–14, 21, 27–8, 46–7, 165–9, 200
faith 13–14, 16–17, 21, 152, 160–1, 185, 196–7, 200, 203
family 12–13, 15–18, 48–9, 125–6, 138, 180
Festival of the Law, his organization of the 107–11
finances, his personal 12–13, 15–18, 29, 36, 86, 89, 125, 180
Fountain of the Innocents, intervention to save the 40–4
Gallo-Roman monuments, desire to preserve and restore 29
Germany, travels in and reflections on 191–9
Greek art and architecture, reflections on 22–3, 25–6, 28–36, 38, 79–82, 131, 167–8
ideal, artistic theory of the 22, 38, 44, 46
imitation, theory of in the arts 33, 38, 44–6, 193–7
improving Paris, his ideas on 12–13, 38–9, 42–3, 46–7, 203–5
Italy, travels in and attitudes towards (including Rome and Sicily) 18–33
language of architecture 33–4, 39–40, 46–7
Legislative Assembly, representative in the 89–114
Letters on the Plan to Abduct Monuments of Art from Italy 8–9, 13–14, 150–1, 154–6, 163–73, 192–4, 201
Manège, Paris, reflections on its architecture 89, 92–3, 202
materialism, his hostility towards 194–8, 200–1

Moral Considerations on the Destination of Artworks 154–5, 203–4
museums and collections, attitudes towards 24, 27–8, 45, 65–6, 83–4, 89, 96–7, 140–1, 154–6, 160–1, 163–4, 168–72, 180–4, 197, 200, 203–7
music, reflections on 21, 38, 44–5, 53–4, 82–3
opera bouffa, reflections on 44–5
Paris architecture, his critique of recent trends in 34, 38–40, 202
Paris Commune, his service as an elected representative 49–54
Panthéon, his vision in 1791 for the 79–84, 87–8
Panthéon, his direction of the 116–34
papacy, admiration for the 13–14, 21, 171–2, 200
Permanent Secretary of the Academy of the Fine Arts, his tenure as the 1, 205–7
philosophy of history 37, 142, 167–8
polchromy in ancient sculpture, theory of 30, 131, 194
prison 135–8
royalist political thought 46–7, 138, 150–3, 172–3, 192–3
sexuality 12
slavery in the colonies, attitudes towards 90–1, 170–1, 189
system of the arts, his theory of the 38, 44, 65–6, 194–5
type, architectural theory of 34–5, 47
Vendémiaire uprising, his role in and reflections on the 138, 146–7, 150–1, 179
Quatremère de Roissy, Jean-Nicolas (1754–1834: writer) 15–16
Quatremère-Disjonval, Denis-Bernard (1754–1830: brother of Antoine Quatremère de Quincy; physician and chemist) 12, 15–16, 138, 176–7, 180, 186, 190–1

Rabault de Saint-Étienne, Jean-Paul (1743–93: Calvinist pastor, historian, and politician) 172
Ramey, Claude (1754–1838: sculptor) 128
Raphael (1483–1520: artist) 73–4, 146–7, 167–70, 176, 206–7
Renou, Antoine (1731–1806: painter) 10, 58, 60–3, 66–8
Restout, Jean-Bernard (1732–97: painter) 56–7, 59, 63
Robert, Hubert (1733–1808: painter) 75, 174–5

Robespierre, Maximilien (1758–94:
   politician) 16–17, 51–2, 133, 137–9, 143,
   145, 150, 158–9, 184
Robin, Jean-Baptiste (1734–1818: painter) 57, 63
Roederer, Pierre-Louis (1754–1835: politician
   and political economist) 1, 119, 160–2,
   167, 185
Roland, Philippe-Laurent (sculptor:
   1746–1816) 108–10, 122
Rome. *See* Antoine Quatremère de Quincy, Italy
Romme, Charles-Gilbert (1750–95: politician
   and mathematician) 95, 100
Rondelet, Jean-Baptiste (1743–1829:
   architect) 29–30, 36–7, 86, 117–18, 129–31
Rossel de Cercy, Auguste-Louis de (1736–1804:
   navy officer and painter) 97–8
Roucher, Jean-Antoine (1745–94: poet) 107, 110
Rousseau, Jean-Jacques (1712–78: author) 59,
   73, 76, 122–3, 140
Royer-Collard, Pierre Paul (1763–1845:
   statesman and philosopher) 186, 190–1, 200
Rubens, Peter Paul (1577–1640: painter) 17, 156,
   182–4

Sainte-Beuve, Charles (1804–69: literary
   critic) 10
Sainte-Chapelle club 70–1
Salon of Painting and Sculpture 17, 50, 56, 58–62,
   65–7, 69–71, 94–5, 100–1, 122, 181–4
Schneider, René (1869–1938: art historian) 3, 193–4
Seneca (*c*. 4BC–AD 65: Roman philosopher) 112
Sérizy, Jean Richer de (1759–1803) 9, 144–5,
   180–1, 185–6
Sieyès, Emmanuel-Joseph (1748–1836: political
   writer and politician) 86, 133, 198
Simonneau, Jacques-Guillaume (1740–92: mayor
   of Etampes) 105–10, 112
Smith, Adam (1723–90: political
   economist) 13–14, 167, 169–71
Soane, John (1753–1837: architect) 1
Soufflot, Jacques-Germain (1713–80:
   architect) 40–4, 68, 72, 74–83, 86–8
Soufflot le Romain, François (1750–1801:
   architect) 77–8, 86, 117–18
Staël, Germaine de (1766–1817: author)
   190–1, 194
Stendhal, Marie-Henri Beyle (1783–1842:
   author) 1
Stolberg, Christian (1748–1821: poet and elder
   brother of Friedrich Stolberg) 193–4
Stolberg, Friedrich Leopold (1750–1819: author
   and translator) 192–5, 200

Stone, John Hurford (1763–1818: printer) 180
Suard, Jean-Baptiste (1732–1817:
   journalist) 40–2, 144–5, 151–2
Suzanne, Francois-Marie (1750–1813:
   sculptor) 25–6, 128

Talleyrand-Périgord, Charles-Maurice de
   (1754–1838: statesman and diplomat) 1, 8,
   64, 68, 190–1
Tardiveau, François-Alexandre (1761–1833:
   lawyer and politician) 110
Théâtre de Monsieur (Théâtre Feydeau) 7, 44–5,
   51–4
Thermes de Julien, Paris 206–7
Thermidorians 141–2, 144–5, 147
Trouvé, Charles-Joseph (1768–1860:
   administrator and diplomat) 176
Tuileries palace and gardens 17, 44, 51, 111–14,
   145–6

Vanderbourg, Charles (1765–1827: translator
   and author) 194–5
Vasari, Giorgio (1511–74: artist and
   biographer) 17, 19
Vattel, Emmerich de (1714–67: Swiss
   jurisconsult) 13–14, 168, 170
Vaubertrand, Jean-Charles (concierge of
   Madelonnettes prison) 135–6, 146
Vaublanc, Vincent-Marie Viénot de (1756–1845:
   politician) 9, 90–1, 101, 113–15, 144–5,
   188–9, 200
Vaudoyer, Antoine (1756–1846: architect) 76
Vernet, Horace (1789–1863: painter) 207
Vernet, Joseph (1714–89: painter) 184
Versailles palace 180–1, 184, 206–7
Vien, Joseph-Marie (1716–1809: painter) 19–20,
   23–4, 57–9, 62–3, 139, 141, 174–5
Villèle, Joseph de (1773–1854: Restoration leader
   of the ultra-royalist faction) 204–5
Villette, Charles Michel (1736–93: writer and
   politician) 73–8, 80–1, 84–6
Vitruvius (*c*. 80 BC–post *c*. 15 BC: architect and
   author) 28, 33, 38, 68, 86
Voltaire, François-Marie Arouet (1694–1778:
   author) 73–4, 77, 84–6, 122–3, 168
Volney, Constantin-François (1757–1820:
   philosopher) 148–9

Wickham, William (1761–1840: spy
   master) 190, 193
Winckelmann, Johann Joachim (1717–68: art
   historian) 1, 22, 32, 35, 37, 45–6, 68, 170–1